THE BARATARIANS
and the
BATTLE OF NEW ORLEANS

by

Jane Lucas de Grummond

with

BIOGRAPHICAL SKETCHES
of the VETERANS
of the BATTALION OF ORLEANS
1814-1815

by

Ronald R. Morazan

Legacy Publishing Company, Inc.
Baton Rouge, Louisiana

Copyright, 1961
Louisiana State University Press
Library of Congress Catalog Card Number: 79-65176
ISBN: 0-918784-23-9
Reprinted with additional material by
Legacy Publishing Company, Inc.
Baton Rouge, Louisiana, U.S.A.
Copyright, 1979

To
Ernest I, II and III

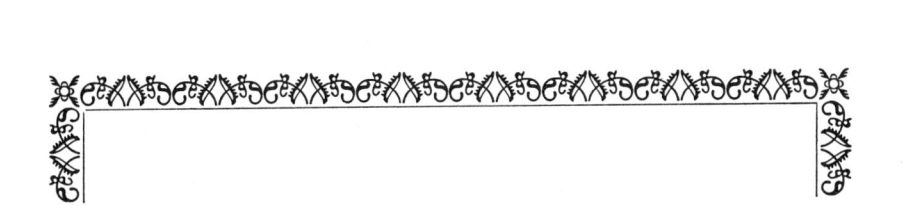

TABLE OF CONTENTS

		PAGE
	Introduction	ix
I	Barataria and the Baratarians	3
II	Barataria's Heyday	16
III	Negril Bay	25
IV	The British approach Jean Laffite	37
V	Andrew Jackson	49
VI	The British camp below New Orleans	64
VII	"They shall not rest on our soil!"	77
VIII	Sir Edward Michael Pakenham	96
IX	The Artillery Duel, January 1	111
X	Bivouac, January 1 to January 8	119
XI	The Battle of the 8th of January	134
XII	Triumph and Trial	142
XIII	Taps	153
	Appendix A	160
	Appendix B	162
	Essay on Authorities	171
	Index	175

LIST OF ILLUSTRATIONS

	PAGE
Andrew Jackson	50
Attack on Fort Bowyer	52
Attack on Fort St. Philip	61
Attack by British Barges on American Gun Boats	67
De La Ronde's Mansion	70
Villeré's Mansion	74
Affair Below New Orleans. Dec. 23rd. 1814	89
Positions of the American and British Armies Near New Orleans. Jan. 8th. 1815.	135
The Old Spanish Cathedral and Government House	144
The Old Court-House	151

INTRODUCTION

MOST ACCOUNTS OF THE BRITISH INVASION OF LOUISIANA describe fully the activities of Tennessee, Kentucky and Mississippi militia and give them the main credit for driving out the enemy. Baratarians and their associates, when mentioned, are disposed of briefly. They did not write the reports that were sent to Washington after the battle was over. From these records and published histories the reader does not realize that victory would have been impossible without the smugglers and privateers.

Jackson had used up all his ammunition and most of his flints during the Creek campaign. When he came to New Orleans at the beginning of December, 1814, he had a few troops, no artillery and no supplies. Yet from the night of December 23, 1814, to January 19 (not January 8), 1815, almost continuous bombardment harassed the British. Baratarians supplied the powder, flints, cannon, cannon balls, flying-angles, ship cannister, and " every description of destructive missile."

Cannon fire from the *Carolina* spearheaded the night attack of December 23. The battles on December 28 and January 1 were artillery duels. Riflemen from the Tennessee Valley were good shots on January 8 but after the first half hour they were not needed. The British retreated—and could not renew the battle because the artillery kept up its bombardment until the British asked for a truce

Introduction

several hours later. Reinforcements from England continued to arrive at the British camp, but eleven more days of bombardment killed any remnant of resistance that remained and caused the enemy to slink away.

Jackson's chief engineer, Major A. Lacarrière Latour, wrote the best account of the battle. This was published in 1816. In this work Latour could not do full justice to the Baratarians because he knew too much about them. He was a patriot during the battle, but he was not before; and soon afterwards he and the Laffites became spys and agents for Spain. In Spain's secret files, Pierre Laffite became No. 13-A or 13-*uno*; Jean Laffite became 13-B, 13 *dos* or 13 *bis.*; Latour travelled under the name of John Williams.

A review of Latour's book which appeared shortly after its publication shows the almost forgotten significance to the people of that generation of the War of 1812. In their eyes " all the disposable forces both sea and land, were directed to these devoted shores, which they (the British) were to overrun, and particular parts were to be retained as permanent acquisitions. An eminent Map-seller in London advised an American gentleman, not knowing him to be such, who applied to him for a map of the United States, to defer the purchase for a few weeks; that he was then keeping all his maps unfinished, as the boundaries would all be changed, and a considerable part of the Union incorporated with the British possessions! " [1]

The United States made many blunders during the war but the enemy committed still greater. When they found themselves unexpectedly relieved from the long contest in Europe, they should have offered peace. " This would have appeared the greatest magnanimity on their part, thus to waive the opportunity of overwhelming us. The capture of the frigates would have been forgotten and we should have escaped from a luckless war, with all the disgrace of our first defeats by land, and in the opinion of the world and perhaps our own, should have thought we owed our

---

[1] *The North American Review and Miscellaneous Journal*, III (July, 1816), 238.

Introduction

escape to the clemency of a generous and powerful foe. . . . They came and were covered with confusion and disgrace." [2]

The author is deeply grateful for the patient help of the Louisiana State Library Staff, especially of the following: Vergil L. Bedsole, Virginia M. Ott and Marcelle F. Schertz, Archives; Elizabeth Welker, Government Documents; Lucy B. Foote, Evangeline M. Lynch and Emeline R. Staples, Louisiana Room; and George J. Guidry, Photoduplications.

Raymond H. Downs, graduate student in history at Louisiana State University, found the roster of the Orleans Battalion in the Louisiana State Archives; he also found the letter in Appendix A.

In New Orleans the following were most helpful in locating documents: George Raffalovich, researcher; Connie G. Griffith, Tulane University Archives; Mary M. Impastato, Secretary, St. Louis Cathedral; Clarence Wagner, United States District Court; and Fordyce L. Perego.

Hazel Rodgers, Beth de Grummond, and Linda Johnson helped with the page proofs and Index.

Finally, mention must be made of Mildred and Darryl Smith with whom I explored Grande Terre; and of Lonie Vizier, " King of Cut Off," with whom I sailed out Barataria Pass in *Boston Bill*.

JANE LUCAS DE GRUMMOND

Baton Rouge, August 11, 1960.

---

[2] *Ibid.*, 237-38.

THE BARATARIANS
AND
THE BATTLE OF NEW ORLEANS

BARATARIA
AND THE BARATARIANS

THE FIRST SETTLERS IN LOUISIANA NEEDED TERMITE-RESISTANT cypress for building their houses and sturdy oaks for building their ships. Across the Mississippi from New Orleans was a lush forest of these timbers in a swamp area which was really an island because it was bounded by the Big Lake of the Ouatchas, the Ouatchas River, the Little Lake of the Ouatchas, and Bayou Pierrot.[1]

However, this swamp forest was inaccessible to those early Frenchmen, so they named it " The Island of Barataria," after that unattainable island kingdom of Sancho Panza in Cervantes' immortal *Don Quixote*.[2] In time the whole area west of New Orleans to Bayou Lafourche and south to the Gulf was called Barataria. One branch of the Ouatchas River snakes almost to the Mississippi where it curves below New Orleans; so the Ouatchas, " the bayou which leads to Barataria," came to be called Bayou Barataria. The bay into which this river, the two lakes, and numerous little bayous disembogue was called Barataria Bay.

This Bay is fifteen miles long and six wide. It is protected from the Gulf of Mexico by Grande Terre and Grand Isle, two islands that

---

[1] A. Lacarrière Latour, *Historical Memoir of the War in West Florida and Louisiana in 1814-1815* (Philadelphia, 1816), 13. On modern maps, Big Lake of the Ouatchas is Lake Salvador, and the other is Little Lake; Bayou Pierrot is Bayou Perot.

[2] Le Page du Pratz, *Histoire de la Louisiane* (3 vols., Paris, 1758), I, 289.

lie almost end to end. The pass between them that leads to the Gulf (Barataria Pass) is only a quarter of a mile wide. Grande Terre is the eastern island. It is about 40 miles due south of New Orleans and 70 miles west-northwest of the mouth of the Mississippi. Here the Laffite brothers established smuggling headquarters for privateers of the Gulf and the Caribbean who were driven from one French island after another.

This was during the period of the Napoleonic Wars when Creole corsairs harassed English shipping until Great Britain set to work in dead earnest to capture their bases. One of the first to fall was the island of Santa Lucia in 1803. During the course of the attack a Creole shot Edward Michael Pakenham in the neck. When this wound healed it drew his head to one side. Six years later Pakenham commanded at the capture of Martinique. Again he was shot in the neck. When this second wound healed it restored his head to its original position.[3]

Guadeloupe, the last of the French islands, fell to the English in February of 1810. After that date, privateers sailing under French commissions no longer had a harbor nor an admiralty court to which they could openly take their prizes. This did not stop them for they had already found Grande Terre. The first smugglers' convention had been held there in 1805. Among those present were Alexandre, Pierre and Jean Laffite, Vincent Gambie, Louis Chighizola and perhaps Renato Beluche also.[4] Jean Laffite emerged as the leader and organizing genius of the privateers.

The Laffite brothers were born at Port-au-Prince, Haiti. Their parents had moved there from Spain to escape the Inquisition which had persecuted and finally killed Mrs. Laffite's father. Alexandre Frederic, the oldest of eight children, was born in 1771. The youngest, Jean, was born in 1782. Pierre was two and a half years older than Jean. These two youngest brothers were inseparable in their play and studies. They did not remember their mother, who

---

[3] *Dictionary National Biography* (22 vols., London, 1949-50), XV, 83-84; Alexander Walker, *Jackson and New Orleans* (New York, 1856), 200-201.
[4] *The Journal of Jean Laffite* (New York, 1958), 38.

died soon after Jean was born, but their Jewish grandmother took her place and dominated their early lives. She planted a deep hatred of Spain in her grandsons; but she was an intelligent, educated woman and saw that they had competent tutors at home until Jean was fourteen. Then the two boys were sent to a private school on the island of Martinique. Later they had military training on another island, Saint Christopher; it was here that Jean became skilled in the use of duelling weapons.[5]

Meanwhile, Alexandre Frederic had become a privateer. Following the usual practice of those who followed this profession, he never revealed his true name or origin. To the enemies of France, upon whose commerce he preyed, he was known as Dominique You or Frederic You.

Dominique was short, not quite five feet four inches tall. His shoulders, twice as broad as the average man's, made him seem strong and stubborn as an ox. He was swarthy, with flashing black eyes and a hawk-like nose. Scars from powder burns on the left side of his face made him look ferocious, yet men soon discovered that he was a likable cuss.

Jean and Pierre were determined to become privateers like Dominique. While he was in France winning fame as a cannoneer, they trained in the Gulf and Caribbean under Renato Beluche who seemed mature to them because he already had twelve years' experience at sea. He was solidly built, with broad shoulders and a strong aquiline nose that showed he was kin to Dominque You. Although he was probably a second cousin of the Laffites and the same age as Pierre, Jean and Pierre called Renato " uncle."

Beluche was a native of New Orleans. He was born there in 1780.[6]

---

[5] *Journal of Jean Laffite*, 10; Stanley Clisby Arthur, *Jean Laffite, Gentleman Rover* (New Orleans, 1952), 283; Henry Adams, *History of the United States* (9 vols., New York, 1890 and 1930), VII, 321; Frank R. Stockton, *Buccaneers and Pirates on our Coasts* (New York, 1898), 281; Gaillard Hunt, *Life in America one hundred years ago* (New York, 1914), 162.

[6] St. Louis Cathedral Archives, New Orleans, Register I. Month and date of birth are not clear. The date appears to be December 15, 1780. Date of baptism is January 7, 1781. The Index to the Archives states the approximate year of the marriage of his

His birthplace was 632 Dumaine Street, the house known today as "Madam John's Legacy."[7]

Beluche was seven when his father died,[8] leaving a pregnant wife, five children, and, as far as property was concerned, one heavily mortgaged plantation and several slaves.[9] Selina, Renato's youngest sister, was born five months later.

Renato went to sea, shipping on fishing boats, smugglers, merchant vessels. He served his term on the governor's flagship and learned how to handle cannon.[10] Within a few years he was part-owner of at least two privateers and sailed under letters of marque from Guadeloupe. This island was the seat of French colonial government in the Lesser Antilles, therefore the source of privateer commissions and the haven to which prizes could be taken and lawfully condemned in admiralty court.

When the blacks in Haiti succeeded in driving out the French armies and establishing an independent republic, French Creoles fled to Louisiana. Jean and Pierre helped to transport many of these as well as their father, their youngest sister Yvonne and her family, and their own families.[11] Then the brothers returned to their privateering.

---

parents as 1767, and adds that the marriage record had been destroyed. His mother was Rosa Laporte of Orleans Parish; his father was Renato Beluche of Tours, France.

[7] George Cable made this house famous. It was the scene of his story about Tite Poulette, daughter of the beautiful quadroon Zalli and Monsieur John. When Monsieur John died, the house became known as "Madam John's Legacy," and that is the name by which it is known today, even though it is now part of the Louisiana State Museum.

Laura Porteous and Samuel Wilson searched the titles to this property. According to their findings, Santiago Lamelle sold the house to Renato Beluche Sr., in 1778; he in turn sold it in 1783 to Don Manuel de Lanzos. "Madam John's Legacy" is reputed to be the oldest house in the Mississippi Valley—built *circa* 1723. *Times Picayune, Sunday Magazine,* July 17, 1949, 13.

The last owner of the house was Mrs. I. I. Lemmann. She gave it to the Louisiana State Museum.

[8] The inscription on his tomb reads: "Renat Beluche, husband of Dona Rosa Laporte, Age 50 years, Died September 3, 1778." Saint Louis Cemetery No. 1, New Orleans.

[9] Cabildo Records, New Orleans, Document No. 2262, Box 55.

[10] Stanley Faye, "Privateers of Guadeloupe and Their Establishment in Barataria," *Louisiana Historical Quarterly,* XXIII (Baton Rouge, April, 1940), 429.

[11] Jean had married Christina Levine in the year 1800 at her home on the island of St. Croix. She was the daughter of Thomas Levine, a merchant through whom privateers

Barataria and the Baratarians

One day in June, 1805, Jean Laffite sailed up the Mississippi and anchored at the Crescent City. Dominique was there to greet him; he had recently returned from France. Anyone watching the two at that moment would never have guessed that the stocky, swarthy Dominique was conversing with his brother. Jean was five feet ten inches tall, but he seemed taller because he was slim and stood proudly erect. Some say he was fair with reddish blond hair and hazel eyes. Others say his hair was dark. Jean tells us that many times he washed his head with potash and gunpowder which made his hair, eyebrows, and mustache a beautiful red color.[12] Whatever the color of his hair, Jean was meticulous about his clothes and elegant in his manners. In fact, he was a handsome, refined gentleman.

Jean told Dominique that he had prize goods and 12,600 English pounds in hard money with him and that he needed an agent to help him dispose of these items in New Orleans. After making discreet inquiries, Jean went to Joseph Sauvinet, a shrewd Frenchman from Bayonne who had lived in New Orleans long enough to become one of its most important businessmen. He employed twenty clerks in his counting house in the suburb Marigny.[13]

Hard money was scarce in New Orleans. The main source of supply had been Mexico, but that had been cut off since 1803 when the United States purchased Louisiana. Spanish and French paper money was available, but citizens had little or no confidence in it. They resisted Governor William C. C. Claiborne's attempt to establish a bank. Such an institution was new to the Creoles. They thought it would issue paper money which to them would be the same as legalized robbery. Had they not already suffered greatly

---

did considerable business. Jean and Christina soon had two sons and, when they fled from Haiti in 1804, Christina died giving birth to a daughter. Jean named the baby Denise Jeannette. His sister Yvonne took the baby while Pierre's wife took the two boys. Pierre's wife was Françoise Sel, the daughter of Jean Baptiste l'Etang Sel, who had been a planter in Haiti. Sel became famous in New Orleans as a portrait and miniature painter. *Journal of Jean Laffite*, 21; Arthur, *Jean Laffite*, 19, 23, 255.

[12] *Journal of Jean Laffite*, 122.

[13] Vincent Nolte, *Fifty Years in Both Hemispheres* (New York, 1854), 207; Arthur, *Jean Laffite*, 20.

from the depreciation of French and Spanish paper? What better results could they expect from American paper?[14]

It was not much wonder that Sauvinet was impressed with Jean's 12,600 hard pounds. He became Jean's partner and told him that, in order to avoid greedy customs officials, he should in the future unload cargoes at a point, which he indicated on a map, down the river below English Turn; and that he, Sauvinet, would get them from that depot to his warehouses. This was the beginning of a contraband commercial venture that was to involve nearly everyone in New Orleans.

When Jean left the city, Dominique sailed with him. They had captured nearly a dozen English vessels by the time they found Pierre in Guadeloupe. Pierre was handsome and fair or dark like Jean, and the same height but he did not seem as tall. He was heavier and careless in appearance; and because he was not as " refined " as Jean, he had a great deal more pleasure with women.

Soon Renato Beluche arrived at Guadeloupe also. In between legitimate runs from New Orleans to Vera Cruz, Pensacola, or Havana,[15] Beluche found his way to the French islands with prizes he had captured. For his privateering ventures, he used a number of aliases—among them Pedro Brugman or variations thereof, and the name Rigmartin.[16]

As the English closed in on the French Islands, more and more contraband was taken to Grande Terre or other islands along the coast and smuggled up the bayous to Donaldsonville and New Orleans. In 1807, Jean acquired a warehouse in New Orleans. He built one the next year at Donaldsonville, and a relay warehouse at the village of Barataria.[17]

---

[14] Charles E. A. Gayarré, *History of Louisiana* (4 vols., New Orleans, 1903), IV, 15.
[15] Customs House Records show that on March 4, 1805, Beluche sailed the schooner *Two Sisters* to Vera Cruz for its owner, Bartholomew Bosque, listed as a New Orleans merchant, and in the fall another to Vera Cruz. Three voyages for other merchants and in other vessels are recorded for the year 1806, two for 1807, and one for 1808. Crew Lists, United States Customs Archives, Port of New Orleans, I (1803-1805), Book 2002, 16, 43, 52, 197; II (1806-1808), Book 2003, 83, 159, 212; Book 2005, 372, 449, 552.
[16] William B. Bollaert, " Life of Jean Laffite," *Littell's Living Age*, XXXII (Boston, March, 1852), 442.
[17] *Journal of Jean Laffite*, 39.

Barataria and the Baratarians

Late in that year, 1808, Jean passed the mouth of the Mississippi sailing west with four captured vessels in tow. One of these he had named the *Tigre*. It was to become Dominique's flagship.[18] The little fleet sailed through Barataria Pass, then turned east and anchored off the broad beach of Grande Terre. This island, six miles long and three wide, was flat, and when Jean first saw it only a few rude huts and scrub bushes broke its smooth contour. Now warehouses (within two years there would be forty of them), slave pens, dwellings, a hospital, and a fort were being built.

Soon a multitude of pirogues and other bayou craft converged at Grande Terre as news of Laffite's arrival spread through the labyrinth of Barataria. The contraband was unloaded on these small vessels. Then they sailed across Barataria Bay, through devious waterways to Little Lake, then up Barataria Bayou to its head across the Mississippi from New Orleans. It took three days for the pirogues to reach this spot. Men and mules were ready to transfer their contraband the short distance overland to the river where it was ferried across to the city. In this way the market was flooded with iron, wine, dry goods, and manufactured goods, as well as slaves. Prices dropped to amounts that people could afford to pay. Pig iron was one dollar per hundredweight. Ladies were happy and honest Anglo-Saxon merchants unhappy as the price of silk stockings dropped to nine dollars a dozen pairs.[19]

Chief among the other privateer captains who nosed along the Louisiana coast to Grande Terre were two Italians: Louis Chighizola and Vincent Gambie. Chighizola was a native of Genoa.[20] He had on his body scars of many a battle, but there was one on his face that made people stare and call him " Nez Coupé " (Cut Nose). A saber thrust had slashed off half his nose.

Vincent Gambie looked like the cruelest assassin alive, and legend and Spanish archives picture him as the blackest villain.[21] His

---

[18] United States District Court of Louisiana, Cases No. 812, No. 816.
[19] Faye, " Privateers of Guadeloupe," 442.
[20] USDC of La., Case No. 816.
[21] Stanley Faye, " Privateersmen of the Gulf and Their Prizes," *Louisiana Historical Quarterly*, XXII (Baton Rouge, October, 1939), 26-27 in the reprint. Faye cites

schooner he had named the *Philanthrope*, which was rather an odd name for a slaver; but perhaps Gambie felt that his black cargo would be better off in Louisiana and Mississippi than in Africa or Cuba.

The privateers were preying on Spanish commerce as well as English, for Spain was now openly allied with England in war against Napoleon. French refugees who had fled from Haiti to Cuba at the time that the Laffites had taken their families to New Orleans now found themselves persecuted. They escaped to Louisiana.

Perhaps it was because of his French Creole wife that Governor Claiborne was at first sympathetic to these French refugees—and did not molest the Baratarians who brought them. Claiborne reported in June, 1809, that "near one thousand people from Cuba have reached this City, and from two to three hundred more have passed the Balize.[22] Some of those arrived in great distress; . . . Their negro's are still detained on Board the Vessels in which they came— I should myself be well pleased if Congress would relax the Law forbidding the importation of Slaves,[23] as relates to these *miserable exiles*. I witness their distress, and would most readily alleviate it, if in my powers." [24]

An act was approved June 28, 1809, which authorized the President of the United States to remit penalties imposed under the exclusion act in cases where the owners of slaves had been expelled from

---

Papeles de Cuba, Legajo 1796, Soto to Apodaca, April 25, 1815, in which Gambie is described as "the cruelest and the greatest assassin among all the pirates."

[22] When the French first came to Louisiana, South East Pass was the only one of the five passes at the mouth of the Mississippi which could be used by vessels drawing fourteen feet of water. The French set up a pilot station at the head of this pass to guide ships seeking the mouth of the river. It became known as the Balize, from the French word for "beacon." Alcée Fortier, *Louisiana* (3 vols., Atlanta, 1909-14), I, 438.

[23] Act of March 2, 1807: "An Act to prohibit the importation of Slaves into any port or place within the jurisdiction of the United States, from and after the first day of January, in the year of our Lord one thousand eight hundred and eight." W. E. Burghardt Du Bois, *The Suppression of the African Slave-Trade to the United States of America 1683-1870* (New York, 1954), 94-108.

[24] Claiborne to Julien Poydras, June 4, 1809, in *The Territorial Papers of the United States*, ed. Clarence Edwin Carter (Washington, 1934—), IX, *The Territory of Orleans 1803-1812* (1940).

Cuba.[25] So slave-owning refugees, and refugees who were free people of color, and free Negroes continued to swell the population of New Orleans.

By July of 1809, the record shows that 5,754 emigrants had come to New Orleans. Of this number 1,798 were white French; 1,977 were free colored and free black; and 1,979 were slaves.[26] By the end of the year the population of New Orleans had doubled and more than half this number were recent French arrivals.[27] The Anglo-Saxon and Spanish elements found themselves very much in the minority, and they resented and feared the French Creoles as their influence dominated not only in the city, but in the whole delta area.

One has only to look at Crew Lists in the Customs House Records to discover where the free colored and free blacks found employment. The 30 or more privateer captains who sailed out of Barataria had small vessels, 120- or 130-ton brigs and schooners, but they manned them with crews of 90 to 170 and sometimes even 200 men. These men were trained as cannoneers as well as deck hands. On a successful cruise a captain might take six or more prizes. Some of these would be sunk or otherwise destroyed after the removal of cargo, but good vessels were saved and had to be manned by prize crews.

A conservative estimate of the number of Baratarians who served on the fleet would be 3,000 men.[28] A similar number must have served on shore to unload goods and get them to distributing centers, to corral captured slaves until they were sold, and to transport powder and flint to ammunition depots in the interior. Some writers estimate that Jean and Pierre Laffite controlled an organization of more than 5,000 men. This is probably an understatement.

---

[25] *Ibid.*, 843.
[26] Gayarré, *History of Louisiana*, IV, 218.
[27] Dunbar Rowland (ed.), *Official Letter Books of W. C. C. Claiborne, 1801-1816* (6 vols., Jackson, 1907), IV, 358-67, 372, 378; Faye, " Privateers of Guadeloupe," 435; William O. Scroggs, *The Story of Louisiana* (Indianapolis, 1924), 204-205.
[28] These figures, as well as the size of vessels and crews, are based on piracy case records in USDC of La. and on Customs House Records.

Commodore Patterson found about 1,000 on Grande Terre alone during his raid in September, 1814.

A new source of privateer commissions and a new port opened to the Baratarians at the close of 1811—Spain's most strongly fortified city in the new world, Cartagena, on the Caribbean coast of South America. This seaport was the capital of Cartagena province, a part of New Granada (today the state of Colombia). Cartagena declared its independence from Spain on November 11, 1811. Immediately Spanish troops cut off her source of supplies from the interior. The President of Cartagena retaliated by sending a vessel with privateer commissions to Grande Terre and by inviting the Baratarians to capture or destroy Spanish shipping.[29] The Baratarians were quick to accept the commissions which they needed to supplement their French ones; but because the United States was not at war with Spain, they still could not legally bring into the United States any prizes they might capture.

This did not alter the operations of Baratarians. They continued to infest all approaches to Cuba, since that island was the center of the slave trade. Soon the Spanish Consul at New Orleans was bombarding Governor Claiborne with complaints of illegal seizures.

Claiborne's young French wife had died after two brief years of marriage and he was now courting Sophronie Bosque, a Spanish señorita.[30] He was beginning to turn against the Baratarians, but the first to take definite action against them was Commodore David Porter of the United States Navy. No special machinery had been provided to enforce the act of March 2, 1807, which prohibited importation of slaves; and at first this duty fell to the Secretary of the Treasury as head of customs collections. Then, through the activity of cruisers, the Secretary of Navy came to have oversight of violations.[31]

Naval officials were stationed at the Balize to prevent the entry

---

[29] José Manuel Restrepo, *Historia de la Revolución de la República de Colombia* (4 vols., Besanzon, 1858), I, 155; USDC of La., Cases No. 746, No. 779, No. 817.

[30] Henry E. Chambers, *A History of Louisiana* (3 vols., Chicago, 1925), III, 370; Fortier, *Louisiana*, I, 214.

[31] Du Bois, *Suppression of Slave-Trade,* 108.

of suspected slavers or contraband, but there was not much they could do at this time because the Baratarians operated through the whole coastal area west of Grande Terre and Grand Isle. Chenière Caminada, the mouth of Bayou Lafourche, Timbalier Island, Cat Island and Isle Dernière all offered easy access to the Baratarian country. So great was the contraband they brought in that every month Laffite built a new warehouse in the area between Grande Terre and New Orleans, and now not only Sauvinet but a whole flock of merchants were his distributors.

Commodore Porter was indignant at the flagrant flouting of the laws of the United States. He reported that "the district attorney apparently winked at piracies committed in our waters and at the open communication kept up between these depredators and the citizens of New Orleans." [32]

Porter was aware of the complaints of the Spanish Consul and of the fact that Cuban merchants had subscribed $60,000 as a reward for three vessels which the privateers had taken.[33] These three vessels (the *Duc de Montebello*, *L'Epine*, and *Intrépide*) arrived at the Balize in the spring of 1810 and asked for "refreshment and repairs."

From the records it is difficult to say who was commanding these vessels. Testimony in piracy cases indicates time and again that captains frequently changed their names and the names of their vessels. Francis Brosquet may have been commanding the *Duc de Montebello*. Ange-Michel Brouard, alias Mentor, and perhaps alias Renato Beluche, was mentioned as the owner.[34] The *Duc de Montebello* brought a sheaf of French commissions. One of these was for Pedro Brugman, which name Beluche most frequently used as an alias.

Beluche was on the *Intrépide* which was listed as Sauvinet's vessel. Marcellin Batigne was serving at this time as master of *L'Epine*.

---

[32] David D. Porter, *Memoir of Commodore David Porter of the United States Navy* (Albany, 1875), 79.
[33] *Ibid.*, 81.
[34] Rowland (ed.), *Claiborne Letter Books,* V, 26; USDC of La., Case No. 363.

The Baratarians and the Battle of New Orleans

As soon as naval officials on duty at the Balize reported the arrival of these vessels to Porter in New Orleans, he went down the river with a force of gun boats and demanded that the privateers surrender. They refused and the District Attorney asked Porter to let the vessels depart. " The many friends of the buccaneers in New Orleans made every exertion to obtain permission for them to depart," reported Porter, " and a direct conflict arose between the civil and naval authority, which culminated when Commander Porter informed the privateer captains that in default of their immediate surrender he should open fire." [35]

The privateers hauled down their colors, and Porter took the three vessels to New Orleans and began proceedings to claim them as prizes in the United States District Court. It was now the duty of the District Attorney to prosecute. Porter began to experience all of the ramifications and procrastinations of expert legal guidance in the courts. His lawyer Edward Livingston, whose wife was from Haiti and whose brother-in-law was from Haiti, must have laughed inwardly at his client's frustrations.

Porter recorded that all three prizes were condemned and sold, but apparently Sauvinet's *Intrépide* went free after paying a $1500 penalty; and when Customs refused her a clearance, she sailed without one.[36] *L'Epine*, " whose complete innocence had been proved," went out with the *Intrépide*.[37]

Porter's share in the prize money was one-fourth or $25,000. He had to pay Edward Livingston 5 per cent of this.[38] Then Porter, with proof of his capture of the three vessels, went to Havana to collect the $60,000 reward that the merchants had offered. He was " kept so long dancing attendance that he was very nearly impoverished." The promised reward was never paid.[39]

By mid-August the *Intrépide* was approaching Barataria with a

---

[35] Porter, *Memoir*, 79.
[36] Faye, " Privateers of Guadeloupe," 437, quoting from *Archivo General de Indias, Papeles de Cuba, Legajo* 1710, Morphy to Someruelos, May 30, 1810; USDC of La., Case No. 379.
[37] *Ibid.*
[38] Faye, " Privateers of Guadeloupe," 437; Porter, *Memoir*, 80-81.
[39] Porter, *Memoir*, 81.

prize when a storm blew the two vessels on the coast. Their cargoes of iron, wine and dry goods were unloaded on small craft and sent up the bayous while the wrecks were burned.[40]

Soon *L'Epine* neared the Mississippi with a prize, the *Alerta*, which had a cargo of slaves. Naval officials seized the *Alerta* and presented claim to its cargo in the United States District Court.[41] The slaves were ordered appraised and sold in accordance with an act passed by the legislature of the Territory of Orleans on March 16, 1810. This act said that slaves imported in violation of the act of March 2, 1807, " should be sold in the manner directed by the said act and that the proceeds of such sale should be delivered into the hands of the Marshal of said Territory, to be afterwards disposed of as the Legislature should deem proper." [42]

The slaves were quartered on Dr. William Flood's plantation on the west bank of the Mississippi and there appraised as follows: [43]

60 men at $400	$24,000
33 females at $325	10,725
51 boys and men, average $200	10,200
1 boy very sick	50
	$44,975

The value of this contraband is significant when one considers that for every prize libelled in court, dozens successfully unloaded at Barataria.

---

[40] *Louisiana Gazette*, July 28, August 23, September 4, 1810.
[41] USDC of La., Cases No. 379, No. 380, No. 381, No. 401.
[42] The act of March 16, 1810, is cited in Case No. 401.
[43] USDC of La., Case No. 380.

BARATARIA'S HEYDAY

SUGAR PLANTERS, COTTON PLANTERS, AND MERCHANTS OF ALL the lower part of the Mississippi Valley went to Grande Terre to buy slaves and British manufactured goods.[1] But Grande Terre was a three-days' journey from New Orleans. It was early in 1812 that Jean Laffite decided to hold an auction at The Temple.

The Temple was a chenière or mound of shells which Indians had built long before white men came to Louisiana. The mound covered a large area and was three or four feet higher than the surrounding marsh land which meant that it was dry. The Temple was located about half way between New Orleans and Grande Terre at the point where Bayou Pierrot and Bayou Barataria empty into Little Lake.

The auction was a huge success. Many more followed and so great was the demand for Baratarian wares that traders gave and received orders for them on the streets of New Orleans with as little secrecy as orders were given for purchases in Philadelphia or New York.[2]

Beluche, Dominique, Pierre Laffite, Gambie, and others paraded the streets of New Orleans arm in arm—singing, carousing in happy-

---
[1] Nolte, *Fifty Years in Both Hemispheres*, 189; Latour, *Historical Memoir*, 15.
[2] Latour, *Historical Memoir*, 15.

Barataria's Heyday

go-lucky fashion. Jean Laffite walked the streets openly but he found entertainment in more select circles. There seemed to be no limit to the success of the Baratarians; but, as in a Greek tragedy, their very success (which seemed like arrogance and insolence to certain Anglo-Saxon merchants who did not patronize them) provoked not " the wrath of heaven," but slow, inexorable Nemesis on the part of federal authorities and Governor Claiborne.

That section of the Louisiana Purchase which had been designated as the Territory of Orleans in 1804, became the State of Louisiana in 1812, and the legislature elected Claiborne as the first state governor. Six weeks after Louisiana became a state, the United States Congress declared war on Great Britain. On that same day, June 18, Congress authorized the President to issue commissions or letters of marque and general reprisal to private armed vessels, in such form as he should think proper and under the seal of the United States, against the vessels, goods, and effects of the government of the United Kingdom of Great Britain and Ireland, their dependencies, and the subjects thereof.[3] Six privateers were duly commissioned in New Orleans. Beluche accepted command of one of them, the four-gun schooner *Spy*, and he was the only one of the six who was successful.[4]

On the 17th of November, Beluche captured the 332-ton *Jane* laden with mahogany and logwood from Honduras. He took his prize to New Orleans and presented his claims in Admiralty Court.

The captain of the *Jane* declared before Judge Dominick Augustin Hall that the pretense upon which the ship was taken was her being British property, that resistance was made at the time of her capture, " that there were twelve carried guns mounted on board said vessel; that there were a few small arms on board, three kegs of powder and different kinds of shot; that she was so armed for the purpose of resisting any cruiser that might attack her." [5]

---

[3] USDC of La., Case No. 552.
[4] Edgar Stanton Maclay, *A History of American Privateers* (New York, 1899), 322.
[5] USDC of La., Case No. 552.

This suit speedily came to an end and Judge Hall decreed that "the said ship *Jane*, her tackle, apparel and furniture, guns and cargo, were rightly and duly taken and seized as aforesaid, and did at the time of the capture and seizure thereof, as far as appears to me, belong to Great Britain, or to some person or persons being subjects of the King of Great Britain . . . and as such ought to be accounted and reputed liable to confiscation and be adjudged as good and lawful prize to the said private armed schooner *Spy*, and the said ship *Jane*, her tackle, apparel and furniture, guns and cargo, be adjudged and condemned as good and lawful prize to the said Reyne Beluche, commander of the said private armed schooner *Spy*." [6]

The ease and quickness with which this case was settled and the fact that Beluche was awarded the captured ship and cargo which he had openly and legally brought into New Orleans should have made privateering for the United States attractive to the Baratarians. But *only six* privateers were commissioned by the federal government in New Orleans. British warships were patrolling the coast and beginning that tight blockade which would cause cotton and sugar of the Mississippi delta to pile up in warehouses for the next two and a half years.

Baratarians found Spanish prizes more numerous and more rewarding than British merchantmen. So the Spanish Consul had plenty of complaints which he filed with Claiborne while the federal government complained of the small customs receipts and the continued illegal importation of slaves, and Anglo-Saxon merchants insisted that something must be done.

So Andrew Hunter Holmes of the United States Army was sent "with a party of between 30 and 40 men . . . for the purpose of aiding revenue officers in preventing the practice of smuggling by means of Lake Barataria." Holmes and his men had proceeded as far as twenty-five miles into the Barataria country without witnessing any violation of the revenue law, when on the night of November 15, 1812, they hailed a pirogue. On its refusing to come on shore

---

[6] *Ibid.*; *Minutes United States District Court 1811-1815* (Typescript, Louisiana State University Library), III, 154.

Barataria's Heyday

Holmes "fired his piece without injurious effects" and the pirogue came to shore. It was found to have on board a small quantity of imported goods which Holmes took out and then "permitted the men to proceed in consequence of their behavoiring well after the capture." [7]

The next night, in the bright moonlight, Holmes and his men saw three or four sail upon the lake " which is the first large one after leaving the Temple." The federal men immediately got in boats and pursued the Baratarians. When they were within hailing distance, the Baratarians asked, "What boat is that?"

Holmes replied, "United States troops!"

Then in broken English a voice warned the troops that if they came nearer the Baratarians would fire into them and kill everyone. Holmes paid no attention to this threat and after a brief battle the Baratarians surrendered. Later a boat tried to escape, but some of the troops fired into it, killed one man and took the rest prisoners. Then all the prisoners and boats were rowed across the lake to Holmes's camp.

One of the boats was found to contain imported goods "consisting of a large quantity of cinnamon and other articles." Then Holmes brought "the whole of the goods and boats and all the prisoners except one who escaped a few miles above the city," to New Orleans.

The names of the prisoners, "as they confessed themselves were: Jean Laffite (jeune), Angel Raballo, Antoine Sennet, Antoine Angelet, Antoine Bormet, Pierre Cadet, Pierre Laffite (ainé), Jean Gentil, Salvador Artugue, Louis Dalhier, Jean Baptiste Soulize, Pierre Terraim, Michel Joseph, Andre Como, Henry Nuñez, Henry Seybardier, Antoine Michel, Manuel Garcia, Jean Herven, Julien Berat, Jean Mayer, Manuel Brazo, Martin Pounce, Antoine Cordier." [8]

This list is significant. It contains not a single Anglo-Saxon name. Most of the names are French, probably aliases, but the names of men from Haiti. Jean, the younger Laffite, and Pierre, the elder,

---

[7] USDC of La., Case No. 573.
[8] *Ibid.*

immediately secured bail. They had the best legal counsel in New Orleans—Edward Livingston.

The capture of the Baratarians was made on November 12, 1812. District Attorney John Randolph Grymes did not file a petition against them until April 7, 1813; that is, after Governor Claiborne had complained to the President and in the press, and had issued a proclamation on March 15, 1813, commanding the Baratarians to cease from their unlawful acts.[9]

Then Grymes most respectfully showed that Jean Laffite of the city of New Orleans was indebted to the United States for the sum of $12,014.52 for 26 bales cinnamon, 54 linen shirts, 3 pieces of Russia sheeting, 7 pieces canvas, 1 bundle twine, 1 piece of handkerchiefs—to the value of $4,004.89; these " being goods, wares and merchandise arriving from a foreign port or place within four leagues of the coast of the said United States and unladed from out of the said ship or vessel before said ship or vessel had arrived at the proper place for the discharge of her cargo or any part thereof and without the authorization of the proper officer or officers of the customs. . . . By virtue of the act of Congress of the United States . . . the said Jean Laffite hath forfeited and become liable to pay to the said United States treble the value of said goods." [10]

United States Marshal Pierre Le Breton Duplessis was given a writ on April 8, which commanded him " to take the body of Jean Laffite, so that he shall appear before this District Court on the third Monday of April." He was given a similar writ for Pierre. On April 19, Duplessis wrote on the writs, " Not to be found." He was given writs a second time on April 29, on which he wrote on July 20, " Not to be found." July 29, he was given a third set of writs. These he kept until October 16, then wrote on them, " Not to be found." [11]

Three times court had convened and Jean and Pierre had not appeared because Marshal Duplessis could not find them. Governor

---

[9] Gayarré, *History of Louisiana*, IV, 289-91; Arthur, *Jean Laffite*, 28.
[10] USDC of La., Case No. 573.
[11] *Ibid*.

Barataria's Heyday

Claiborne issued a second proclamation denouncing the Baratarians as bandits and ordering them to break up their establishment. Then throughout the city, he had the following notice posted:

> I, governor of the state of Louisiana, offer a reward of five ndred Dollars which will be paid out of the Treasury, to any person c..ivering John Laffite to the Sheriff of the Parish of Orleans, or to any other Sheriff in the State, so that he, the said John Laffite, may be brought to justice.
>
> Given under my hand at New Orleans on the 24th day of November, 1813.
>
> William C. C. Claiborne.[12]

Two days later citizens guffawed as another handbill appeared in public places. It read something like this:

> I, Bos of Barataria, offer a reward of five thousand dollars which will be paid out of my treasury, to any person delivering Governor Claiborne to me at Isle au Chat (Cat Island) west of Grande Terre, near the mouth of Bayou Lafourche.
>
> Given under my hand at Grande Terre on the 26th day of November, 1813.
>
> Jean Laffite.[13]

---

[12] Gayarré, *History of Louisiana*, IV, 302-303; Arthur, *Jean Laffite*, 31, cites the entire proclamation Claiborne issued that day against the Baratarians—what appeared on the handbill was the last part of that proclamation; Rowland, *Letter Books of Claiborne*, VI, 279-280.

[13] Letter of Walker Gilbert to Thomas Freeman. Donaldson Ville, February 18, 1814 (written about three months after the incident), Records of the Eastern District, State Land Office of Louisiana (see Appendix A); Letter of Major General Flournoy who succeeded General James Wilkinson as commander of the 7th military district to J. F. H. Claiborne, undated, J. F. H. Claiborne, *Life and Times of Gen. Sam Dale The Mississippi Partisan* (New York, 1860), 87-89. In part this letter says:

> ... A man called Laffite, reputed to be connected with smugglers and pirates, I determined to apprehend. I had a consultation with the governor, and we fixed a plan. I learned that he kept a mistress on Conti Street, and that he was expected to visit her on a certain night. I sent a corporal and six men to arrest him, but failed. The next day I ascertained that Laffite was in the house and in bed at the time, but, on hearing the approach of my guard, had leaped out of a window and into a well close by, where he remained, with his head only out of water, until the guard retired. I likewise received a message about him, stating that he knew me well; that he crossed me on my walks every night, and could slay me, or have me slain, at any moment, either in the streets or in my quarters; but that, as he knew I was acting from a sense of duty, he would spare me if I would take no farther cognizance of him. Having failed in my plan, Governor Claiborne said he would see what he

The Baratarians and the Battle of New Orleans

Meanwhile, the British tried several times in that year of 1813, to invade Barataria; but the privateers were better gunners and the British retired suffering losses. In August, Dominique, Gambie and Jean Marotte attacked an English convoy in the neighborhood of Barbados. After a hot battle they succeeded in detaching two slavers which they captured and brought to Grande Terre. Then the British tried different tactics. Just a few days before Claiborne published his proclamation offering a $500 reward for Jean Laffite, a British man-of-war appeared at Grande Terre and one of its officers tried to get permission for the British to fortify channels so that they could pass secretly through Barataria to New Orleans. Jean told the officer that warships of the United States were nearby at Timbalier Island. The man-of-war hastily sailed away.[14]

In early April, 1814, Dominique sailed from Grande Terre in the *Tigre* searching for prey. He spied sail to the west and followed for a day when he discovered he was chasing a British armed merchantman. On the Mexican coast north of Vera Cruz, off the port of Nautla, the *Tigre* attacked the merchantman. Dominique's cannon were deadly and the battle was soon over. Delirious with joy, the jubilant buccaneers celebrated.

"Whiskey! For all hands!" roared Dominique.

Suddenly the roistering crew was knocked sprawling to the deck. The *Tigre* had wrecked on a shoal. Shocked sober, the sailors looked lugubriously at one another.

"Don't look like that," pleaded Dominique. "Sapristi! I can get another ship. There are plenty more where this one came from."

High spirits returned as the Baratarians scrambled to shore. Some men from Nautla had been watching them and asked who they were. "Baratarians," was the reply.

could do in the matter; that Laffite had comrades who would betray him. He offered a reward of five hundred dollars for his apprehension. Next, day, a proclamation, signed Laffite, appeared, offering *five thousand dollars* for the governor's head! He added a postscript, however, stating that this was a mere *bagatelle*. He was subsequently pardoned by the governor, and assisted in the defense of New Orleans. I know not what became of him thereafter.
(The author is indebted to Fordyce L. Perego of New Orleans for this citation.)
[14] *Journal of Jean Laffite*, 50-51.

Barataria's Heyday

The men from Nautla knew about Grande Terre. They were Mexican patriots and had captured a Spanish felucca which they wanted Dominique to take and bring back loaded with arms and ammunition. General Juan Pablo Anaya was to accompany them and pay them $10,000 in silver.[15]

Dominique jumped at the chance to make such a deal. Hard money was still scarce in New Orleans. He knew that merchants, bankers, and others would be only too glad to take part in such commerce.

And so it was at this time that the New Orleans Association took definite shape. Edward Livingston was the directing genius of the group which included John Randolph Grymes, district attorney; Abner L. Duncan, former territorial attorney general at Natchez; John K. West, Duncan's business partner; United States Marshal Pierre Le Breton Duplessis; Benjamin Morgan, bank president; Captain Henry Perry, quartermaster and ordnance officer in New Orleans, and a number of others.[16] This group of men saw that Laffite's magazines were filled with powder and flints.

So Dominique was able to load the felucca with 80,000 pounds of gunpowder and return to Nautla by June 20. This was the beginning of a flourishing trade between the New Orleans Association and the Mexican patriots.[17]

While Dominique was busy along the Gulf coast, Beluche was at Cartagena, transporting troops for the new republic and helping rescue survivors of an expedition against the Spaniards at Santa Marta. For this service he was rewarded with the rank of *teniente de navío* in the Cartagenan navy.[18] Then he raided Spanish shipping.

At this time he had two vessels: *La Popa*, his favorite which he

---

[15] Faye, "Privateersmen of the Gulf and Their Prizes," 22; USDC of La., Case No. 817.

[16] Stanley Faye, "Commodore Aury," *Louisiana Historical Quarterly*, XXIV (Baton Rouge, July, 1941), 21 in the reprint.

[17] Faye, "Privateersmen of the Gulf," 22; USDC of La., Case No. 817.

[18] Hoja de Servicio, Archivo Nacional, Bogotá; Restrepo, *Historia de Colombia*, I, 177-78, 198-204; Renato Beluche, *R. Beluche, Capitán de navío de la República de Colombia* (Caracas, 1824; reprinted by Isidro Beluche in Panama, 1954), 4 in the original.

usually commanded himself and which had a crew of a hundred men; and the *Piñeres*, commanded by Charles Lominé. Beluche soon had a third ship. On October 2, 1813, he captured the 1012-ton *La Caridad*, alias *La Cubana*, as she was coming from New Haven to Cuba. Beluche changed her name to *Atalanta*, and later changed it again to *General Bolivar*.[19] This vessel was commanded by different captains or perhaps by the same captain under different names.

Beluche's service record says that during the three years he sailed under the flag of Cartagena he destroyed more than a million dollars worth of Spanish shipping. He prowled in the Bahama Channel, the Gulf, and the Caribbean, and kept Grande Terre supplied with commissions from Cartagena.

Gambie, with a fresh Cartagenan commission, was cruising along the Mexican coast in May, 1814. His good *Philanthrope* had a prize in tow, the schooner *Marcela*. Then off the bar of Tampico he captured another, the Spanish brig *Fernando VII*, Captain Vincente Quintanilla, of Campeche.

Back at Grande Terre the two prizes yielded their rich cargo. A few days later the Spanish Consul in New Orleans found a note on his desk written by Captain Quintanilla. It said: " Captain Gambie brought us to Grande Terre where he sold the cargo of my ship and that of the schooner *Marcela*. After keeping us twenty-eight days in the most cruel situation, this man had the kindness to give us the schooner *Marcela* in order that we may go to Campeche, our home port."[20]

Gambie usually was not so considerate. In fact, he had little respect for Jean Laffite's regulations against piracy. On one occasion the two clashed after Gambie attacked a merchantman of the United States.[21] Laffite won this battle of wills and in a few days Gambie seemed to have forgotten the incident as other events demanded attention.

---

[19] USDC of La., Cases No. 746, No. 760.
[20] Faye, " Privateersmen of the Gulf," 26-27, citing *AGI, PdeC, Legajo* 1836, Quintanilla to Morphy, June 29, 1814.
[21] Saxon, *Laffite the Pirate*, 49-51.

NEGRIL BAY

THE WAR OF 1812 WAS IN ITS THIRD YEAR BEFORE LOUISIANA became the theater of operations, but citizens there had been following developments with interest. They knew that peace overtures had been made almost as soon as the war began. However, it was not until the fall of 1813 that England agreed to meet American commissioners at some neutral city in Europe.

American commissioners arrived at Ghent in Belgium in the spring of the next year and cooled their heels waiting for their opponents. "England was gathering her strength to bludgeon America into submission and the British Cabinet was organizing as great an effort as they believed the British taxpayers would endure."[1] It was summer before the English commissioners arrived and with demands that took away the breath of the Americans.

They demanded a new boundary line between Canada and the United States which placed part of Maine, Vermont, and New York in Canada. From there the proposed line ran from the St. Lawrence to the Lakes, through Lake Erie to the head of the Allegheny River, down that river to the Ohio, from the Ohio to the Mississippi, and up the Mississippi to the Missouri, and following that river to the Rocky Mountains. The United States was to cede New Orleans,

---
[1] C. S. Forester, *The Age of Fighting Sail* (New York, 1956), 202.

The Baratarians and the Battle of New Orleans

" in order to insure us the enjoyment of our privileges to navigate the Mississippi."[2] These demands indicated that England still refused to recognize the Louisiana Purchase as legitimate.

So unthinkable were the British terms that the five Americans rejected them without even referring them to their government. The English commissioners stalled, waiting to hear that Great Britain was in possession of the Atlantic seaboard, Louisiana, and the whole Mississippi Valley. The course of war in Europe as well as in America gave them every reason to hope for such a result. Napoleon had been defeated. Britain's military might and all the resources of her Empire could now be used for a last stupendous effort to crush the United States.

The British press set to work to marshal opinion against the United States as it had against Napoleon. The London *Courier*, usually the first to receive information from the British ministry, reported January 27, 1814, on President Madison's annual message to Congress, saying that it was " a compound of canting and hypocracy, of exaggeration and falsehood, of coarseness without strength, of assertions without proof, of the meanest prejudices, and of the most malignant passions; of undisguised hatred of Great Britain, and of ill-concealed partiality and servility toward France."

The London *Times* on May 24, called Madison a liar and an imposter. It said, " Mr. Madison's dirty, swindling manoeuvres in respect to Louisiana and the Floridas remain to be punished. . . . With Madison and his perjured set no treaty can be made, for no oath can bind them." When British commissioners were ready to start for Ghent in June, the *Times* on the second of that month instructed them saying: " Our demands may be couched in a single word,—Submission."

On September 3, after the capture and burning of Washington (August, 1814), the *Sun* spoke of Americans as " worthless, lying, treacherous, false, slanderous, cowardly. . . . Were it not that the

---

[2] A London pamphlet entitled " compendious view of the points to be discussed in treating with the United States . . ." quoted in *Niles' Register* (76 vols., Baltimore, 1811-49), VII (December 10, 1814), 218.

(26)

course of punishment they are undergoing is necessary to the ends of moral and political justice, we declare before our country that we should feel ashamed of victory over such ignoble foes. The quarrel resembles one between a gentleman and a chimney-sweeper; the former may beat the low scoundrel to his heart's contentment; but there is no honor in the exploit, and he is sure to be covered with the soil and dirt of his ignominous antagonist."

As this hate campaign continued, the English were so sure of conquering the United States that the day after the news of the burning of Washington reached Europe, Paris newspapers reported Lord Castlereagh as saying: " I expect at this time most of the largest seaport towns in America are laid in ashes, that we are in possession of New Orleans, and have command of all the waters of the Mississippi and the lakes, so that now the Americans are little better than prisoners at large in their own country." [3]

Because of a change in naval command in 1814, the British offensive against the Atlantic coast was much more aggressive and effective than it had previously been. At the beginning of April Vice-Admiral Sir Alexander Cochrane arrived in Bermuda to supercede Admiral John Warren in command of the North Atlantic, Leeward Islands, and Jamaica stations.

Admiral Cochrane dispatched the *Orpheus*, Captain Pigot, to Apalachicola to negotiate with the Creeks and other Indians. The *Orpheus* arrived at Apalachicola May 10th, and within ten days Pigot estimated that 2,800 Creek warriors, perhaps as many Choctaws, and 1,000 others were ready to take up arms with the British. They would be easy to train because they were good horsemen and familiar with firearms. Pigot felt also that the Negroes of Georgia would join the British wholesale, once the movement started.

He suggested to Cochrane that, since Mobile was the only post held by the United States between Pensacola and Baton Rouge, a few British troops cooperating with Creeks and Choctaws could get possession of Baton Rouge. This would cut off New Orleans from

---

[3] *Niles' Register*, VII (February 18, 1815), 389.

The Baratarians and the Battle of New Orleans

the interior and make it easier to occupy that city and the lower Mississippi area.[4]

Cochrane felt that Pigot was right, so he reported to the Admiralty that not more than 3,000 British troops would be needed to drive Americans out of Louisiana and the Floridas. The 3,000 British troops could be landed at Mobile where Indians and disaffected French and Spaniards would join them.[5]

Meanwhile, Cochrane sent Colonel Edward Nicholls to Pensacola with 4 officers, 11 noncommisioned officers and 97 privates of the Royal Marines to train the Indians. They were dispatched in the *Hermes* and *Carron*. These sloops carried two howitzers, a field-piece, 1,000 stand of arms and 300 suits of clothing for the Indians. At the same time the brig *Orpheus* anchored at Apalachicola with 22,000 stand of arms, ammunition, blankets and clothing.[6]

While Nicholls was preparing the Florida thrust toward Louisiana, and while 10,000 veteran troops in Canada were ready to invade New York from Montreal by way of Plattsburgh and Lake Champlain, Cochrane terrorized the Atlantic coast to divert attention and military support from the two main targets of the British. His forces started on the coast of Maine, raided, ruthlessly looted, and worked their way south.

In August Cochrane's forces were augmented by the arrival of Admiral Malcolm and his fleet with additional regiments from Europe. It was not at all unusual for women to accompany such expeditions and there were women with this one. Balls and other public entertainments had been held through the fleet while crossing the Atlantic.

One night a grand ball was held on the Admiral's flag ship, the *Royal Oak*. It was opened " by Admiral Malcolm and the Honour-

---

[4] A. T. Mahan, *Sea Power in its Relations to the War of 1812* (2 vols., Boston, 1905), II, 383.
[5] *Ibid.*, 384.
[6] Latour, *Historical Memoir*, 10-11; Adams, *History of the United States*, VIII, 319-20; George Laval Chesterton, *Peace, War and Adventure* (2 vols., London, 1853), I, 213; Benson Earle Hill, *Recollections of an Artillery Officer* (2 vols., London, 1836), I, 299.

Negril Bay

able Mrs. Mullens, in a country dance."[7] It is well to note the popularity of Mrs. Mullens with superior officers because it may have had some bearing on the truculence of her husband, Colonel Mullens, later at the battle of New Orleans.

After burning Washington and attacking Baltimore, Admiral Cochrane and his fellow officers agreed in conference that they had fulfilled their mission—harrying the Atlantic coast. Now it was time to withdraw from this diversionary movement and concentrate forces for the invasion of Louisiana.

On the west coast of Jamaica are two headlands eight miles apart. which protect an expanse of sea where ships can ride safely at anchor. This roadstead is called Negril Bay. Here British naval and military forces concentrated in November of 1814. Orders for this operation were written *after* peace commissioners had assembled at Ghent.

An English subaltern recorded that after the fleets had reached Negril Bay, " seventy or eighty sail of vessels . . . lay . . . so closely wedged together that to walk across the decks, from one to the other, seemed, when at a little distance, to be far from impracticable."[8]

Fifty of those vessels were warships, carrying 1,000 guns. The rest were merchant ships, chartered to carry to England the rich booty in New Orleans. English speculators estimated the value of cotton, sugar, Kentucky whiskey, flour, port, and other produce stored there as $15,000,000.[9] An itemized list in *Niles' Register* arrives at a larger total value.[10]

Baratarians tried but had been unable to get much produce out of the country. In 1811, Beluche had made a run to Bordeaux in

---

[7] George Robert Gleig, *A Narrative of the Campaigns of the British Army at Washington and New Orleans, under Generals Ross, Pakenham, and Lambert, in the Years 1814 and 1815* (London, 1826), 65.

[8] *A Subaltern In America: Comprising His Narrative of the Campaigns of the British Army, at Baltimore, Washington, & &, During the Late War* (Philadelphia, 1833), 187-88.

[9] Latour, *Historical Memoir*, xv; Walker, *Jackson and New Orleans*, 208.

[10] VII (February 18, 1815), 390; VIII (April 15, 1815), 113-14.

the 128-ton *Jenny*.[11] He cleared New Orleans again for Bordeaux on March 5, 1812; but the British caught him after he had crossed the Atlantic and detained him at Plymouth. This happened in May, the month before the United States declared war on Great Britain.[12] After this experience Beluche hurried back to New Orleans and accepted one of the six privateer commissions issued there by the United States.

Now, at Negril Bay, "while horses of the artillery, caught in America, were landed and turned out to pasture," Cochrane's officers were hiring all the small craft they could.[13] These would be needed in shallow coastal waters of the United States and for communication between the warships and shore.

Cochrane's armada was to transport an army such as Louisiana had never seen before. In addition to the four regiments that had vandalized from Maine to the Chesapeake, there were the four regiments Kean had brought direct from the battlefields of Europe and two regiments of Negro troops he had collected in the West Indies. These eight regiments totaled approximately 8,000 troops. The fleet would furnish 1,500 marines and 10,000 sailors.[14] Altogether, the invasion force numbered 20,000, avid for the promised " beauty and booty." [15]

Civil officers were already on board to conduct the government of Louisiana. The Honorable Mr. Elwood from Trinidad was to be lieutenant governor. A gentleman from Barbados was to be collector of the Port of New Orleans. He had with him his five, blond daughters. They were a glut on the market in Barbados, but in

---

[11] *Louisiana Gazette*, April 5, 1811.
[12] From Lloyd's List in *Louisiana Gazette*, July 21, 1812.
[13] Chesterton, *Peace, War and Adventure*, I, 167; Hill, *Recollections of an Artillery Officer*, I, 295.
[14] Latour states that after the arrival of Lambert, December 28, 1814, with 2,200 more troops, the total effective force, exclusive of sailors, was 14,450. *Historical Memoir*, Appendix No. LXIV, cxxxvi.
[15] The appetite for plunder of British troops had been whetted along the Chesapeake, in France, and in Spain. They had no reason to suppose they could not do the same in New Orleans. British prisoners and deserters reported that the " parole and countersign of the enemy's army was *beauty and booty.*" Latour, *Historical Memoir*, 255-56; *Niles' Register*, VII (February 25, 1815), 410; VIII (April 22, 1815), 133.

Negril Bay

Creole New Orleans their blond beauty would surely get them rich husbands.[16]

An attorney general, an admiralty judge and a secretary for the colony had been sent directly from England. The Superintendent of Indian Affairs had come from Canada.[17]

The list of civil officers was complete except for the choice plum. Who was to be governor of Louisiana? The man who had been shot in the neck twice by privateers. In due time he would appear. Meanwhile, officers' wives and other females with the expedition anticipated a gay season in New Orleans. They made life merry with music and dancing and other entertainment.

A government editor and printing press were part of the retinue. The editor would print and broadcast proclamations and other announcements which would explain English policy to the benighted inhabitants of New Orleans, and publish orders of the new government.

English peace commissioners at Ghent knew all this, knew that the orders of the expedition were to occupy Louisiana, ascend the Mississippi, make a junction with the 10,000 troops in Canada, and choke what was left of the United States. The invasion and occupation of Louisiana, they thought, would be easily and quickly accomplished.

---

[16] During the last part of January, 1815, Thomas Shields, Purser at the New Orleans naval station, captured some of these civil officers. They became a subject of correspondence between Master Commander Daniel T. Patterson and Admiral Cochrane. Patterson sent the whole packet, including Shields's report, to the Secretary of the Navy March 3, 1815. These are to be found in the National Archives, Naval Records. Other sources for the civil officers are Gleig, *Campaigns of the British Army*, 1826 London edition, 340, 1836 London edition, 349; Latour, *Historical Memoir*, xv; James Parton, *Life of Andrew Jackson* (3 vols., New York, 1861), II, 40; William M'Carty, *History of the American War of Eighteen Hundred and Twelve* (Philadelphia, 1816), 234; and items like the following from *Niles' Register*, VII (February 25, 1815), 411: " The Plantagenet 74 arrived at Havana a little while since . . . it is notorious that they had also with them a comptroller, collector, printing presses and apparatus, and everything else that belonged to the *permanent* establishment they originally designed to have made at New Orleans."

[17] The Indian administrator was a son of the notorious Colonel Dockstadter of Tory fame in the Revolutionary annals of the Mohawk Valley. Augustus C. Buell, *History of Andrew Jackson* (2 vols., New York, 1904), II, 72-73.

The Baratarians and the Battle of New Orleans

Therefore, the English peace commissioners declared to the Americans: "We do not admit of Bonaparte's construction of the law of nations. We cannot accept it in relation to the subject-matter before us." [18] This meant the Treaty of Ghent would not apply to what they called the *province* of Louisiana because they did not recognize it as belonging to the United States.

The American commissioners were uneasy. Perhaps they would have felt better had they known that watchdogs like Beluche, Dominique You, Vincent Gambie, Chighizola and others were well aware of British activity. In fact, Lieutenant George Robert Gleig of the British Eighty-fifth Regiment reported that "the West Indian seas at this time swarmed with American privateers, and it was of great consequence to keep the storeships and heavy transports in the middle of the squadron." [19]

One morning one of the privateers approached a British transport, and an officer on the transport observed that: "The decks of this vessel were crowded with a group of piratical independent-looking fellows, of all sorts of complexions. While carelessly lounging in every possible posture, some leaned over the gunwale, whilst others stood erect with arms folded or akimbo. These men wore red and striped shirts; many of their sleeves tucked above the elbows of their brawny arms; their heads cased in various colored handkerchiefs or hairy caps, and other outlandish gear; hardly one of the piratical-looking fellows wore a jacket, owing to the genial warmth of the atmosphere.

"At first they hailed us in French through a hoarse speaking trumpet, a language we pretended not to understand; they then questioned us in English. But finding that we were only a transport, they took no further notice, and ploughed through the water to reconnoitre the body of the convoy." [20]

The "piratical, independent-looking" fellows did indeed go after

---

[18] *Ibid.*, II, 75-77; Adams, *History of United States*, IX, 9-11.
[19] *Campaigns of British Army*, 1836 London edition, 215.
[20] John Henry Cooke, *A Narrative of Events in the South of France and of the Attack on New Orleans, in 1814 and 1815* (London, 1835), 190-91.

Negril Bay

better game, the small war vessel *Volcano*. They " set more sail and ran to windward, moving just out of gunshot, in a parallel direction to us," reported Gleig who was on the *Volcano*.

It was now necessary to fall upon some plan of deceiving him, otherwise . . . he would attack. . . . The height of the bulwark served to conceal some of our men. . . . Captain Price, in order to give his ship a still greater resemblance than it already had to a merchantman, displayed an old faded scarlet ensign, and drew up his fore and mainsail in what sailors term a lubberly manner.

As yet the stranger had shown no colours, but from her build and rigging, there was little doubt as to her country. She was a beautiful schooner, presenting seven ports on a side, and apparently crowded with men,—circumstances which immediately led us to believe that she was an American privateer. The Volcano, on the other hand, was a clumsy strong-built ship, carrying twelve guns; and the Golden Fleece (the transport) mounted eight; so that, in point of artillery, the advantage was rather on our side; but the American's sailing was so much superior to that of either of us, that this advantage was more than counterbalanced.

Having dogged us till eight o'clock and reconnoitred with great exactness, the stranger began to steer gradually nearer and nearer, till at length it was judged that she had arrived within range. A gun was accordingly fired from the Volcano, and another from the transport, the balls from both of which passed over her, and fell into the sea. Finding herself thus assaulted, she instantly threw off her disguise, and hung out an American ensign; when, putting her helm up, she poured a broadside, with a volley of musquetry, into the transport; and ran alongside of the bomb (Volcano), which sailed to windward.

As soon as her flag was displayed, and her intention of attacking discerned, all hands were ordered up, and she received two well-directed broadsides from the Volcano, as well as a warm salute from the Golden Fleece. But such was the celerity of her motion, that she was alongside of the bomb in less time than can be imagined; and actually dashing her bow against the other, attempted to board. Captain Price, however, was ready to receive them. The boarders were at their posts in an instant, and the enemy discovering, when it was too late, the mistake into which he had fallen, left about twenty of his men upon the Volcano's bowsprit, all of whom were thrown into the sea; and filling his sails, sheered off with the same speed with which he had borne down. In attempting to escape, he unavoidably fell somewhat to leeward, and exposed the whole of his deck to the fire of the transport. A tremendous discharge of musketry saluted him as he passed and it was almost laughable to witness the haste with which his crew hurried below, leaving none upon deck except such as absolutely wanted to work his vessel.

The Volcano had by this time filled, and gave chase, firing with great precision at the privateer's yards and rigging, in the hope of disabling him. But as fortune would have it, none of his important ropes or yards were cut; and we had the mortification to see him, in a few minutes, beyond our reach.[21]

The Baratarians had friends on the coast of all the West Indian islands and these quickly reported any rumors or facts; so Cochrane's destination, which was supposed to be a profound secret, was soon known to the Baratarians. As one artillery officer complained: " The negociations made by the admiral for the hire of small craft," was the way in which " many persons who ought to have remained in ignorance were aware that New Orleans was the intended scene of action." [22]

The subaltern had another explanation of how the secret became known. He said: " I believe the truth to be as follows. The conquest of New Orleans was from the first the grand object . . . and so anxious were ministers to effect this, that though a general rendezvous at Jamaica, of the invading army, had been long planned out, not a hint of the matter was dropped to the naval officer commanding there, till the forces, both from England and the Potomac, were ready to set sail.

" It unhappily occurred, however, that in the interval, the Admiral on the Jamaica station died, and the dispatches designed for him were necessarily put into the hands of the senior captain. That gentleman, with a singular absence of all common prudence, opened these dispatches in the presence of a Jew merchant; and, like a perfect simpleton, informed him of their contents. . . . He fitted out a fast sailing schooner without delay, and dispatched them to the enemy." [23]

Some of the Baratarians had also been watching the British infiltration under Colonel Nicholls at Pensacola and along the

---
[21] Gleig, *Campaigns of British Army*, 1836 London edition, 220-22.
[22] Hill, *Recollections of an Artillery Officer*, I, 295.
[23] *A Subaltern in America*, 1833 Philadelphia edition, 187-88.

Negril Bay

Florida coast. Nicholls had been successful in getting an alliance with the Creek Indians. They were smarting from their recent chastisement at the hands of Andrew Jackson. Now they would get even with " Old Sharp Knife " who had forced them to sign a treaty whereby they ceded to the United States 23,000,000 acres in Georgia and Alabama.[24] The British high command counted greatly on the aid of the Creeks. Lord Bathurst wrote in his instructions from England: " With their favor and cooperation . . . we may expect to rescue the whole province of Louisiana from the United States." [25]

It may have been Renato Beluche who sent an anonymous report on this sector to Jean Laffite. Beluche was the most literate of the Baratarians, and this letter is in the same style as hundreds of his in Archives at Bogotá. Moreover, the mayor of Pensacola was his brother-in-law.[26] This report, dated from Havana, August 8, 1814, was as follows:

> Dear Sir
>
> I embrace the opportunity offered for Pensacola, to inform you, that an expedition has sailed from Bermuda for Mobile, who touched and left this on the 11th instant, under the command of colonel Nicholls of the artillery, a brave officer well known in the European wars.
>
> They touched here for aid in gun-boats, small vessels, &c. and for leave to land at Pensacola, all of which were refused by the captain-general. However, I learn that they are determined to land at Pensacola with or without leave, where they will embark their park of artillery. The colonel was conveyed with his troops in two sloops of war, the Hermes, commanded by the hon. W. H. Percy, and the Caron, commanded by the hon. P. Spencer, who, with such vessels as may be on the station, will cooperate with the land forces.
>
> The brig Orpheus, some time past, landed arms and some officers at Apalachicola to arrange with the Creek nation for future operations against Mobile, New Orleans and that district of the country, which they effected, and caused the breaking off the treaty.
>
> The whole nation are ready to join the British troops under colonel

---

[24] Marquis James, *Andrew Jackson The Border Captain* (Indianapolis, 1933), 187-90.
[25] Bathurst to Ross, September 28, 1814; MSS in the British Archives, cited in Adams, *History of United States*, VIII, 313.
[26] *AGI, PdeC, Legajo* 1874, cited in Faye, " Privateersmen of the Gulf," 16 in the reprint.

Nicholls, who will immediately on his arrival issue his proclamation, declaring all slaves who will join their standard free and liberated forever from their masters. He will also issue another to the Indians, promising all the tribes who will join him, to reinstate them in all their lands taken from them by the United States, and to guarantee the same to them forever. Having thus prepared the minds of the negroes and Indians, he will on arrival of two or three black regiments from Nassau, &c. of fine troops, calculated for that climate (who may pass by this next week) push for New Orleans—first having secured and fortified Mobile point, and taken Mobile, as well as placed a force at every point on the lakes, of any importance, as well as Plaquemines in order to cut off all trade of the Mississippi.

This force with him is small, but he will soon be re-enforced from Bermuda, &c.—the flying artillery appears well calculated for his operations in that country.[27]

Jean Laffite was well informed when he was approached by agents from Colonel Nicholls.

---

[27] Latour, *Historical Memoir*, Appendix No. 2, v-vi.

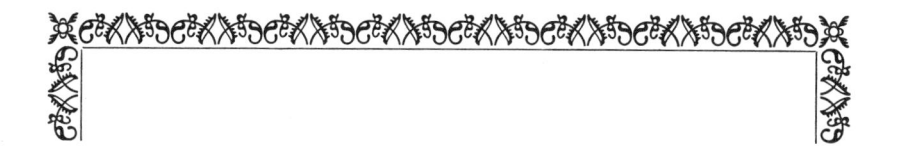

THE BRITISH APPROACH

JEAN LAFFITE

EARLY ON THE MORNING OF SEPTEMBER 3, 1814, GRANDE TERRE was aroused by a cannon shot coming from the direction of the Gulf. Two hundred Baratarians ran to see what was up. A British sloop had fired a gun at one of their ships about to enter the Pass and had forced her to run aground. The sloop anchored at the entrance.

Four Baratarians quickly manned a boat and rowed Jean Laffite to the scene.[1] A tender bearing British colors and a flag of truce came toward them. Captain Nicholas Lockyer, commander of the sloop, and Captain McWilliams of the army were in the tender.

"Is Mr. Laffite at home in the bay? I have important communications for him," said Captain Lockyer.

"You will have to come to shore if you want to see Mr. Laffite," replied Jean. "Follow me," he added, and the boats rode through the Pass and into the harbor.

Two hundred glowering Baratarians watched every move. Now the Englishmen were in Jean Laffite's power. "I am Jean Laffite," he said.

Captain McWilliams handed him a packet addressed to "Mr. Laffite—Barataria."

---

[1] USDC of La., Case No. 746, testimony of E. Williams.

(37)

The Baratarians and the Battle of New Orleans

"Make them prisoners," growled the Baratarians.

"You had better come into my house while we discuss this matter," Jean said to the Englishmen. Then he turned to the Baratarians saying, "These men have come under a flag of truce. We must respect it."

"They're spies! They have come to spy out the coast so they can invade and plunder the country," was the general cry. "We should make them prisoners and send them to New Orleans."

"Let me talk to them first and find out what is in the papers. You can keep guard to see that there is no communication with the sloop until I am through," answered Jean.[2]

The surly mob agreed and Jean led the Englishmen to his headquarters. He broke the seal on the first communication. It was Colonel Nicholls' proclamation to the citizens of Louisiana and it said:

> Natives of Louisiana! On you the first call is made to assist in liberating from a faithless, imbecile government, your paternal soil. Spaniards, Frenchmen, Italians, and British, . . . on you I call to aid me in this just cause. The American usurpation in this country must be abolished, and the lawful owners of the soil put in possession.
>
> I am at the head of a large body of Indians, well armed, disciplined, and commanded by British officers—a good train of artillery with every requisite, seconded by the powerful aid of a numerous British and Spanish squadron of ships and vessels of war.
>
> Be not alarmed, inhabitants of the country, at our approach. The same good faith and disinterestedness which has distinguished the conduct of Britons in Europe accompanies them here. You will have no fear of litigious taxes imposed on you for the purpose of carrying on an unnatural and unjust war; your property, your laws, the peace and tranquility of your country will be guaranteed to you by men who will suffer no infringement of theirs. Rest assured that these brave red men only burn with an ardent desire of satisfaction for the wrongs they have suffered from Americans, to join you in liberating these southern provinces from their yoke and drive them into the limits formerly prescribed by my sovereign.
>
> The Indians have pledged themselves, in the most solemn manner, not

---

[2] This conversation is based on such accounts as Latour, *Historical Memoir*, 17-18; and Walker, *Jackson and New Orleans*, 40-43.

The British approach Jean Laffite

to injure in the slightest degree, the persons or properties of any but enemies.[3]

As Jean Laffite read this proclamation, not a muscle of his face moved. The Englishmen had not the slightest hint of his reaction. Jean reached for the second document—a letter from William H. Percy, Captain and Senior Officer in the Gulf of Mexico. It said:

> Having understood that some British merchantmen have been detained, taken into, and sold by the inhabitants of Barataria, I have directed Captain Lockyer, of His Majesty's sloop *Sophia*, to proceed to that place and inquire into the circumstances with positive orders to demand instant restitution and, in case of refusal, to destroy to his utmost every vessel there, as well as to carry destruction over the whole place, and at the same time to assure him of the co-operation of all His Majesty's naval force on this station.
>
> I trust at the same time that the inhabitants of Barataria, consulting their own interests, will not make it necessary to proceed to such extremities— I hold out at the same time a war instantly destructive to them; and, on the other hand, should they be inclined to assist Great Britain in her just and unprovoked war against the United States, the security of their property, the blessings of the British Constitution—and should they be inclined to settle on this continent, lands will, at the conclusion of the war, be allotted them in His Majesty's colonies in America. In return for all these concessions on the part of Great Britain I expect that the directions of their armed vessels will be put into my hands (for which they will be remunerated), the instant cessation of hostilities against the Spanish government, and the restitution of any undisposed property of that nation. . . .[4]

"In this letter," said Jean, "Great Britain threatens to destroy Barataria unless we help her invade the United States. If we do help, my men are to be considered British subjects and will be rewarded with lands taken from the Americans; but what will my reward be?"

"The Governor of Louisiana has declared you and your men to be outlaws," answered Captain Lockyer. "Your brother Pierre is

---
[3] Latour, *Historical Memoir*, Appendix No. III, vii-viii. This proclamation has been quoted by many authors. The original is in Bibliotheca Parsoniana: La.-Am. MSS, No. 1023.
[4] *Ibid.*, Appendix No. III, ix-x; Bibliotheca Parsoniana: La.-Am. MSS, No. 1024.

at this very moment loaded with irons in the jail of New Orleans.[5] We will free your brother. Moreover, you will receive a reward of $30,000 and be made a captain in the British service. This will mean a great career before you in England's new colony. Do not let slip this opportunity of acquiring fortune and consideration."[6]

Thirty thousand dollars—what a paltry bribe to offer Jean Laffite. At that very moment his thatched-roof warehouses on Grande Terre alone were bursting with prize goods worth more than a million dollars.

"You saw how ominous my men were when you came in," Jean answered calmly. "I will need a little time to persuade them to accept this offer. But first, let us dine."

The amazed Englishmen soon found themselves drinking choice wines and eating exotic foods served with elegance on silver plates and priceless damask. Jean persuaded them to be his guests for the night. Actually, they were his prisoners.

---

[5] Writs were still out against Jean and Pierre Laffite when Pierre brazenly showed himself in the streets of New Orleans. So the Marshal could certify on July 8, 1814, that he had "committed Pierre Laffite to prison for want of bail."

It was at this time that Grymes resigned as district attorney to become Pierre's lawyer. However, he was unable to get him out of the Cabildo. In August he petitioned the Court to have a physician make an inquiry into the state of the prisoner's health "and to report on the expediency of relieving him of irons in his confinement." Drs. William Flood and Lewis Heermann "in compliance with the directions of the Honorable Dominique A. Hall" examined Pierre and reported:

> That said Pierre Laffite appears to have suffered about two years ago an apoplectic fit succeeded by palsy of the left side and that he is habitually subject to paroxysms resembling hysteria.
>
> We further report that the said Laffite is at present entirely free from any symptoms indicating the probability of an early return of apoplexy, and that lowness of spirit from agitation of mind appears to be the only indisposition he labors under.
>
> With due regard, therefore, to every indulgence of a prisoner, we are of the opinion that there is no apparent necessity of relieving him of irons which have been applied, as a means of security; and as far as may be consistent with safety, we would beg leave to recommend that he should be reasonably indulged in taking as much exercise as his confinement within the walls of the jail will admit of.
>
> Lewis Heermann
> Wm Flood

August 10, 1814
USDC of La., Case No. 574.

[6] Latour, *Historical Memoir*, 19.

The British approach Jean Laffite

Later, Jean consulted with his captains. The next morning Baratarians surrounded the house and made threatening demonstrations. Jean told the Engishmen that they had better go back to their ship while he calmed the Baratarians. "You will have my answer within a very short time," he assured them.

True to his word, Jean sent Captain Lockyer his answer. It was written in French and said:

Sir

The confusion which prevailed in our camp yesterday and this morning, and of which you have a complete knowledge, has prevented me from answering in a precise manner to the object of your mission: not even at this moment can I give you all the satisfaction that you desire; however, if you grant me a fortnight, I would be entirely at your disposal at the end of that time—this delay is indispensable to send away the three persons who have alone occasioned all the disturbance—the two who were the most troublesome are to leave this place in eight days, and the other is to go to town—the remainder of the time is necessary to enable me to put my affairs in order—you may communicate with me, by sending a boat to the eastern point of the pass, where I will be found. You have inspired me with more confidence than the admiral, your superior officer, could have done himself; with you alone I wish to deal, and from you also I will claim, in due time, the reward for the services which I may render to you.

Be so good, sir, as to favour me with an answer, and believe me yours, &c.

Laffite [7]

Jean and his captains held a consultation. They decided to send all the communications from the British to Jean Blanque, who had come to Louisiana in 1803 with his cousin Pierre Clément Laussat, whom Napoleon had sent as his prefect. Jean Blanque was not only the owner of a number of ships the Baratarians sailed; he was also a member of the legislature and a man of influence in New Orleans. "It was impossible to hear him without remembering all that he had said, so correct was he. In habitual commerce with men he was patient, kind, human and serviceable. After being received as a lawyer at the bar, he pleaded without remuneration," [8] In a country

---

[7] Bibliotheca Parsoniana: La.-Am. MSS, No. 1031.
[8] Blanque was married to Delphine Macarty, widow of Don Ramón López y Angula,

where the power of the word dominated, the Baratarians could not have selected a better champion. Laffite sent this explanation to Jean Blanque:

> Though proscribed by my adoptive country, I will never let slip an occasion of serving her, or of proving that she has never ceased to be dear to me. Of this you will here see a convincing proof. Yesterday, the 3rd of September, there appeared here, under a flag of truce, a boat coming from an English brig, at anchor about two leagues from the pass. Mr. Nicholas Lockyer, a British officer of high rank, delivered me the following papers: two directed to me, a proclamation, and the admiral's instructions to Captain Lockyer; all herewith inclosed. . . . I make you the depository of the secret on which perhaps depends the tranquility of our country; please to make such use of it as your judgment may direct.
>
> Our enemies have endeavoured to work on me by a motive which few men would have resisted. They represented to me a brother in irons, a brother who is very dear to me, whose deliverer I might become, and I declined the proposal. . . . I have asked fifteen days to settle my affairs, assigning such plausible pretexts, that I hope the term will be granted. I am waiting for the British officer's answer, and for yours to this. Be so good as to assist me with your judicious counsel in so weighty an affair.[9]

When Laffite had finished this letter, he sent for Raymond Ranchier, his swiftest messenger, and gave the packet to him to deliver.[10] Ranchier travelled by "courier pirogue." Ten husky slaves rowed him across Barataria Bay and through the lakes. They were relieved by the next relay which took Ranchier past The Temple and up Bayou Barataria to its head, where he got on a horse and galloped to the river. A waiting pirogue ferried him across the

---

Consul General for Spain. Blanque's "stature was above the ordinary. He was well made. His face was oval; his beard and his fine eyes black; his nose aquiline; his manners were the manners of a son of good family who had never ceased to frequent good society. Add to all that, he was always ready to draw sword or pistol. His diction was remarkable in spite of a Southern accent. His oxordium invited a hearing. His narration was clear and connected. His peroration warm and filled with metaphors." Typescript translation of Bernard de Marigny, *Reflection on the Campaign of General Andrew Jackson, in Louisiana 1814 and 1815* (New Orleans: W.P.A., 1938), 18-19; originally published in French by J. L. Sollée (New Orleans, 1848).

[9] Bibliotheca Parsoniana: La.-Am. MSS, No. 1022.

[10] *Journal of Jean Laffite*, 47.

The British approach Jean Laffite

Mississippi, and Ranchier appeared before Jean Blanque 24 hours after he left Grande Terre.[11] This trip normally took three days.

Jean Blanque read the letters and immediately took the packet to Governor Claiborne. "I must confer with a committee of the legislature," said Claiborne.

This committee soon assembled. Some of the members were Major Jacques Villeré, commander of the Louisiana Militia; Commodore Daniel T. Patterson of the United States Navy;[12] Colonel George Ross, commanding the 44th United States Infantry; and Pierre Du Bourg, Collector of United States Customs. Claiborne presented the letters. They were read. Then the governor said: "The council must decide two questions: first, are these letters genuine; second, is it proper for the Governor of Louisiana to enter into any correspondence with Jean Laffite or any of his associates?"[13]

One member of the committee sprang to his feet and cried, "These letters are a ruse on the part of Jean Laffite to get Pierre out of jail and make us look ridiculous."

Commodore Patterson spoke up and said, "My instructions from the Secretary of the Navy are to disperse the Baratarian association. The schooner *Carolina* has been sent here for that purpose. Colonel Ross and I have made preparations to carry out these instructions."[14]

Colonel Ross told the committee that his instructions were to cooperate with Commodore Patterson; and Collector Du Bourg shouted, "The smugglers' stronghold should be attacked and destroyed, now![15]

Only one member spoke in defense of the Baratarians. "I know them," said Major Villeré. "They are not pirates, they are privateers. Their ships sail under the flag of Cartagena. They can not bring their

---

[11] Arthur, *Jean Laffite*, 65.
[12] Patterson's rank was master commander, one grade lower than a naval captain. The rank of commodore was not created in America until 1862, and is a grade higher than that of captain. Jackson and other contemporaries of Patterson called him "commodore." John Spencer Bassett, *The Life of Andrew Jackson* (New York, 1925), 165.
[13] Latour, *Historical Memoir*, 253.
[14] *Ibid.*
[15] *Ibid.*; Arthur, *Jean Laffite*, 73.

(43)

The Baratarians and the Battle of New Orleans

prizes into our ports legally. The only crime which can be charged against them is that they have disposed of their prize goods by illegal means. The United States is their adopted country. They see it threatened by an enemy they hate. These documents are true. We must believe the Baratarians." [16]

But Major Villeré was "a voice crying in the wilderness." Claiborne paid no heed to him. True, the governor did not vote but neither did he speak in behalf of the Baratarians. Claiborne was a transplanted Virginia politician who had swung the Tennessee vote for Jefferson in the presidential election of 1800. As a reward he had been sent to the Spanish frontier to govern Louisiana. He had been on that frontier ten years, long enough to develop frontier instincts. But perhaps because the Laffites had wounded his vanity and perhaps because of the importunities of his Spanish wife and her people, Claiborne was blind when opportunity knocked at his door. He missed greatness because he did not champion the Baratarians. Instead, he let the committee decide what should be done and he abided by that decision.

The committee, with Major Villeré dissenting, decided the letters were a ruse to get Pierre out of jail. Commodore Patterson was directed to carry out the mission for which he had been sent to Louisiana—destroy the Barataria establishment on Grande Terre.

Meanwhile, Laffite's friends and perhaps even J. H. Holland, the jailor, managed Pierre's escape from the Cabildo so that Pierre returned to Grande Terre with Jules Ranchier.[17] The next day Holland put a notice in the papers and placed posters throughout New Orleans stating that:

1000 Dollars Reward

Will be paid to whoever arrests Pierre Laffite, who last night, broke from the parish prison and escaped. The said Pierre Laffite is five feet, ten inches tall, and of robust stature, light complexion, and somewhat

---

[16] Latour, *Historical Memoir*, 254; Walker, *Jackson and New Orleans*, 45; Francois Xavier Martin, *The History of Louisiana* (2 vols., New Orleans, 1827-29), II, 239.

[17] Arthur, *Jean Laffite*, 71. Jules Ranchier in *The Journal of Jean Laffite* is cited as Raymond Ranchier.

The British approach Jean Laffite

cross-eyed. It is believed that a more complete description of the said Laffite is useless as he is so well known in this city.[18]

This was not only to cover up his own action in the escape, but Holland's way of informing the Creoles. When Pierre arrived at Grande Terre with Ranchier, Jean was worried about the effect of the escape on Claiborne. He wrote to the governor the best letter he ever composed. One can feel his concern in the unusual deference to Claiborne as one reads the letter which was as follows:

Grande Terre, 10 September, 1814

A Son Excellence Monsieur
Wm. C. C. Claiborne, Gouverneur
de l'Etat de la Louisiane;

Monsieur—

In the firm persuasion that the choice made of you to fill the office of first magistrate was dictated by the esteem of your fellow citizens and was conferred on merit, I confidently address you on an affair on which may depend the safety of this country.

I offer to you to restore to this state several citizens who, perhaps in your eyes, have lost that sacred title. I offer you them, however, such as you could wish to find them, ready to exert their utmost efforts in defense of the country. This point of Louisiana which I occupy, is of great importance in the present crisis. I tender my services to defend it and the only reward I ask is that a stop be put to the proscription against me and my adherents, by an act of oblivion for all that has been done hitherto.

I am the stray sheep wishing to return to the flock. If you were thoroughly acquainted with the nature of my offenses I should appear to you much less guilty and still worthy to discharge the duties of a good citizen. I have never sailed under any flag but that of the republic of Carthagena, and my vessels are perfectly regular in that respect. If I could have brought my lawful prizes into the ports of this state, I should not have employed the illicit means that have caused me to be proscribed.

I decline saying more on the subject until I have the honour of your excellency's answer, which I am persuaded can be dictated only by wisdom.

In case, Monsieur le Gouverneur, your reply should not be favourable to my ardent wishes I declare to you that I will leave so as not to be held

---
[18] *Louisiana Courier*, September 7, 9, 12, 28, 1814.

The Baratarians and the Battle of New Orleans

to have co-operated with an invasion on this point, which cannot fail to take place, and puts me entirely at the judgment of my conscience.

Jai l'Honneru d'etre,
M. le Gouverneur
Jn Laffite [19]

After dispatching Ranchier to New Orleans with this letter, Jean supervised the transfer of arms and ammunition stored on Grande Terre to warehouses hidden in the vicinity of The Temple. The slaves in the barracoons were sent elsewhere. Then several ships were loaded with important papers, maps Jean had collected, hard money, and the most valuable merchandise. Jean expected the British would be vindictive when they learned he had been stalling for time, so none of those things which might help the enemy were left on the island. The two weeks he had asked for were almost gone when Jean sailed with his loaded vessels to Isle Dernière, about forty miles west of Grande Terre. Pierre was ill. He traveled by pirogue to a plantation on Bayou Lafourche to convalesce.[20]

Dominique You was left in charge at Grande Terre. If the British attacked he was to bombard them from the fort at the Pass and set fire to warehouses and whatever ships were in the harbor. Many writers assume that Renato Beluche was with Dominique at this time and he may have been.

Meanwhile, Commodore Patterson was sailing down the Mississippi with six gunboats, one launch, and the *Carolina*, equipped for battle and carrying part of the 44th Regiment.[21]

On the morning of September 16, Dominique's sentinels sighted Patterson's squadron approaching. Dominique was expecting the British. His cannon were ready to fire. When the vessels were close enough so that he could make out the flag, Dominique stopped short. He could not fire on the flag of the United States. Instead, he ordered his men to set fire to the warehouses and the ships.

From the *Carolina* Patterson could see the action on Grande Terre.

---

[19] Stanley Arthur's translation, *Jean Laffite*, 71-72.
[20] Latour, *Historical Memoir*, 254.
[21] USDC of La., Case No. 734.

(46)

The British approach Jean Laffite

"I perceived that the pirates were abandoning their vessels and were flying in all directions," he testified later in court.[22]

About 500 Baratarians did escape before Patterson landed and took possession of the ships and the island. Dominique surrendered. He and 80 Baratarians were made prisoners. Patterson did not have room for any more. He and his men spent the next four days loading the 26 captured vessels and their transports with the loot they rescued from burning warehouses.[23]

On Patterson's last day at Grande Terre, one of Beluche's vessels approached the island. It was the *General Bolívar* arriving from Cartagena. The captain at this time, according to the ship's papers, was Joseph Clement. He could not know what had been going on in Barataria Bay, but he did see a strange ship lying outside the Pass. The strange ship was the *Carolina*. Her commander sighted the *General Bolívar* and immediately gave the signal to chase.

Clement altered the course of the *General Bolívar*, firing several shots at the pursuing vessel. "The Carolina gaining fast, the General Bolivar changed its course again and bore away for Grande Terre. The Carolina hoisted her colors and continued to fire until the General Bolivar was grounded." Clement and his crew "immediately abandoned ship and got on shore and disappeared." The commanding officer of the *Carolina* "did thereupon seize and take possession of the General Bolivar with her apparel, guns and appurtenances and therein departed therewith" for New Orleans.[24]

Patterson reported to the Secretary of the Navy his regret that the Baratarians had not fought him. "But," he added, "it is a great subject of satisfaction to me to have effected the object of my enterprise; viz. capturing all their vessels in port, and dispersing their band without having one of my brave fellows hurt. The enemy had mounted on their vessels twenty pieces of cannon of different calibre...."[25]

---

[22] *Ibid.*, Case No. 760.
[23] Arthur gives the names of the captured vessels. His list is accurate; it was compiled from federal court records. *Jean Laffite*, 87-88.
[24] USDC of La., Case No. 760.
[25] *Historical Military Data, Louisiana Militia 1811-1814* (Jackson Barracks, New Orleans, 1941).

The Baratarians and the Battle of New Orleans

When Patterson and his flotilla reached New Orleans, he charged the Baratarians with piracy and they were jailed in the Cabildo. Dominique You was chained to heavy irons. Then Patterson filed suit for himself and his men, claiming the vessels and stores seized at Grande Terre.[26]

However, it was not long before plaintiffs and defendants suspended the suit to deal with a common enemy.

---

[26] Private letters said the goods captured by Patterson at Barataria were worth $500,000. *Niles' Register*, VII (October 27, 1814), 111. Jean Laffite says the value was $600,000. *Journal*, 54.

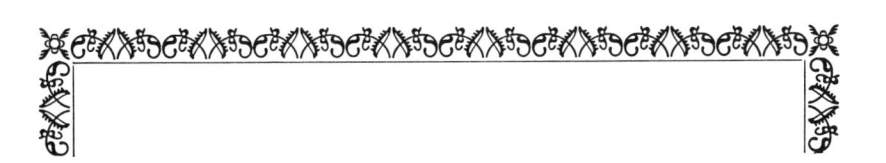

ANDREW JACKSON

DURING 1813 AND 1814 ANDREW JACKSON MADE HOSTILE CREEKS on the Florida frontier wish they had never heard of him. By the summer of 1814 they were ready to make peace.

At this point William Henry Harrison resigned from the United States Army. The powers that controlled promotions dared not give the vacant commission to any one but " Old Hickory." So he was made commander of Military District No. 7. This included the states of Tennessee and Louisiana and the Mississippi Territory. Headquarters for this district were at Mobile, since Jackson's main duty would be to protect the Gulf coast.

Jackson did not proceed to Mobile until after the Creeks had signed the treaty whereby they ceded what is today one-fifth of the state of Georgia and three-fifths of Alabama to the United States. This area was added to Jackson's command.

The Secretary of War had assigned five regiments of the United States Infantry to the defense of this district. They were the Second, Third, Seventh, Thirty-ninth and Forty-fourth. They totalled 2,378 men. The Seventh and Forty-fourth were mostly Creoles from Louisiana.[1]

Jackson left central Alabama on August 11, and going down the

---

[1] Marigny, *Reflection on the Campaign*, 13.

ANDREW JACKSON.

Andrew Jackson

river of that name, reached Mobile on August 15. Two large river systems empty into Mobile Bay—the Alabama and the Tombigbee. If the English should get into the bay, they could penetrate the United States for hundreds of miles up these rivers and their tributaries.

Thirty miles across the bay from Mobile was Fort Bowyer. It was on a narrow, sandy peninsula that almost closed Mobile Bay from the Gulf of Mexico. Fort Bowyer, on the tip of this peninsula, controlled the narrow entrance to the bay from the Gulf.

Jackson found Fort Bowyer abandoned!

He sent Major William Lawrence with 160 men, all he could spare, to repair the fort and strengthen its defenses. Lawrence and his men worked like Trojans. They found twenty cannon which they remounted. While they worked, the British burned Washington, raided the Chesapeake, then dispatched vessels to the West Indies to collect black troops, and extend their beachheads at Pensacola and Apalachicola.

As Jackson entered the critical theater of war operations against Great Britain, he could get no help from Washington. United States government officials fled while the city burned. When the Secretary of War finally sent dispatches to Jackson, they did not arrive until after the war was over. The same was true of supplies. A government contractor was supposed to bring some from Pittsburgh down the Ohio and the Mississippi, but he did not get to New Orleans until two months after the war was over.

Jackson knew within 48 hours after arriving at Mobile that the English at Pensacola, 60 miles away, had landed marines, seized the city, and were recruiting Creek Indians. Western and Southern newspapers raged about the assistance the Spanish governor of Pensacola was giving the British.

"Old Hickory" wanted to go right after the British and drive them from Florida but he could not. He did not have enough troops. He had to send to Tennessee, Kentucky (this state was outside his jurisdiction), and the Mississippi Territory for them and *wait* two months until they arrived.

The Baratarians and the Battle of New Orleans

Meanwhile, the *Sophie* which Sir William H. Percy had sent with dispatches to Jean Laffite returned to Pensacola. Percy decided to attack Mobile without waiting to see whether or not Jean Laffite and his men would aid the British. He boasted that he would make the fort surrender within twenty minutes.[2]

So it happened that on the morning of September 12, 1814, an outpost at Fort Bowyer reported the British had landed marines and Indians a few miles east of the fort. That evening the little garrison saw four British war vessels anchor six miles from them.

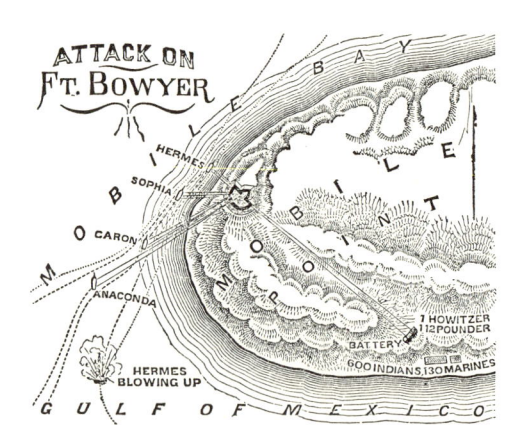

Two days later, at 4:30, the *Hermes* ran broadside into the channel and dropped anchor within musket shot of the fort. The rest of the ships followed and anchored one behind the other. Then a thundering cannonade burst from enemy guns. It was answered by only 12 of Fort Bowyer's 20 guns. Eight were not in position to use.

Marines and Indians opened fire behind a bluff. A few shots from the south battery silenced them and kept them away. Colonel Nicholls lost an eye when a splinter lodged in it.[3]

A lucky shot from the fort cut the cable of the *Hermes*. The current turned her bow to the fort and for twenty minutes a terrible

---
[2] Adams, *History of United States*, VIII, 323; Latour, *Historical Memoir*, 39-41; Buell, *History of Andrew Jackson*, I, 344.
[3] Washington *Daily National Intelligencer*, October 15, 1814.

fire raked her from stem to stern. Then she ran aground. Commander Percy transferred his wounded to the *Sophie*, set fire to the *Hermes*, and abandoned her.

Then Sir William H. Percy, minus one ship, and Colonel Edward Nicholls, minus one eye, proceeded to Pensacola. Two marines deserted. They told Major Lawrence the British casualties were 162 killed and 70 wounded, including Colonel Nicholls.[4]

Major Lawrence took stock. Four dead in the fort, four wounded in battle and six when some cartridges burst. Seven hundred cannon balls had been shot, two guns had been knocked off their carriages, four cracked beyond repair; and three hundred holes had been made in the fort.[5]

Because the British had not taken Fort Bowyer, they determined to bypass Mobile. Their instructions said to occupy the *province* of Louisiana by advancing directly on New Orleans, or move into the back parts of Georgia and the country of friendly Indians. They decided to make a direct approach to New Orleans.

At that moment Jean Laffite and his Baratarians were contributing to the security of the United States by refusing to guide the English through bayous west of the Mississippi. A glance at the map will show that the easiest access to New Orleans from the Gulf is up Bayou Lafourche or through the bays and bayous of Barataria. If Jean Laffite had sided with the enemy, British troops could have moved easily and rapidly to a point above New Orleans. Then the city could have been cut off from all communication with the interior.

Convinced that the Baratarians had tricked them, and afraid of a possible trap, the British abandoned all idea of including Barataria in their theater of operations. Without Laffite's small ships they could not navigate the bayous even though they could find their way.

So the British top command narrowed the field of operation and eliminated the best approach to New Orleans. The only one left was from below the city: up the Mississippi itself, which meant bucking 120 miles of currents and curves, to say nothing of winds

---
[4] Latour, *Historical Memoir*, 40; Adams, *History of United States*, VIII, 323-24.
[5] Parton, *Life of Jackson*, I, 608.

The Baratarians and the Battle of New Orleans

and calms, or through some bayou that emptied into Lake Borgne and the Gulf.

After the British were defeated at Fort Bowyer, Jackson received Jean Laffite's packet of letters which Claiborne had forwarded to him. Jackson read Colonel Nicholls' "Proclamation to Louisianians" and one can almost see "Old Hickory" rushing to broadcast a proclamation also. It said:

> Louisianians!
> The base, perfidious Britons have attempted to invade your country—they had the temerity to attack fort Bowyer with their incongruous horde of Indians and negro assassins—they seem to have forgotten that this fort was defended by freemen—they were not long indulged in their error—the gallant Lawrence, with his little spartan band, has given them a lecture that will last for ages; he has taught them what men can do when fighting for their liberty, when contending against slaves. He has convinced Sir W. H. Percy that his companions in arms were not to be conquered by proclamations; that the strongest British bark is not invulnerable to the force of American artillery, directed by the steady nervous arm of a freeman.
> Louisianians! The proud Briton, the natural and sworn Enemy of all Frenchmen, has called upon you, by proclamation, to aid him in his tyranny, and to prostrate the holy temple of our liberty. Can Louisianians, can Frenchmen, can Americans, ever stoop to be the slaves or allies of Britain?

Then Jackson pounced upon the British offer to the Baratarians as he continued:

> I ask you, Louisianians, can we place any confidence in the honour of men who have courted an alliance with pirates and robbers? Have not these noble Britons, these honourable men, colonel Nicholls and the honourable captain W. H. Percy, the true representatives of their royal master, done this? Have they not made offers to the pirates of Barataria to join them, and their holy cause? And have they not dared to insult you by calling on you to associate, as brethren with them, and this hellish banditti.[6]

"Hellish banditti"—that was what Jackson thought of the Bara-

---

[6] John Spencer Bassett (ed.), *Correspondence of Andrew Jackson* (7 vols., Washington, 1926-35), II, 57-58.

Andrew Jackson

tarians. He self-righteously ignored them. He did not know then that Jean Laffite and his Baratarians had contributed greatly to the security of the United States by refusing to cooperate with the British.

Jackson was worried, fussing and fuming while waiting for the volunteers from Kentucky, Tennessee, and Mississippi. Six inactive weeks he waited. His dysentery got worse and his body wasted to skin and bone, but nothing could conquer the indomitable spirit that gleamed from his cadaverous eyes.

General John Coffee with 1,800 Tennesseans arrived first, then Thomas Hinds and his Mississippi mounted rifles, about a hundred and fifty strong. These, with his seven hundred regulars, a hundred or more volunteers from Mobile and Captain Pierre Jugeat with his two hundred and fifty Choctaws gave Jackson a grand total of 3,000 troops. Early in November he distributed rations for eight days and marched his troops to Pensacola. When he prepared to storm the city it surrendered.

The British held Fort Barrancas, 14 miles away at the mouth of the bay. The Spanish governor, González, sent them a written order to surrender, that Jackson and his men would take command the next day.

That night the British blew up Fort Barrancas and departed. They left disillusioned Spaniards and Indians behind. Where had they gone? Back to mutilated Fort Bowyer to capture Mobile while Jackson was absent with his troops?

Jackson evacuated Pensacola and dashed to Mobile. He saw no sign of the British but heard increasing rumors of the invasion fleet. "Old Hickory" waited 11 days at Mobile and still no sign of the British. Then he thought he had better look into the situation at New Orleans. He did not think the British would be so foolhardy as to attack New Orleans directly, but they might.

Jackson's " Proclamation " and other sources had made known the contents of Laffite's letters and the people of New Orleans had become panicky. Livingston and Governor Claiborne had been writing Jackson, describing the defenseless city and urging him to come. The legislature was wasting time in endless debate. The

The Baratarians and the Battle of New Orleans

Creole faction, on general principles, blocked every move Governor Claiborne's supporters tried to make.

The legislature had appointed a defense committee to work with Claiborne and Commodore Patterson, but concerted action was frustrated not only by personal jealousies, but by another defense committee. Citizens, having no confidence in the governor nor in the legislature, had appointed their own defense committee. Livingston was chairman. The two defense committees worked at cross purposes with each other.

Creoles could not believe that the recently arrived Americans loved New Orleans enough to risk their lives in its defense. Their bulging warehouses represented great wealth. Surely the yankee owners would make a bargain with the enemy to preserve this treasure. English and Spanish agents raised a crop of subversive rumors that added to the general suspicion and undermined confidence.

Claiborne himself helped to maintain the feeling of panic. His correspondence during the nine months preceding the British invasion seemed to be preparing the President of the United States and his cabinet for the possibility of losing Louisiana. He reported rumors of " design on the part of the enemy to wrest Louisiana from the hands of the United States and restore it to Spain! "

Claiborne teetered back and forth between confidence in the free people of color and fear of them. When Jackson issued his " Proclamation to Louisianians," he issued one also to the free colored inhabitants of Louisiana in which he said:

> Through a mistaken policy you have heretofore been deprived of a participation in the glorious struggle for national rights in which our country is engaged. This no longer shall exist.
>
> As sons of freedom, you are now called upon to defend our most inestimable blessing. . . .
>
> To every noble-hearted, generous freeman of colour, volunteering to serve during the present contest with Great Britain, and no longer, there will be paid the same bounty in money and lands, now received by the white soldiers of the United States (viz. one hundred and twenty-four dollars in money, and one hundred and sixty acres of land). The non-commissioned

officers and privates will also be entitled to the same monthly pay and daily rations, and clothes furnished to any American soldier.[7]

This proclamation was sent to Claiborne. He did nothing about it for a whole month. On October 17, he wrote to Jackson: "The publication of your address to the free people of color is delayed a few days. An unfortunate misunderstanding between the officers of the battalion of color, which excites much interest, is the subject of investigation before a court of inquiry now sitting."[8]

So Claiborne did nothing constructive. He wrote down all the alibis that would excuse defeat and put himself in a position to be accepted by whichever side won. The difference between Jackson and Claiborne was that Jackson had made up his mind to defeat the British and he did not waste any energy inventing excuses for failure. Instead of deprecating the free men of color as a source of strength, Jackson was determined to use them. But before he went to New Orleans to clear up the mess there and organize the city for defense, Jackson moved to their stations the men on his half of the checkerboard of war.

He sent one thousand Tennessee horsemen to scour the Florida coast and keep the English from making a beachhead there. Major Lawrence and his valiants were to remain at Fort Bowyer, while three regiments of regulars (2nd, 3rd, 39th) were kept at Mobile. This was the main body of Jackson's force, but surely the British would try again to take Mobile and penetrate to Baton Rouge. General Coffee was sent with twelve hundred mounted troops to Baton Rouge, to protect New Orleans from a possible British breakthrough and attack from above. The Seventh Regiment joined the Forty-fourth at New Orleans.

Meanwhile, Jackson had sent messengers to Kentucky, Tennessee, and Mississippi, pleading for more volunteers and urging them to hasten to New Orleans. On the 22nd of November, he put his dysentery-wracked body on a horse and travelled by land, 125 miles, to have firsthand knowledge of points at which the enemy might

---

[7] Latour, *Historical Memoir*, Appendix No. XVII, xxxi-xxxii.
[8] Gayarré, *History of Louisiana*, IV, 365-66.

effect a landing. When he was halfway to New Orleans, Cochrane's invasion fleet left Negril Bay, Jamaica; and as Jackson entered the city of New Orleans, the British passed Cuba and headed for the Florida coast. There they lay at the entrance to Pensacola Bay for nearly 48 hours, wind-bound by a westerly gale.

Early on the morning of December 2, 1814, Jackson and his escort reached Fort St. John at the point where Bayou St. John empties into Lake Pontchartrain. This was the back door to New Orleans, which was only six miles away. Jackson dispatched a courier with a letter to Bernard de Marigny de Mandeville within the city. The courier met Marigny at the corner of Chartres and St. Louis Streets and gave him the letter. Marigny opened it and found it was from his father-in-law, Don Juan Ventura Morales, Governor of the Floridas.

Don Juan had been the Spanish Intendent at New Orleans before Louisiana was transferred to the United States, and had continued to act as Intendent (making concession and sales of land in territory in dispute between the United States and Spain) until 1806, when he went to Pensacola.[9] When Jackson took that city, Morales insisted on being his host and as Jackson left, gave him the letter for his son-in-law.

After Marigny had read it, the courier asked if it would be agreeable for General Jackson to establish headquarters at his home the next day. Marigny replied that he " would receive with great pleasure the Conqueror of the Floridas, and of Colonel Nicholls, who had maltreated his old compatriots in Pensacola and had carried away a great number of their slaves." Then he sent the courier back to Jackson with the message that he would receive General Jackson the next day and that breakfast would be awaiting him.[10]

Meanwhile, Jackson and his escort rode up the muddy road along the bank of Bayou St. John until they came to a villa near the junction of Canal Carondelet which connected the bayou with the

---

[9] *Ibid.*, 70-73, 113.
[10] Marigny, *Reflection on the Campaign*, 20.

Andrew Jackson

city. The villa was the suburban retreat of J. Kilty Smith, a rich merchant. Here the horsemen dismounted and had breakfast.

After breakfast Mr. Smith supplied a carriage in which Jackson rode into the city. Governor Claiborne, Mayor Nicholas Girod (" a rotund, affable, pleasant old French gentleman, of easy, polite manners "), the citizens' defense committee, and the legislature's defense committee hastened to meet him. They led him to a three-story building at 106 Royal Street.

Soon Royal Street was filled with people and Jackson appeared on the second story gallery to speak to them. Livingston was by his side and translated Jackson's words into French. Marigny was with the crowd below. He heard the General say: " I have come to protect the city. I will drive our enemies into the sea or perish in the effort. Good citizens, you must all rally around me in this emergency, cease all differences and divisions, and unite with me in patriotic resolve to save this city from dishonor and disaster which a presumptuous enemy threatens to inflict upon it." [11]

Bernard de Marigny de Mandeville, with that clarity and logic peculiar to Frenchmen, was able to put into words how the citizens of New Orleans felt when they heard and saw Andrew Jackson. They all had wanted to fight but there had been " a sense of uneasiness arising from a defect of organization. Governor Claiborne was a very honest man of personal bravery, but he had not the energy necessary to give a great impulse to the population of Louisiana." Here was a man who could.[12]

Edward Livingston, his brother-in-law August de Castera Davezac, and John Randolph Grymes, members of the *citizens'* defense committee, immediately attached themselves to Jackson and became part of his staff. They spoke French and neither Jackson nor any of his regular adjutants understood the language.

Bernard de Marigny did not try to become one of Jackson's aides-de-camp. His pride was hurt when the General decided to make

---
[11] Walker, *Jackson and New Orleans*, 14; Parton, *Life of Jackson*, II, 29.
[12] Marigny, *Reflection on the Campaign*, 2; Gayarré, *History of Louisiana*, IV, 398.

The Baratarians and the Battle of New Orleans

106 Royal Street his headquarters. So Marigny, chairman of the *legislative* defense committee, joined Claiborne's staff.

Jackson immediately wanted to know the military strength of the city. He reviewed the Battalion d'Orleáns with its five companies of militia—287 men. Their captains, four Frenchmen and one Irishman, were all naturalized citizens. Captain J. B. Plauché, a Creole of Louisiana, commanded the Carabiniers d'Orleáns, the best-equipped and best-trained company. Little five-foot Baron Henri de Saint-Gème, with a foot-high plume in his cap, put his Dragons à Pied through their paces. St. Gème was an emigrant from Haiti, and Dominique You's partner.

Captain Jean Hudri of the Francs and Captain Auguste Guibert of the Chasseurs were the other Creole commanders. The Irish captain, Maunsel White, was the "Ajax of the army. In spite of his tall stature, increased by a high plume, he never bowed his head to bullets nor Congreve." [13] His corps was made up entirely of Irishmen.

These were the available white troops. The population of New Orleans, as given by different authorities, varied between 18,000 and 20,000 at this time. The sources agree that 5,000 of these were slaves. Subtracting these and women, children, old and infirm, and the sick, meant that about 2,000 men (white and free people of color) were available for militia or regular troops. Marigny says that, of these 2,000, not more than 300 were Anglo-Saxons.[14]

The New Orleans Militia, the City Rifles which were soon to be organized, and the 7th and 44th Regiments totaled approximately 1,200.[15] The difference of 800 represented the free people of color who, due to Claiborne's dilatory tactics, had not been organized as a battalion.[16]

Jackson had confidence in the militia troops and told them so; but he did not let them see his concern because there were no guns

---
[13] Marigny, *Reflection on the Campaign*, 12.
[14] *Ibid.*, 17.
[15] *Ibid.*; Adams, *History of United States*, VIII, 334.
[16] Bassett, *Life of Andrew Jackson*, 156-57.

(60)

for his army except 500 old muskets and 7,500 flint pistols obtained from the Baratarians. He did have two mortars. They had been landed from bomb-ketches which had been condemned. But there were not 100 bombs of the caliber required for these mortars.[17]

Meanwhile, all the engineers of New Orleans were called together so that Jackson could consult with them about topography and defense. Then Jackson sent detachments " to fell timbers against every small bayou and creek through which a passage for boats and barges could be afforded; and to increase the obstruction, by sinking large frames in their beds, and filling them with earth." [18]

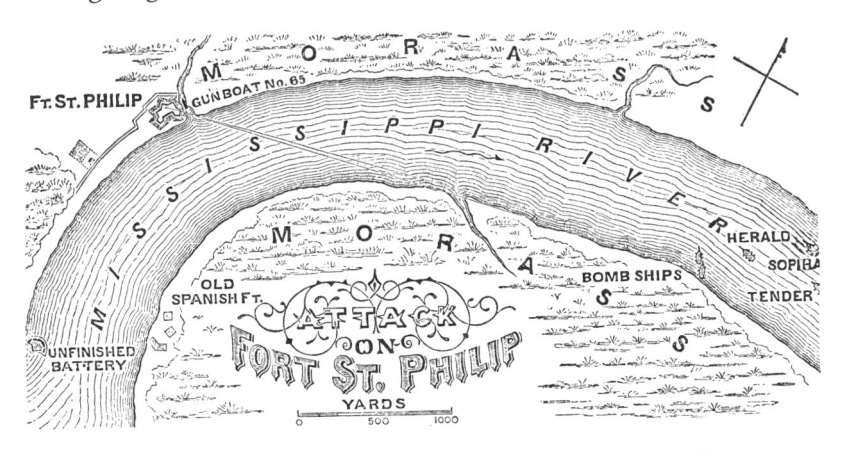

Commodore Patterson had by this time stationed on Lake Borgne his old gig, the *Alligator*, and the five gunboats that had been used against the Baratarians. Trusting in these " eyes and ears " to give warning of any enemy approach, Jackson with Patterson, Livingston and other aides, and two engineers sailed down the Mississippi on an inspection tour.

Because of the nature of the river, no defense was attempted below Fort St. Philip, fifty miles from the mouth. Jackson gave instructions for strengthening this fort and then came back up the river. He

---
[17] Bassett (ed.), *Correspondence*, II, 110; Adams, *History of United States*, VIII, 334; Gayarré, *History of Louisiana*, IV, 385.
[18] John Henry Eaton, *The Life of Andrew Jackson* (Philadelphia, 1824), 274.

The Baratarians and the Battle of New Orleans

stopped at English Turn and ordered batteries of heavy cannon placed so as to destroy any armed vessel that might try to pass. No vessel could round the Turn without waiting for a proper wind. During the wait a few guns could destroy any enemy ship.

Jackson and Patterson were back in New Orleans by December 9. A friendly Choctaw handed Patterson a letter. It was in French and unsigned. The Choctaw said the man who sent it was " dark-complexioned, had a long mustache, and spoke like a Frenchman." [19] The letter was dated Pensacola, December 5, 1815, and said:

Sir
I feel it a duty to apprize you of a very large force of the enemy off this port, and it is generally understood New Orleans is the object of attack. It amounts at present to about eighty vessels, and more than double that number are momentarily looked for, to form a junction, when an immediate commencement of their operations will take place. I am not able to learn how, when, or where the attack will be made; but I heard that they have vessels of all descriptions, and a large body of troops. Admiral Cochrane commands, and his ship, the Tonnant, lies at this moment just outside the bar; and probably no means will be left untried to obtain their object. The admiral arrived only yesterday noon.[20]

Patterson took the letter to Jackson. He considered it trustworthy, so Patterson sent these instructions to Tac (Thomas Ap Catesby) Jones, lieutenant in command of the gunboat flotilla on Lake Borgne: " Proceed to Pass Christian for reconnaissance. If the enemy force tries to cut off the gunboats, retreat to the Rigolets. There with the protection and help of Fort Petites Coquilles, sink the enemy or be sunk." [21]

Then Jackson visited the area back of the city. He rode along Bayou Sauvage or Gentilly to its confluence with Chef Menteur— one mile from where Chef Menteur disembogues into Lake Borgne and Lake Pontchartrain in such a way that it forms a pass between the two lakes. Jackson ordered a fort to be built at the point where Bayou Sauvage joins Chef Menteur. This would command the

---
[19] Buell, *History of Jackson*, I, 370.
[20] Latour, *Historical Memoir*, Appendix No. XVIII, xxxii.
[21] *Ibid.*, 57-58.

(62)

Andrew Jackson

Gentilly plain which was high ground and gave easy access to the city. A few miles to the east was another pass between the two lakes, Pass Rigolets, and its unfinished fort, Petites Coquilles.

By this time Jackson knew the worst. He had approximately 500 militia, two infantry regiments, Fort St. Philip on the Mississippi, a sloop of war and a schooner on that river, Fort Petites Coquilles on the Rigolets, five gunboats and the *Alligator* on Lake Borgne, Fort St. John on Lake Pontchartrain back of the city, and a very small supply of arms and ammunition with which to defend New Orleans and the 600 miles of Louisiana coast.

THE BRITISH CAMP BELOW NEW ORLEANS

While Jackson thought all his orders were being executed, Admiral Cochrane's invasion fleet approached Chandeleur Island. On December 8, his 74's anchored off that island while the rest of the fleet took a position between Ship and Cat Island.[1] Only the lighter vessels could navigate from this point which was the entrance to Mississippi Sound—the shoal coastal waters between Mobile and Lake Borgne.

Cochrane had a good understanding of the area, not only from maps and books published a few years earlier by English observers in America but also from information which certain Spaniards, formerly residents of New Orleans, gave him. This was confirmed by Spanish fishermen who had a village of 20 or 30 huts about one mile from the mouth of Bayou Bienvenu which emptied into Lake Borgne.

The British could not attack New Orleans from the mouth of the Mississippi. Vessels dependent upon sails could not hope to pass Fort St. Philip and English Turn against the strong current of the river. Neither could they enter Lake Pontchartrain and attack New

---

[1] There are two Cat Islands along the coast: this one in the Mississippi Sound and the other in the large bay west of Bayou Lafourche delta where Laffite operated. The bay west of Lafourche is called Cat Island Lake.

(64)

The British Camp below New Orleans

Orleans from the rear because Cochrane thought Fort Petites Coquilles defending the entrance to Lake Pontchartrain had 40 pieces of artillery mounted and 500 troops. These would be sufficient to annihilate any force that tried to enter the lake through the Rigolets.[2]

Cochrane decided to bypass the Rigolets and attack New Orleans from a point which he could reach by crossing Lake Borgne and ascending Bayou Bienvenu. The mouth of this bayou was 60 miles from where his ships were anchored. His plan was to land all the troops on Isle-aux-Pois which was midway between the ships and the mouth of the bayou. He had only enough small vessels to transport one-third of his troops at a time. From Isle-aux-Pois the landing craft, guided by Spanish fishermen, could transport troops in relays the 30 remaining miles to Bayou Bienvenu.[3]

Meanwhile, Tac Jones and his five gunboats had been studying the concentration of British ships between Ship and Cat Island.[4] The British sighted the gunboats on December 12. They would have to be captured because Cochrane's troops had to be ferried 60 miles in open boats. Jones saw that the British had discovered him and scurried before the wind, hoping to make the 50 miles to Fort Petites Coquilles on the Rigolets.

In hot pursuit was Captain Lockyer (the same Captain Lockyer who had been sent to Jean Laffite) with 45 barges, 43 cannon and 1,200 sailors and marines. This flotilla pursued the gunboats two days.[5]

---

[2] William James, *A Full and Correct Account of the Military Occurrences of the Late War Between Great Britain and the United States of America* (2 vols., London, 1818), II, 358; Mahan, *Sea Power and the War of 1812*, II, 388.

[3] Mahan, *Sea Power and the War of 1812*, 388-89.

[4] Jones had stationed his gunboats and the *Alligator* at Bay St. Louis where there were public stores and a schooner, the *Seahorse*, sailing master William Johnson, commander. On the morning of December 13, Jones sent the *Seahorse* into Bay St. Louis to bring away public stores from the position he had evacuated. Johnson, finding it impossible to escape, blew up the schooner, set fire to the stores on shore, and escaped with his crew by land. Latour, *Historical Memoir*, Appendix No. XIX, xxxii-xxxvi; Robert B. M'Afee, *History of the Late War* (Lexington, 1816), 505-506.

[5] Tac Jones's letter to Benjamin W. Crowinshield, Secretary of the Navy, March 12, 1815, reporting the battle, is quoted in various sources: William James, *Military Occurrences*, II, 526-28; *Niles' Register*, VIII (April 22, 1815), 126, 345; Latour, *Historical*

The Baratarians and the Battle of New Orleans

On the morning of December 14, Jones and the gunboats had bad luck. The wind died away completely at 1 A. M. The gunboats were between Malheureux Island and Point Claire on the mainland. Jones stationed the gunboats in line across the channel and waited.

About 9:30 Captain Lockyer saw Commodore Porter's old gig, the *Alligator*, trying to join the five gunboats. He detached four boats with nearly 200 men to capture this cockle-shell. In his report he described his splendid prize as "an armed sloop." [6]

One hour later the enemy came within range and the gunboats deliberately opened fire. The battle lasted three hours. Ten Americans were killed and 35 wounded. All the gunboat captains except one were wounded. The British captured the gunboats at a cost of 17 men killed and 77 wounded.[7] They returned to Cat Island with their prisoners and captured gunboats.

Jones and the other wounded were put on the *Gorgon*, a large storeship. There a tall and gentlemanly individual conversed freely with them "respecting his future arrangements for the discharge of his duty." He was to be the future "collector of the revenue of his Britannic Majesty in the Port of New Orleans." [8]

Memoir, Appendix No. XIX, xxxiii-xxxv; John Henry Eaton, *The Life of Andrew Jackson* (Philadelphia, 1824), 275-81.

[6] Nicholas Lockyer to Admiral Cochrane, December 17, 1814, quoted in Latour, *Historical Memoir*, Appendix No. LXVI, cxl. This "armed sloop" mounted one 4-pounder and carried eight men.

The English navy has been greatly overrated, perhaps, because it dominated European seas where it had little competition. One English captain, during service in America at this time, wrote: "I was placed as a supernumerary on the books of the *Magnificent*, and very shortly after received my commission as commander of a ten-gun brig. These vessels are so admirably constructed as neither to be able to fight or fly, as occasion may require. They are the most useless class of vessels ever constructed, and are admirably calculated to depress the courage of our seamen, and to heighten that of our adversaries. There is not a ten-gun brig in the service which is a match for any smart American schooner with a long gun on board. . . . The same remarks are applicable to the little, short, useless, leewardly class of ships called Jack-ass frigates, out of compliment to the proposer or builder, I know not which, of these deformed vessels. An American sloop of war ought to take them with a certainty." Frederick Chamier, *The Life of a Sailor* (2 vols., New York, 1833), II, 127.

[7] Report of Captain Lockyer, quoted in Adams, *History of United States*, VIII, 336; Eaton, *Life of Jackson*, 281; Latour, *Historical Memoir*, Appendix No. LXVI, cxlii-cxliii.

[8] Walker, *Jackson and New Orleans*, 109-10.

The British Camp below New Orleans

As soon as Patterson heard about the gunboat battle, he sent two men under a flag of truce to the British fleet. They were Thomas Shields, purser of the New Orleans naval station, and Dr. Robert Morrell. Shields was to try to get the prisoners released on parole and Morrell was to attend the wounded. Admiral Cochrane thought the real purpose of these two was to get information. He questioned them without learning anything important. However, observing that Shields was deaf, Cochrane had Shields and the doctor placed in a room where their conversation could be overheard.

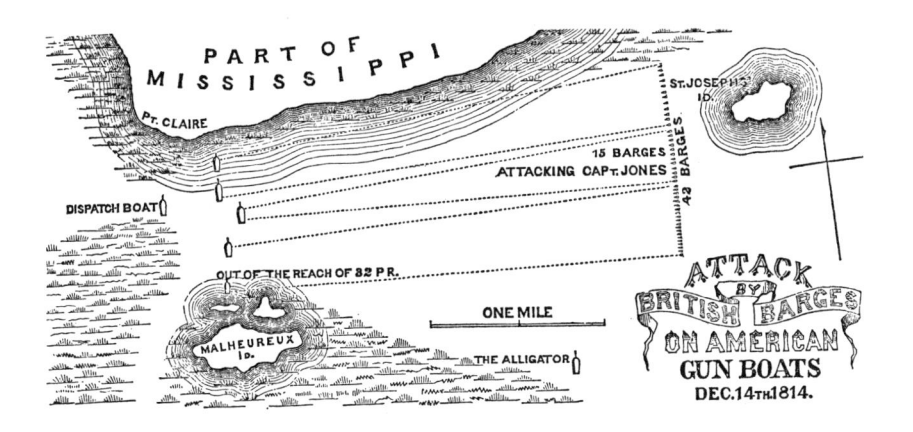

[Map: ATTACK BY BRITISH BARGES ON AMERICAN GUN BOATS DEC. 14TH 1814. Showing Part of Mississippi, Pt. Claire, Dispatch Boat, Malheureux Id., St. Joseph Id., 15 Barges attacking Capt. Jones, 42 Barges, The Alligator, Out of the reach of 32 P.R., One Mile]

The two suspected this purpose. After everyone had retired and all was quiet, they began to speak in loud voices of why they had been detained and how they had not given any vital information. " How greatly these gentlemen will be disappointed in their expectations," said Shields, " for Jackson with the twenty thousand troops he now has, and the reinforcements from Kentucky which must speedily reach him, will be able to destroy any force that can be landed from these ships." [9]

Major General John Keane, who was in temporary command of the British army, and Admiral Cochrane pondered this information.

---
[9] Eaton, *Life of Jackson*, 287-88.

The Baratarians and the Battle of New Orleans

The next day Shields and Morrell were sent to the *Gorgon*, and they were not released until January 12, 1815.[10]

One British officer who had witnessed the gunboat battle said, " I have always regarded this affair as a wanton sacrifice of human life, merely to maintain the idle boast of bull dog pertinacity." [11] However, the victory was necessary. It gave the British command of Lake Borgne, which meant that during the next nine days they landed troops and made their beachhead without being discovered or disturbed.

While troops were assembling on Isle-aux-Pois, Admiral Cochrane sent an embassy to the Choctaws whose allegiance had wavered after Jackson drove the British from Pensacola. Gleig went along and found the expedition amusing. The Englishmen had to stay overnight with the Choctaws for they would not be hurried. Then, having presented the warriors with muskets and ammunition, the British departed, taking with them the two chiefs at their own request. " For this journey they had equipped themselves in a most extraordinary manner; making their appearance in scarlet jackets, which they had obtained from Colonel Nicholls, old-fashioned steel-bound cocked hats, and shoes. Trowsers they would not wear, but permitted their lower parts to remain with no other covering than a girdle tied round their loins; and sticking scalping knives in their belts, and holding tomahawks in their hands, they accompanied us to the fleet, and took up their residence with the Admiral." [12]

These chiefs joined others already on the flagship. Captain Benson Earle Hill says that on its quarter-deck he saw, " for the first time the Indian chiefs, who we were led to believe, would prove valuable allies to us in the present undertaking. A British officer, Colonel Nicholls of the Marines, had for some time past been domesticated with them; from his account of their prowess, and attachment to our cause, most favourable results were anticipated." [13]

---

[10] Latour, *Historical Memoir*, 75-77.
[11] Chesterton, *Peace, War and Adventure*, I, 179.
[12] Gleig, *Narrative of Campaigns*, 1821 London edition, 264-70.
[13] *Recollections of an Artillery Officer*, I, 299.

The British Camp below New Orleans

George Laval Chesterton, another officer, was shocked when he saw his friend Colonel Nicholls look " so strangely care-worn." And when Nicholls urged him to help him with his Indians, Chesterton " adroitly referred Nicholls to Colonel Dickson " and privately expressed to that colonel his " earnest desire to be spared the horrors of so questionable a service." Dickson thereupon told Nicholls that he could not spare Chesterton and hence for Chesterton " all danger of marauding and scalping was obviated." [14]

In the meantime, Cochrane had sent two officers in a boat to reconnoiter the area below New Orleans via Bayou Bienvenu. They were disguised as fishermen and some of the Spanish fishermen were their guides. They reached the bayou and ascended to the village of the fishermen.

Why had this bayou not been obstructed? Jackson had given particular orders with regard to Bayou Bienvenu. This important assignment had been committed, " in the first instance, to a detachment from the 7th Regt.—afterwards to Col. de Laronde of the Louisiana militia, and lastly, to make all sure, to Majr. Genl. Villeré commanding the district between the river and the lakes, and who being a native of the country, was presumed to be best acquainted with all those passes." [15]

Perhaps the fishermen had something to do with the situation. They were accustomed to fish in Lake Borgne and then to take their fish in pirogues to the canals of De Laronde's and Villeré's plantations and thence by wagons up the River Road to New Orleans.

At the village the two Englishmen got into a pirogue and with their guides ascended Bayou Bienvenu to its main branch, Bayou Manzant, and up that branch to the canal which drained Villeré's plantation. At its head the Englishmen jumped out and walked to the Mississippi—1,000 yards away.

They were nine miles below New Orleans. The road along the

---

[14] *Peace, War and Adventure*, I, 213-14.
[15] Jackson to Secretary of War Monroe, Camp below New Orleans, December 27, 1814, Bassett (ed.), *Correspondence*, II, 126-27.

levee and the firm strip of plantation land next to the river would make a good spout through which to funnel the invasion army into the city. The officers decided that the best place for the British to establish their encampment would be on Villeré's plantation, Lacoste's plantation, and De Laronde's plantation.

DE LA RONDE'S MANSION.

They questioned the fishermen, saying, "How many men does General Jackson have in New Orleans?"

"Not many," was the answer, "not more than two thousand."

All the fishermen except one went with the officers back to Isle-aux-Pois. The one left behind was sick.

By December 21, all the British troops had been landed on Isle-aux-Pois. No women were taken to the island. They remained on the larger ships. The women of Captain Crawford's company were left on the *Anne*, a transport.[16] While Major General Keane reviewed his troops on Isle-aux-Pois, Major Gabriel Villeré sent a picket of eight men and a sergeant to the fishermen's village.

---

[16] Chesterton, *Peace, War and Adventure*, I, 203.

The British Camp below New Orleans

"All the others are out in the lake fishing," the sick fisherman told them. The sergeant in command did not question this statement. He posted a sentinel, sent a man at intervals two or three miles into the lake, and learned nothing.

Meanwhile, along the beach of Isle-aux-Pois boats from every ship in the fleet were assembling to move the troops. A subaltern gives us a vivid description of the procedure. He records that "to protect the rear against annoyance, each launch, as well as some of the barges, was armed with a twelve-pound carronade in the bows; whilst the six cutters lately captured from the enemy, with all the tenders and small craft brought from the Chesapeake, prepared to accompany them. After everything, even to the captain's gigs, had been put in requisition, it appeared that hardly one-third of the army could move at a time; but even thus our leaders determined upon entering immediately upon the business." [17]

The 22nd of December dawned cold and rainy. At nine o'clock in the morning

> the advance of the army, under the command of Colonel Thornton, stepped into the boats. It consisted in all of about fifteen hundred infantry, two pieces of light cannon, and a troop of rockets, and it was accompanied by General Keane in person, the heads of the engineer and commissariat departments, a competent number of medical officers, and the Indian chiefs. . . .
> The boat in which Charlton and myself were embarked was a man-of-war's barge, rowed by six oars of a side, and commanded by a midshipman. Besides the seamen, there was crowded into it not fewer than sixty men and four officers, so that the full complement amounted to seventy-eight souls. Under these circumstances the space granted to each individual was not very commodious. It was by no means an easy task to shift our postures after they had once been assumed, for we were as completely wedged together as were ever a child's bricks in their box, or a bundle of logs in what is called a cord of wood. As long, however, as it continued dry overhead, the inconvenience thence arising was little felt; but we had not proceeded more than a mile from the place of embarkation, when the black clouds suddenly opened, and the rain fell as if a thousand shower-baths had been all at once opened upon us. Then our situation became comfortless

---

[17] *A Subaltern in America*, 1833 Philadelphia edition, 206.

The Baratarians and the Battle of New Orleans

enough. In the difficulty of adjusting ourselves at all, cloaks and greatcoats necessarily lost their clasps, and the neck and shoulders were left bare. Water ran down our backs and shoulders like the sewers in Ludgate Hill after a thunder-storm, yet was there much in the appearance of all about us calculated to carry our thoughts beyond the present moment,—at all events, to make us think lightly of present grievances. Not fewer than an hundred boats, of all shapes and sizes, were making way in regular column over the surface of the lake; they were all filled, to repletion, with armed men, and not a sound issued from them, except that which the rowing occasioned, and an occasional word of command uttered by those in authority. The boats moved in lines of ten a-breast; a little way a-head of them sailed a couple of cutters; the like number protected each of the flanks; and the rear was covered by three traders. . . . Sir Alexander Cochrane, in a light schooner, kept just so far apart as to see at a glance how things were going, and to superintend the whole. . . .

But the prospect of passing the night cramped and cooped up as we were, was certainly not hailed by any one with either satisfaction or indifference. The rain had fallen in such quantities, as not only to saturate the clothing of every individual, but seriously to incommode us, by creating a pool ankle-deep in the bottom of the boat, while, on account of our crowded state, we could not succeed in baling it. It ceased, however, at last, and was succeeded by a keen frost, and a northerly wind as sharp and cutting as any mortal would desire to face. . . .

As day dawned, a singularly wild and uninviting waste of country opened out before us. We were now within a stone's throw of the American shore, and ran along its edge in search of the mouth of the creek. It was a complete bog. A bank of black earth, or rather black mud, covered with tall reeds, constituted the single feature of the landscape. Not a trace of human industry, not a tree or bush of any kind or description, not even a mound or hillock, served to break in upon the sameness of scene. One wide waste of reeds alone met the eye, except at the very edge of the water, where the slime which nourished them lay slightly exposed. . . .

At length the mouth of a creek or inlet, wide at first, but rapidly narrowing, presented itself. Towards it the Admiral immediately directed his course; but the schooner in which he was embarked drew too much water, and in a few minutes went aground. We could not make any effort to relieve him from his awkward situation, for this was not a moment at which serious delay could be tolerated, and our boats were all too heavily laden already, to admit of their taking additional passengers on board. Onwards, therefore, we swept, the banks on either hand closing in upon us more and more as we proceeded, till first we were necessitated to con-

The British Camp below New Orleans

tract our front, from five boats a-breast to three, and finally only one. We were now steering up a narrow cut, which measured at its widest spot, not more than twenty feet across, and which, in some parts, became so exceedingly narrow, that the rowers ceased to dip the oars in the water, and propelled us by punting alone. Yet it was an admirable spot for the conduct of a secret expedition. As far as we could judge from the appearance of the soil, the bogs on either hand seemed quite impassable even for infantry. It was covered by reeds, so lofty as to obscure any object which could float in the canal. No eye could therefore watch our proceedings; and though we, too, were shut out from beholding all other objects besides our own line of boats and the blue sky, there was not a man amongst us who entertained the slightest apprehension that danger could be near.[18]

In the small hours of the morning of December 23, a sentinel at the fishermen's village heard something. He aroused the picket. They saw five barges full of men ascending the bayou.

The Americans hid behind the cabins until the barges passed. Then they silently entered a small boat and rowed for the lake. Occupants in one of the English barges looked back. They saw the escaping Americans, chased after the little boat, and captured it. One man contrived to escape. He floundered in the swamps for two days before he found his way to Jackson's army.

The captured men were shut up in a cabin. An officer came in, looked them over and pointed to Joe Ducros. The redcoats put Joe in a small boat and took him to Major General Keane for questioning.

"How many men has General Jackson in New Orleans?" Keane asked.

"Maybe twelve, maybe fifteen thousand. He has about four thousand at English Turn," Joe answered.[19]

Keane was disturbed. Jackson must have 20,000 troops. That doctor and purser sent by Commodore Patterson under a flag of truce had said so, and now Ducros said the same thing. They could not possibly have talked with Ducros.

Meanwhile, Colonel Thornton advanced to the edge of Villeré

---
[18] *Ibid.*, 207-12.
[19] Walker, *Jackson and New Orleans*, 123-24.

VILLERÉ'S MANSION.

plantation. Under cover of an orange grove, he and his men approached the "Big House," Major Gabriel Villeré was sitting on the gallery facing the Mississippi, watching his brother Célestin clean a gun. He looked up and saw the redcoats and almost immediately the two brothers were made prisoners.

Major General Keane arrived and decided to halt. Thornton pleaded with him to move on. He pointed out that the fishermen were right about Jackson's strength—2,000 troops—and that in two hours they could be in New Orleans. The troops were fresh, in excellent spirits, and full of confidence.

Major General Keane would not be persuaded. If the fishermen were wrong and Jackson did have 20,000 troops, the British might be attacked and cut off by overwhelming numbers before reinforcements could reach them. "We can afford to wait," he told Thornton. "In twelve hours two thousand more troops will be here and soon after that the rest of the army. Place your men next the levee. We will bivouac here tonight and attack in the morning."

Thornton was shocked, but he put his troops in postition one

The British Camp below New Orleans

hundred yards from the river and sent men to post handbills on buildings and fences. These had been printed in French and Spanish on the invasion press. They said:

> Louisianians! Remain quiet in your houses. Your slaves shall be preserved to you, and your property respected. We make war only against Americans.
>
> Admiral Cochrane
> Major General Keane [20]

Several parties were sent in all direction to reconnoitre. They returned with an account that no enemy, nor any traces of an enemy, could be discerned.

The troops were accordingly suffered to light fires, and make themselves comfortable; only their accoutrements were not taken off, and the arms were piled in such form as to be within reach at a moment's notice.

As soon as these agreeable orders were issued, the soldiers proceeded to obey them both in letter and in spirit. Tearing up a number of strong palings, large fires were lighted in a moment; water was brought from the river, and provisions were cooked. But their bare rations did not content them. Spreading themselves over the country as far as a regard to safety would permit, they entered every house, and brought away quantities of hams, fowls, and wines of various descriptions; which being divided among them, all fared well, and none received too large a quantity. In this division of good things, they were not unmindful of their officers; for upon active warfare the officers are considered by the privates as comrades, to whom respect and obedience are due, rather than as masters.

It was now about three o'clock in the afternoon, and all had as yet remained quiet. The troops having finished their meal, lay stretched besides their fires, or refreshed themselves by bathing, for to-day the heat was such as to render this latter employment extremely agreeable, when suddenly a bugle from the advanced posts sounded the alarm, which was echoed back from all in the army. Starting up, we stood to our arms, and prepared for battle, the alarm being now succeeded by some firing; but we were scarcely in order, when word was sent from the front that there was no danger, only a few horse having made their appearance, who were checked and put to flight at the first discharge. Upon this intelligence, our wonted confidence returned, and we again betook ourselves to our

---

[20] Latour, *Historical Memoir*, 91.

The Baratarians and the Battle of New Orleans

former occupations, remarking that, as the American had never yet dared to attack, there was no great probability of their doing so on the present occasion.[21]

---

[21] Gleig, *Narrative of Campaigns*, 1821, London edition, 282-83.
". . . the English army dominated the whole extent of territory from Chalmette plantation to Terre-au Boeufs and in following Terre-au-Boeufs to Lake Borgne. Consequently all inhabitants below Chalmette plantation were prisoners of the English, who had the right to seize all the provisions of the inhabitants as well as the power to force them to bring it to the camps in their carts. But, instead of seizing the provisions and animals without paying for them, they paid for them more than they were really worth originally. In a word, they did what the American army did in New Mexico on its march to Vera Cruz and until their moment of embarkation to return to the United States." Marigny, *Reflections on the Campaign*, 8.

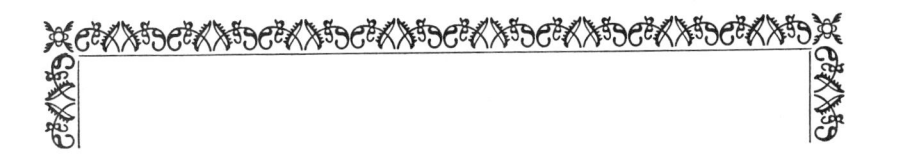

"THEY SHALL NOT REST ON OUR SOIL!"

NEWS OF THE CAPTURE OF THE GUNBOATS ARRIVED IN New Orleans on the afternoon of December 15. Jackson was not in the city, he was on his way there from Chef Menteur. Rumors spread by the enemy caused the city to panic. When Jackson arrived he issued a General Order which looked the danger square in the face and convinced the citizens that this man could and would command the situation.

Then Jackson called out the Louisiana State Militia. Major General Jacques Villeré—he whose plantation the British were approaching—was in command of the first division. He had already rallied men in the outlying areas and soon " from all the parishes the inhabitants could be seen coming with their hunting guns for in the city there were not enough guns in the magazines of the United States to arm the citizens." [1]

Major Pierre Lacoste—whose plantation was next to Villeré—had already organized and drilled a battalion of free men of color. These were sent with two pieces of cannon down the Gentilly road to erect a battery at the confluence of Bayou Sauvage and Chef Menteur. So pleased was Jackson with this battalion that he had ordered another organized. Savary, a colored man from Haiti who

---

[1] Marigny, *Reflection on the Campaign*, 3.

The Baratarians and the Battle of New Orleans

had served as an officer under the French Republic and who was known as a man of great courage, organized this second battalion and then in accordance with Jackson's policy handed it over to a white man, Major Louis Daquin.[2]

Feliciana dragoons hurried after Lacoste and his battalion to help cover the Gentilly plain. They had been quartered in the upper suburb of the city for some time and had already reconnoitered passes toward Chef Menteur and settlements below Villeré's plantation at Terre-aux-Boeufs.[3]

Pierre Jugeat was sent to organize a company of friendly Choctaws. Jugeat was the son of a Creole French trader by a half-breed Choctaw woman whose white blood was also French. He had received some education at a Catholic academy in New Orleans but he had also lived among the Indians. He was " a man of unusual intelligence, fine personal appearance and a thorough gentleman in deportment. Living among the Indians, speaking all their dialects and well acquainted with their leading men, he was invaluable to Jackson as a scout during the Creek War." [4]

Jackson had not concentrated his forces, he dared not, until he knew where the British would strike. He was certain of the approximate target by the day the gunboat battle was fought, for on that date he ordered Brigadier General John Coffee in the neighborhood of Baton Rouge to come immediately to New Orleans.

Coffee was in camp at the mouth of Sandy Creek which flows into the Amite. His men had been foraging without much success because he did not have cash with which to buy at a low price. Jackson's orders reached him at 8 P. M., December 16. At four the next morning he was writing Jackson saying: " Shall move my command this morning at sunrise. . . . I think we will reach you in four days, say by the evening of the 20th instant. . . . My arms are in bad condition . . . we have from 2 to 4 hundred that are not good . . . all my powder was destroyed by the rains." [5]

---
[2] *Ibid.*, 12; Gayarré, *History of Louisiana*, IV, 406; Latour, *Historical Memoir*, 64.
[3] Bassett (ed.), *Correspondence*, II, 84, 91.
[4] Buell, *History of Jackson*, I, 245.
[5] Bassett (ed.), *Correspondence*, II, 117.

"They shall not rest on our soil!"

The matter of arms and ammunition was getting more and more critical. During the summer Jackson had written the Secretary of War asking that such be sent to New Orleans. They should have arrived in October. It was not until November that part of a supply was sent from Pittsburgh. When Major General Carroll and his Tennesseans arrived at Natchez at 10 P. M., December 13, there was a keelboat behind him " freighted with about 14.00 stand of Arms and ammunition for the use of the Army." These were the Pittsburgh supplies. William Carroll sent a messenger to Jackson saying, ". . . a great number of my Men being badly armed, and many others not armed at all, I wish to ascertain if you will not permit me to furnish them from this boat." [6]

Meanwhile, Major General John Thomas was on his way with Kentucky Militia. Kentucky was not within Jackson's military district, but the governor of Kentucky had cooperated with his request and had mustered into service 2,300 men and officers, who, under the command of Thomas, were at the mouth of the Cumberland River on December 8. Thomas wrote Jackson that it would take 20 or 25 days to get as far as Natchez.[7]

While militia from Kentucky and Tennessee, Hinds's Mississippi Dragoons, and Coffee's brigades were on their way, Jackson was not idle. Before the gunboat battle Patterson had complained that he did not have enough seamen, so Jackson had asked the legislature to suspend the writ of habeas corpus in order that seamen might be impressed. Louis Louaillier was chairman of the committee to which this request was referred. The committee decided that men forced into the service would not be good defenders of the country. This may have been the beginning of that antagonism between Jackson and Louaillier that would have repercussions later.

Jackson requested a second time that the writ of habeas corpus be suspended. Not only did the legislature refuse this request but it also refused to adjourn because conditions might arise when the intervention of the legislature might be necessary. Apparently, the

---
[6] *Ibid.*, 113.
[7] *Ibid.*, 115.

The Baratarians and the Battle of New Orleans

legislature did not believe that Jackson could solve Louisiana's defense problem. Jackson did not quibble with it. On December 16, he proclaimed strict martial law. Notices were posted containing the rules that would be rigidly enforced.

Not a voice was raised in protest and so great was the confidence in Jackson that not a shop, not a warehouse was closed, nor any valuables removed from the city.[8] Private hospitals were established and the women formed committees to provide all that was necessary. Citizens contributed lint, clothing and bed linen. The old men under Gaspard De Bruys organized themselves to protect the city.[9] A company of volunteer riflemen was formed "under the command of a Mr. Beale, a man of advanced years, a native of Virginia. . . . This company was principally made up of Americans from the northern states, and people of some instruction: it numbered among its ranks Mr. B. Lewis, Judge of the District Court in Louisiana, B. Chew, Director of the Custom House, Messrs. Montgomery & Touro, wealthy and respectable merchants, the merchants Story, Kenner, and Henderson, the lawyer Pouter de Peyster, and many others." [10]

All able-bodied men except Englishmen were pressed into service.

Even the legislature fell into line. It adopted measures designed to aid citizens who had " to leave their private affairs in a state of abandonment, which might expose them to great distress." It passed an act to grant delays which provided that no notes or bills of exchange could be legally collected for 120 days, that no property should be sold during the same space of time, and that no civil suit or action should be commenced and that all pending suits should cease until the first of May, 1815.[11]

On one point, all the citizens disagreed with their general—they could not understand why he would have nothing to do with the Baratarians. They set to work to get that stubborn soul to relent,

---

[8] Latour, *Historical Memoir*, 73.
[9] Marigny, *Reflection on the Campaign*, 3.
[10] Nolte, *Fifty Years in Both Hemispheres*, 206.
[11] Gayarré, *History of Louisiana*, IV, 412-13.

(80)

"They shall not rest on our soil!"

"to remove the antipathy he had conceived against the Baratarians." Major Villeré was their first spokesman. He pointed out that Patterson had no sailors to man the *Louisiana* and the *Carolina*, and that Jackson had very few artillerymen. If he would only say the word, he would have the best sailors in the world and the most skillful gunners. But Jackson would not say the word and Villeré left him feeling that he had failed. However, Jackson's frontier instinct was telling him that he had misjudged the Baratarians, that it would be folly to persist in his mistaken notion.

So the next day when Bernard de Marigny and his defense committee broached the subject, Jackson replied, " The Baratarians are now being prosecuted by civil officers of the United States. Many are in prison and I cannot do anything in the matter." [12]

Taking the hint, the committee went to Judge Dominick Augustus Hall and told him what Jackson had said. " I am general in these circumstances," replied Judge Hall. " Present at once a resolution in the legislature demanding that the procedures against these men be suspended for four months and I will immediately give my orders to the District Attorney of the United States." [13]

This resolution was presented the next day and passed unanimously. Prosecution ceased and Judge Hall immediately released Dominique You and the rest of the Baratarians who were in the Cabildo.

Baratarians and their leaders appeared from everywhere. Patterson soon had splendid crews on his two ships. Dominique and Jean Laffite hastened to Jackson. They ran into him on the corner of St. Philip and Royal Street.[14]

Jean Laffite assured Jackson that he could supply cannon and all the ammunition that his army needed. At headquarters Laffite placed his maps and knowledge at the general's service, and sent his agents to deliver the war matériel. Dominique and Beluche set to work organizing three companies of artillery.

---

[12] Marigny, *Reflection on the Campaign*, 3.
[13] *Ibid.*, 4.
[14] *Journal of Jean Laffite*, 58.

The Baratarians and the Battle of New Orleans

Jackson held a review of the city militia and the newly organized company of men of color on December 18. Then he sent Plauché with his five companies of the Battalion d'Orléans to Fort St. John on Lake Pontchartrain behind the city. Both Dominique You and Beluche and one company of artillery went with Plauché. The other two companies of Baratarian artillery were sent elsewhere—one to Fort Petites Coquilles and the other to Fort St. Philip.

The work of obstructing bayous west of the Mississippi was under the command of Major Michael Reynolds. His headquarters were at The Temple, in the very heart of the area where Laffite had munition depots. Jackson's powder magazine was on the west side of the Mississippi, at a point a short distance below New Orleans. Nothing must happen to interrupt or destroy the delivery of powder to Jackson's magazine. Jean Laffite knew the network of vital communications better than any one else. Jackson sent him to Reynolds with this letter: "Mr. Jean Laffite has offered me his services to go down and give you every information in his power. You will therefore please to afford him the necessary protection from Injury and Insult and when you have derived the information you wish furnish him with your passport for his return dismissing him as soon as possible as I shall want him here."[15]

Coffee and his men came in on the 20th. He had commenced his march with 1,250 men, having left behind at Sandy Creek 300 who were on the sick list. The weather was cold and rainy, the terrain difficult, but 50 miles were covered the first day. The terrific pace slowed down 500 of his mounted. Coffee gave orders that all who were able were to advance with him, the rest to follow as fast as their exhausted horses permitted. Coffee and 800 men rode 70 miles the next day. They camped 15 miles from New Orleans and early the next morning halted four miles above the city at the place Jackson had designated.

Coffee's weather-beaten men were tough, hardened veterans with the ability to take care of themselves in any emergency. They were all good shots who thought nothing of bringing down a squirrel

---

[15] Bibliotheca Parsoniana: La.-Am. MSS, No. 1019 (December 22, 1814).

"They shall not rest on our soil!"

from the top of the tallest tree with a rifle. They did not look very military "in their woolen hunting-shirts, of dark or dingy color, and copperas-dyed pantaloons, made, both cloth and garment, at home by their wives, mothers and sisters, with slouching wool hats, some composed of skins of raccoons and foxes, the spoils of the chase . . . with belts of untanned deer-skin, in which were stuck hunting-knives and tomahawks—with their long unkempt hair and unshorn faces." [16]

Hinds and his Dragoons came in from Woodville, Mississippi, right on the heels of Coffee's men. They had covered 230 miles in four days.

The next day, December 21, "when the orders that had been given for obstructing the different canals of the bayous below Manchac were presumed to have been executed, a detachment of the 3d regiment of militia, consisting of eight white men and a serjeant, two mulattoes and one negro, with a single boat, were sent by major Villeré [son of the owner of the plantation] to the village of the Spanish fishermen." [17]

(On that same day the British held a review of all their troops on Isle-aux-Pois. The next day Thornton and his advance guard crossed Lake Borgne and, on December 23rd, established themselves on Villeré's plantation.)

While Villeré's picket was on its way to the Spanish fishermen's village and while the British were parading on Isle-aux-Pois, Carroll arrived at the outskirts of New Orleans with 3,000 Tennesseans. His division had left Nashville on the Cumberland River on November 19. Just before they embarked, "that river, which is seldom boatable at that season of the year, was suddenly swelled by unexpected rains and torrents." [18] The flood had swept them into the Ohio and down the Mississippi in record time.

Most of Jackson's men (with the exception of Thomas and his Kentuckians who would arrive about New Year's Day) were now

---
[16] Walker, *Jackson and New Orleans*, 154-55.
[17] Latour, *Historical Memoir*, 77-78.
[18] Walker, *Jackson and New Orleans*, 155.

within a radius of four miles from the city. Coffee's Tennesseans were above the city on Avart Plantation; Plauché's battalion with Dominique You and Beluche and their gun crews were at Fort St. John; Claiborne with two regiments of Louisiana militia and Lacoste with half of the free colored battalion were on Gentilly plain;[19] the Regulars (7th and 44th) were at Fort St. Charles on the lower river corner of the city and in barracks nearby; Jugeat and his Choctaws were not far away.

In addition to these land forces, Jackson had the schooner *Carolina* and the larger *Louisiana*, a merchant vessel which was being prepared as a sloop of war. These two vessels had been transporting ammunition from the "Grand Magazine of Powder" across the river which Laffite's men kept filling.[20] The *Louisiana* was not ready for immediate action; the *Carolina* was.

The stage was now set, Jackson and his men were in the wings waiting for their cue. A preliminary one came on the evening of December 22, when Colonel Denis de Laronde of the third Louisiana militia sent Jackson word that several sails of vessels had been seen off the point of the three bayous behind Terre-aux-Boeufs. Jackson ordered engineer Lacarrière Latour and engineer Howell Tatum to find out whether or not this report were true and to examine very particularly all the communications from Terre-aux-Boeufs to Lake Borgne. They left town at eleven o'clock on the morning of Friday, December 23.

Meanwhile, Gabriel Villeré, a prisoner nine miles below New Orleans, watched and waited. Then he saw his chance. He leaped

---

[19] Claiborne complained to Jackson that he did not really know how many men were in the militia. He explained why, saying: "I have not accurate information as to the Present Condition of the Battalion of uniformed militia, at Present under your immediate orders; It has of late been much added to by Recruits from the Regular militia, and indeed *the practise* of leaving one company to join another, has of late become *so common*, that to prevent the total destruction of some corps, and much derangement, to others, I have deemed it proper to forbid it, in General militia orders." Bassett (ed.), *Correspondence*, II, 120-21.
Claiborne lacked the tact and power to make himself obeyed. Bassett, *Life of Jackson*, 158.
[20] Bassett (ed.), *Correspondence*, II, 53, 132.

"They shall not rest on our soil!"

through a window, jumped a picket fence and escaped in spite of shots and pursuing redcoats. Crossing the river in a small boat, he encountered Colonel de Laronde on the other side. The two found horses, galloped up the west side of the Mississippi, recrossed, and at 1:30 in the afternoon reached 106 Royal Street.

A sentinel announced the mud-spattered fugitives. "Gentlemen, what news do you bring?" asked Jackson.

"Two thousand British are on my plantation," said the excited Villeré. "More are expected. They will camp tonight and attack in strength in the morning."

"By the Eternal!" roared Old Hickory. "They shall not rest on our soil!" [21]

Meanwhile, engineers Latour and Howell Tatum had reached the boundary between Bienvenu and de Laronde plantation,[22] and had met several people hurrying to the city who told them the British were at Villeré's and that Major Villeré and others were prisoners. Tatum immediately galloped back to inform Jackson while Latour went ahead until he stepped over the boundary of Villeré's plantation from which point he watched British troops "occupying the ground from the commencement of the angle made by the road in that place to the head of the canal."

Latour was no ordinary observer. He was a man of great stature, with black eyes that illuminated the dusky skin of his big round face. His black hair and bush of beard and whiskers were streaked with white, the only indication of his forty-five years. Intelligent, astute, a graduate of the Paris Academy of Fine Arts, he was a talented engineer and architect.[23]

This Frenchman approached within rifle shot and judged the number of British to be sixteen or eighteen hundred. He noted the

---

[21] Walker, *Jackson and New Orleans*, 151.
[22] Six plantations were to be the main theater of action during the next few weeks. Beginning with Macarty and going down the river they were: Macarty, Chalmette, Bienvenu, de Laronde, Lacoste, and Villeré.
[23] Stanley Faye, "The Great Stroke of Pierre Laffite," *Louisiana Historical Quarterly*, XXIII (Baton Rouge, July, 1940), 25 in the reprint. In the spring of 1816, Latour became a Spanish spy.

position they were taking. Such exact information could not have been gained by any ordinary scout. It was then 1:30 in the afternoon. Within 25 minutes he reported at headquarters.[24]

Jackson knew he could rely on this information. He knew now that for a few hours at least he would slightly outnumber the enemy; moreover, he had the advantage of the *Carolina* and *Louisiana* and their guns. Turning to his aides he said, "Gentlemen, we must attack tonight!"

He sent couriers in all directions: to Coffee, Carroll, and Hinds above the city; to the Feliciana Dragoons on Gentilly; to Jugeat and his Choctaws, and to Plauché who was at Fort St. John. With the exception of Carroll, they were all to come with haste to Fort St. Charles where they would be inspected and provided with ammunition. Apprehending a double attack by way of Chef Menteur, Jackson sent Carroll and his whole brigade to reinforce Claiborne in the Gentilly plain.

Jackson's messengers found Patterson and Captain John Henley at Fort St. John, examining batteries being erected by Beluche's and Dominique's gun crews. The Baratarians were to hold that fort alone—Plauché and the Battalion d'Orléans were on their way to Jackson. Patterson and Henley hurried back to the city to get their ships ready to take up a position downriver opposite the enemy's camp. Because of calm, the big *Louisiana* could not steer in the stream, so Patterson instructed Lieutenant C. B. Thompson to follow when he could. Then he and Henley boarded the *Carolina* whose Baratarian crew had the ship ready to get under weigh.

After Jackson had given his orders, he ate a little rice and lay down to rest while the troops assembled. As he slept, Feliciana Dragoons scouted the enemy. They were the few horsemen whom the British subaltern had said "were checked and put to flight at the first discharge."

By 2:30 a detachment of artillery under Colonel William MacRea, with two 6-pounders commanded by Lieutenant Samuel Spotts; the

---

[24] Adams, *History of United States*, VIII, 343-44; Latour, *Historical Memoir*, 88.

"They shall not rest on our soil!"

7th Infantry Regiment under the command of Major Henry D. Piere; and a detachment of marines were all formed on the river road near Montreuil's plantation, the third one below the city. At 3:00 o'clock Jackson arose, went to Fort St. Charles and stationed himself at the gate through which the troops would pass to get on the river road. Jean and Pierre Laffite, Livingston, Grymes, Duncan and Davezac were in his escort. Troops came pouring through the narrow streets and filed by them. Hinds and his Mississippi Dragoons were the first to appear. They were sent ahead to reconnoiter. Coffee and his mounted rifles came next, then the 44th Infantry, Jugeat and his Choctaws and Major Daquin's battalion of free men of color.

After them came Beale's Rifles, a corps of sixty-odd men, carrying long rifles. They were just out of sight when Jackson spied a body of men coming on the double quick down one of the side streets to the fort. "Ah! There come the brave Creoles," he cried.

Major Plauché's battalion had run all the way from Fort St. John. Jackson smiled as they passed him, then he glanced at the River. He saw that the *Carolina* was moving. It was only five o'clock, but the darkness of December night had already fallen as Jackson and his aides galloped down the road after his little army.

Most authorities estimate its strength at about 2,000. Latour's figures are:[25]

Hinds's Mississippi Mounted Rifles	107
Coffee's Tennessee Mounted Rifles	563
Beale's Rifles (lawyers and merchants)	62
Seventh U. S. Infantry	465
Forty-Fourth U. S. Infantry	331
Jugeat's Choctaws	18
Daquin's Company, Haitian colored	210
Plauché's Battalion	287
Marines	66
Light Artillery with two 6-pounders	22
	2131

---

[25] Latour, *Historical Memoir*, 103-104; William James, *Military Occurrences*, II, 361-62; Cooke, *Narrative of Attack on New Orleans*, 189.

The Baratarians and the Battle of New Orleans

Opposed to Jackson would be Colonel Thornton with the light brigade already landed which consisted of:

part of the 85th regiment of infantry	650
part of the 95th rifles—Captain Hallen	500
a detachment of sappers and miners	100
a detachment of the rocket brigade commanded by Captain Lane	80
the 4th regiment or King's own	750
	2080

On the supposition that each regiment had left a party on board to take care of the baggage, there would remain about 1,800 effectives. However, while Jackson's line was forming, the odds against him were increasing as a second brigade landed which consisted of:

21st regiment, fusileers	900
44th regiment, fusileers	750
93rd regiment, fusileers	1100
artillerists	150
	2900

Again assuming that some were left on board, 4,500 effectives had been landed on the 23rd of December before nine o'clock P. M.[26]

Jackson's line formed on De Laronde's plantation. Only one plantation, Lacoste's, separated the Americans and the British. Enemy pickets, 500 yards away, heard nothing as Jackson's troops silently took their position. Colonel de Laronde and Pierre Laffite guided Coffee, followed by Beale's Rifles and Hinds's Dragoons to the swamp side of the plantation. When the signal came, Coffee's command was to turn the British right and drive it to the river. He formed his men along the edge of the cypress swamp, perpendicular to a ditch which was the boundary of Lacoste's plantation. Coffee's men dismounted and turned their horses loose. Beale's Rifles were behind them and in the rear Hinds's Dragoons remained on their horses.

---

[26] *Ibid.*

"*They shall not rest on our soil!*"

Jackson's right formed perpendicular to the river, stretching from a boat landing on the levee along an avenue of oaks to Versailles, Colonel de Laronde's home. Artillery and marines occupied the levee road. To their left was the 7th, then Plauché's battalion and Daquin's men of color. Jugeat's Choctaws and the 44th were on Jackson's left end. Colonel Ross, the same who with Patterson had destroyed the Baratarian establishment on Grande Terre, commanded the militia battalions.

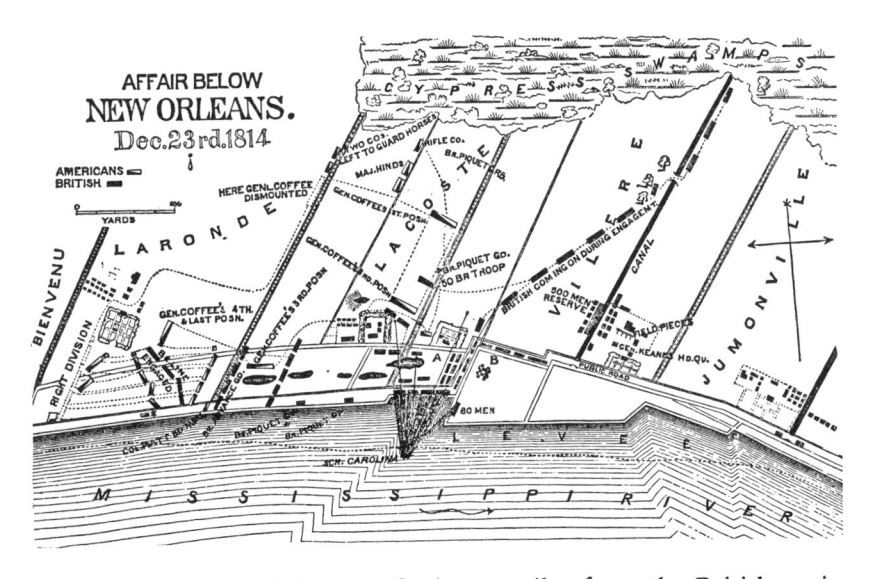

AFFAIR BELOW NEW ORLEANS. Dec. 23rd. 1814

As Jackson joined his right flank two miles from the British position, Hinds's scouts reported that some of the redcoats were cooking their suppers over little fires while others were sleeping.

Because of the precedent Americans had set along the Atlantic coast, at Washington, and at Baltimore, the English acted on the supposition that no danger threatened unless they sought it. They fully expected the French and Spanish to be passive or join them. They knew there was some activity in front of them, but they were so sure it could only be Jackson's advance guard that they built their fires and moved around without the least qualm.

So secure did they feel that they paid no attention to the *Carolina*

The Baratarians and the Battle of New Orleans

and her cargo of cannon moving downstream. They thought she was just an ordinary vessel making her usual trip down river. At 6:30 Jackson sent Livingston to Patterson to tell him to take up his position abreast the enemy camp and start bombarding it. When he sent up a red, white, and blue rocket, that would be the signal for the troops to start firing.

The *Carolina* carried five 6-pounders on each broadside and two long twelves on pivots, one foreward and the other aft. Her broadside then, would be seven guns: two twelves and five sixes. Her crew of 90 men were mostly Baratarians, skilled in the use of cannon.

At 7:30 the *Carolina* was in position and ready to fire. All was quiet in the British camp. Suddenly the redcoats heard a shout rising out of the waters of the Mississippi: "Now, damn their eyes, give it 'em!" [27]

All Hell broke loose, or so thought the confounded British as a storm of 6-pound shot and grape flashed down on them "like so many thunder-bolts, the balls boring down whole piles of arms, knocking kettles off the fires, scattering blazing beams of wood about, maiming some soldiers, and sending others whence no traveller returns. . . . The levee being only three feet above the level of the water, was no screen. . . . Round after round, and ball after ball, were vomited forth, driving the troops into most dire confusion, which caused a ten-fold panic during the darkness, and the confusion beggars all description; no mob could be in a more utter state of disorganization. . . . Officers were buckling on their swords, and throwing down knives and forks, and calling on their soldiers. Soldiers were looking after their arms or buckling on their knapsacks, and calling to their officers. Bugle-horns were sounding, while the soldiers were striving to gather together . . . all the time under the fire of this floating battery at point-blank range, and without any effective aim to silence these seven noisy monsters, the fire of which was assisted, when some of the fires were extinguished, by the confusion of voices amongst the soldiers." [28]

---

[27] Cooke, *Narrative of Attack*, 191.
[28] *Ibid.*, 191-92.

(90)

"*They shall not rest on our soil!*"

Colonel Thornton, probably the most able British officer, kept his head. He ordered the 95th to rush to the support of its pickets along the river, and the 85th to support its outposts spread across Lacoste's plantation to the right of the 95th. The 4th or King's own was sent back to Villeré's house to act as reserve.

The *Carolina* fired seven broadsides in rapid succession, then sent up the red, white, and blue rocket signal. Jackson's sector was in motion. Lieutenant Spotts with his artillery supported by 60 marines had moved down the road next the levee. Major Piere, leading the 7th, was moving in column. Jackson was near the 7th. Ross's brigade—Plauché's battalion, Daquin's colored, and the 44th led by Major Baker—marched in extended line. This was all right at first, but soon the river inclined to the left and pushed the 7th inward on Plauché's battalion while on the other side De Laronde's house and a grove of orange trees pressed the 44th against Daquin's men. Thus Plauché and Daquin with their commands were pushed back of the line. This could not be corrected because of darkness and the momentum of the advance.

Colonel Piatt and a company of the 7th had by this time filed through a gate of De Laronde's plantation and advanced as far as the boundary of Lacoste's plantation when an outpost of the enemy—80 men of the 95th Rifles under Captain Hallen—opened fire. Hallen's men were in a ditch behind a fence. The 7th and 44th moved in the direction of the fire and forced them to retire. Meanwhile, the artillery blazed away. The British, reinforced by more of the 95th, regained their position and started for the two guns. The marines recoiled under their heavy fire. Wounded horses overturned one of the guns. "Save the guns, boys!" yelled Jackson.[29]

Part of the 7th dashed forward, rescued the marines and guns, and drove back the enemy. Because of numerous ditches, the redcoats were able to reform. Seeing the 44th weakened, they attacked

---

[29] Jackson would later say, when complimented on the gracefulness of his bow, that he learned the art on the night of the twenty-third when, though the British thought differently, he never wasted so much politeness in his life in bowing to their bullets as they whistled around his head. Walker, *Jackson and New Orleans*, 172.

it. The 44th was mostly young boys. Plauché's Creoles and Daquin's Haitians rushed from behind and with the 44th drove the British back.

Jackson's right wing had been in action about an hour when he sent a scout to discover Coffee's position. He had not as yet had any news from his left wing. Coffee, meanwhile, had deployed his men next the swamp and was opposite the *Carolina* when she sent up her rocket signal. With his dismounted and Beale's Rifles parallel to the river, he started west like a broom toward the enemy. Hinds's cavalry remained in the rear—they would ruin their horses if they attempted, in the dark, to maneuver over terrain cut up with ditches and bayous.

The 85th was closer to Coffee than he had expected—it had retired two or three hundred yards into the open field where darkness was some protection from the belching *Carolina*. Coffee had advanced only 100 yards when the 85th opened fire. He had ordered his men not to fire unless they were sure of felling an object. Their aim was accurate; they fired faster than the redcoats. The 85th retreated, rallied and charged, and retreated again until they reached an orange grove. Here they formed to fight. Coffee's men were overpowering them when four companies of the 21st Royal North British Fusileers came up from the boats.

The subaltern said: " There cannot be a doubt that we should have fallen to a man had not the arrival of fresh troops at this critical juncture turned the tide of affairs." [30]

The reinforcements formed for battle. Their fire revealed their position. Coffee's men charged, forced them toward the river. Beale's Rifles had been separated from Coffee by a fence. When Coffee moved right, Rifles on the extreme left did not observe the movement because of gun smoke and darkness. They kept going straight ahead and found themselves in a trap.

Some of the British 85th had been very quiet, catching their breath after Coffee turned to the right. They saw a small column

---

[30] *A Subaltern in America*, 1833 Philadelphia edition, 225.

"*They shall not rest on our soil!*"

advancing toward them. The subaltern said: " We were at this time amply supported by other troops . . . and willing to annihilate the corps now approaching. We forbade the men to fire till it should be mingled with us. We did even more than this. Opening a passage for them through our center we permitted some hundred and twenty men to march across our ditch, and then wheeling up with a loud shout, we completely enclosed them. Never have I witnessed a panic more perfect or more sudden than that which seized them. They no sooner beheld the snare into which they had fallen, than with one voice they cried aloud for quarter; and they were to a man made prisoners on the spot. The reader will smile when he is informed that the little corps thus captured consisted mainly of members of the legal profession. The barristers, attorneys and notaries of New Orleans . . . were all made prisoners. The circumstance was productive of no trifling degree of mirth amongst us; and to do them justice, the poor lawyers, as soon as they recovered from their first alarm, joined heartily in our laughter." [31]

By this time Coffee had most of the 85th on the run toward the river. They took refuge behind sections of an old levee. Thick fog from the river obscured everything. Coffee wanted to charge, but one of his officers had discovered the advantage of the British and persuaded Coffee it would be too hazardous, that the enemy " could be driven no further, and would, from the point they occupied, resist with the bayonet, and repel with considerable loss, any attempt that might be made to dislodge them." [32] Furthermore, Coffee's men would be exposed to fire from the *Carolina*.

At this point Jackson's messenger reached Coffee and told him that Jackson feared the consequences, under the circumstances, of further prosecution of a night attack on troops then acting together for the first time. Coffee was to withdraw to the position on De Laronde's plantation where he had been when the battle started.

The battle had raged for an hour and a half over one square mile of plantation fields and ditches. In the obscurity of gun smoke and

---

[31] *Ibid.*, 226-27.
[32] Eaton, *Life of Jackson*, 315.

The Baratarians and the Battle of New Orleans

fog, " such confusion took place as seldom occurs in war—the bayonet of the British and the knife of the American were in active opposition at close quarters during this eventful night. . . . The darkness was partially dispelled for a few moments, now and then, by flashes of fire-arms; and whenever the outlines of men were distinguishable, the Americans called out ' don't fire, we are your friends! ' prisoners were taken and retaken. The Americans were litigating and wrangling, and protesting that they were not taken fairly, and were hugging their fire-arms and bewailing their separation from a favourite rifle that they wished to retain as their lawful property."

"The British soldiers likewise, hearing their mother tongue spoken, were captured by this deception; when such mistakes being detected, the nearest American received a knock-down blow; and in this manner prisoners on both sides having escaped, again joined in the fray, calling out lustily for their respective friends." [33]

So Coffee retired to the swamp end of De Laronde's plantation and Jackson's right wing to the main entrance of that plantation near the river. Meanwhile, 350 Louisiana Militia under General David Morgan who were stationed at English Turn (seven or eight miles below the British) knew the redcoats were on Villeré's plantation almost as soon as Jackson did. They wanted to attack immediately, but Morgan refused to give the order since he did not know Jackson's wishes. When the night battle started and they heard the firing, Morgan could restrain his men no longer; so he gave the necessary orders and led them through muddy roads and darkness to Jumonville's plantation which was immediately below Villeré's.

It was about 11:30 when some of his scouts came across enemy outposts and fired. The fire was returned. Then Morgan ordered his men into a field until they could reconnoiter. They were unable to learn anything and at three o'clock they started back to their post at English Turn.

During the night opposing generals estimated their losses. Keane officially reported the British losses at 46 killed, 167 wounded and

---

[33] Cooke, *Narrative of Attack*, 195.

"They shall not rest on our soil!"

64 missing.[34] Jackson's losses were 24 killed, 115 wounded and 74 prisoners.[35]

At four o'clock on the morning of December 24, Jackson began to move his army back to Rodriguez Canal between Chalmette and Macarty plantations. Carroll with 1,000 of his men was already there. Jackson knew the British were 6,000 strong and that more troops were still coming up the bayous.

He did not know that on that day, the day before Christmas, British and American peace commissioners were signing a peace treaty at Ghent in Belgium. It provided for the *status quo ante bellum*. The British interpreted this to mean that before the war Louisiana did not belong to the United States; therefore, Louisiana's future status would be determined after the invasion force had rolled into New Orleans and up the Mississippi valley.

The British peace commissioners could not know that Jackson's night attack, the opening round in the Battle of New Orleans, had convinced Major General Keane and Admiral Cochrane that the army defending the city was really larger than it was. Therefore, they would wait until their force assembled in all its power and majesty before attacking the "backwoods rabble."

The delay gave Jackson time to dig a ditch.

---

[34] Keane's report, December 26, 1814, cited in Adams, *History of United States*, VIII, 350-51. *A Subaltern in America*, 1826 Philadelphia edition, 292, says the British loss was enormous, that not less than 500 men had fallen.
[35] Latour, *Historical Memoir*, 102-103; Adams, *History of United States*, VIII, 350-51.

SIR EDWARD
MICHAEL PAKENHAM

THERE WAS NO FIGHTING ON THE 24TH. JACKSON DECIDED IT would be foolhardy to send his troops, most of whom had no bayonets, against six or seven thousand redcoats skilled in the use of them.[1] No, there was too much danger on the open plain. His men needed something to shield them. They could dig out the old grass-grown Rodriguez Canal and throw up the mud into breastworks.

Old Hickory requisitioned every spade, shovel, axe, saw, wheelbarrow, cart, and wagon in New Orleans. Hundreds of slaves

---

[1] " It had been Jackson's anxious desire to renew at daybreak the conflict, which night had interrupted, and to attack the British vigorously. But he learned from scouts, that the English Major-General Keane . . . had received a reinforcement of 3500 men. Jackson was, nevertheless, as much as ever disposed to assail the English with his small force of inexperienced militia, but his aide, Livingston, very prudently advised him to consult Major St. Gème. The latter had gone about a good deal with Moreau, when the latter visited New Orleans a few years before, and had examined its situation with the critical eye of a tactician; had studied its capabilities for defence in case of hostile attack, and, hence, was peculiarly fitted to give Jackson some excellent advice. This he did, and had the great merit of making Jackson comprehend that Keane, with his 6,000 men, would, in the open field, surround, defeat, and capture him and his small force of raw levies, who had not much more of the soldier about them than the mere name; he then pointed out the canal or channel . . . behind which we had assumed our position, as the very spot that Moreau himself had indicated as the best one adapted to a defence of the city, particularly by unpractised troops. Jackson listened to this advice." Nolte, *Fifty Years in Both Hemispheres*, 213.

(96)

Sir Edward Michael Pakenham

helped in the hand-blistering work.² While Mississippi and Feliciana horsemen patrolled the fields in front of Jackson, and while the *Carolina* kept up an irritating fire, work progressed on the barricade which extended from the river to the cypress swamp. Empty barrels and sugar casks were lined up at intervals along Rodriguez Canal and the apertures between them filled with earth. This formed a temporary screen. The canal, ten feet wide, protected the barricade in front.³

After deepening the ditch three feet, the toilers struck water and the excavated soil began sliding back into the canal. Cypress logs were cut (from the plentiful stand nearby) and laid crib fashion. Dirt was hauled in from some distance to thicken the watery mud which was thrown into the cribs. Slowly the mud piles grew. By nightfall they were three and four feet high the whole length of the line. As the ditch was deepened in the week that followed, Jackson's parapet on its outer face (including the depth of the ditch) was everywhere at least seven feet, and in many places eight feet high.⁴

Throughout the 24th the British made no move. Perhaps Major General Keane was waiting to shift responsibility to the commander in chief who was on his way. The *Louisiana*, the *Carolina*, and Jackson's road battery were not insuperable obstacles. On this day Keane could have marched his troops along the cypress swamp— one mile from the ships and Jackson's two sixes—to New Orleans. Jackson's barricade was in its infancy and open behind. But Keane preferred to keep his troops under an irritating fire.

By the next morning, Christmas, all the British troops from Isle-aux-Pois had been landed. Their chief occupation seemed to be eying the *Carolina* " whose sides still smoked by day, and at night vomited iron harbingers from its port into the bivouac of the British, so that the city of New Orleans and General Jackson now became only a secondary consideration, and the discussion was how to get rid of this watery dragon." ⁵

---

[2] Buell, *History of Jackson*, I, 400-402.
[3] Cooke, *Narrative of Attack*, 201-202.
[4] Buell, *History of Jackson*, I, 401.
[5] Cooke, *Narrative of Attack*, 201.

The Baratarians and the Battle of New Orleans

Then cannon shots broke the quiet of Christmas day. Ditchdiggers dropped their shovels and ran for cover. Jackson sent Hinds to find out the cause of the disturbance. He returned to say that the British were jubilant, a new commander had arrived from England, someone very important, perhaps the Duke of Wellington himself.

"Who's afraid of the Iron Duke?" shouted Old Hickory. "Here we shall dig our stakes and not abandon them until we drive the red coats away. Men, get back to your shovels." [6]

The new commander was not the Iron Duke but his brother-in-law, Major General Sir Edward Michael Pakenham, the second most popular military commander in England. (This was the same Pakenham who had already had his neck adjusted twice by French Creoles.) Major General Samuel Gibbs, second in command, an efficient staff, and 3,000 reinforcements came with Pakenham. When they had left England at the end of October, English and American commissioners at Ghent were in their third month of peace negotiations.

Rumor had already spread among the English troops that Sir Edward had in his dispatch case a commission as governor of Louisiana and the promise of an earldom when he occupied that province.[7]

It was not British policy to reward and maintain such meritorious but penniless conquerors as Sir Edward with money from England. Pakenham's earldom would be supported by the $15,000,000 in cotton, sugar, corn, and whiskey in New Orleans warehouses. This wealth would be used to dazzle Louisianians with the splendor of British pageantry. The merchant fleet would carry this wealth to England.

---

[6] Walker, *Jackson and New Orleans*, 211.

[7] There was a lady on board one of the ships in Lake Borgne who expected to become the "governess" of Louisiana. Letter of Pierre Favrot to his wife, January 21, 1815, Howard-Tilton Memorial Library, New Orleans. The author is indebted to Connie G. Griffith for her typed transcript of this letter. She asked, "Who was the lady?" The author could only point out that Pakenham was not married. He had been engaged to Lady Milbanke, but she had jilted him when she learned there was insanity in the family. At that very moment Lady Milbanke was getting ready to marry Lord Byron, who had a club foot. They were married one week later, January 2, 1814.

(98)

Sir Edward Michael Pakenham

Once established, the system would work—as it was working in India. Mississippi Valley cotton would be manufactured into cloth and sent back for the natives to buy at England's price. Here was a splendid opportunity for many Englishmen to make their fortunes. One officer on Villeré's plantation saw the situation thus: "The conquest of New Orleans would have proved the most valuable acquisition that could be made to the British dominions, throughout the whole western hemisphere. In possession of that post, we should have kept the entire southern trade of the United States in check; and furnished means of commerce to our own merchants, of incalculable value." [8]

Pakenham rode forth to survey his encampment and the position of the Americans. He could see nothing of Jackson's army except Hinds's horsemen galloping over the cane-stubble fields in very unmilitary fashion. They would rush up to British outposts, shoot as they whizzed by, then yell like savages and wheel in the opposite direction. Pakenham looked toward New Orleans but "the town was completely hid, nor was it possible to see beyond the distance of a very few miles, either in front or rear, so flat and unbroken was the face of the country." [9]

Pakenham called his staff together in Villeré's house and gave vent to his feelings. "With the forces at our disposal," he said, "our entrance into New Orleans should have been swift and easy. I regret the defeat of our forces due to the error made on the 23rd of December. Our troops should have advanced to New Orleans immediately on taking Villeré's plantation. However, that is past. Let us look to our present position. I do not like it. Never have troops been found in so strange a position, the Mississippi from eight hundred to a thousand yards in breadth on our left flank, an impassable wood on our right, the Americans less than three-quarters of a mile in front, and the fleet only supplying enough boats to carry off one-third of the force collected on this spot." [10]

---

[8] Gleig, *Campaigns of British Army*, 1836 London edition, 385.
[9] *Ibid.*, 1826 London edition, 303.
[10] Cooke, *Narrative of Attack*, 203.

The Baratarians and the Battle of New Orleans

Admiral Cochrane interrupted angrily, " We were not defeated," he cried, " and there is nothing wrong with our position. If the army shrinks from attack here, I will bring up my sailors and marines from the fleet. We will storm the American lines and march into the city. Then the soldiers can bring up the baggage." [11]

Stung by this taunt, Pakenham gave up the idea of changing the theater of operations. His next suggestion met with better success. It was to bring guns from the ships and blow the *Carolina* from the water. Then the British could make a formidable display of military power and discipline which would overwhelm the " backwoods rabble."

And so Sir Edward, instead of making an instantaneous attack, " set himself down to lay siege to the American schooner, the destruction of which had no more to do with the capture of New Orleans than the most foreign thing in nature; besides, a ship with more guns lay higher up the river to dispute the further march to the city *by the road.* . . . There was no harm in blowing both of them up as soon as possible, but there was no occasion for the whole army to await the event; for while time was lost in disposing of these annoyances, the barricade was rising out of the earth like enchantment as a real stoppage to take the place of an imaginary one." [12]

All that day and the next sailors labored with incredible toil in December cold and rain to bring nine field pieces, two howitzers, one mortar, a furnace for heating balls, and a supply of ammunition from the ships in Lake Borgne, sixty miles away, and then up the bayou and through mud to the river bank.

On Christmas Day Jackson sent orders to General Morgan to evacuate his position at English Turn. He was to send a garrison of 100 men with the artillery across the river to Fort St. Leon. The rest of his men were to cross the river also, but they were to ascend its right bank and go into camp opposite Jackson's line on the plantation of " big fat Dr. Flood."

---
[11] *Ibid.*, 212.
[12] *Ibid.*, 203-204.

Sir Edward Michael Pakenham

The river was rising. This gave Jackson an idea. He sent engineers to cut the levee both above and below Villeré's plantation. Water began to flow through the cut, then the river fell. Instead of flooding the British camp, the cuts let enough water into canals and bayous so that it was easier for the enemy to bring heavy artillery up the waterways.

Winter rains chilled both camps. Jackson kept his men busy at the ditch. He was surveying the work next the cypress swamp when Jean Laffite pointed out that the line was not long enough, that it should be carried through the cypress woods and into the swamp itself. Otherwise, the enemy might turn the left end of Jackson's line.[13]

Old Hickory agreed with Jean, so engineers directed men to anchor logs to trees for a platform behind whatever barrier they could erect. Meanwhile, Jackson had no regular chain of outposts like the British. But, every morning before daylight, mounted horsemen spread themselves over the plain to watch British movements.

At night Jackson's "rabbit hunters" took over with their own special system of irritation that made night hideous for the British. They stalked and killed sentinels and picked off officers going the rounds. Worse still, groups would silently approach an outpost, fire simultaneously, and drive in. Then they would lie on their bellies in the cane stubble, convulsed with silent mirth as they watched developments. The aroused British would form in column and prepare to meet the whole American army. After all, it *had* attacked at night on the 23rd. Then the officers would discover there was no army in front of them, and command the soldiers to lie down, only to arouse them again and again because of the same false alarm.

Officers complained bitterly of this unsportsmanlike conduct. "Those savages have no knowledge of how war should be fought," whined one of them. "In Europe, when two armies face each other, the outposts of neither are molested. Nay, so far is this tacit good understanding carried out that I myself have seen French and English

---

[13] Bassett (ed.), *Correspondence*, II, 125.

The Baratarians and the Battle of New Orleans

sentinels not more than twenty yards apart. These ' dirty shirts ' entertain no such chivalric notions." [14]

What that English officer failed to understand was that the " dirty shirts " could not afford to have chivalric notions such as his. The " dirty shirts " were by now three thousand citizens contending against ten thousand veteran soldiers and marines come to murder, and seize the produce of their peaceful industry so that Pakenham could establish himself in pomp and glory as their master and make them slaves of England.

On the evening of December 26, Hinds reported to Jackson, saying, " Enemy batteries on the levee seem to be completed."

Jackson notified Patterson and he sent word to Captain Henley to get the *Carolina* up river out of danger. Captain Henley made every possible exertion to move the vessel, but without success " the wind being N. N. W. and blowing fresh, and too scant to get under weigh, and the current too rapid to move her by warping." [15]

The Macarty mansion, one hundred yards behind his ditch, was Jackson's headquarters. His best observation post was from a second story window of the mansion. At daylight on the morning of December 27, Jackson was stationed there with a spy glass an old Frenchman had sent him. He looked for the *Carolina*. She was near the far bank of the river but still opposite the British camp. The *Louisiana* was closer to the American position, still she was only one mile above the *Carolina* and within range of British guns.

Suddenly Jackson saw, and then heard those guns concentrate their fire on the *Carolina*. The bombardment knocked down the bulwarks, rigging and spars. Hot shot lodged in the schooner's main hold under her cables in such a way that sailors could not quench the burning cables. The cabin and filling room contained a considerable quantity of powder. Expecting every moment that the *Carolina* would blow up, Henley reluctantly gave orders for the crew to

---

[14] Gleig, *Campaigns of British Army*, 1836 London edition, 313-14.
[15] Henley to Patterson, New Orleans, December 28, 1814, Master Commandant's Letters.

Sir Edward Michael Pakenham

abandon her. This was effected with the loss of one killed and six wounded. A short time after Henley "had the extreme mortification of seeing her blow up." [16]

English and American soldiers lined the levee watching the destruction. Among the crowd of spectators were the Indian chiefs who appeared deeply interested in the proceedings.[17] Then the *Carolina* blew up, the redcoats shouted and yelled in glee. They had suffered four days from that terrible floating battery.

Meantime, Lieutenant C. C. B. Thompson was straining every nerve to get the *Louisiana* beyond reach of British batteries. She was loaded with powder.[18] Wind and current were against her. Americans and British and their Indian allies saw the Baratarians get into boats, fasten two lines, take up oars. Tensely they waited. Then a great shout escaped the Americans as they saw the *Louisiana* move. Baratarians towed her beyond reach of the enemy.

The British were foiled again! And because of their own error. They should have opened fire on the *Louisiana* first, then they could have taken care of the *Carolina*. Charred timber of this vessel had well-nigh reached the Gulf of Mexico before Pakenham took the offensive.

During the night of the 27th he established batteries on the river road and formed his phalanx into two brigades.[19] These brigades moved in the dark across De Laronde's plantation. By superiority of numbers they obliged Jackson's advance guard to fall back. Old Hickory had ordered Colonel MacRea, commander of artillery, to fire and blow up all the buildings on Chalmette and Bienvenu so they could no longer protect the enemy from artillery fire. MacRea and his outfit succeeded in destroying all the buildings on Chalmette

---

[16] *Ibid.*
[17] Hill, *Recollections of an Artillery Officer*, 328.
[18] Latour, *Historical Memoir*, 114.
[19] One brigade under Gibbs consisted of the 4th, 21st, and 44th Regiments and the 5th West India black corps; the other under Keane consisted of the 85th and 93rd Regiments, the remains of the 95th Rifle Corps, and the 1st West India black corps. A squadron of the 14th light dragoons and the artillery were to support Keane. Cooke, *Narrative of Attack*, 206; Gleig, *Campaigns of the British*, 1836 London edition, 312.

The Baratarians and the Battle of New Orleans

and were stuffing those on Bienvenu with combustibles when they heard the British coming and escaped without being detected.

Meanwhile, Jean Laffite had returned to the Macarty mansion from an inspection of the powder and shot supply. Perhaps it was he who convinced Jackson that Beluche and Dominique You, the best cannoneers in the western hemisphere, should not be used any longer for sentry duty at Fort St. John. At any rate, Jackson sent for them to come immediately to the mud ramparts.

As Jean Laffite supervised the installation of two twenty-fours, the number of cannon on the American line increased to five. The two 6-pounders used on the 23rd were designated Battery No. 1 and placed on the levee. A 6-pound howitzer, Battery No. 2, was planted so that it commanded the river road. Laffite's two twenty-fours, fifty yards from No. 2, became Batteries No. 3 and No. 4.[20]

As the gun emplacements were being built, a French engineer had suggested filling up the hollowed redoubts with cotton bales three or four deep.[21] Wooden platforms could then be placed over them and made secure for heavy cannon. The crenellated openings on both sides of the redoubt could be constructed with six or eight bales fastened to the main body of the redoubt by iron rings.

Jackson approved this plan and his men seized the nearest supply which was on a ship that had been loaded before the invasion. Most of the cotton belonged to Vincent Nolte. When he recognized his marks on the bales he was somewhat vexed at the use made of his good cotton. He told Livingston that there was plenty of cheaper cotton in town which should have been used. Livingston replied, " Well, Mr. Nolte, if this is your cotton, you at least will not think it any hardship to defend it." [22]

At daybreak on the morning of December 28, Pakenham's troops

---

[20] It is difficult to be accurate about these batteries. Latour makes the 6-pounders and the howitzer Battery No. 1. He does not mention a Battery No. 4 for the 28th of December. *Historical Memoir*, 122; Parton, *Life of Jackson*, II, 136; Walker, *Jackson and New Orleans*, 226.

[21] Perhaps the French engineer was H. S. Bonneval Latrobe. Latour, *Historical Memoir*, 120.

[22] Nolte, *Fifty Years in Both Hemispheres*, 215-16.

Sir Edward Michael Pakenham

formed in order of attack. Gibbs placed his brigade in column along the cypress wood throwing out skirmishers halfway across the plain. Keane did the same with his troops along the river road. His men were preceded by several pieces of artillery and his right was covered by the rifle corps which in extended order met the skirmishers from Gibbs's line.

The frosty morning was clear and bright. In spite of harrassment during the night by " dirty shirts," expectations of success were high as the whole army started to move. On it went without any halt or hindrance, but as it came from behind the buildings on Bienvenu, it was not unseen.

Jackson had been at his observation post before dawn, waiting for the first streak of light. Hinds had informed him that enemy guns were in position and the army on the move. Jackson was relieved and thrilled when he saw Dominique and Beluche with their gun crew coming on the run, their red shirts stained with perspiration and splattered with mud. Gambie, Chighizola, and Raymond Ranchier were among the crew. Clowning, joking, they loped easily along. Men on the line cheered them, but the Baratarians did not pause; they went right to work swabbing and charging the twenty-four at No. 3.

Behind them came the Baratarian crew of the destroyed *Carolina*. They were in two groups, one under Lieutenant Crawley and the other under Lieutenant Norris. Crawley's group manned the howitzer and Norris and his Baratarians took over the twenty-four at No. 4.[23]

Jackson saw that the *Louisiana* had moved a little way downstream and anchored so that her guns would command the whole field in front of his line. Then he saw Hinds's observation corps falling back and the British coming from behind the Bienvenu plantation buildings, their bright colored uniforms and shiny muskets glittering in the winter sunlight. The whole army was in two strong columns: one by the river and one by the swamp. The swamp!

---

[23] Walker, *Jackson and New Orleans*, 226-27; Parton, *Life of Jackson*, II, 136.

The Baratarians and the Battle of New Orleans

Jackson's weakest sector! The ditch there was only a couple of feet wide and the breastworks were barely noticeable.

Jackson raced down the steps and ran to his horse. Abner Duncan galloped up and stopped him before he could ride away. " The legislature is going to give up the country to the British," shouted Duncan. " Governor Claiborne wants to know what to do." (According to Marigny, Jackson had forbidden Claiborne to come to camp.) [24]

" Tell him to investigate. If he finds this is true, tell him to blow up the legislature," yelled Jackson as he raced against time along his line. He saw Jugeat who by now had nearly sixty Choctaws. " Get into the swamp," ordered Jackson. He knew the Choctaws could maneuver on logs like alligators.

It was 8:25 when enemy field artillery opened up with shells, hot shot, and Congreve rockets.[25] " Dirty shirts " and " rabbit hunters " had never seen Congreve rockets before. Pakenham expected to frighten them and throw them in confusion. The Americans were used to bullets which they could not see coming but which hummed as they passed. But the rockets were a different matter. Each rocket made a roaring swoosh. The " swooping thing was dreadfully personal. It appeared to be darting directly at each watching soldier, making him shake in his boots, turning his knees to water. Only when he saw it strike the ground some distance in front could he believe it was not aimed at him. Even then the menace of the thing with a pointed iron head and an eight-foot stick was not ended. Smoking and sputtering, it writhed through the grass like a serpent.

---

[24] *Reflection on the Campaign*, 5.

[25] As early as 1232, Chinese had used rockets in warfare, firing them from bamboo tubes. As cannon developed, rockets declined. However, in the 18th century they were used in India against the British. Sir William Congreve became interested in this recoilless weapon and improved it. Wellington used more than 20,000 Congreve rockets in 1807 when he beseiged and burned Copenhagen. Congreve rockets made their American debut at the Battle of Lundy's Lane in July, 1814. They were used at Bladensburg in August. Francis Scott Key, watching the bombardment of Fort McHenry on the morning of September 13 " in the rocket's red glare," saw " bombs bursting in air." Fairfax Downey, *Sound of Guns* (New York, 1955), 68-77.

Sir Edward Michael Pakenham

Then a time fuse burst its black powder charge with a sharp report and a spurt of acrid smoke." [26]

Congreve rockets rained down between the first line at Rodriguez Canal and the second line on Canal Dupré. Jackson placed them in their proper place when he yelled, " Pay no attention to the rockets boys, they are mere toys to amuse children." [27]

For a moment there was no reply from the Americans. Jackson's aides had warned his men to hold their fire. The enemy came nearer and nearer. Then suddenly the *Louisiana* and the four land batteries let loose. Cannon balls, striking Keane's column, knocked down soldiers and tossed them into the air like old bags. One single ball from the *Louisiana* killed fifteen men. Jackson's batteries stopped enemy field artillery, killing or wounding all the gunners. Red-hot shot struck the buildings beside Keane's men and set them on fire. Blazing wood scorched panic-stricken soldiers as bright uniforms flattened in the mud of plantation ditches.

The British column by the swamp had better luck. Gibbs had no respect for what he described with contempt as the " mere rudiments of an entrenched camp." Why, his men could easily jump that miserable ditch!

A detachment of Carroll's riflemen came out from behind the breastworks—they were itching for action. British rifles, concealed in the edge of the swamp, killed five and wounded eight. Then Jugeat and his Choctaws came to the rescue. They leaped lightly from one log to another, came upon the British from behind, fired their rifles at short range. Redcoats peered into the moss-draped cypress forest. Not an Indian could they see. Colonel Rennie led his rifles away from the swamp and was about to turn Carroll's flank when Gibbs sent him word that Pakenham had commanded a retreat. Both Gibbs and Rennie were disgusted. They knew they could have overcome the Tennesseans and gotten behind Jackson's line.

Pakenham had ordered his proud army to retire, but how ? File

---

[26] *Ibid.*, 71-72.
[27] Walker, *Jackson and New Orleans*, 257; M'Afee, *History of Late War*, 514.

(107)

The Baratarians and the Battle of New Orleans

to the rear in small squads as rapidly as possible. Jackson's gunners were watching. Jeering, booing, they shot at each running group; never missing their mark. One 9-pound shot hit a retreating soldier on the knapsack and dashed him to pieces. Captain Collings got up from the ditch where he was lying and took only a few steps before a cannon ball struck his head and knocked it off his shoulders.[28]

Seven hours passed before the cannoneers relented and ceased firing. Seven hours of lying low in wet ditches did something to the mud-soaked survivors who had boasted they would sleep in New Orleans that night. They were glad when the shades of night concealed their humiliation from prisoners and slaves.

"Thus, without as much as one effort to force through them, was a British army baffled and repulsed by a horde of raw militiamen, ranged in line behind a mud wall, which could have hardly protected them from musketry, far less from round-shot. There was not a man among us," said the subaltern, "who failed to experience both shame and indignation, when he found himself retreating before a force for which he entertained the most sovereign contempt." [29]

No official British report was published concerning the killed and wounded on that day, December 28. Most estimates placed the number of casualties at 200. Considering that the only weapons used by the Americans were those of the artillery, the chances are that few of the wounded ever recovered. The American loss was nine killed and eight wounded.[30]

Patterson praised the Baratarian gunners in his report to the Secretary of the Navy saying: "You will have learned from my former letters that the crew of the Louisiana is composed of men of all nations (English excepted) taken from the streets of New Orleans not a fortnight before the battle, yet I never knew guns better served, or a more animated fire, than was supported from her."

---

[28] *A Subaltern in America*, 1833 Philadelphia edition, 235-36.
[29] *Ibid.*, 235.
[30] Walker, *Jackson and New Orleans*, 233.

Sir Edward Michael Pakenham

But, in his very next sentence, the commodore belittled this praise when he attributed the skill and bravery of the Baratarians to Lieutenant C. C. B. Thompson, who, said Patterson, " deserves great credit for the discipline to which in so short a time he had brought such men, two-thirds of whom do not understand English.".[31]

Those Baratarians would have known what to do even without direction from Lieutenant Thompson. They probably gave their own orders—in French. The British had been very much astonished on the night of the first attack, to hear the word of command given in French; for they did not expect the French inhabitants would fight against them.[32]

Only yankees sent in reports to the War Department and to the Navy Department concerning the Battle of New Orleans. They mentioned by name only Anglo-Saxon Americans. Jackson, in his general orders and in a very few of his letters, did mention Creoles by name.

When the fire of battle had ceased on December 28, Jackson returned to his headquarters at Macarty house and found Marigny with " a heart enraged " waiting for him. Marigny had gone to the legislature about eleven o'clock that morning and had met Magloire Guichard, Speaker of the House, coming down the steps with tears rolling down his cheeks.

" We are accused of treason," he said, " the doors of the legislature are closed by order of General Jackson."

Jackson listened patiently to Marigny's story of what had happened. Then he took Marigny by the hand and said: " Return to the city. Reassure your colleagues. It is all a misunderstanding. I was occupied in fighting when I sent word to Governor Claiborne to blow up the legislature if he was sure it wanted to capitulate." [33]

One cannot read the record of the investigation which followed

---

[31] Patterson to Secretary of Navy, United States ship *Louisiana*, four miles below New Orleans, December 29, 1814, Master Commandant's Letters, Vol. II, 1814.

[32] Letter from a Yankee to his " Dear Brother," written December 30, 1814, Boston *Daily Advertiser and Repertory*, February 4, 1815.

[33] Marigny, *Reflection on the Campaign*, 5-6.

The Baratarians and the Battle of New Orleans

without feeling that there were some "summer soldiers and sunshine patriots" in the legislature. Only four of its members were at the front.[34] A faction of the legislature was concerned about the rumor that Jackson would fire the city if the British drove him back. This group was ready to capitulate to the British rather than see the wealth in their warehouses destroyed. If they did not remember, British agents reminded them that "loyalists" had been well repaid during the revolution of the thirteen colonies. Take the case of Benedict Arnold. He had received 6,315 pounds in cash, an annual pension of 500 pounds for his wife, army commissions for his three oldest sons, and pensions of 100 pounds each for his five youngest children.[35]

Neither Jackson nor Claiborne considered the charge of treason as being very serious. The next day the legislature was in session as though nothing unusual had happened.

---

[34] "We regret not knowing the name of one of these persons: those we have learned are general Garrique Flojack, major Eziel, and Mr. Bufort." John Reid and John Henry Eaton, *The Life of Andrew Jackson* (Philadelphia, 1817), 322. The fourth was Sebastian Hiriard of the Senate "who served a considerable time in the ranks of the volunteer battalion, and afterwards as adjutant of the colored troops." Jackson's address to the army, January 21, 1815, *Niles' Register*, VII (February 25, 1815), 404.

[35] Richard B. Morris, editor, *Encyclopedia of American History* (2 vols., New York, 1953), I, 104. British magazines published Arnold's address of October 7, 1780, in which he explained why he could not be silent as to the motives which induced him to join the king's arms. The editor of *Niles' Register* pointed out the resemblance of a number of passages "to a multitude of speeches, essays, and paragraphs of the present day.... Indeed one might be inclined to think that several of our orators had borrowed their ideas from Benedict: his abuse of congress, his terror of France, his eulogies on Great Britain." *Niles' Register*, V (January 29, 1814), 357-58.

(110)

THE ARTILLERY DUEL, JANUARY 1

JACKSON COULD AFFORD TO BE MAGNANIMOUS WITH THE LEGISlature. His army had won victories; its elation knew no bounds. His troops were " so warm for the attack " that he had to make a speech to them to keep them quiet. One soldier, writing to his brother, said: "Although the New Orleans troops are constantly under arms, such is the spirit which prevails among them, that they submit to the fatigues of the camp with the greatest cheerfulness, and it appears more like a party of pleasure, than the encampment of an army in hourly expectation of being led into battle. The Tennessee troop are equally brave and confident of success with those from the city, and the French and Americans appear to vie which shall give each other the most praise. Indeed, an Aid-de-camp of the general said he could not get a man of them to stop to keep clear of the shot and rockets which were flying among them. They volunteer and go out in parties of 20 or 30 men, and pick off the British when they get a chance. . . . The deserters say that there would be a great many more desert, if they were not afraid of ' those fellows with dirty shirts,' but soon as they see any coming up to them, they shoot them with their rifles, so that many of the deserters cannot get near enough to our pickets to cry out *a friend*." [1]

---

[1] Unsigned letter to "Dear Brother," Boston *Daily Advertiser and Repertory*, February 4, 1815.

The Baratarians and the Battle of New Orleans

By night, rabbit hunters varied their tactics. Sometimes they carted 6-pounders within cannon shot of British outposts, then fired at any living object they could see. They terrorized the whole British camp. Jugeat's Choctaws also helped keep the British nerves on edge. They patrolled the edge of the swamp, leaping unperceived from one log to another. As they surveyed the enemy they shot every redcoat who came within rifle range. "Not less than fifty British soldiers were killed and many more severely wounded by this method of assassination." [2]

The *Louisiana* dropped down river each day to gall the British and to destroy any emplacements they might have made during the previous night. After Pakenham had complained of "those contemptible militia" mistaking a reconnaissance in force for a real attack, Admiral Cochrane had cryptically retorted: "Now that the infantry has failed to scare the Americans from their line, we must bring more heavy artillery from the ships. If we fail to blast them from behind that ditch, then we must storm their little mud piles." [3]

Gibbs was bitter. "And if the cannon fail," he asked, "how are you going to make regular approaches in this ground where you can't dig more than two feet without making a well of water? How can parallels and zigzags be pushed in such soil?"

Pakenham replied, "The operation can be conducted by sap-rolling. We will use hogsheads filled with raw cotton for saps." [4]

Gibbs left the council in despair.

So now more cannon were being brought from the fleet. Sailors—Cochrane's tough sailors—rowed boats filled with wounded soldiers sixty miles out to the ships, then rowed back those sixty miles with guns and ammunition. Soldiers manning long dragropes hauled the guns over a road the British had constructed along Bayou Bienvenu. This road through the cypress swamp was soft and miry everywhere and corduroyed where otherwise the swamp would have been impassable.

---

[2] Buell, *History of Jackson*, I, 416.
[3] Adams, *History of United States*, VIII, 357.
[4] Buell, *History of Jackson*, I, 412-13. In this reference Buell quotes from an edition of Gleig which this writer could not secure.

The Artillery Duel, January 1

It took three days—the last three days of 1814—to get the additional guns to British headquarters. As those days passed Jackson was apprehensive. What was Pakenham waiting for? Choctaws had thoroughly scouted the north and west shores of Lake Borgne and had found not the slightest sign of activity to indicate an attack by way of Chef Menteur and the Gentilly plain.

Maybe the British would cross the river and attack on the west bank! Jackson sent Latour with 150 Negroes to establish a line behind Morgan's camp. To be effective this line would have to reach from the river to the swamp on the west.

Meanwhile Patterson was busily establishing a marine battery on the levee behind this new line on the west bank of the Mississippi. He took a 24-pounder from the *Louisiana* and on December 30 found that this land gun was more effective than guns on the *Louisiana*. So the next day, December 31, he removed two more guns (12-pounders) from the ship. Then he learned from a deserter that the British were getting hot shot ready to destroy the ship on her next sally. Patterson now sent the *Louisiana* up river out of range but detailed most of her Baratarians to man his land battery.

That night, the last night of the year, sounds of hammering came from the enemy lines. Hinds and his men investigated and reported that the British were erecting batteries within 700 yards of Jackson's line.

The redcoats were building three new batteries and having trouble. Digging for earth they struck water. Under the delusion that sugar would prove as effective as soil in checking the progress of cannon balls, they decided to use the sugar stored in plantation warehouses. Thousands of pounds worth of American sugar went into the British war effort as full hogsheads were rolled into position. While this work was in progress, enough powder and ball for six hours of continuous cannonading were brought to the batteries.[5]

By dawn the British had in place no less than 24 guns and perhaps, as the subaltern says, 30 guns. Battery No. 6 on the levee opposite

---

[5] Gleig, *Campaigns of British Army*, 1833 London Edition, 344; *A Subaltern in America*, 1833 Philadelphia edition, 248.

The Baratarians and the Battle of New Orleans

Patterson's marine battery had two (four?) guns. Battery No. 7 and Battery No. 8 on the levee below Battery No. 6 had seven guns. Three batteries on the plain 700 yards from Jackson's line were No. 5, No. 4 and No. 3. They mounted fifteen guns. Not counting the guns in Battery No. 1 and Battery No. 2 (behind and to the right of No. 5, No. 4 and No. 3), one gets a total of twenty-four (twenty-six?) guns. These would be served by regular artillerists and would throw a greater weight of metal than Jackson's fifteen guns.[6] Three of Jackson's fifteen guns (Patterson's marine battery) were three-quarters of a mile from the main British battery of six 18-pounders. However, Dominique You and Renato Beluche (each now commanding a twenty-four) were directly opposite the six enemy 18-pounders.

---

[6] *Ibid.*, 249.

British guns would throw at least 350 pounds to Jackson's 224. Adams, *History of United States*, VIII, 361-62. On his main line Jackson had seven effective batteries by January 1. They were:

Battery No. 1, seventy feet from the bank of the river, was commanded by Captain Humphreys of the United States Artillery. It consisted of two brass 12-pounders, served by soldiers belonging to the regular artillery; and a 6-inch howitzer on field carriages, served by dragoons of St. Gême's company.
3 guns

Battery No. 2, ninety yards from No. 1, was a 24-pounder commanded by Lieutenant Norris of the navy and served by part of the Baratarian crew which had manned the *Carolina*.
1 gun

Battery No. 3, fifty yards from No. 2, contained two 24-pounders. Dominique You and Renato Beluche with their Bartarians manned these guns.
2 guns

Battery No. 4, twenty yards from No. 3, had a 32-pounder. Lieutenant Crawley of the navy and part of the *Carolina* crew manned this gun.
1 gun

Battery No. 5, one hundred and ninety yards from No. 4, had two 6-pounders. Colonel Piere and Lieutenant Kerr of the artillery commanded.
2 guns

Battery No. 6, thirty-six yards from No. 5, was a brass 12-pounder. It was commanded by Garriques Flaujeac—one of the four members of the legislature at the front—and served by a company of Francs under Lieutenant Bertel.
1 gun

(114)

The Artillery Duel, January 1

In addition to more guns and a greater weight of metal, the British had another advantage over the Americans. When they were ready they could concentrate their fire on the point or points they chose. Moreover, since Jackson's batteries were on high platforms, they were much easier targets than the low British batteries. With Jackson's guns dismounted, Pakenham's infantry could go through the breach and get behind the American line.

Jackson was prepared for such a contingency. Two miles behind his breastworks he had thrown up a second line on Dupré plantation; and one and a half miles behind this a third line was begun on Montreuil plantation.

Old Hickory was up early on January 1. By the time he had completed his inspection it was daylight. A heavy winter fog made it impossible for him to see more than a few feet in any direction. He knew there could not be any action until the fog lifted. Someone suggested that since it was New Year's Day there should be a parade. Jackson agreed and then went into Macarty mansion to rest a little.

Soon the camp had a festive air as bands tuned up and played "Yankee Doodle" and the "Marseillais." Many visitors arrived from New Orleans to see their relations and friends. They milled around in the field where tents were pitched.

In the opposite camp, a hundred yards or so behind British batteries, lay Pakenham's infantry, anxiously waiting for the sun to rise; and, as the subaltern said, "confidently anticipating that long before his setting, we should be snugly housed in the city of New Orleans. But the sun . . . was slow of making his appearance;

---

2 guns Battery No. 7, one hundred and ninety yards from No. 6, had a long brass 18-pound culverine and a 6-pounder. These were commanded by Lieutenant Spotts and Chauveau and served by gunners of the United States Artillery.

Battery No. 8, sixty yards from No. 7 and on the edge of the woods, was a small brass carronade with an imperfect carriage; therefore it was not very effective.

Latour, *Historical Memoir*, 147-48.

The Baratarians and the Battle of New Orleans

a heavy mist obscured him; and the morning was far advanced before it cleared away." [7]

When the fog lifted the American camp was fully exposed to the British. They had heard bands playing and now they could see the different regiments on parade, mounted officers riding backwards and forwards through the ranks, colors floating in the air.

British gunners nearest the river had their batteries ready to fire at Macarty House where they hoped to entomb Jackson and his staff. All the rest had their aim set for the batteries which had destroyed their guns on December 28—the twenty-fours of Dominique and Beluche. That was where the British expected to make a breach through which the infantry would storm.[8]

The instant the signal was given, all the British guns and rocket tubes let go. Their thunderous crash made the delta tremble. A hundred balls, rockets, shells struck Macarty House. Bricks and splinters flew in every direction. One man was knocked down by a flying splinter but no one was hurt.

Jackson and his staff ran for the line. They found Humphrey at Battery No. 1 calmly chewing his cigar. Norris and his Baratarian crew were at No. 2. At No. 3 Dominique was standing on the parapet studying the enemy through a spy glass. A cannon ball whizzed by and scorched his arm. He screamed a curse and shook his fist, crying in French, " I'll make you pay for this! " [9]

Then the little Frenchman calmed himself, gave orders to his crew " to cram their gun to the mouth with terrible chain-shot and ponderous ship cannister, and every description of destructive missile." His shot knocked the biggest British gun to pieces, collapsed the flimsy sugar foundation and killed six men. Beluche fired his twenty-four while Dominique's crew reloaded. These two kept up a steady, alternate fire.[10]

---

[7] 1833 Philadelphia edition, 249.
[8] *Ibid.*; Latour, *Historical Memoir*, 132; Nolte, *Fifty Years in Both Hemispheres*, 218.
[9] *Ibid.*; Walker, *Jackson and New Orleans*, 258.
[10] *Ibid.*; Nolte, *Fifty Years in Both Hemispheres*, 218. Captain R. N. Hill said: " The battery of theirs that did us by far the most damage was the third one from the

The Artillery Duel, January 1

Within forty minutes Jackson's batteries dismounted five enemy guns and disabled eight more so that they could not be pointed. With only nine guns left, enemy fire began to slacken. The invaders had a ten minute start in this artillery duel. When they blew up a caisson which contained a hundred pounds of powder, they thought they had made their breach. British troops in the ditches and at the batteries gave three cheers. Then American artillery answered and their shots became more terrible as the British realized too late that they were firing too high and had used up most of their "hardly-collected ammunition."[11] Cannon balls which did hit the soft earth of Jackson's line sank in easily and reinforced the breastwork. One ball struck a cotton bale, set it on fire and knocked it over the embankment. Its smoke blinded the gunners. Some of Plauché's men slid into the ditch and put out the fire.

Meanwhile, Patterson's marine battery silenced enemy guns on the levee.[12] The British infantry never had a chance to get started. In the afternoon Pakenham gave orders to withdraw from the 600-yard line. His men retired baffled and discouraged. That night working parties were sent to retrieve the guns. The subaltern said: "It was my fortune to accompany them. The labour of dragging a number of huge ships' guns out of the soft soil into which they had sunk, crippled, too, as most of them were in their carriages, was more extreme by far than any one expected to find it; indeed, it was not till four o'clock in the morning that our task came to a conclusion, and even then it had been very imperfectly performed."[13]

Pakenham's costly effort had only slightly hurt the Americans. Three of their guns had been damaged, two caissons blown up and

---

right. . . . This battery mounted 24-pounders which were fired alternately with great deliberation and with unvarying effect." Quoted in Buell, *History of Jackson*, I, 419.
[11] Admiral Sir Edward Codrington, quoted in Adams, *History of United States*, VIII, 364.
[12] In reporting this battle, Patterson again did not name a single Baratarian. Instead he made haste to say: "I beg leave particularly to name lt. Campbell, acting sailing-master John Gates, acting midshipman Philip Philibert, of the Louisiana, and sailing-master Haller, of the late schooner Carolina." To Secretary of Navy, Marine batteries five miles below New Orleans, January 2, 1815, Master Commandant's Letters, 1815.
[13] *A Subaltern in America*, 1833 Philadelpia edition, 251.

The Baratarians and the Battle of New Orleans

34 persons killed or wounded. Eleven of these casualties were persons going to or returning from camp.[14] The British loss was greater. Captain Hill said there were 31 killed and 39 wounded, "the great disproportion of killed to wounded being due to the fact that all the hits were by round shot or heavy grape—no small arms being used on either side."[15]

Admiral Cochrane's official report was laconic. It said: "On the 1st instant batteries were opened; but our fire not having the desired effect, the attack was deferred until the arrival of troops under Major-General Lambert."[16]

---

[14] Latour, *Historical Memoir*, 134-35; Adams, *History of United States*, VIII, 364.
[15] Buell, *History of Jackson*, I, 420. Cooke says the British loss was 142, *Attack on New Orleans*, 212; British return of casualties between the 1st and 5th of January, 1815—76 killed and wounded, 2 missing, James, *Military Occurrences*, II, 543.
[16] Admiral Codrington, quoted in Adams, *History of United States*, VIII, 365.

BIVOUAC,
JANUARY 1 TO JANUARY 8

JACKSON WAITED SEVEN DAYS FOR THE ATTACK OF THE ENEMY. He was compelled to wait. He could not take the offensive and destroy or capture the British army because *he did not have enough guns.*[1]

At the first hint that the British intended to invade Louisiana, Jackson informed the Secretary of War that he did not have arms for his volunteers and had suggested that they be sent immediately. Secretary Monroe then ordered a supply to be shipped from Pittsburgh. But the contractor, instead of shipping the guns on a steamboat, sent them on a slow flatboat which stopped on the way to traffic and trade the different articles with which it was laden.[2]

On January 1, but after the battle of that day, the second division of Louisiana Militia arrived—500 men from the parishes above Baton Rouge. They did not have guns.[3] Jackson ordered them to camp behind Piernas Canal near his second line. The first regiment of Louisiana Militia was already in position in the wood on the

---
[1] Jackson to Monroe, Camp four miles below New Orleans, January 9, 1815, Bassett (ed.), *Correspondence*, II, 136-37; Reid and Eaton, *Life of Jackson*, 1817 edition, 272; Latour, *Historical Memoir*, 142-43; extract of a letter from Claiborne to Eligins Fromentin, Boston *Daily Advertiser*, February 7, 1815.
[2] Reid and Eaton, *Life of Jackson*, 271-72; Monroe to Willie Blount, November 3, 1814, Bassett (ed.), *Correspondence*, II, 85.
[3] Reid and Eaton, *Life of Jackson*, 333.

The Baratarians and the Battle of New Orleans

banks of this canal. It was important to guard Piernas Canal since it was the only water route by which the enemy could penetrate behind Jackson's main line. Schooners, after ascending Bayou Bienvenu, could come up Piernas Canal.[4]

Major General John Thomas arrived on Wednesday, January 4, with about 2,250 Kentucky Militia. Included in this number were 45 volunteers from Indiana.[5] The northern campaigns had drained Kentucky of firearms, so that two-thirds of the Kentuckians came without any arms, expecting to be supplied in New Orleans.[6]

Jackson was stunned. "I don't believe it," he cried. "I have never in my life seen a Kentuckian without a gun, a pack of cards and a jug of whiskey."[7]

Jackson sent John Adair with 500 of the Kentuckians who had arms to support Carroll on the main line, but there was nothing he could do with the remaining 1,750 except place them with the unarmed Louisiana Militia on his second line and, "by the show they might make, add to his appearance and numbers, without at all increasing his strength."[8]

Several days before this, a search had been made in every house in New Orleans for guns. Only a few ancient Spanish muskets were found. The four companies of old men guarding the city gave up their guns and armed themselves with fowling pieces and pikes, so that 400 more Kentuckians were armed by January 7.[9]

However, Jackson's army behind the mud ramparts of Rodriguez

---

[4] Latour, *Historical Memoid*, 129.
[5] Buell, *History of Jackson*, II, 45.
[6] John Frost, *Pictorial Life of Andrew Jackson* (Philadelphia, 1847), 302; Latour, *Historical Memoir*, 141.
[7] Buell, *History of Jackson*, I, 423.
Not only were the Kentuckians without arms, they were almost naked and half-starved. The people of New Orleans and the river parishes remedied their "deplorable want of clothing in the inclement weather." They contributed $16,000 with which they bought blankets, woolen cloth, and shoes stored in warehouses. The blankets and woolens were distributed among the ladies of New Orleans. Within one week they made 1,200 blanket cloaks, 275 waistcoats, 1,127 pairs of pataloons, and 800 shirts. Latour, *Historical Memoir*, 142.
[8] Reid and Eaton, *Life of Jackson*, 333.
[9] *Niles' Register*, VII (February 11, 1815), 376; Bassett (ed.), *Correspondence*, II, 129 n.; ———, *Life of Jackson*, 190.

Bivouac, January 1 to January 8

Canal was impregnable because the *cannoniers* had plenty of ammunition. Ever since the night battle of December 23, the artillery had annoyed and impeded the enemy. Latour says, and other eyewitnesses agree, that " whenever a group of four or five men showed themselves, they were instantly dispersed by our balls or shells. The advantage we derived from that almost incessant cannonading on both banks of the Mississippi, was that we exercised our gunners, annoyed the enemy to such a degree that he could not work at any fortification, nor indeed come within the reach of our cannon by day, and was deprived of all repose during the night." [10]

An Ordnance Report for October, 1814, says there was in New Orleans at this time

> 37 cannon mounted
> 3,335 cannon cartridges, filled and empty
> 56,108 pounds gunpowder
> 28,746 cannon shot of different sizes
> 21,867 musket cartridges
> 12,321 flints

This report was made *after* Patterson's descent on Laffite's establishment at Grande Terre. Since the spring of 1814, the Baratarians had been delivering ammunition to Mexican rebels for New Orleans

---

[10] Latour, *Historical Memoir*, 143.

The French genius of Jackson's *canonniers* is evident in the names of those who directed the gun crews: Dominique You, Renato Beluche, Garriques Flaujeac, Bertel, and Chauveau. Jackson's 10-inch mortar was useless until Jules Lefevre, one of Napoleon's eagles and a veteran marine artillerist, took command of it. At some of the batteries, an Anglo-Saxon and a Frenchman commanded, but Jackson's aides usually gave all credit to the Anglo-Saxon, as at Battery No. 7 where Spotts and Chauveau commanded. Reid and Eaton say, for example, that on January 8, " Battery No. 7 was ably served by lieutenant Spotts." This was true, but it was also true that Battery No. 7 was ably served by the Frenchman Chauveau.

A gentleman from New Orleans, writing to a member of Congress, January 13, 1815, said: " Many men distinguished themselves at our batteries whose names until lately were unknown; the privateering class, formerly yclept *Baratarians,* have produced a corps of skillful artillerists. Behind our entrenchments, the discipline of the English troops is not feared, nor our want of it felt; the more regular they are in approaches and attacks, the greater is the loss they sustain, and perhaps the very irregularity of our fire makes it more destructive." *Niles' Register*, VII (February 11, 1815), 375.

[11] George Bomford, Lieutenant Colonel, United States Ordnance to Hon. James Monroe, Secretary of War, Boston *Daily Advertiser*, February 25, 1815.

merchants. The first shipment was 80,000 pounds.[12] Baratarians were skilled in making gunpowder and Laffite had full magazines near New Orleans. Laffite was not bragging when he told Jackson he could furnish ammunition for an army of 30,000.[13]

Because the Baratarians wholeheartedly cooperated in the war effort, Patterson was able not only to keep the *Louisiana* loaded with ammunition to supply his battery on the west bank of the Mississippi; but also, as Claiborne reported to President Madison, Patterson was able to furnish promptly " to the army and militia such supplies of arms and ammunition as could be spared from the naval stores, or prepared by his marines—," which would be the Baratarians.[14]

Apparently Claiborne was not so prompt in forwarding these supplies to Jackson. Nolte says: " The first week of the new year was occupied in strengthening our defences, and it was particularly ordered to have plenty of ammunition in readiness. The munitions were in charge of Gov. Claiborne, who was so frightened that he could scarcely speak. On the first of January ammunition was wanting at batteries Nos. 1 and 2. Jackson sent in fury for Claiborne, who was with the second division, and said to him, ' By the Almighty God, if you do not send me balls and powder instantly, I shall chop off your head, and have it rammed into one of those field-pieces.' "[15]

While Jackson barked at " Clabo," Pakenham was waiting for supplies, guns, and reinforcements. On the first of January he had sent the *Dictator 64* to Havana with about 400 passengers—" soldiers wives, and sick and wounded or disabled soldiers, to relieve the enemy's camp of its ineffectives, and also to obtain provisions for those that remained. The Captain of the *Dictator* immediately contracted for, and began to take on board with all haste 4000 barrels of flour, at 23 dollars *per barrel*."[16]

---

[12] Faye, " Privateersmen of the Gulf," 22; USDC of La., Case No. 817.
[13] *Journal of Jean Laffite*, 60.
[14] Patterson to Secretary of the Navy, Marine Battery Five Miles below Neworleans [sic], January 13, 1815, Master Commandant's Letters, 1815; Rowland (ed.), *Claiborne Letter Books*, VI, 335.
[15] Nolte, *Fifty Years in Both Hemispheres*, 219.
[16] *Niles' Register*, February 4, 1815, 356; February 11, 1815, 378.

Bivouac, January 1 to January 8

An observer at Havana reported that a brig from New Providence had been permitted to take from the royal arsenal at Havana "18 pieces of brass cannon for the use of the enemy at New Orleans, and that they were carried thence in the night to save appearances."[17]

Pakenham was waiting also for the arrival of Major General John Lambert with two regiments, the 7th and 43rd, "mustering upwards of seventeen hundred bayonets." The British expetced much from these troops who had not suffered "the galling and unmilitary trials that their fellow soldiers had been put to." After landing, these troops were reviewed with their backs turned towards the enemy's line. Pakenham did not appear at this review because "he was up in a tree in the pine-wood, examining the works of the Americans."[18]

These reinforcements, together with more sailors and marines from the fleet increased Pakenham's force to eight thousand men—"a force which in almost any other quarter of America would have been irresistible."[19] But in Louisiana the flower of the British army had found itself "living targets set up before the elite of the round-hatted Americans." Fatigue, frustration, and hunger were undermining the confidence of those who had pillaged in Spain and France and along the Chesapeake. They no longer had the cocksureness of that Major Mitchell, one of the prisoners taken on the night of December 23, who, when offered clean linen "politely declined it on the ground that his own baggage would be up in a few days."[20] Instead, "some-

---

[17] *Ibid.*

[18] Cooke, *Narrative of Events*, 215-16.
One of the new arrivals was fascinated with the two hundred or so Indians camped at the left of his hut. After describing the men, he said: "The married women or squaws, are in a state of nudity, with the exception of one petticoat reaching to the middle of the calf of the leg; the daughters of twelve years of age are entirely without covering, and squat in the white ashes cross-legged, like their parents; and when they have occasion to move about, the ashes from the fire sticking like feathers to their posteriors, and as dame nature has cast the part in so many moulds, no further description can be requisite to assist the tittering faculties." *Ibid.*, 166.

[19] *A Subaltern in America*, 1826 London edition, 320. The 1836 London edition, page 330, states that the new arrivals increased Pakenham's force to 6,000 men. A collation of the different editions brings out some interesting alibis.

[20] Letter from a gentleman in New Orleans to a member of Congress, *Niles' Register*, VII (February 11, 1815), 375. This same correspondent noted also that "many of the English officers have brought their families with them, and it is said they have a

(123)

thing like murmuring began to be heard in the camp."[21] Perhaps the main reason was that stomachs were empty.

The "long-suffering sailors" had brought guns, ammunition, and troops from the fleet, but very little food. Officers still had small rations of salt beef, a few biscuits, and a little rum. Soldiers had less. Until they learned better, they tried to stave off hunger by eating raw sugar from hogsheads—"a thick, sticky mass of black stuff, full of grit and little splinters of cane; having a sickish flavor and leaving a bad taste in the mouth, besides producing nausea or diarrhaea (*sic*) if taken in any quantity."[22]

The men in Jackson's camp were well-fed. New Orleans was full of flour, corn meal, meat which had not been exported because of the blockade and which continued to come from up river. Jackson had impresssed every horse, mule, and wagon for transport service. These brought a daily supply of cornbread, sweet potatoes, bacon, and other food from the city. Creoles drank coffee while westerners drank whiskey.

Letters written in Jackson's camp show a different spirit from the memoirs written by Pakenham's subalterns. Instead of complaining, as did the British, about not being able to sleep because of the continuous shower of cannon balls, a militiaman in Jackson's camp wrote on the day before the final battle:

> We have become so used to the sound of cannon within these two weeks past that no one appears to attach any importance to it, and even women who never heard of a camp before, will enter it in the heat of battle without fear. I think now, all I have read of wars and battles is mere stuff— that its terrors are more horrid in imagination than in reality. Some of the most cowardly fellows are among our first rate warriors ... but practice makes everything familiar to the human mind, and I do really believe that our troops are now so familiarized to scenes of blood, that they would not hesitate, if commanded, to march in column up to the mouth of a cannon. I cannot conceive how the men at Washington allowed the same cowardly Englishmen to alarm them when they attacked at Bladensburg. ...

---

collector aboard. Everything proclaims their intention of a permanent establishment and their confidence of ultimate success."
[21] *A Subaltern in America*, 1826 London edition, 318.
[22] Cited from account of R. N. Hill in Buell, *History of Jackson*, I, 420.

Bivouac, January 1 to January 8

You will laugh at my calling the British soldiers cowardly. I don't know if the epithet may be applicable to the whole army, but to the divisions we have seen it appertains with great justice. On the first assault the enemy made upon our entrenchments, on the 28th ult., they came in three columns, first on the right, second to the center, and third to the extreme left. They marched up in solid mass, until they came within about 400 yards, they then halted and displayed; we then saluted them with grape and cannister shot; they immediately formed solid column again, but with all the thrashing that the officers could give them, not a man would advance another inch—in this situation they stood until we gave them another round of cannister and grape, when down they fell upon their bellies and laid there until dark, and then sneaked off under cover of night.[23]

If any of Jackson's troops had cause to complain, it was Coffee's Tennesseans. From the 24th of December until the 20th of January they worked and slept in mud, and never showed the least symptoms of discontent or impatience. Jackson's ramparts on Rodriguez Canal stretched in a fairly straight line *on firm ground* from the river to fifty yards beyond Battery No. 8—a distance of about 700 yards. Fifty yards beyond Battery No. 8 the line was not visible to the enemy because it plunged into the woods for 750 yards, still in a fairly straight line. Then, because the land inclined away from the river, the woods became impassable. Enormous holes full of water from the canal made it necessary to turn the line at a 90 degree angle and bend it back 200 yards. Coffee's Tennesseans guarded the 750-yard sector in the woods and the 200-yard end. To do so they had to camp there. The ground was so low and difficult to drain that the Tennesseans literally lived in water, walking knee deep in mud. Several tents were pitched on small isles surrounded with mud or water. The 200-yard end had to be guarded constantly for the enemy, under cover of bushes, might otherwise get behind Jackson's line.[24]

Jackson was anxious about possible British penetration from that end back to Piernas Canal; so on January 3, he sent Reuben Kemper

---
[23] Letter dated January 7, 1815, *Niles' Register*, VII (February 11, 1815), 377-78.
[24] Latour, *Historical Memoir*, 149-50.

The Baratarians and the Battle of New Orleans

from Feliciana (parish above Baton Rouge) and eleven Louisiana volunteers on a scouting expedition. They descended Piernas Canal in boats to Bayou Bienvenu and proceeded down that bayou to its junction with Bayou Manzant. They stopped occasionally and climbed trees to see whether or not they could locate the British. They had almost reached Bayou Manzant before they discovered the fortified enclosure Pakenham's troops had built at its junction with Bienvenu. Kemper left five men to guard his boats while he and the rest went to reconnoiter from the prairie. They had gone about half a mile when they saw the enemy coming up the bayou in five vessels. They saw sailors looking out from the mast head and when the vessels got near Kemper's boats, the British fired on them. Four of Kemper's men escaped but one was taken prisoner.

The British set fire to the prairie as they went on up the bayou " so that whoever happened to be in it had to run from the flames rapidly gaining on the grass . . . which was . . . as thick as wheat in a field." Kemper and his men worked their way toward Villeré's Canal. Where it enters Manzant, they discovered a strong force behind breastworks guarding magazines. Kemper and his scouts were back in camp by January 5.[25] Only men like Kemper and his Louisianians could have found their way through the swamps and trembling prairies and circle back with precise reports to Jackson in less than two days.

Jackson and his troops were able to see some actvity in front of them. After the battle on New Year's Day they saw the British working on a large quadrilateral redoubt. Its interior dimensions were 80 feet × 62 feet × 108 feet × 70 feet. It was located near the woods on Bienvenu plantation. Jackson's heavy pieces of artillery did not cease firing on the working parties, but they made some progress because the officer commanding them stood upon the parapet; and as soon as he saw the fire of Jackson's guns, he gave a signal to his men who instantly flattened behind the parapet.[26]

British workmen also were constantly galled as they built a square redoubt at the ditch separating Bienvenu and Chalmette plantations.

---

[25] *Ibid.*, 138-40.   [26] *Ibid.*, 136.

Bivouac, January 1 to January 8

This redoubt was in front of Jackson's Battery No. 7. Not until the night of January 7, Saturday night, did Pakenham re-establish the batteries that had been destroyed the previous Sunday, the batteries on Chalmette plantation. Shortly after nightfall hammer strokes of the Brtish resounded even within the American lines and gave a "note of preparation." Jackson's outposts reported this activity and also that British guards had been reinforced.

Meanwhile from other sources Jackson knew the British were about to attack on both sides of the Mississippi. A brig from Jamaica had been captured near Chef Menteur. It was loaded with rum, bread, and munitions. Ten prisoners from this brig told Jackson of the arrival of Lambert with reinforcements. Deserters from the British camp confirmed this report and added that a water passage was being dug to the Mississippi. All week long the British made Negroes of the planatations in their possession cut through the levee and continue Villeré's Canal until by Saturday it connected with the river.

On that day there was a great deal of activity in front of the British camp but the distance was so great that Americans could not see distinctly what the enemy was doing. Jackson took his old telescope to the second story of Macarty House and was able to see that on Laronde's (three plantations away) soldiers were making fascines and ladders. Beyond that on Lacoste's and Villeré's plantations troops continually marched and maneuvered so that they concealed operations behind them. Jackson sent word to Patterson to go down his side of the river and look across at the British.

Patterson and Morgan were responsible for the defense of the west bank. Immediately after the battle of New Year's Day, Jackson had sent his chief engineer, Latour, across the river to assist Morgan in choosing an advanced position for a line of defense. Latour surveyed the situation and chose a place where the distance between the river and the impassable woods was only 900 yards wide. Several cannon and 500 men behind breastworks here could hold the line. It could not be turned because to attack the line the enemy would have to advance on the open plain.[27]

---

[27] *Ibid.*, 166-68.

The Baratarians and the Battle of New Orleans

When Latour went to advise Morgan he found Patterson with him. Patterson's batteries (three twenty-fours and six twelves) were strung out for a mile along the river edge. Some were below Latour's projected line. Patterson's guns were placed to enfilade Pakenham's troops if they came up the levee or the plain on Jackson's side of the river. It seems as though Patterson wanted to be sure that he played with the big boys. His guns were not in position to cover his own bank against attack from below.[28]

Morgan rejected Latour's proposed 900-yard line and chose a line 2000 yards long (longer than Jackson's line on Rodriguez Canal which from the river to the woods was 700 yards and on which there were eight batteries) below Patterson's batteries along the shallow Raguet Canal. This selection was made early in the week, probably on Monday. By Saturday 200 yards of breastworks had been thrown up beginning at the river. These were protected by one 12-pounder and two 6-pounders. Behind these breastworks were Morgan and 500 Louisiana militia. Nine-tenths of the line (1800 yards) had no protection except a shallow ditch.

This was the situation on Saturday afternoon, January 7, when Patterson dropped down river to see what the British were doing. He looked across and still was not much concerned about his own side of the river. He reported to Jackson saying, " The British have dug out Villeré's Canal to the River, and from the number of men, soldiers and seamen, I apprehend they will get their Boats into the River tonight." In another note he added: " Be assured that no exertion on my part shall be wanting to defeat the attempts of the Enemy, but we are extremely weak on this side, require a strong reinforcement. . . . I consider the firing of the Enemy this evening, as a feint to draw your attention from their operations below, which I apprehend they will carry into execution to-night; but I hope and trust they will meet defeat. Come when they may, my Guns shall roar long and loud depend upon it! "[29]

---
[28] Adams, *History of United States*, VIII, 370; M'Afee, *History of the Late War*, 519-20; Bassett, *Life of Jackson*, 198-99.
[29] West bank of Mississippi, January 7, 1815, Bassett (ed.), *Correspondence*, II, 132.

Bivouac, January 1 to January 8

Jackson paid some attention to Patterson's plea. He ordered Adair to send 400 Kentucky militia to reinforce Morgan's camp. This order Adair gave to Colonel Davis at 7 P. M. Colonel Davis immediately marched 400 men to New Orleans—about five miles. There 170 of them were armed. Some of the muskets had no flints. Those who had such guns would have to substitute pebbles. The unarmed Kentuckians returned to camp below New Orleans.[30]

Colonel Davis and his 170 armed men were ferried across the river; then they marched five more miles over bad roads, sometimes knee-deep in mud, and reached Morgan's camp at 4 A. M. General Morgan was glad to see them. Keeping his Louisiana Militia behind the line, he immediately sent the Kentuckians a half mile down the river beyond the breastworks to meet the enemy.

Meanwhile, in the British camp, a soldier who had escaped from Jackson's line on the night of January 6 told Pakenham about the unarmed condition of many of Jackson's troops; and, " pointing to the centre of general Carroll's division, as a place occupied by militia alone, recommended it as the point where an attack might be most safely made." [31]

The next day, Saturday, January 7, Pakenham called his last council of war. Admiral Cochrane was there. He was the one who had suggested that Pakenham send enough troops across the river to seize Patterson's guns and turn them on Jackson's army while the main British force stormed the American line.[32] Admiral Malcolm was also present, the same who had held a ball on his flagship, the *Royal Oak*, as the fleet crossed the Atlantic; and who " with the honourable Mrs. Mullens " had opened the ball with a country dance.[33]

---

[30] John Adair to Governor Isaac Shelby, New Orleans, March 20, 1815, *Niles' Register*, VIII (April 29, 1815), 157; Latour, *Historical Memoir*, 170; Bassett, *Life of Jackson*, 197-98; Adams, *History of United States*, VIII, 370-71.
[31] Reid and Eaton, *Life of Jackson*, 334-35; S. Putnam Waldo (ed.), *Memoirs of Andrew Jackson* (Hartford, 1819), 244; Colyar, *Life and Times of Jackson*, I, 335.
[32] Adams, *History of United States*, VIII, 367.
[33] *A Subaltern in America*, 1826 London edition, 65. " Mrs. Mullens, an elegant lady then in the fleet, had come over to grace the fashionable circles of New Orleans. She

The Baratarians and the Battle of New Orleans

Pakenham and his generals and admirals reviewed the strategy of their simultaneous attack on both sides of the river which was to take place two hours before dawn the next day while it was still dark enough to conceal their movements. Major General Gibbs with 2,200 men would lead the main attack against Carroll's center which was behind Batteries No. 7 and No. 8. (These batteries the English did not fear.)

Major General Keane would lead 1,200 troops in a sham attack to the right along the river. This column would draw the fire of Jackson's heavy batteries (Nos. 1, 2, 3 and 4) until Gibbs could break through at Battery No. 7.[34] There were no cannon on the 750 yards of Jackson's line in the cypress woods. Gibb's column could approach Battery No. 7 under cover of those woods to within 200 yards of the Americans. A regiment of West Indian Negroes would support Gibbs's right. They would advance through the woods and distract Coffee and Jugeat's Choctaws so that they would not go to the aid of Carroll.

Major General Lambert with 1,400 reserves would be in the rear center. Thus 5,300 men would be ready to assault Jackson's line while Colonel Thornton with 1,400 men across the river captured Patterson's guns and turned them on Jackson's west flank. Seamen and troops detailed for other duties swelled the total of the attacking force to about 8,000.[35]

Pakenham appointed the 44th to lead Gibbs's column. These 400 men were to advance over broken ground and unseen obstacles lugging fascines (made of ripe sugar cane and therefore heavy) and ladders ten feet long so that troops behind them could cross Jackson's

---

had been the life of the squadron, contributing by her fascinating manners and vivacity, to brighten many of the dull and gloomy hours of the long voyage. But her husband was far from being the soul of the army. Son of a lord, he had obtained his promotion more by influence than merit. . . . He had received one honorable wound at Albuera, and that sufficed to fill the measure of his ambition." Walker, *Jackson and New Orleans*, 323.

[34] Gleig, *Campaigns of British Army*, 1836 London edition, 331.
[35] Adams, *History of United States*, VIII, 373; Bassett, *Life of Jackson*, 192-93.

Bivouac, January 1 to January 8

ditch and scale his slippery mud wall. Lieutenant Colonel Mullens (he was only a captain in the regiment) commanded the 44th. Captain Hill was sent before sunset to instruct the "Honorable Colonel Mullins (*sic*) of the 44th, respecting the redoubt in which the fascines, etc were placed," and to report the result of his interview. Hill found Mullens, read the directions from headquarters to him, and then asked, "Do you thoroughly understand the instructions?"

Mullens replied, "Nothing could be clearer." A little later he cried out, " My regiment has been ordered to execution. Their dead bodies are to be used as a bridge for the rest of the army to march over!"[36]

This cry sounds as though Mullens thought he was to be another Uriah the Hittite whom the captain of the armies had sent to sure death at the front so that King David could have Bathsheba, the wife of Uriah the Hittite. That night, as Mullens led the 44th to the front, he hâlted for ten minutes at the redoubt where the fascines and ladders were scattered about; but no engineer officer came to point out the equipment. A commanding officer even of a regiment is only a secondary person to the engineer department on such occasions. Mullens passed on and stationed his troops in the lead position without any fascines or ladders.[37]

During the night the rest of the troops moved forward and Pakenham's engineers placed six 18-pounders in position about 700 yards from the Americans to cover the British attack.[38] Jackson's outposts observed and silently moved back as the enemy advanced. In his camp " all was composure," except that Jackson was uneasy about the half-moon shaped redoubt on the river in front of his line. Two of his officers had insisted on Thursday (January 5) that this

---

[36] William James, *Military Occurrences*, II, 374-80 (this account is based on the court maritial of Mullens) ; *A Subaltern in America*, 1826 London edition, 371; Parton, *Life of Jackson*, II, 185, 191 (this account quotes Captain Hill) ; Buell, *History of Jackson*, II, 3.
[37] Cooke, *Narrative of Attack*, 247-48.
[38] *Ibid.*, 224-25 ; Adams, *History of United States*, VIII, 372.

(131)

The Baratarians and the Battle of New Orleans

bastion for two 6-pounders should be established there to rake a charging column coming up the river road since Battery No. 1 was 70 feet from the Mississippi.[39]

The troops behind Jackson's guns from the redoubt to Battery No. 6 were the 7th regiment next the river, then Beale's Rifles, Plauché's battalion of volunteer uniform companies, Major Lacoste's battalion of Louisiana men of color, Major Daquin's battalion of Haitian men of color, and the 44th. All these corps—from the 7th on the river to the 44th beyond Battery No. 5—were under the command of Colonel Ross and numbered about 1,300 men.

Carroll's 1,400 Tennesseans, supported in their rear by Adair with 520 Kentuckians, were behind Batteries No. 6 and No. 7. To the right of No. 7 were 50 marines under the command of Lieutenant Bellevue. Carroll's command extended fifty yards beyond Battery No. 8 at which point the line entered the woods. Coffee's brigade and Jugeat's Choctaws, about 800 men, were in the woods.

The troops defending Jackson's line totalled approximately 4,000. Behind the line were four small cavalry groups and a strong row of sentries. Along the edge of the woods were some Louisiana Militia.

Jackson started to survey his line shortly after one o'clock on Sunday morning. He began at the right on the river. His face clouded as he looked at the unfinished redoubt 30 yards in front of his line. "I don't like that redoubt. I didn't want it in the first place," he growled, "but my young officers talked me into it."

His spirits lifted when he saw Beale's Rifles and a company of the 7th Infantry ready to defend the redoubt. Battery No. 1 was in good shape. There was Colonel Humphrey with his cigar and St. Gème without his plumed cap. His dragoons and the rest of the 7th were behind the battery. Lieutenant Norris of the navy and Baratarians from the *Carolina* had Battery No. 2 well in hand.

Jackson sniffed. A delicious aroma was coming from Battery No. 3. The Baratarians were making coffee. Odd what a ritual those Frenchmen observed in making coffee. They had to have a

---

[39] Latour, *Historical Memoir*, 144-45; Bassett, *Life of Jackson*, 190.

Bivouac, January 1 to January 8

special drip pot of tin-coated iron. This was placed in a kettle of simmering water so the pot and contents would keep hot but would not boil. A spoonful of the hot water was carefully ladled on the coffee. It must not channel through the grounds but soak them evenly. The first little bit of water barely moistened the coffee. Then a second spoonful of water was added and allowed to drip before the next was added, and the next and the next. It seemed to take a Frenchman hours to make a pot of coffee.

As Jackson approached Dominique You he said. "That smells like better coffee than we can get. Where did you get such fine coffee?" Then he suggested slyly, "Maybe you smuggled it in?"

"Mebbe so, général," grinned Dominique as he handed Jackson a small tin cup full.

Jackson drank the coffee with gusto, thanked the Baratarians, and moved on to complete his inspection. Later, when he again saw Dominique and his battery in action—as he had on December 28th and on New Year's Day, Jackson said to his aides, "If I were ordered to storm the gates of hell, with Captain Dominique as my lieutenant, I would have no misgivings of the result." [40]

---

[40] Saxon, *Laffite the Pirate*, 181.

THE BATTLE

OF THE 8th OF JANUARY

A LITTLE BEFORE DAYBREAK JACKSON'S OUTPOSTS CAME IN without any noise and reported the enemy moving forward in great force. The whole line was tense, expectant. In a few moments there was light, but a heavy mist reduced visibility to 200 yards. The Americans could not see 50 armed boats crossing the river below them.

Those boats were supposed to have reached the west side at midnight, but the banks of the newly dug canal had caved in and choked the channel. The boats had to be dragged through mud. Six hours behind schedule, Thornton, with only 340 troops and 100 seamen and marines (instead of a total of 1,400 men), moved across the river. His seamen rowed in silence with oars muffled and, thanks to the mist, gained the opposite bank without having been perceived. However, the current of the Mississippi had dragged them downstream so that Thornton landed five miles below Patterson's guns which were to be fired on Jackson's line as the starting signal for the battle.

At daybreak Pakenham, mounted on horseback, was on the levee in a central position where he could listen for Thornton's shots and direct the main attack. The mist was the luckiest screen possible, for otherwise the Americans would have seen and opened fire on

The Battle of the 8th of January

the boats and on the columns formed only 400 yards in front of Jackson's line.

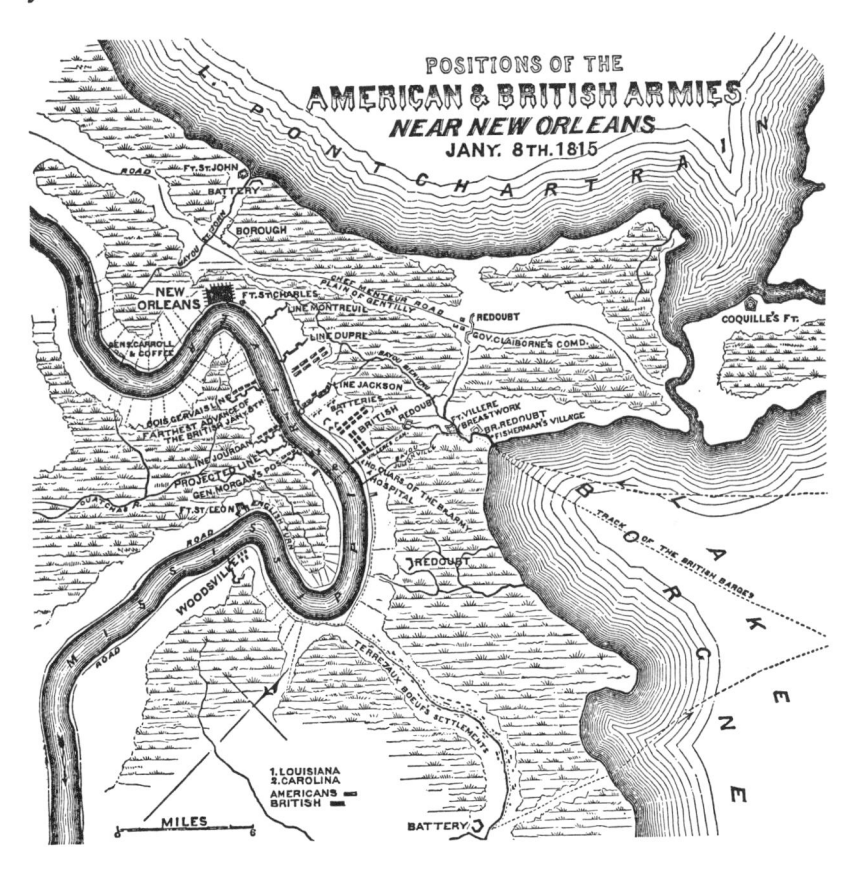

Then the mist began to clear. No sound came from across the river. Pakenham galloped toward his lines. He saw his troops in battle array but not a ladder nor a fascine was upon the field. Gibbs rushed up and cried, "If I live till tomorrow, I'll hang Mullens on the highest tree in the cypress swamp." [1]

Pakenham ordered Mullens to take 300 men and rush back to

---

[1] Colyar, *Life and Times of Jackson*, I, 344; *Niles' Register*, VIII (April 22, 1815), 133.

The Baratarians and the Battle of New Orleans

the redoubts—nearly a quarter of a mile—for fascines and ladders. Breathless with running, only half of them had returned and regained their position when Pakenham gave the signal for attack. Mullens was not one of those who returned. Historians say he was incompetent; but according to his lights he was using common sense.

Confused, many of the 44th threw down their burdens and began to fire. Gibbs's men fired too—they forgot that they were to rush Jackson's line with bayonets. Gibbs rallied his troops. At that instant Jackson's gunners at Battery No. 6 perceived the enemy column moving in formation sixty abreast. They fired their 12-pounder.

Gibbs's troops gave three cheers and charged. Jackson yelled to his men, " Give it to them boys, let's finish this business today! " [2]

Instantly Jackson's whole line was ablaze with cannon fire. Grape shot and cannister ploughed through Gibbs's column. On it came. In a moment it was within easy musket range. Carroll's men fired—a constant rolling fire. The echo from the cannonade and musketry was so tremendous in the forests, " that the vibration seemed as if the earth was cracking and tumbling to pieces, or as if the heavens were rent asunder by the most terrific peals of thunder that ever rumbled; it was the most awful and the grandest mixture of sounds. . . . the woods seemed to crack to an interminable distance, each cannon report was answered one hundred fold, and produced an intermingled roar surpassing strange. . . . The flashes of fire looked as if coming out of the bowels of the earth. . . . The reverberation was so intense towards the great wood, that any one would have thought the fighting was going on there." [3]

Gibbs's column recoiled, fled to the woods, to the ditch from which it had started. A captain on the 700 yard line saw " the dark shadows of men, like skirmishers, breaking out the clouds of smoke which slowly and majestically rolled along the surface of the field."

---

[2] *Niles' Register*, VII (February 11, 1815), 376; Washington *National Intelligencer*, February 6, 1815.
[3] Cooke, *Narrative of Attack*, 234-35.

The Battle of the 8th of January

He was so astonished at the panic he saw that he asked a retiring soldier, " Have we or the Americans attacked? " [4]

Gibbs shouted to the 44th. They did not heed but continued their retreat. He galloped a short distance to Pakenham in the rear and cried, " The troops will not obey me! " [5]

Pakenham rode to the 44th and yelled for Mullens but that officer was not to be found. The commander in chief took Mullens' place—dashed to the head of the column and moved it forward 30 or 40 yards. Then a musket shot wounded his knee and killed his horse. Pakenham jumped on another and almost instantly grape shot from Battery No. 8 mortally wounded him.[6]

Gibbs tried to rally the column as the dying Pakenham was carried to the rear. His command was annihilated and 20 yards in front of Jackson's ditch, Gibbs was mortally wounded. A few men did cross the ditch and climb the slippery parapet only to be killed or captured.

Meanwhile, Keane's column had advanced between the river and the levee. Patterson's battery across the river enfiladed the column and killed most of the advance, but Colonel Rennie, leading the remnant, stormed Jackson's unfinished redoubt. Rennie was crawling toward Battery No. 1 when one of Beale's Rifles shot him. He and his followers died in the redoubt.

Keane had held most of his men back. He was watching Gibbs. When he saw confusion in the main attack, Keane obliqued across the field to the rescue. He was wounded and carried from the field as his men fell to the ground.

Within 25 minutes after the battle had started, the three main British commanders were carried off the field and Chalmette plantation was covered with dead and wounded redcoats. Lambert was

---
[4] *Ibid.*, 235.
[5] Bassett, *Life of Jackson*, 194.
[6] *Ibid.*, 195. " The death of the general was a fortunate event for the British. His character was irretrievably ruined if he did not take New Orleans or perish in the attempt . . . the opinion of a British officer taken on the 8th of January." *Niles' Register*, VIII (April 22, 1815), 133.

The Baratarians and the Battle of New Orleans

now commander in chief. He tried to make his 1,400 reserves attack but he could not. So he ordered retreat.

Jackson's musketry blazed away until 8:30. His cannonade did not stop until two in the afternoon.[7] Then the roar of artillery gave place to the most profound silence.

Thornton's attack on the west side of the Mississippi did not get started until musketry fire had ceased on Jackson's line. Then the Americans heard Thornton's guns and looked across the river. They saw the flotilla of enemy boats carrying carronades and cannon, keeping close to the bank and firing on the Kentucky Militia while Thornton's troops on shore drove them back. The Kentuckians returned the fire as they retreated to Morgan's line. There they were given a 300-yard sector of the unfinished 1,800 yards to protect. Thornton's redcoats steadily charged in two columns. One of these moved toward the woods and turned the right of the Kentuckians. Patterson could not fire on the redcoats without killing his own men. With no protection and muskets that were not much good, outflanked on the right and cannonaded with grape-shot on the left, the Kentuckians fled from the points of enemy bayonets. This left the Louisiana Militia exposed. They fled. Patterson spiked his cannon and threw his ammunition in the river.

Thornton chased the Americans until he held the west bank for a mile above Jackson's line. Then he received an order from Lambert to bring his men back across the river.

---

[7] Cooke described the hours during which Jackson's cannoneers plied him and his men with grape and round shot. He says: "Some of the wounded managed to crawl away; but every now and then some unfortunate man was lifted off the ground by round shot, and lay killed or mangled. . . . A wounded soldier, who was lying amongst the slain two hundred yards behind us, continued without any cessation, for two hours, to raise his arm up and down with a convulsive motion, which excited the most painful sensations amongst us; and as the enemy's balls every now and then killed or maimed some soldiers, we could not help casting our eyes toward the moving arm, which really was a *dreadful magnet* of attraction. . . . A tree, about two feet in diameter and fifteen in height, with a few scattered branches at the top, was the only object to break the monotonous scene. . . . The Americans, seeing some persons clustering around it, fired a thirty-two pound shot, which struck the tree exactly in the centre, and buried itself in the trunk with a loud concussion. Curiosity prompted some of us to take a hasty inspection of it, and I could clearly see the rusty ball within the tree." *Narrative of Attack*, 240-41.

The Battle of the 8th of January

In the afternoon Lambert sent a flag of truce to ask permission to bury his dead. Jackson granted a suspension of arms for only two hours. This was wise because the British had command of the west bank, 50 boats in the Mississippi, a blockade at the mouth of the river, and they were approaching Fort St. Philip (50 miles above the mouth of the Mississippi) with two bomb vessels, one sloop, one brig, and one schooner.[8]

A truce line was agreed upon, 300 yards from Jackson's breastworks. No British soldier was to come over this line. Jackson detailed men to help the British gather up their killed and wounded.[9] There were 1,971. The Americans had six killed and seven wounded.[10]

The English buried their dead on a section of Bienvenu plantation. Some of the officers were buried in Villeré's garden. The remains of Pakenham and Gibbs were disembowled and put in casks of rum to be sent to England. About three hundred of the wounded were carried into the American camp. Then they were taken to New Orleans and lodged in the barracks. Captain De Bruys, commander of the city, " represented to the citizens the wants of those unfortunate victims of British ambition, and immediately one hundred and forty matresses, a great number of pillows, with a large quantity of lint and old linen for dressing their wounds, were procured by contributions from all quarters, at a moment when such

---

[8] On the 9th, the enemy opened fire on Fort St. Philip which they continued without much intermission until the morning of the 18th when they withdrew.

[9] As he was helping to gather up the wounded, a Tennessean looked at the long corpse of an Englishman and saw that two bullets had gone through his head. One had struck him over the left eye and passed out back of the right ear. The other hit him between the right nostril and the eye and had come out through the left ear. Either wound must have been instantly fatal. "A little lead wasted there," said the Tennessean. Buell, *History of Jackson*, II, 34-35.

[10] Bassett, *Life of Jackson*, 197. Most of the newspaper accounts say there were between two and three thousand British casualties. Total British casualties since the night of December 23 were 3,326. Total American casualties were one-tenth that number. Latour, *Historical Memoir*, Appendix No. XXIX, lii-liv; Buell, *History of Jackson*, II, 41; Bassett (ed.), *Correspondence*, II, 136-38; *Niles' Register*, VII (February 18, 1815), 386.

The Baratarians and the Battle of New Orleans

articles were extremely scarce in New Orleans, where not a truss of straw could be purchased." [11]

During the next ten days Jackson's artillery annoyed the enemy. Major Hinds wanted to attack with his cavalry; but after consulting with Adair and Coffee, Jackson decided against such a maneuver for Adair had said: " My troops will fight when behind breastworks or in the woods, but do not hazard an attack with raw militia in the open plain." [12]

The British army seemed to be inactive but it was not. Lambert's engineers were building a road to the lake over which the army could withdraw since there were not enough boats to carry off the troops in a body. It took nine days of hard, unceasing labor to construct the semblance of a road. The route was along the margin of the bayous, but there was little room for firm footing. Reeds, cane, and boughs of trees were laid across deep mud holes.

Trimming their fires on the evening of January 18, " and arranging all things in the same order as if no change were to take place, regiment after regiment stole away, as soon as darkness concealed their motions; leaving the piquets to follow as a rear-guard, but with strict injunctions not to retire until daylight began to appear. As may be supposed, the most profound silence was maintained; not a man opening his mouth, except to issue necessary orders, and even then speaking in a whisper." [13]

While the soldiers were still on firm ground the retreat was easy, but as they entered the trembling prairies their troubles began. The first corps beat the flimsy path to pieces. Those who followed floundered along the best they could where the path had been. Not only were the reeds torn asunder and sunk by the pressure of those who had gone before, but the mud had been so churned that at every step soldiers sank to their knees. The night was dark, there was no moon, and it was difficult to follow the soldier ahead.

When one cried, " Help! Help! " a lieutenant started to the rescue

---

[11] Latour, *Historical Memoir*, 177.
[12] Bassett, *Life of Jackson*, 203.
[13] Gleig, *Campaigns of British Army*, 1836 London edition, 349-50.

The Battle of the 8th of January

but he too began to sink in mud up to his breast. He felt himself being smothered but managed a feeble cry of "Help!" Someone threw him a leather canteen strap and dragged him out just as the man he had tried to save sank from view.[14]

Mud was not the only terror. Alligators who inhabited that mud resented the intrusion of these humans. They made the night hideous for the British and obsessed them during the day.

On the morning of the nineteenth a British surgeon came to Jackson and gave him a letter from General Lambert. It announced that the British had left, but that there were eighty soldiers who were too badly wounded to be moved. Would General Jackson please look after them?

Jackson immediately dispatched Dr. David C. Kerr, his surgeon general, with helpers to take care of the eighty; and then with his aides rode to the deserted camp. He saw cannon, thousands of cannon balls, and the public and private possessions left behind by the departing British—mute testimony of the complete victory of his little army.

---

[14] *Ibid.*, 351-52.

TRIUMPH AND TRIAL

The British had covered their dead with Louisiana soil but rains soon caused bodies to rise toward the surface. Legs, arms and heads appeared in many places above ground. The effluvia was insupportable. Jackson decided to move the main part of his army to New Orleans, so on Saturday, January 21, his troops were drawn up behind their ditch ready to march as soon as General Orders were read. Their hearts stirred within them as they listened to these words from their chief:

> The enemy has retreated, and your general has now leisure to proclaim to the world what he has noticed with admiration and pride—your undaunted courage, your patriotism and patience, under hardships and fatigues. Natives of different states, acting together for the first time in this camp, differing in habits and language, instead of viewing in these circumstances the germs of distrust and division, you have made them the source of an honourable emulation. . . . This day completes the fourth week since fifteen hundred of you attacked treble your number of men, who had boasted of their discipline, and their services under a celebrated leader . . . attacked them in their camp, the moment they had profaned the soil of freedom with their hostile tread, and inflicted a blow which was a prelude to the final result of their attempt to conquer, or their poor contrivances to divide us. . . .
>
> Let us be grateful to the God of battles who has directed the arrows of indignation against our invaders, while he covered with his protecting

Triumph and Trial

shield the brave defenders of their country. . . . The consequences of this short but decisive campaign are incalculably important. The pride of our arrogant enemy humbled, his forces broken, his leaders killed, his insolent hopes of our disunion frustrated—his expectation of rioting in our spoils and wasting our country changed into ignominious defeat, shameful flight, and a reluctant acknowledgment of the humanity and kindness of those whom he had doomed to all the horrors and humiliation of a conquered state. . . .

Then Jackson praised every corps: the regulars, Coffee's Tennesseans, Hinds and his Mississippi cavalry, the Kentucky Militia, Jugeat and his Choctaws, the Louisiana Militia, the two corps of colored volunteers, distinguished foreigners, and the Baratarians. Of these last he said:

They performed their duty with zeal and bravery. . . . Captains Dominique and Belluche, lately commanding privateers at Barataria, with part of their former crew and many brave citizens of New Orleans, were stationed at Nos. 3 and 4. The general cannot avoid giving his warm approbation of the manner in which these gentlemen have uniformly conducted themselves while under his command, and of the gallantry with which they have redeemed the pledge they gave at the opening of the campaign to defend the country. The brothers Laffite have exhibited the same courage and fidelity; and the general promises that the government shall be duly apprized of their conduct.[1]

As the troops marched toward the city that clear, cool Saturday morning, Nature seemed to smile upon the heroes who had fought and conquered to save their country. The aged, the infirm, women, children—all went out to meet the men. " The scene was splendid and delightful—it was perhaps the most unmixed triumph that ever occurred on this globe; so few men had fallen in the contest that private regret did not impair public joy. Every eye beamed, every heart beat high. Parents and children, husbands and wives, brothers and sisters were again united, rendered dearer to each other by the peril and danger past." [2]

---

[1] Latour, *Historical Memoir*, Appendix No. LXIX, clxxxii-clxxxvii.
[2] Letter dated New Orleans, January 21, 1815, in Boston *Daily Advertiser*, February 24, 1815.

THE OLD SPANISH CATHEDRAL AND GOVERNMENT HOUSE.

Two days before the return of the army to the city, Jackson had written Father Dubourg requesting that a service of public thanksgiving be performed in the Cathedral. This could not be done immediately on the return of the troops to the city because "the first display was too wild to be controlled by any regular method or system," and because the ladies needed more time to complete their arrangements for a ceremony "sprung from female gratitude and arranged entirely by the ladies." [3]

On the morning of January 23, all was ready and New Orleans was awakened by salvos of artillery. Soon the streets were filled with people on their way to witness the pageantry of Jackson's entrance into the Cathedral.

In the middle of the Place d'Armes and facing the main door of the Cathedral was an arch of triumph with six Corinthian columns, all twined with laurel. From either side of the arch, laurel festoons supported by eighteen pillars (nine on each side) formed an aisle through which General Jackson would walk. On each pillar was a

---

[3] *Niles' Register*, VIII (May 6, 1815), 163.

medallion with the name of a state surrounded by wreaths of various hues. In front of each pillar stood a young girl in white with a lace veil on her head, "tastefully confined by a white satin bandeau, finished on the left by a golden star." On her left hand she carried a white basket with blue ribbon ornaments and filled with artificial flowers.

Two little girls, each standing on a pedestal, were to suspend a laurel wreath over Jackson's head as he passed under the arch. Near each child was another little girl. One represented Liberty and the other Justice.

Mothers stood behind their daughters ("the states"), and a short distance back of these matrons several very handsome uniform companies were drawn up to keep the people from "incommoding" those taking part in the ceremony. A full band of military music announced the approach of the beloved general, followed by his staff officers. They entered the square by the river gate and when Jackson was under the arch "the little girls managed their wreath to admiration." Miss Louisiana, Dr. Kerr's eight-year-old daughter, stepped forward and presented an address handsomely ornamented, the composition of Mrs. Ellery.[4] Jackson deposited this document in his bosom and then flowers were strewn in his path as he walked down the aisle, bowing to "the states." These fell in line behind him and then their mothers joined the procession.

Father Dubourg, attended by priests, met Jackson at the entrance to the Cathedral and entreated him to remember that his splendid achievements were to be ascribed to Him, to whom all praise is due. "Let the infatuated votary of blind chance," said the prelate, "deride our credulous simplicity; let the cold hearted atheist look for the explanation of such important events to the mere concatenation of human causes; to us, the whole universe is loud in proclaiming a Supreme Ruler who, as he holds the hearts of men, holds also the thread of all contingent occurrences. Whatever be his intermediate agents, still on the secret orders of His all-ruling providence depend

---
[4] *Ibid.*; Bassett (ed.), *Correspondence*, II, 163.

the rise and prosperity, as well as the decline and downfall of empires." [5]

When Father Dubourg finished his address he presented Jackson with a wreath of laurel which he desired him to accept as "the prize of victory, and the symbol of immortality."

Jackson accepted the pledge and said: "Reverend Sir, I receive with gratitude and pleasure the symbolical crown which piety has prepared. I receive it in the name of the brave men who have so effectually seconded my exertions for the preservation of the country— they well deserve the laurels which their country will bestow." [6]

Then Jackson was escorted to a chair near the altar and Father Dubourg began the mass. While *Te Deum* was sung and the organ played music composed especially for the occasion, one of the mothers silently observed Jackson and later wrote: "I was seated in the very place I would have selected if my choice had been offered me of all the seats in the chapel—one person separated me from the dear old general, who sat on a chair rather apart, and I had a fine opportunity of contemplating his profile. I did not give the general one flower, but I could have given him many tears—one of the ladies reproved me laughingly for defrauding the general, whilst I stood unconsciously grasping the flowers which had been given me to strew." [7]

After the service was over, Jackson returned to his quarters to renew the defense of New Orleans and Louisiana. He sent reinforcements to the right bank of the river, and orders to keep a strict watch to his outposts on Bayou Lafourche and to Major Reynolds at The Temple. Some Kentucky troops and Louisiana Militia were stationed below the city while other Louisiana Militia guarded the Chef Menteur sector. The Tennesseans were sent to their previous camp on Avart plantation four miles above New Orleans. Baratarians and Mississippians prowled at large and kept Jackson informed of movements of the British. Because of the information they brought him, Jackson did not dare relax martial law.

---

[5] Latour, *Historical Memoir*, Appendix No. XXV, lxxi-lxxiii.
[6] *Ibid.*; Frost, *Pictorial Life of Andrew Jackson*, 399.
[7] Letter dated New Orleans, February 3, 1815, in *Niles' Register*, supplement to Vol. VIII, 163.

Triumph and Trial

The British were on Lake Borgne. Lambert and Cochrane were planning to take Mobile in an attempt to reach the Mississippi overland from that direction. First, they would have to take Fort Bowyer. Jackson did not know of these plans but Baratarian scouts had informed him that on the 20th of January transports had arrived bringing two regiments of infantry from England. By March 10th, the total of reinforcements arriving on British transports was five regiments of infantry, three companies of garrison artillery, and a company of engineers—a total of 5,600 reinforcements.[8]

On February 8, the British made their first move against Fort Bowyer. Two and a half miles east of the fort, Lambert landed the second brigade, 1,200 strong, and 450 artillerists, sappers, miners, and marines. These established a line across the peninsula to cut off reinforcements from the mainland and at the same time they fortified sand mounds which the American gunners could not destroy.

Major Lawrence's garrison of 366 men had no protection against explosives thrown into the fort from the land side. At ten o'clock on the morning of February 11, Lambert sent a flag of truce with the demand that the fort surrender. Lawrence asked for time to consider and after consulting with his officers agreed to surrender the following day.

Meanwhile, Jackson had sent Livingston with a committee to the British fleet to negotiate for the exchange of prisoners and the return of nearly 200 slaves which had been taken away by the British army. Livingston and his committee arrived just as Lambert and Cochrane were preparing to take Fort Bowyer. They were received on the flagship and detained several days.

Two days after the surrender of Fort Bowyer, the British sloop *Brazen* arrived with news of peace. Then Livingston and his committee were permitted to return to New Orleans. They told Jackson about the peace. Jackson replied that the Treaty of Ghent had not been officially announced, that it was not valid until ratified by our government, and that they must not be thrown off guard. In other

---

[8] Buell, *History of Jackson*, II, 47-48.

The Baratarians and the Battle of New Orleans

words: Jackson could not disband his army while the enemy were in force on the coast, and martial law was still in effect.

Until this unofficial news of peace arrived, the civil authorities had not openly protested martial law and not too many militiamen had deserted their posts. But now Governor Claiborne appealed to Jackson to disband the army.

Jackson resented this interference and refused to comply, but the Creole volunteers and militia who lived in New Orleans wanted to return to their homes. As Marigny explained: " They wished to see their wives or mistresses; and they wanted to relate what they had done and what they had seen." [9]

These troops began to leave their stations with or without leave. A sharp reprimand from Jackson halted this method of escape but the Creoles thought of another. They went to Louis de Tousard, the French Consul, registered as French citizens and then applied to Jackson for discharge from military service. The first of these applications were granted but as the number increased Jackson's temper flared. He ordered all French citizens to retire into the interior, to a distance not nearer than Baton Rouge. Travel distance between New Orleans and Baton Rouge at this time was one hundred and twenty miles.

Tousard went to Governor Claiborne to get protection for French subjects. Jackson heard of this and ordered Tousard out of the city also. He went.

The French were indignant. Was this their reward for winning the Battle of New Orleans? Jackson could have done nothing without them—" he had been guided entirely by French officers in all his measures of defence. Were not the fortifications planned by Lafon, Latour and others? Was not Captain St. Gème of the dismounted dragoons, always at his elbow, and suggesting all his military movements? Had not Flaugeac, Beluche, Dominique and Laffite won the battle of the 8th of January with their artillery? " [10]

An anonymous letter appeared in *La Courrière de la Louisiane*

---

[9] Marigny, *Reflection on the Campaign*, 7.
[10] Gayarré, *History of Louisiana*, IV, 582.

Triumph and Trial

which accused Jackson of abusing his authority when he ordered all Frenchmen residing in New Orleans to leave within three days and to keep at a distance of one hundred and twenty miles. As Jackson read the letter he fumed at what he considered defiance of military power. He ferreted out the author—Louaillier, the same who in December had defied him in the legislature—and had him arrested. Louaillier's counsel applied to Judge Hall for release on a writ of habeas corpus. Judge Hall granted the writ " to liberate the person of M. Louaillier."

Jackson grimly declared that this was a violation of his jurisdiction under martial law, so he had the judge arrested and conducted beyond the limits of the city with orders not to return until such time as peace was officially announced or the enemy had departed from the coast.

While this little squall was becoming a tempest, Gambie rounded up thirty Baratarians and walked off with two of Jackson's cannon— a 6-pounder and a 9-pounder. Perhaps Gambie felt he was only taking cannon which had been loaned for the defence of New Orleans. He got his men and cannon across the Mississippi to pirogues at the head of the bayous. There he learned that the mouths of the bayous were still obstructed by Jackson's orders. There was no point in trying to get to Grande Terre by way of Bayou Lafourche because it was very shallow at this time. The best route would be to get by Major Reynolds at The Temple and after that it would be easy to clear Degruy's Canal and reach the Gulf.

The main obstacle was Major Reynolds. He had strict orders to let no one pass without permission from General Jackson. Gambie knew this. He felt the pocket of his shirt. Yes, the paper was still there. His little fleet continued on to The Temple. When Major Reynolds stopped it, Gambie pulled the paper from his shirt and handed it to the major. It was a passport from General Jackson's headquarters giving Gambie permission to take men and two guns to Chernière Caminada for the defence of that place. The passport was signed by Edward Livingston, Jackson's chief aide.[11]

---

[11] USDC of La., Cases No. 817, No. 844.

Major Reynolds let the pirogues pass but he had his doubts when he saw Gambie and his men scramble to open Degruy's Canal. He immediately sent a report to General Jackson. Jackson's blood pressure went up. He stamped the floor in his rage (witnesses testified in court that he did so), but Jackson could do nothing. Official news of peace arrived and ended his military rule.

Judge Hall returned to the city. He waited until the rejoicings over peace had died down before he issued a writ summoning Jackson "to shew cause, on Friday next, the 24th March, at 10 o'clock A. M. inst., why an attachment should not be awarded against him, for contempts of this Court, in having disrespectfully wrested from the clerk aforesaid an original order of the Honorable the Judge of this Court, for the issuing of a writ of Habeas Corpus in the case of a certain Louaillier, then imprisoned by the said Major General Andrew Jackson, and for detaining the same, also for disregarding the said writ of Habeas Corpus when issued and served, in having imprisoned the Hon. the Judge of this Court, and for other contempts as stated by the witnesses." [12]

Jackson's aide-de-camp, John Reid, represented Old Hickory at the bar. He began to read a formal protest which said that contempt had not been committed in court, that the proceedings were illegal and unconstitutional, and that if Jackson were guilty of any statutory offence he had the right to trial by jury and not by a single judge. Only a few sentences of this defence had been read when the judge interrupted and ordered "the attachment to be sued out;" the process to be returnable on the 31st of March.

On that day an immense throng filled Royal Street in front of the little red-tiled court house. Dominique, Beluche, and about fifty Baratarians pushed their way into the crowded building. They didn't like Judge Hall. They had been hailed before him on too many occasions in this very court room. Jackson, dressed as a private citizen, had nearly reached the bar before Dominique spotted him.

"Général!" he yelled, "say the word and we pitch the judge and the bloody courthouse in the river!" [13]

---

[12] *Ibid.*, Case No. 791.   [13] Gayarré, *History of Louisiana*, IV, 620.

THE OLD COURT-HOUSE.

Pandemonium broke loose. Yells and shrieks rocked the room and the crowd outside wondered at the uproar. Jackson climbed on a bench and raised his hand. The tumult subsided and he spoke to the Baratarians of the respect due to public authorities and said that if they had any regard for him they would on this occasion forbear expressing their feelings and opinions.

In the silence that followed Judge Hall directed the clerk to proceed. He called the case: "The United States versus Andrew Jackson."

Then the District Attorney presented nineteen interrogatories to Jackson saying: "Did you not arrest Louaillier? Did you not arrest the judge of this court? Did you not seize the writ of habeas corpus? Did you not say a variety of disrespectful things to the judge?"

Jackson informed the court that he would not be interrogated. He said: "You would not hear my defence. . . . Under these circumstances, I appear before you, to receive the sentence of the court, and have nothing further to add." [14]

---

[14] Reid and Eaton, *Life of Jackson*, 387.

The Baratarians and the Battle of New Orleans

Since Jackson did not answer the interrogatories the court had no alternative but to adjudge him in contempt. As Judge Hall pronounced the sentence—a fine of $1,000—he said that the duty was unpleasant, that he could not forget the important services of the the defendant to his country, and that in consideration thereof he would not make imprisonment a part of the punishment. " The only question," he added, " is whether the Law should bend to the General or the General to the Law." [15]

Jackson bowed to the judge and started to walk away, but Dominique and Beluche and others lifted him on their shoulders and bore him triumphantly from the room. They placed him in a carriage from which the horses had been unhitched and " amidst the huzzas of an immense concurse " Jackson was taken by his admirers to the Exchange Coffee House.

There he spoke to them saying: " During the invasion I exerted every one of my faculties for the defence and preservation of the Constitution and the laws. On this day, I have been called on to submit to their operation under circumstances which many persons might have thought sufficient to justify resistance. Considering obedience to the laws, even when we think them unjustly applied, as the first duty of the citizen, I did not hesitate to comply with the sentence you have heard pronounced, and I entreat you to remember the example I have given you of respectful submission to the administration of Justice." [16]

---

[15] Bassett, *Life of Jackson*, 229.
[16] Gayarré, *History of Louisiana*, IV, 625.

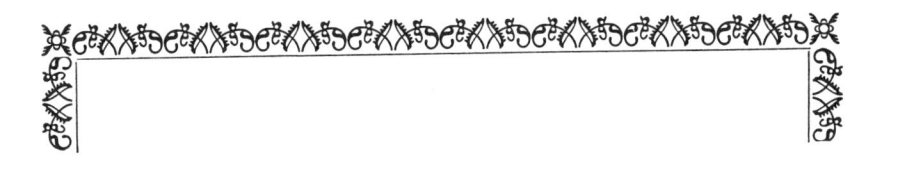

TAPS

GENERAL JACKSON AND THE LEGISLATURE OF LOUISIANA earnestly recommended to the President of the United States that the Baratarians be given a full pardon. Not only did James Madison grant this pardon; but he also authorized that all suits, indictments and prosecutions against them " be stayed, discontinued and released."

However, it was difficult for most of the Baratarians to settle down to the humdrum of legitimate business. Gambie never did. His ship the *Philanthrope*, which Patterson had taken as prize to New Orleans when he destroyed the establishment on Grande Terre, had been sold to Julius Caesar Amigoni and renamed *Le Petit Milan*. Amigoni was just a front. The real owners were New Orleans merchants and lawyers who belonged to the Mexican Association. They wanted Mexico to become independent of Spain so that they could trade with that country and be paid in hard money, still a very scarce item in the United States.[1]

Many Mexican patriots had been in New Orleans throughout the battle and their leader, General José Alvarez de Toledo, was able to persuade Jackson that important dispatches must be sent to

---

[1] This paragraph and the following are based on testimony found in USDC of La., Cases No. 817, No. 821, No. 824, No. 844.

patriots in Mexico. Early in February Jackson granted permission for *Le Petit Milan* to sail with these dispatches on condition that she go without arms and commit no depredations on Spanish commerce. Toledo agreed to this *in writing*. Then *Le Petit Milan* dropped innocently down river with Julius Caesar Amigoni in command. The vessel went out Southwest Pass and headed for Grande Isle.

Gambie was there with his two cannon. He mounted them on the vessel, took on board twenty men from Grande Isle and the ones he had brought with him, changed the name of the ship to *L'Aigle*, and sailed against Spanish shipping under a Mexican privateer commission. Along the coast between Tampico and Vera Cruz he captured a vessel with a cargo of flour, beef, tallow, sheep, and a bag containing $1,000.

Gambie landed on the coast and sold the ship and its cargo to Mexican patriots. He kept the $1,000 and the clothing of the crew. Two days later at seven o'clock in the morning, he made another prize, *La Santa Rita*. She was laden with brandy, wine, and dry goods. Gambie transferred her crew to the hold of *L'Aigle* and put a prize crew on board *La Santa Rita*.

At seven that night he captured another vessel, *El Presidente*, with a cargo of dry goods, oil in jars, iron, and white wine in barrels.

Gambie sailed east with his two prizes. He passed Isle Dernière and came to Cat Island where he anchored when he saw a number of small craft there. Within three days he was able to unload his loot and get it smuggled up Bayou Lafourche and across to New Orleans. Then United States gunboats appeared and took possession of Gambie's three schooners. Gambie asked permission to go on shore and get oysters for his crew. He did not return. This happened in the month of April.

Early in May the United States Marshal was ordered to bring Vincent Gambie into the Federal District Court because he did " illegally fit out and arm or was knowingly concerned in the fitting out and arming of a certain schooner called *The Eagle*, alias *Petit Milan*, alias *Philanthrope*, with intent that said schooner should be employed in the service of some foreign prince or state to cruise or commit hostilities upon the subjects, citizens or property of another foreign prince or state, with whom the United States are at peace."

On May 6, a Federal Grand Jury indicted Gambie for piracy. Étienne de Boré, the famous Étienne de Boré who had made Louisiana sugar granulate, went Gambie's bail for the sum of $8,000. But then, De Boré had nothing to fear because, as Vincent Nolte said, no man in the United States knew better than Edward Livingston how to draw up a bond so that the sum mentioned never could be demanded by law from the bailer.[2]

Gambie was tried in the red-tiled court house on Royal Street. The verdict was, "Not guilty."

For the next few years, Gambie sailed on his own and there is no record of his piracy other than hearsay. Then one day he was sailing north of Haiti when he spotted a sail. As it came closer he recognized Jean Laffite. Gambie's smouldering revenge burst into flame and he ordered his crew to fire on Jean Laffite. Jean's guns answered and the battle raged till dark. Both captains made repairs during the night and at the crack of dawn Gambie attacked again. Within two hours the battle was over and Laffite watched Gambie and his ship sink beneath the waves.

After the Battle of New Orleans, Beluche and perhaps two hundred Baratarians raided Spanish shipping under letters of marque from Cartagena. There is no way of knowing how many prizes they made during 1815. The only ones for which there are records are those which were libelled in federal court.

Two of Beluche's vessels, *La Popa* and the *Piñeres*, sailed through the Spanish blockade and into Cartagena Bay in August, 1815. They were laden with provisions for starving patriots. Soon the Spanish army had possession of all land approaches to the city while forty of their vessels blockaded Cartagena by sea. The patriots asked

---

[2] *Fifty Years in Both Hemispheres*, 230.

The Baratarians and the Battle of New Orleans

Beluche to take a letter to Simón Bolívar who was then in Jamaica. Beluche, in *La Popa*, thumbed his nose at the Spanish, got through the blockade and delivered the letter to the Liberator.

Bolívar and Beluche decided to go first to Les Cayes in Haiti where they hoped to find supplies and ammunition before sailing for Cartagena.[3] Soon after they arrived at Les Cayes four hundred refugees reached there and told them of the fall of Cartagena. While Bolívar organized them for an invasion of South America, Beluche outfitted the ships—rounding up crewmen and supplies in his usual manner. Prowling to the west of Haiti, he spied the *Santa Rosa*. She had taken on a merchant cargo at Jamaica and had left the port of Kingston on January 5, 1816. Beluche captured her the next day. He put the crew in chains but let the captain and supercargoes go free. Sailing back to Haiti, Beluche signalled outside the harbor of Les Cayes to one of the privateers who joined him and then the three vessels sailed to the bay of Haquen.

There, marks on the boxes and bales were erased and new ones put in their places. While this was being done, the value of the cargo was estimated to be $40,000. It was landed and sold for $30,000 to a Frenchman who speculated in such merchandise. Soon Beluche took another prize. Then an American schooner hailed him and the captain informed Beluche that a Spanish warship from Cartagena was after him. This made Beluche laugh and say, " I would like to meet that warship." [4]

Beluche returned to Les Cayes and found that his *Piñeres* had arrived. President Petion gave orders to the Governor of Les Cayes to let Bolívar have powder, lead, muskets, and a printing press. In addition, he ordered three Haitian transports to accompany Bolívar's expedition. These with two Cartagenan schooners and

---

[3] Alfredo Boulton, *Miranda, Bolívar y Sucre* (Caracas, 1959), 48-55.

[4] When the captain of the captured *Santa Rosa* reached Cuba, he reported that Beluche's *La Popa* had a crew of 100 and was armed with one 16-pound cannon, one 12-pound swivel, 12 small bronze cannon, and 50 muskets. The captain referred to Beluche as " Mr. Pierry." This was one of several aliases used by Beluche. Corráles, *Documentos para la historia de Cartagena*, II, 295-300.

Taps

Beluche's two made a grand total of seven little vessels which left Les Cayes at the end of March, 1816, "to begin the conquest of half a continent."

La Popa now had a new name, the *General Bolívar*, and being the best armed and the fastest, became the flagship. Bolívar and most of his officers sailed on the flagship—and so Beluche started on his fabulous career as the most famous admiral in Bolívar's navy. But that story will fill another volume.

After South America's wars for independence were over, Beluche became a Venezuelan citizen and to the end of his long life was always involved in turbulent episodes. He died and was buried in Puerto Cabello. The slab over his grave bears this inscription:

General Renato Beluche
Octubre 4, 1860
79 años [5]

Chighizola and other Baratarians returned to the peaceful life of oyster fishing and sailing shrimp boats. Chighizola became the patriarch of Grande Isle and his descendants there today will show visitors with pride the tomb that covers his remains.

For several years Jean and Pierre Laffite held together a privateer establishment at Galveston, but this was abandoned in 1821. Later Jean changed his name to John Lafflin and dropped out of sight. He must have laughed many times to himself as the Laffite legend grew. His brother Pierre died in 1844 in the small Missouri town of Crèvecoeur and was buried in the Wesleyan Cemetery of St. Louis.

Jean's son wrote in the family Bible on May 5, 1854, at Alton, Illinois:

---

[5] When Beluche received top ranking in the navy, he was given the title of general and not admiral because he was expected to fight on land as well as on sea; and perhaps also because of the sorry career of the only officer who had been given the title of admiral—Luis Brion.

The Baratarians and the Battle of New Orleans

> Our father died. Will be with
> our brother Glenn Henri: Will be
> with Uncle Pierre in Heaven.[6]

And what about the little man who had been born in Haiti and christened Alexandre Frederic Laffite but who, as Dominique You, had carried Andrew Jackson on his shoulders?

Dominique could not forget the words of praise bestowed on him when Jackson reviewed the troops and said: " Captains Dominique and Belluche . . . were stationed at Nos. 3 and 4. The general cannot avoid giving his warm approbation . . . of the gallantry with which they have redeemed the pledge they gave at the opening of the campaign to defend the country."

Dominique *was* an American patriot. He sailed a few times for his brothers and then returned to New Orleans where he acquired a tavern at the end of St. Anne Street.

For a few years Dominique was happy. Then head injuries he had received in the past and evil effects of the months spent in a damp Cabildo cell began to take their toll. Headaches and body pains became more frequent. The last ten years of his life were a slow, torturous death. His tavern became neglected, squalid.

Dominique You died on November 14, 1830.

Flags were lowered to half-mast and all business houses closed. That afternoon *L'Abeille* and other newspapers published notices calling on all friends of Dominique to attend his funeral. Under large headlines cannoneers of the Battalion of Artillery and the Louisiana Legion were notified to assist at the funeral next day.

Dominique's earthly remains were taken to the Cathedral for the rites of the Catholic Church. Then a military escort and a great throng of people accompanied them to St. Louis Cemetery No. 2 where he was interred with full military honors.

When the last gun had been fired, a little group of men gathered around the tomb as Masons are wont to do.[7] One of them stepped forward to deliver the oration.

---

[6] Arthur, *Jean Laffite*, 238-53, 256, 279.
[7] Dominique was a member of lodge La Concorde No. 3. Arthur, *Jean Laffite*, 234.

Taps

"My friends," he said, "the worthy citizen, the brave warrior, the intrepid seaman, captain Dominique You, ceased to exist yesterday. . . . The authorities wishing to render funeral honors which were due to his remains, caused his corpse to be carried to the Cathedral Church; and thence you have seen him transported to his last abode, attended by the officers of the military and soldiers under arms, carrying their flag. . . . There only remains for us to repeat the words pronounced on his tomb by the worthy pastor Moni: *Requiescat in pace*; Rest in peace. . . . This is the solemn wish of Louisianians in memory of the services rendered by captain Dominique, in the engagements of the 23rd of December, 1814, and 8th of January, 1815, the time of the defeat of the English."[8]

When the oration was finished, each man in the circle slowly filed by the tomb, dropped a sprig of evergreen, and said: "Alas! My brother!"

---

[8] *Ibid.*, 234-35.

APPENDIX A

Donaldson Ville Feb. 18th 1814

Dear Sir:

I rec^d your letter of the 4th instant by Mr Gilmore yesterday—Nothing could give me more pleasure than to here of your intention to communicate to our Government a statement of this banditti, the most base and daring ever known in any country on Earth—this outlawd crew of which you have requested information are established on an Island known by the name of Cat Island situated about fifteen miles to the west of the mouth of the La Fourche, their force consists of five or six armed vessels, carrying from 12. to 14. guns each and from 60 to 90. men—They have some heavy cannon on the Island and also a gun Brig sunk in the pass on which they have a battery of 14. guns.— From the best information I can obtain their crews when collected amount to from 5. to 600, men, and I have not a doubt but the advantage of their position triple their force against an offensive operation which could be carried on only in Barges, for the numerous shoals form a barrier against vessels of any considerable size without a correct chart—The quantity of goods brought in by this banditti is immense: I have not a doubt but they have entered & secured for more than a million of dollars within this last six months.—When once their goods are deposited in New Orleans they apprehend no danger of being detected, for they even offer them at public auction, and they have but few difficulties in getting them transported there, for nine tenth of the community are proud to support and protect this infernal crew:— I am informed, that as many as 500, hundred [sic.] inhabitants, & citizens of New Orleans have been seen at one time on this Island to purchase and brig away goods—What depravity!—Men in office; Citizens hitherto of

(160)

Appendix A

undoubted integrity and first respectability, uniting with a piratical band and sharing with them their ill gotten booty—When officers no longer regard their oaths citizens may (with) impunity lay aside their integrity and the opposition to law and justice consequently become meratorious:— Such, I conceive to be our present situation, and him who, once placed unbounded confidence in the loyalty of his subjects has this day proofs sufficiently demonstrative of his error, and in my opinion if things do not change, will ere long be obliged to claim protection of the General Government for his own personal safety This will not be credited, but a fact well known, that a reward of five hundred dollars having been offered by the Gov. to any person that would apprehend Le Fitte was sneered at as being contemptable and in reply 5000. $. was offered by Le Fitte & Party, for the apprehension and safely conveying to the Isle *au Chat* his Excellency—and I firmly believe that the Gov. runs a greater risk of being taken to Cat Island and tried for his life than Le Fitte does of being punished for his crimes in the State of Louisiana— It is a fact they have at this time several men attached to the custom house in close confinement and a custom house officer sentenced to ten years hard Labor with a 56. pound weight hung to his leg—their unherd of depredations will not be believed but they are facts and some of the most enormous I have been an eye witness—

I am Sir,
With the highest esteem & respect
your obed[t] Serv[t]
Walker Gilbert

Thos. Freeman Esquire
Records of the Eastern District, State Land Office of Louisiana

APPENDIX B

The original copy of the Roster of the Orleans Battalion is contained in the Louisiana State Department of Archives, Baton Rouge, Louisiana.

Translation of title:

Staff of the Troops of the Orleans Battalion under the orders of Major J. B. Plauché on December 20, 1814.

État Major de la Force du Bataillon d'Orléans sous les ordres du Major J. B. Plauché le 20 Décembre 1814.

État Major

J. B. Plauché   Major   C. Sainet   Quartier Mai
F. M. Reynaud   adjt.   J. Le Monnier Chirurgi
Casper Joy   "

Compagnie
des Carabiniers

Pierre Roche	Capt.	Soldats.
Coeur de Roy	1er Lieut	B. Génois
B. Grima	2. "	Obignon
C. Roche	3. "	Chaumette
A. Tourla	1er Sergt	J. Bozant
Soubercaze	2. "	Daphrémont
J. Desvignes	3. "	B. Bozant
Guady	4. "	Millaudon
Turlin, ainé	5. "	Jean Bart
A. Choppin	6. "	Papet
Lanaux	7. "	Vicena
S. Alvarez	Fournier	Michel Armat
A. Liautand	1er Caporal	Tricou
Marchand	2. "	Chastant
Trémoulet	3. "	Bacas
Bel ainé	4. "	Labarre
Guesnard	5. "	Garcia
C. Forstall	6. "	Cohn
Isnard	7. "	Vanel
Rondeau	8. "	Lucas

Appendix B: Roster of the Orleans Battalion

A. Lemoine	J. B. Voisin
Durel aîné	Sagory

Musiciens

Pommier	Foucher
Maurice	Valentine
Cahony	Trimé
J. B. Fagot	Dufilho
Cruzel	Carry
A. Fernandez	Cronin
Tessier	Puech Jr.
Desforges	B Fauchet
Denis	Lacroix

Compagnie des Dragons
(à pied)

May. St Geme	Capt	Defourge	
J. St Jean	1er Lieut	C. Belot	
Benetaud	2 "	C. Lemaitre	
Dulcot	3 "	S. Cohn	
Huet	4 "	Enard	
A. Bonneval	M. Logis chef	Hanbert	
J. B. Joublanc	" "	Brelet	
J. B. Lattens	" "	Durand fils	
Gautier	1er Brigadier	David	
Nicston	2 "	Porte aîné	
Dubignon	3 "	Ferrand	
J. B. Hacker	4 "		

(164)

Appendix B: Roster of the Orleans Battalion

Pasand
Syler
Ducayet
Ferrera
Orteing
Turpin Jr.
J. Sibilot
Pillerin
St Cyr
Desforges
N. Darel
Devize
Jourdain
Moree
V. Jourdain
Delarue
J. Hart
Trépagnier
Desmarates
Pidesclaux
P. Pidesclaux
P. Lanauf
J. H. Shepherd
Barthelmy
P. De Buys
W. De Buys
M. Sarge
Barbarin
G. Musson
Moro
J. Marchand
Drouet

St Armand
Garridel
La Borde
Morel
S. Paxton
H. McCall
C. J. Vizinier
F. Duplessis
Foucher
Berluchaux
Golis
Porche fils
Seignouret
Morin
Détour
Tete
Avart
J. R. Stringer
Coignard
F. Funel
Fagot
Liberal
Busac
A. Gervais
P. Wale
H. Mercier
St Avid
V. Nolte
Roland
Tremoulet
A. Prieur
V. Lessassier

(165)

Appendix B: Roster of the Orleans Battalion

Compagnie des Chasseurs.

A. Guibert, Capt.

J. C. de St. Romes	1st Lieut.	Lamothe fils	5 Sergt
Louis Pilié	2 "	St Cyr	6 "
Gueronard	1 Sergt.	Cavaillée	Fourrier "
Couvertié ainé	2 "	Nadaud	1. Capr.
Couvertié jeune	3 "	Pesson	2 "
Pidoux	4 "	Ducayet	3 "
		Bouny	4 "

Soldats.

Schomberg	J. Montamat
Mahé	Lavan
J. B. Lefvetre	Gourjon
Lesconflair	Gilly
Macoin	Barbarin
Mariot	Michault
Duhy	N. Parisien
Chazal	Leminard
B. Glaumé	Nicaud
Mc Clelland	C. Lefevre
Baptiste	A. Gravier
Dufuy	A. Richard
Daunoy	J. B. Blanchard
M. Meilleur	Maison Rouge
S. M. Lafue	Fort
Galliot	Verron
Lemoine père	J. Berluchaux
Bournos	Bonabel
Delamothe	Nice
Maurian	V. Lefevre
Carraby	Lafferandrie

(166)

Appendix B: Roster of the Orleans Battalion

Rivaux   Riviere
Clairvaux   Badigée
Bicombelle   Jerome
Lebros   Badin

Compagnie des Francs

J. Audry	Capt	A. Robert	4 Sergt
E. Fremont	1 Lieut	Bible	2 Fourriers ..
E. Bertel	2 "	E. Touchet	1. Capor.
Chevalow	Sergt Major	E. Sperrier	2 "
Jerome Tourni	2 Sergt	N. Vassel	3 "
Giraudau	3 "	J. Guerin	4 "

Soldats

Bayard   J. Sifflet
N. Molé   Cuvillier
F. Thercout   Bonnaventure
T. Hoffman   L. Ayot
M. Thomas   Lanschagrun
G. Rolland   Charles Gé
J. Lemaitre   Desbans
Miniche   P. Landreaux
E. Sibet   Grégoire
B. Rolland   T. Duricon
T. Ribard   Bolence
Hyp. Dubanoir   F. D. Henry
L. Hugot   J. Freinder
C. Mayer   J. Toledano
C. Toledano   A. Grimden
A. Toledano   F. Hoffman
B. Frederic   J. Muller

(167)

Appendix B: Roster of the Orleans Battalion

Dragons

Saulet	Lambert
M. Destouche	Bide
Despris	B. Desonges
Marans	Simillien
Marin	Le Bon
Pons	La Barrière
Mercier	Poele
N. Frederic	Menard
Borillet	Barnett
Cadion	S. Marat
Ducoin	Camas
Michel	Duheron
Theon	Noise
Raymond	Marcenat
Jeriet	Calabour
Cruzel	Raymond
Durand	Corotolles ainé
Michel Gautier	Corotolles cadet
Rouchet	Cérisol
Guignan	Juette
Ardit	Barthelemy
B. Andigé	Piquerin
Le Beau	Murol
Chattagne	Duplantier
J. Perier	Ramel
Charleville	Lauzun
Pellier	A. Larin
Danse	J. B. Nipot
Leloup	St Jean
Mouton	L. Nicolas

(168)

Appendix B: Roster of the Orleans Battalion

Joe. Bourgeois   A. Guillemin
St Germain   L. Lafitte
         Grosset.

Compagnie de Louisiana Blues.

     Mansel White,   Capitaine

J. S. Girault	1 Lieut	Garlick	3. Sergt
N. Thompson	2 "	W. J. Gorham	Fourrier
J. Philips	1 Sergt	Scott	1. Caporal
R. Nisbett	2 "	Goforth	2 "

       Soldats

McFarland	J. Hull
Durive	J. Major
Packwood	Hubbard
Deruse	T. Laidlaw
Cotton	Carnico
W. illon	J. C. Nichols
J. Hagan	Bronsen
Jones	Armstrong
C. Dameron	J. Belize
J. Prior	John Scharf
Hays	Moore
J. Muggat	J. McClelland
H. W. Palfrey	Lee White
J. Wedney	W McClelland
Smith	Jourdan
D. P. Ruff	R. Dobbs
J. Lambert	E. Beans
	Nichols

(169)

Appendix B: Roster of the Orleans Battalion

J. B. Sel.	Guerin
L. Vallé	Bourque
Brouet	Moren
Gervais	Lambert
Rolland	B. Duchamp
Sibilot	Sibilot aîné
T. Veau	Hachard
A. Peuroux	Mennier
Castinet	S. Hiriart
Ch.t Duchamp	Bournos aîné
Dufouchard	De Guy

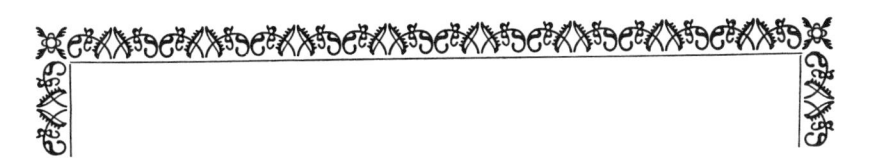

ESSAY ON AUTHORITIES

The richest primary sources for information on the Baratarians are: Archives of the United States District Court of Louisiana District in New Orleans; United States Customs Archives for the port of New Orleans; National Archives, Washington, D. C., *Sección Venezolana del Archivo de la Gran Colombia*, Caracas; *Archivo Nacional*, Bogotá; *Archivo General de Indias*, Seville (typescripts, Edward E. Ayer Collection, Newberry Library, Chicago); Saint Louis Cathedral Archives, New Orleans; Cabildo Records, New Orleans; Howard Tilton Memorial Library Archives, New Orleans; Louisiana State University Archives, Baton Rouge; *Journal of Jean Laffite* (New York, 1958); and Laffite papers in the *Bibliotheca Parsoniana* which was in New Orleans at the time this study was made.

The United States District Court of Louisiana District was established in New Orleans in 1806. In its archives are Case Papers, Minute Books, and other documents pertaining to trials and indictments. Lyle Saxon's *Laffite the Pirate* has fascinated readers since it was first published in New York in 1930; however, it is a loss both to scholarship and literature that Saxon did not use the mass of federal court records in New Orleans. His devotees say they were not available. Under the Work Projects Administration, Louisiana State University sponsored a survey of federal archives in the state. Stanley Clisby Arthur, state supervisor of this project, directed the preparation of an indexed typescript of *Conspicuous Cases in the United States District Court of Louisiana*. Five copies were made in 1940, and one set is in the Louisiana State University Archives. Arthur's *Jean Laffite, Gentleman Rover* (New Orleans, 1952), has great merit since it is based on court records and on some of the Jean Laffite papers in the possession of John A. Laffite.

The Laffite correspondence concerning British intrigue was filed with Case

(171)

Essay on Authorities

Papers in the USDC of La. These were acquired by E. A. Parsons and in his article "Jean Laffite in the War of 1812," in *Proceedings of the American Antiquarian Society*, L, Part 2 (Worcester, October 16, 1940), he gives their exact location in *Bibliotheca Parsoniana*.

United States Customs Archives for the Port of New Orleans contain "Crew Lists," "Ship Registers and Enrollments," and "Returns of Seamen for Marine Hospital Tax." From time to time customs records have been sent to the National Archives, Washington, D. C. After examination there, some have been kept and the rest returned to New Orleans.

From late 1811 until the fall of Cartagena to the Spanish in December, 1815, Baratarians sailed under letters of marque from that place. Not only did they destroy Spanish shipping, but many served in the Cartagenan navy. Outstanding among these was Renato Beluche, a native of New Orleans, who after the fall of Cartagena outfitted a fleet for Simón Bolívar which sailed for South America in 1816. The expedition succeeded in making the island of Margarita a base from which Bolívar or his officers could issue privateer commissions. Not only Beluche but other Baratarians sailed under these licenses for the next eight or nine years. Nearly all the original records that have survived are in the *Archivo Nacional* at Bogotá. Included are hundreds of letters to and from Beluche and service records for him and other privateers who helped South America win its independence from Spain.

The author has examined other archives in Haiti, Caracas, Lima, Guayaquil, Quito, and Panama, only to find that Bolívar and his secretaries had sent most of the records to Bogotá. Three times the author went to Bogotá to investigate the tons of records there, and each time felt helpless and frustrated. She could only skim the small part which had been catalogued or bound in large volumes which contain a thousand or more items.

The *Fundación John Boulton* was organized in Caracas in 1950 by H. L. Boulton y Co., S. A. It has completed microfilming all items in the Bogotá archives that have any bearing on Venezuelan history. This is now the *Sección Venezolana del Archivo de la Gran Colombia* and contains more than 210,000 photographs. These are being placed on microcards, analyzed and catalogued. When they have been processed, the microcards will be available to any researcher.

This author has only a few photostats of documents in the *Archivo General de Indias*. She has relied on the pioneer research of Stanley Faye in the sections that concern privateers. Faye published the following articles in the *Louisiana Historical Quarterly*, Baton Rouge: "Privateersmen of the Gulf and Their Prizes," XXII, No. 4 (October, 1939); "Privateers of Guadeloupe and Their Establishment in Bataria," XXIII, No. 2 (April, 1940); "The

Essay on Authorities

Great Stroke of Pierre Laffite," XXIII, No. 3 (July, 1940); and "Commodore Aury," XXIV, No. 3 (July, 1941).

Between 1845 and 1850, Jean Laffite wrote a diary in French. He requested his heirs not to let it be published for 107 years. His direct descendant, John A. Laffite, published an unedited, English translation in New York in 1958. That part of *The Journal of Jean Laffite* which deals with the years 1804 to about 1825 is an amazing complement to Case Papers in USDC of La. and to material in the other archives mentioned above. This *Journal* needs to be edited by a historian thoroughly familiar with the period 1800 to 1850.

The last three volumes of Henry Adams, *History of the United States of America* (9 vols., New York, 1890 and 1930), deals with the United States during the administration of James Madison. These volumes are still the best history of the War of 1812. A. T. Mahan, *Sea Power in its Relation to the War of 1812* (2 vols., Boston, 1905), rates second. English historians have more or less ignored this war. One exception is the mediocre work of William James, *A Full and Correct Account of the Military Occurrences of the Late War Between Great Britain and the United States of America* (2 vols., London, 1818). More recently, Winston S. Churchill, *The Age of Revolution* (New York, 1957, vol. 3 of *A History of the English-Speaking Peoples*), deals with the war in a brief ten-page chapter which charges that the War Hawks were responsible for causing it because they wanted Canada and had no conception of affairs in Europe. C. S. Forester, *The Age of Fighting Sail* (New York, 1956), reads well.

For the invasion of Louisiana as reported by the defenders, Major A. Lacarrière Latour, *Historical Memoir of the War in West Florida and Louisiana in 1814-15*, with an *Atlas* (Philadelphia, 1816), heads the list. Vincent Nolte, *Fifty Years in Both Hemispheres* (New York, 1854), describes the episode as a business man saw it. The edited correspondence of two principal figures in the Battle of New Orleans gives an insight into the character and achievement of each. John Spencer Bassett (ed.), *Correspondence of Andrew Jackson* (7 vols., Washington, 1926-1935); and Dunbar Rowland (ed.), *Official Letter Books of W. C. C. Claiborne, 1801-1816* (6 vols., Jackson, 1907), have been frequently cited.

The reports that Jackson's aides and the naval officers sent to Washington and to newspapers must be taken with a grain of salt. These men gave themselves credit for victory over the British. Only rarely did they mention Baratarians or Creoles. They failed, for example, to file a single memorandum on such an important item as how many cannon, cannon balls, muskets, and flint, and how much cannister, round-shot, grape, bullets, and powder Laffite and his Baratarians supplied. Without these the outcome would have been different. Creoles and Baratarians were justly incensed as the legend grew that

Essay on Authorities

Kentucky and Tennessee rifles had won the Battle of New Orleans. Bernard de Marigny, in his *Reflection on the Campaign of General Andrew Jackson in Louisiana 1814 and 1815*, typescript translation, WPA (New Orleans, 1939)—orignally published in French by J. L. Sollée (New Orleans, 1848)—was one of the few who cried out in print against this misrepresentation.

More reliable than official reports are the letters written in camp below New Orleans or in that city and sent to relatives and friends in eastern cities. Many of these were given to newspapers and periodicals. The most complete coverage of the defence of New Orleans with regard to these letters and to official reports as well, is to be found in *Niles' Register*, Vols. VI, VII, VIII (Balitmore, 1814-1815); and the 1815 issues of the Boston *Daily Advertiser and Repertory*.

For the British point of view on the invasion of Louisiana, one has to depend on memoirs of English officers who took part in the Chesapeake and Louisiana campaigns. The ones this author was able to locate are: Frederick Chamier, *The Life of a Sailor* (2 vols., New York, 1833); George Laval Chesterton, *Peace, War and Adventure* (2 vols., London, 1853); John Henry Cooke, *A Narrative of Events in the South of France and of the Attack on New Orleans, in 1814 and 1815* (London, 1835); Benson Earle Hill, *Recollections of an Artillery Officer* (2 vols., London, 1836); and a work of which there have been many editions, but of which this author has been able to collate only six: G. R. Gleig, *The Campaigns of the British Army at Washington and New Orleans, under Generals Ross, Pakenham, and Lambert, in the Years 1814-15* (London, 1821, 1826, 1833, and 1836)—published also without the author's name under the title *A Subaltern in America; Comprising His Narrative of the Campaigns of the British Army, at Baltimore, Washington, & &, During the Late War* (Philadelphia 1826 and 1833). The later editions have significant omissions and changes.

Many biographies of Jackson have appeared since the Battle of New Orleans, but only a few need be mentioned. Two works written by men who were close to the event and who knew the main characters were Alexander Walker, *Jackson and New Orleans* (New York, 1856); and James Parton, *Life of Andrew Jackson* (3 vols., New York, 1861). A third outstanding biography was published a half century later—Augustus C. Buell, *History of Andrew Jackson* (2 vols., New York, 1904). Then came John Spencer Bassett, *The Life of Andrew Jackson* (New York, 1925); and finally Marquis James, *Andrew Jackson, The Border Captain* (Indianapolis, 1933).

The illustrations are taken from Benson J. Lossing, *The Pictorial Field-Book of the War of 1812* (New York, 1869).

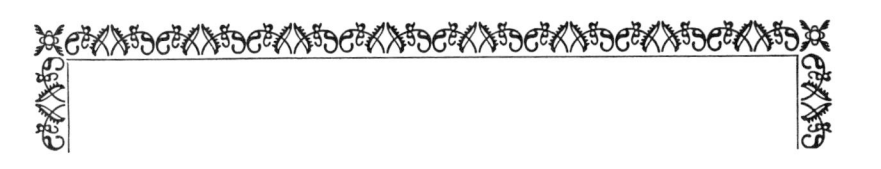

INDEX

Adair, John, 120, 132, 140
Amite River, 78
Apalachicola, 27, 28, 51
Avart plantation, 146

Balize, 10, 12, 13, 14
Barataria, 11, 14, 15, 39; island of, 3; Bayou, 3, 9, 16; Bay, 3, 9, 42; village of, 8; attempts of British to invade, 22; *see* Grande Terre
Barataria Pass, 4, 9; fort at, 46
Baratarians, xi, 13, 18, 22, 29, 34, 44, 53, 61, 150, 158; Latour's account of, xii; number of, 11; commissions of, 12; capture of, 20; threaten English, 38, 40, 41; " hellish banditti," 54–55; gun crews of, 105; Patterson's praise of, 108; Patterson's failure to mention, 117; as artillerists, 121; delivering ammunition to Mexicans, 121–22; skilled in making gunpowder, 122; from *Carolina*, 132; making coffee, 132–33; accuracy of, as cannoneers, 138; Jackson's praise of, 143; scouting of, 146–47; pardon of, 153
Barbados, 22, 30
Battalion d'Orleans, 60, 82
batteries, of British, 113–15, 127, 130, 131
batteries, of Jackson, 104, 113–15, 122, 125, 127, 130–32, 136

Beale's Rifles, 87, 88, 132, 137; capture of, 92
Beluche, Renato, 13, 16, 18, 35, 46, 148, 150; description of, 4, 5; birth of, baptism of, birthplace of, 6; aliases of, 8; voyages of, 8; as United States privateer, 17; at Cartagena, 23; ships of, 23, 24; Bordeaux run, 29, 30; artillery company of, 81; at Fort St. John, 82, 84; leaves Fort St. John, 104; at Battery No. 3, 105, 107, 114, 116; Jackson's praise of, 143; raids Spanish shipping, 155; at Les Cayes, 156; Pierry, alias of, 156; death of, 157
Bertel, Lieutenant, 121; at Battery No. 6, 114
Bienvenu, Bayou, 64, 65, 120, 126; not obstructed, 69
Bienvenu plantation, 104, 126, 139
Blanque, Jean, description of, 41–42; consults Claiborne, 43
Bolívar, Simón, 156
Brugman, Pedro, alias of Renato Beluche, 8, 13
Brouard, Ange-Michel, alias of Renato Beluche, 13; alias Mentor, 13

Carolina, xi, 84, 100; in attack on Barataria, 46–48; transports ammunition, 85; in night attack, 89–93; irritating

(175)

Index

fire of, 97; destruction of, 102–103; crew of, 105–114
Carroll, Major General William, 86, 130, 132, 136; at Natchez, 79; arrival of, 83; riflemen of, 107
Carron, 28, 35
Cartagena, 155, 156; commissions from, 12, 24
Cat Island, in Mississippi Sound, 64, 66
Cat Island (*Isle au Chat*), west of Bayou Lafourche, 3, 64, 160, 161
Cayes, Les, 156, 157
Chalmette plantation, 95, 126, 127, 137
Chef Menteur, 62, 77, 78, 86, 113, 127
Chenière Caminada, 13, 149
Chighizola, Louis, 4, 9, 105, 157
Choctaws, 55, 84, 86, 87, 89, 130, 132; 143; embassy to, 68; on December 28, 106–107; terrorize British, 112; as scouts, 113
Claiborne, William C. C., 12, 18, 22, 39, 55, 59, 109, 110, 161; attempt of, to establish bank, 7; report of, on French refugees, 10; elected governor, 17; proclamation of, 20–21; considers Jean Laffite's letters, 43, 45–46; political career of, 44; defense activities of, 56; on free people of color, 56–57; dilatory tactics of, 60; at Gentilly, 84, 86; in charge of munitions, 122; appeals to Jackson, 148
Cochrane, Vice Admiral Sir Alexander, 31, 95, 100; arrival in Bermuda, 27; terrorizes Atlantic coast, 28; at Negril Bay, 29, 30; off Pensacola, 62; approaches Chandeleur Island, 64; embassy of, to Choctaws, 68; questions Shields and Morrell, 67–68; sends officers to Bayou Bienvenu, 69; lands invading forces below New Orleans, 72; questions Joe Ducros, 73; handbill of, 75; retort of, to Pakenham, 112; brings cannon from fleet, 112–113; report of January 1, 118; at Mobile, 147
Coffee, John, 55; to Baton Rouge, 57; in camp at Sandy Creek, 78; on way to New Orleans, 79; camps at Avart Plantation, 82–84; with Jackson, 86; during night attack, 92–94; Tennesseans of, guard end of line, 125, 140, 143
Congreve rockets, 106–107, 106n.
Court House, New Orleans, 150–51
Courrière de Louisiane, 45, 148
Crawley, Lieutenant, 105, 114
Creeks, treaty with United States, 49; British recruit of, 51

Daquin, Major, 87, 91, 92
Davezac, August de Castera, 59, 87
De Bruys, Gaspard, 80, 139
Degruy's Canal, 149, 150
De Laronde, Colonel Denis, 84, 85 88; plantation of, 69, 70, 127; Versailles, home of, 89
Dictator 64, 122
" dirty shirts," 106; tactics of, 101–102, 112
Dockstadter, Colonel, 31n.
Donaldsonville, 8, 21, 160
Dubourg, Father, 144, 145, 146
Ducros, Joe, questioned by Cochrane and Keane, 73
Duncan, Abner L., 23, 87, 106
Duplessis, Pierre Le Breton, 20, 23
Dupré Canal, 107
Dupré plantation, 115

English Turn, 8, 62, 64, 94

fascines, 130, 131, 135, 136
Favrot, Pierre, letter of, 98n.
Feliciana dragoons, 78; scout the enemy, 86; patrol of, 97
fishermen, Spanish, 65, 69, 70, 83
Flournoy, Major General Thomas, 21–22
Flaujeac, Garriques (Flojack), member of legislature at Battery No. 6, 110, 114, 121, 148
Flood, Doctor William, 15, 40, 100
Forts
  Barancas, 55
  Bowyer, abandoned, 51; attack on, 52–53; garrison of, 57; surrender of, 147
  Petites Coquilles, 62, 63, 65, 82
  St. Charles, 84, 86
  St. John, 58, 63, 86, 104

(176)

Index

St. Leon, 61, 64
St. Philip, 82, 139

Gambie, Vincent, 4, 16, 22, 105, 149, 153; description of, 9–10; prizes of, 24, 154; trial of, 154–55; death of, 155
General Bolivar, alias *La Caridad*, alias *La Cubana*, alias *Atalanta*, 24, 47
General Bolivar, alias *La Popa*, 157
Gentilly, 62, 63, 78, 113
Ghent, peace commissioners at, 25, 26, 32; signing of peace treaty at, 95; Treaty of, 147
Gibbs, General Samuel, arrival of, 98; in action, December 28, 105, 107; bitter, 112; to lead main attack, 130; threatens Mullens, 135; column of, recoils, 136–137; mortally wounded, 137; remains of, to England, 139
Gilbert, Walker, letter of, 21n., 160–61
Girod, Nicholas, 59
Gleig, George Robert, describes Baratarians in action, 32–34; reports on Colonel Nicholls, 68; describes British camp, 75–76; value of conquest of New Orleans, 99; complains of "dirty shirts," 101–102; describes British use of sugar, 113; describes British retreat, 140–41
Gorgon, 66, 68
Grand Isle, 3, 13, 154
Grande Terre, 3, 4, 12, 13, 16, 22, 23, 24, 44, 121, 149; description of, 9; British approach, 37
Grymes, John Randolph, 20, 23, 59, 87, 88
Guibert, Auguste, 60

Hall, Judge Dominick Augustin, 17, 18, 40; releases Baratarians, 81; grants writ to Louis Louaillier, 149–50; issues writ summoning Jackson, 150; interrogatories of, 151; sentences Jackson, 152
Heermann, Lewis, 40n.
Henley, Captain John, 86, 102
Hermes, 28; destruction of, 52–53
Hill, Captain Benson Earle, complains of lack of secrecy, 34; describes Indian allies, 68, 103; reports on battle of January 1, 118
Hinds, Thomas, 55, 140, 143; dragoons of, 79; arrival of, above New Orleans, 83, 86; with Jackson, 87, 88; reports to Jackson, 102; scouting of, December 28, 105; reconnoiters, December 31, 113
Holland, J. H., 44, 45
Holmes, Andrew Hunter, 18, 19
Hudri, Jean, Captain of Francs, 60
Humphrey, Colonel, 114, 116, 132

Isle-aux-Pois, 65, 70; British troops assembled on, 68; boats at, 71; review of British troops at, 83
Isle Dernière, 13, 46, 154

Jackson, Andrew, Creek campaign of, xi; lack of supplies, xi; "Old Sharp Knife," 35; war of, against Creeks, 49; commander Military District No. 7, 49; no help from Washington, 51; receives Laffite correspondence, 54; proclamation to Louisianians, 54; ignores "hellish banditti," 54–55; marches to Pensacola, 55; evacuates Pensacola, 55; on free people of color, 56–57; plea for volunteers, 57; enters New Orleans, 58; headquarters of, 59; reviews militia, 60–61, 82; obstructs bayous, 61; inspection tour, 61; instructs Patterson, 62; orders concerning Bayou Bienvenu, 69; estimate of troops of, 73; activities of, December 15, 77; concentrates forces, 78; shortage of arms and ammunition, 79; asks suspension of habeas corpus, 79; proclaims martial law, 80; confidence in, 80; accepts Baratarians, 81; powder magazine of, 82; plans to attack, 85–86; at Fort St. Charles, 87; night battle of, 88–95; establishes line on Rodriguez Canal, 96–97; learns of arrival of Pakenham, 98; cuts levee, 101; witnesses destruction of *Carolina*, 102–103; sends for Dominique and Beluche, 104; on December 28, 105–108; trouble with legislature, 106, 109; on New Year's Day, 115–18;

(177)

Index

lack of guns, 119; munitions supply, 122; food supply, 124; observes British from Macarty House, 127; sends Kentucky Militia to west bank, 129; river redoubt of, 131–32; troops of, on January 8, 132; surveys line, January 8, 132; praises Dominique, 133; outposts of, 134; in battle of January 8, 136–38; truce line of, 139; casualties of January 8, 139; surveys British camp, 141; General Orders of, January 21, 142–43; return of, to city, 143; triumph of, 144–46; sends Livingston to British fleet, 147; accused in *La Courrière*, 148–49; arrests Judge Hall, 149; ends martial law, 150; writ summoning, 150; contempt of court, 150–52; fined, 152; allows departure of *Le Petit Milan*, 153–54

Jones, Thomas Ap Catesby, 62, 65

Jugeat, Captain Pierre, 55, 84, 86, 87, 89, 130, 132, 143; organizes Choctaws, 78; on December 28, 106–107, terrorizes British, 112

Keane, Major General John, 30, 97; commands British Army, 67; reviews troops, 70; questions Joe Ducros, 73; decides to halt, 74; handbill of, 75; report of, on night battle, 94–95; receives reinforcements, 96; on December 28, 105; column of, along river, 130, 137; wounded, 137

Kemper, Reuben, reconnoiters, 125–26

Kentucky Militia, xi, 79, 83, 120, 146; on west bank, 129, 138; on Jackson's line, 132; Jackson's praise of, 143

Lacoste, Major Pierre, plantation of, 77, 88, 127; on Gentilly plain, 84; night battle on plantation of, 91; battalion of, 132

Laffite, Alexandre, 4, 5; *see* You, Dominique

Laffite, Denise Jeannette, 7n.

Laffite, Françoise Sel, 7n.

Laffite, Jean, 4, 5, 11, 17, 19, 35, 43, 52, 148, 155; Spanish spy, xii; description of, 7; warehouses of, 13; auction of, at The Temple, 16; debt of, to United States, 20; writ for, 20; handbill of, 21, 161; magazines of, 23, 82; clash with Gambie, 24; well informed, 36; British approach, 37; bribe offered to, 40; answers British, 41; letter to Jean Blanque, 42; letter to Claiborne, 45–56; refuses British offer, 53; with Jackson, 81, 87; at The Temple, 82; advice of, on defense line, 101; installs 24's, 104; alias John Laffin, 157; death of, 157

Laffite, Maria Zora Nadrimal, 4

Laffite, Pierre, 4, 11, 16, 19; Spanish spy, xii; description of, 8; writ for, 20; in jail, 39–40, 43; escapes from jail, 44; reward for, 44; with Jackson, 87, 88; guides Coffee, 88; death of, 157

Lafourche, Bayou, 13, 46, 53, 146, 149, 154

Lakes
  Borgne, 62, 63, 64, 68, 113, 147
  Ouatchas, Big Lake of, 3; Little Lake of, 3, 16
  Pontchartrain, 58, 62, 64, 82
  Salvador, 3

Lambert, Major General John, arrival of, with two regiments, 123, 127; with reserves in rear, 130; commander in chief, 137–38; sends truce flag, 139; engineers of, build road, 140; retreat of, 140–41; at Mobile, 147

Laporte, Rosa, 6n.

Latour, Major Arsène Lacarrière, Spanish spy, xii; book of, xii, 3; reconnoiters, 84, 85, 86; description of, 85; estimates Jackson's forces, 87; on advantage of cannonading, 121; west bank defense of, 127–28; planned fortifications, 148

Lawrence, Major William, defense of Fort Bowyer, 51–53; remains at Fort Bowyer, 57; surrenders Fort Bowyer, 147

Levine, Christina, 6n.

Levine, Thomas, 6n.

Livingston, Edward, 20, 149; attorney

Index

for David Porter, 14; director of New Orleans Association, 23; describes defenseless New Orleans, 55; chairman of citizens' defense committee, 56, 59; aide to Jackson, 61, 87; reply to Nolte, 104; brings news of peace, 147
Lockyer, Captain Nicholas, 37, 39, 41, 42, 65
Louaillier, Louis, 79, 149, 150, 151
Louisiana, legislature of, debates of, 55–56; defense committee of, 56; refuses to suspend habeas corpus, 79; refuses to adjourn, 79; measures of, 80; closed on December 28, 106
Louisiana Militia, 77, 119, 120, 129, 132, 138, 143, 146
Louisiana, 85, 102, 108; transports ammunition, 84; rescued, 103; in battle of December 28, 105–107; galls British, 112; guns of, removed, 113

Macarty mansion, 104, 109, 115, 116, 117
MacRea, Colonel William, 86, 103
Madison, James, 26, 122, 153
Malcolm, Admiral Pulteney, 28, 129
Malheureux Island, 66, 67
Manchac, Bayou, 83
Manzant, Bayou, 69, 126
Marigny de Mandeville, Bernard de, 42, 106, 148; letter to, 58; remarks on Jackson, 59; joins Claiborne's staff, 60; plea of, for Baratarians, 81; on closing of legislature, 109–10
Martinique, island of, 4, 5
Masons, 158–59
Mexican Association, 153
Mississippi Dragoons, xi, 55, 143, 146; arrival of, 83; with Jackson, 87; patrol of, 97
Mobile, 27, 28, 35, 49, 51
Monroe, James, 119
Montreuil plantation, 115
Morgan, General David, 94, 100, 127–28, 129, 138
Morrell, Doctor Robert, on British fleet, 67–68
Mullens, Lieutenant Colonel, to command 44th, 131; Gibbs threatens, 135; disappears, 136; Pakenham yells for, 137
Mullens, the Honourable Mrs., 29, 129, 130

Navy Department, reports to, xi, 108, 109, 117
Negril Bay, 25; departure of British from, 58
New Orleans, 5, 14, 27, 34, 35, 38; population of, in 1809, 11, 60; militia of, 60; on January 23, 1815, 144
New Orleans Association, 23
Nicholls, Colonel Edward, 28, 34, 36, 54, 58; alliance with Creek Indians, 35; proclamation of, 38–39; lost an eye, 52, 53; with Choctaws, 68-69
Nolte, Vincent, describes Beale's Rifles, 80; relates advice of St. Gême, 96n.; relates Jackson's anger at Claiborne, 122; comments on De Boré and Livingston, 155
Norris, Lieutenant, 105, 114, 116, 132

Orpheus, 27, 28, 35
Ouatchas River, 3

Pakenham, Edward Michael, 4, 96; arrival of, 98; calls staff meeting, 99–100; plans attack on *Carolina*, 100; on December 28, 104; orders army to retire, 107–108; complains of militia, 112; waiting, 113; orders withdrawal January 1, 117; waits for supplies, 122; orders cannon from Havana, 123; force of, increased, 123; food supply of, 124; fort of, on Manzant, 126; re-establishes batteries, 127; calls last council of war, 129–30; at daybreak, January 8, 134; yells for Mullens, 137; death of, 137; remains of, to England, 139
Patterson, Daniel T., 12, 31, 60, 67, 90; rank of, 43; prepares to destroy Barataria, 44; attack on Barataria, 46–48; gig of, 61; letter to, from Choctaws, 62; praises Baratarians, 108; batteries of, 113, 117, 137; fails to report on Baratarians, 117; arms and ammuni-

(179)

Index

tion of, 121–22; defenses of, 127–28; reconnoiters British position, 128; guns of, 130; spikes cannon, 138
Pensacola, British beachhead, 51; Jackson evacuates, 55
Percy, William H., 35, 39, 53, 54
Perry, Captain Henry, 23
Philibert, Philip, 117
Piere, Major Henry D., 87, 91, 114
Piernas Canal, 119–20, 125, 126
Pierrot, Bayou, 3, 16
Pigot, Captain, 27, 28
Piñeres, 24, 155, 156
Plauché, J. P., commander of Carabiniers, 60; to Fort St. John, 82, 84, 86; during night attack, 87, 91, 92; on January 8, 132
Point Claire, 66, 67
Popa, La, 23, 155, 156, 157
Port-au-Prince, Haiti, 4
Porter, Commodore David, 12, 13, 14

Quintanilla, Captain Vincente, 24

"rabbit hunters," 106; tactics of, 112
Raguet Canal, 128
Ranchier, Raymond (Jules), 42, 43, 44, 45, 105
Reid, John, 150
Rennie, Colonel, 107, 137
Reynolds, Michael, 82, 146, 149–50
Rigmartin, alias of Renato Beluche, 8
Rigolets Pass, 63, 65
Rodriguez Canal, 95, 128; Jackson's line at, 96–97; mud ramparts of, 120–21, 125
Ross, Colonel George, 43, 89, 132
Royal Oak, 28, 129

Saint Gème, Baron Henri de, 96, 132, 148; partner of Dominique You, 60
Saint John, Bayou, 58
Saint Louis Cathedral, 5, 144, 159
Sauvage, Bayou, 62, 77
Sauvinet, Joseph, 7, 8, 13
Seahorse, 65n.
Sel, Jean Baptiste l'Etang, 7n.
Shields, Thomas, 31, 67–68
Smith, J. Kilty, 59
Sophia, 39, 52, 53

Spotts, Lieutenant Samuel, 86, 91, 115, 121
Spy, 17, 18
Subaltern, 34; describes troop movements, 71–72; describes night attack, 92–94; account of December 28, 108; account of New Year's Day, 115–16, 117

Tennessee Militia, xi, 55, 57, 79, 107, 111, 132, 143
Terre-au-Boeufs, 76, 78
Thomas, Major General John, 79, 83, 120
Thompson, C. C. B., 86, 103, 109
Thornton, Colonel William, 71, 88; on Villeré plantation, 73–74; crosses Lake Borgne, 83; during night attack, 91; to cross river, 130; behind schedule, 134; attack on west side, 138; ordered to retire, 138
Timbalier Island, 13, 22
Tousard, Louis de, 148

Villeré, Célestin, 74
Villeré, Gabriel, 69; sends picket to fishermen's village, 70–71, 83; made prisoner, 74; escape of, 84–85
Villeré, Major Jacques, 77; defends Baratarians, 43, 44, 81; plantation of, 69, 70, 94, 127; canal of, 126, 127, 128, 139

Washington, burning of, 26, 27, 29, 51
White, Maunsel, "Ajax of the army," 60
Williams, John, alias of Latour, xii

You, Dominique, 4, 7, 8, 16, 121, 148, 150; description of, 5; delivers gunpowder to Nautla, 22, 23; burns warehouses on Grande Terre, 46; made prisoner, 47; in irons in Cabildo, 48; released from Cabildo, 81; organizes artillery company, 81; leaves Fort St. John, 104; at Battery No. 3, 105, 107, 114, 116; serves coffee to Jackson, 133; Jackson's praise of, 143; death of, 158; funeral of, 158–59; burial of, 158–59

BIOGRAPHICAL SKETCHES
of the
VETERANS
of the
BATTALION OF ORLEANS,
1814-1815

by

Ronald R. Morazan

Legacy Publishing Company, Inc.

1979

Legacy Publishing Company, Inc.
Copyright, 1979
Library of Congress Catalog Card Number: 79-65180
ISBN: 0-918784-51-4

*To
Rosana and Dennis*

FOREWORD

With the continuing development of the Chalmette National Historical Park, Professor Ronald R. Morazán's publication of biographies of the members of Major Jean Baptiste Plauché's Uniformed Battalion of Orleans Volunteers is timely.

Though muster rolls and payrolls of the Battalion are on file in the National Archives no accurate roster has been published. The listing and signatures are difficult to read and some names appear on one roll but not on another of the same company. The strength return for the battalion for December 23, 1814 and January 8, 1815 shows two hundred and eighty seven men for the first date and two hundred eighty nine for the latter date. It is probable that these numbers cover only those present on the battle line.

One researcher concluded that the rolls cover over four hundred individuals. These rolls show the first names of about one hundred fifty men and only the family name is given for about one hundred twenty five others. The remainder for the most part have only one initial. The difficulty of identifying these and others without initials is apparent. The historical importance of the battalion justifies the hundreds of hours Professor Morazán spent in reviewing old newspapers, succession records, pension lists and other sources seeking to add to our knowledge of the unit.

The Uniformed Battalion of New Orleans Volunteers had its origins back in the French and Spanish militia and one or two of its companies were the first volunteer units given official recognition after the area was transferred to the United States. It was placed at the disposal of General James Wilkinson at the time of the so-called Burr conspiracy scare in 1806-1807. It was called out in the slave revolt of January 1811. After serving in the War of 1812 it formed the nucleus of the famous Louisiana Legion which existed as the elite unit of New Orleans until its dissolution in 1862 in the Civil War reorganization of the Louisiana militia.

Volunteer units such as the Orleans Battalion had selective membership. The volunteers usually drilled weekly and bought their own arms and distinctive uniforms. Major Pierre François Dubourg, a prominent merchant of New Orleans, commanded the Orleans Battalion from the start of the American period until 1814. During the British invasion Dubourg served as adjutant and inspector general of militia on Governor Wm. C. C. Claiborne's staff. The Battalion was commanded by Major Jean Baptiste Plauché who was later to become a general officer in the militia and lieutenant governor of the State.

At the time of the Battle of New Orleans the Battalion was comprised of a staff, a band, Captain Pierre Roche's Company of Carabiniers or Grenadiers (the senior unit), Captain Auguste Guibert's Company of Chasseurs, Captain Henri St. Geme's Compagnie Dragons D'Orleans, Captain Jean Hudry's Compagnie Franche and Captain Mausell White's Company of Louisiana Blues.

Personnel of the Battalion were largely from the leading families of New Orleans and of French extraction except in White's company where the names are largely Anglo-Saxon. Hudry in later years said that most of his men were former artillerymen in the French army. His company was organized shortly before the British invasion and he bought its uniforms. Hudry died on January 21, 1835 in Washington D. C. while seeking to have Congress reimburse him for his expenses.

Shortly after General Andrew Jackson arrived in New Orleans in

December 1814 he addressed the Battalion saying that its skill in evolutions was rarely attained by veterans. He also said that its ranks increased with the approach of danger.

On the afternoon of December 23, 1814 when it became known that British troops were on the Villere plantation below New Orleans, the Battalion came at a trot from the bridge over Bayou St. John (near the present day entrance of City Park) to Fort St. Charles to join Jackson's forces moving down river to attack the British. They conducted themselves well in the night attack alongside the 7th and 44th U. S. Regiments of Infantry and D'Aquin's Battalion of Free People of Colour.

The next morning they took a position on Jackson's main line along the Rodriguez canal remaining there until after the Battle on January 8, 1815. The Mississippi River has eroded part of Jackson's line and the present levee crosses the left portion of the sector of the line held by the Orleans Battalion. Its center was in front of the Rodriguez house and Captain Dominique You's two-piece battery was on its right. The 7th U. S. Infantry and Beale's Company of Orleans Riflemen were further to the right. Due to its position on the line the points of attack by the British were generally out of range for the battalion. Some served as cannoneers and some as ammunition carriers.

The Orleans Battalion was in service from December 16, 1814 to March 20, 1815. The officers used their influence with the tempestuous Jackson to have him suspend his order which sent all French males except for the French consul of military age to the lines or to Baton Rouge.

Jackson's report of December 27, 1814 states that the battalion "realized my anticipations and behaved like veterans." The members of the battalion were silent during the attacks made on Jackson because of his flouting of judicial orders, and on March

16 the officers sent him a warm address stating that they would leave to others matters of legal argument and be ever grateful for his services. In reply he spoke of their distinguished bravery, exact discipline, ardent zeal and important services.

In ending his letter he said, "The offered friendship of each individual comprising it (the battalion), I receive with pleasure and with sincerity reciprocate. I shall always pride myself on a fraternity with such men, created in such a cause."

It was a pledge of close friendship mutually kept throughout General Jackson's life to be renewed each time he again visited New Orleans.

Lt. Col. Powell A. Casey

PREFACE

The writer has undertaken the task of writing brief biographical sketches of the veterans of the Battalion of Orleans who participated during the War of 1812. The sketches are not intended to be comprehensive, for it would have been beyond the scope and range of the book. Rather, the writer has attempted to include genealogical information relative to the immediate family of the soldier, where he lived, what type of work he did, to what organization he belonged, the place and date of his birth, and the date of his death.

The writer has attempted to include all of the names of the soldiers who were cited in the original muster rolls, payrolls, and major compilations by Powell A. Casey, Marion John Bennett Pierson, Mrs. J. B. Pelletier, and a compilation in the possession of Dr. Jane L. DeGrummond, which first appeared in the appendix of her book on the Baratarians. The most reliable compilations are the originals, and those by Powell A. Casey and Marion J. B. Pierson.

The compilation by Mrs. J. B. Pelletier appeared on August 23, 1908, in the *Times-Picayune,* and was reprinted the same year in the *Southern Historical Society Papers.* The list was acclaimed to have been the most complete of all known compilations, which allegedly was written by Louis Melchoir Reynaud, one of the adjutants of the Battalion of Orleans, and was discovered by Mr. J. B. Pelletier, an antique dealer on Bourbon St. in New Orleans.

Unlike the originals and those compilations by Casey and Pierson, which include mostly the surnames, and sometimes the first name or just the initial for the first name, the list by Pelletier was very complete, for in most cases it included the surnames, first names, and middle initials of the soldiers. The writer investigated all of the names in the compilation by Pelletier, and in the majority of the cases the first names cited for the soldiers were in contradiction to those cited in the original rolls, and those by Casey and Pierson. It is possible that the first names given by Pelletier were fictitious, for the writer was unable to locate them in the records of people living during the period. Furthermore, some of the names included by Pelletier of soldiers who were included by the other compilers as having served in other units rather than in the Battalion of Orleans, but that could have been possible, for many soldiers transferred without proper procedure; but also she included soldiers who were not cited by any of the other compilers as having served in any unit during the War of 1812.

The writer is indebted to other researchers in the field, to those who made the research facilities available, those who helped him in preparing the manuscript, and those who encouraged him to undertake the project. He would like to extend his appreciation to Nancy G. Morazán, his wife, who typed, edited, and proofread the manuscript; Dr. Jane L. DeGrummond, Professor Emeritus, Louisiana State University, who encouraged the writer to undertake the project which originally was her idea; Powell A. Casey, the most knowledgeable researcher on the military aspects relating to Louisiana during the War of 1812, for encouraging him and giving him guidance to the various sources available which the writer found very useful; Professor John Kemp, and Miss Rose Lambert of the Louisiana Historical Center, Louisiana State Museum Library; Ms. Harriet Callahan, Ms. Pat Leeper, and Ms. Jackie Campbell of the Louisiana Division of the Louisiana State Library; Mr. Collin B. Hamer, Jr., of the Louisiana Division of the New Orleans Public Library; Mr. Bertin O. Barrose, Secretary of the Society of the Sons of the War of 1812; Mr. George Sénac Rapier, who provided the writer with genealogical information of two of his ancestors; and the personnel of the archives at Louisiana State University and Tulane University.

Ronald R. Morazán is Associate Professor of History at Southern University, Baton Rouge. He is the author of several scholarly articles and book reviews dealing with the Spanish colonial period in Louisiana, author of the weekly newspaper column carried by the New Orleans *Times-Picayune* and the Baton Rouge *Sunday Advocate* entitled "The Louisiana Bicentennial Almanac, 1776-1777," editor for the section of the Spanish period for a book of readings designed for the college-level courses to be published by the Louisiana Historical Association, and Program Chairman for the 1976-1977 meeting of the Louisiana Historical Association which was held in Biloxi, Mississippi, in a joint effort with the Mississippi Historical Society.

Latour's map of the seat of War in Louisiana and West Florida.

Table of Contents

	page
Explanatory Notes	(xi)
Biographical Sketches	(1)
Index and Name Guide	(245)
Bibliography	(291)

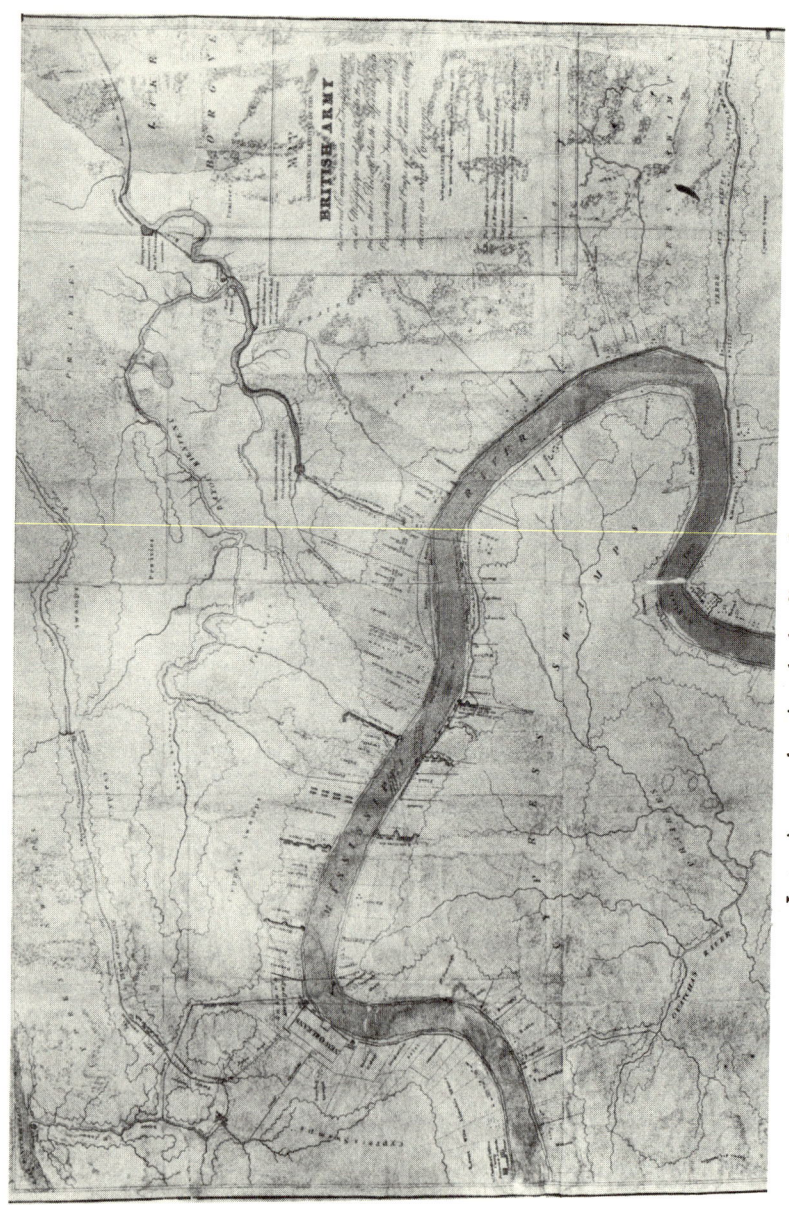

Latour's map showing the landing of the British army.

Explanatory Notes

In order to conserve space, the writer has utilized various symbols in the text and the footnotes. The reader will have to turn to the bibliography in the back of the book to be able to get the full citation of the footnotes.

For Example:
BRAVAXT (BRAVAT), Jacques   Musician   Carabiniers*
Jacques BRAVAXT (BRAVAT) was born in 1775, a native of Auch, France, and son of Jean BRAVAT and Perrine THOMAS. Jacques was married to Marie Lucie TOMACHICHI, from which union several children were born. He was a cigar maker living in New Orleans at 4 Poydras St., but later moved his residence to 48 Main St. He was one of the signers of a petition addressed to General Andrew JACKSON asking for an early discharge from military duty of Lt. Wm [William] A. AUDEBERT, a teacher who was serving in the 2nd Regiment under Colonel Zénon CAVELIER. Jacques died in New Orleans on November 9, 1828. I-A, lix; I-Bf; I-E, 17; II-A; III-D, 6; III-K, 7; VI-Da, January 21, 1815; VIII-B, October 28, 1813.

1. Entry
   BRAVAXT (BRAVAT), Jacques   Musician   Carabiniers*
   The entry includes the name of the soldier, his rank or position, and the company in which he served. If he was a private, then the rank or position will be left blank.

2. **Symbols**
   a. ( ) The parentheses enclosing the name (BRAVAT) indicate that the writer was able to determine that the correct spelling for the name of the soldier cited as BRAVAXT should be BRAVAT.
   b. [ ] The brackets are used to enclose incidental material which might make it clearer to the reader. For example, the name of the teacher was cited in the original document as Wm A AUDEBERT, and after consulting various sources, the writer confirmed that the "Wm" stood for [William]. A second example in using the brackets is in citing the name of the country as it is known today, such as St. Domingue [Haiti], from where many of the soldiers and their families came.
   c. * The asterisk is used to indicate that the name of the soldier is not cited in the compilation which appears in the appendix, but that the writer located his name in other compilations or rosters which are cited in the footnotes.

3. **Footnotes**

   Using as an example the footnotes for Jacques BRAVAT, the symbols in the footnotes can be interpreted by turning to the bibliography in the back pages of the book for the full citation.

   I-A, lix   It indicates that the reference is to Powell A. Casey, *Louisiana in the War of 1812* (Baton Rouge, 1963), page lix.

   I-Bf   It indicates that the reference is to the Payroll Sheet of 10 December 1814 to 20 March 1815, in Powell A. Casey Papers in the Howard-Tilton Memorial Library [Tulane University], New Orleans, Louisiana.

   I-E, 17   It indicates that the reference is to Marion John Bennett Pierson (Comp.), *Louisiana Soldiers in*

II-A the War of 1812 (Louisiana Genealogical and Historical Society, 1963), page 17. It indicates that the reference is to the vertical files of the "St. Louis Cemetery Number One of New Orleans," at the Louisiana Historical Center, Louisiana State Museum Library, New Orleans, Louisiana.

III-D, 6 It indicates that the reference is to *Whitney's New-Orleans Directory and Lousiana & Mississippi Almanac for the Year 1811* (New Orleans, 1810), Page 6.

III-K, 7 It indicates that the reference is to Ronald V. Jackson, et al (eds.), *Louisiana 1830 Census Index* (Utah, Accelerated Indexing Systems, Inc., 1976), page 7.

VI-Da It indicates that the reference is to the Andrew Jackson Papers, 1767-1845, Reel No. 15, January 21, 1815. Microfilm copy at Louisiana State University, Baton Rouge Louisiana.

VIII-B It indicates that the reference is to the issue of October 28, 1813, of the *Courrier de la Louisiane*.

4. Index

In order to expedite the research conducted by the reader, the writer has included in the index all the names and surnames of related families, associates, acquaintances, and others cited in the text in relation to the soldiers. Thus the citations in the index will read as follows:

AUDEBERT, William A.   See Jacques BRAVAXT
BRAVAT, Jean   See Jacques BRAVAXT
THOMAS, Perrine   See Jacques BRAVAXT
TOMACHICHI, Marie Lucie   See Jacques BRAVAXT

(xiii)

Portrait of Gen. Jean Baptiste Plauche, commanding officer of the Battalion of Orleans.

A

ACART [See HACHARD, Pierre]

AILLOT, Etienne Louis [See AYOT]

ALVAREZ, Philip   [Corporal and Quartermaster of Carabiniers] Philip ALVAREZ was born in 1765. He lived in New Orleans on 31 Esplanade in 1822, but later moved his residence to 392 Bourbon St. He became the new manager of the new Exchange Commercial Coffee-House in 1814, which was formerly managed by Bernard TREMOULET. The Exchange was used by businessmen to transact deals as well as for socializing. ALVAREZ died on May 18, 1850, at the age of eighty-five. Although the muster roll in the appendix cites an "S. ALVAREZ" who could have been Simon D. ALVAREZ who lived on Casa-Calvo St. or a Santiago ALVAREZ, a shoemaker who lived on D'Enghein St., three other muster rolls cite a P. or Philip ALVAREZ as the corporal. I-A, lix; I-D, 5; I-F; 2; II-A; III-E, 4; III-G, 15; VIII-B, November 14, 1814.

ANDIGE (AUDIGE), Bernard [Pierre]   Dragoons
Although two muster rolls cite a B or Bernard AUDIGE, the others mention only the surname. The earliest AUDIGE mentioned in the records for the period was one named Pierre who was a carpenter living on Bayou Road in 1811 and later moving to 115 Champs-Elysées in New Orleans. Pierre AUDIGE was born in St.

Domingue [Haiti] in 1775. He was the son of Guillaume AUDIGE and Marie Thérèse FOUNEE [FOUREE]. Pierre died on January 18, 1825 at the age of fifty-three and his father, Guillaume died on November 3, 1825 at the age of eighty-five. I-A, lx; I-D, 9; I-E, 5; II-A; III-D, 5; III-E, 4; III-I, 3; III-J, 1-2; V-Ba, 144; VIII-B, May 1, 1816.

ARMAS, Christoval Guillermo de   Carabiniers
Christoval Guillermo de ARMAS is cited by Powell A. Casey as belonging in the Carabiniers. Marion John Bennet Pierson, however, placed him in the First Regiment under Colonel Jean B. DEJAN. Christoval Guillermo was the son of Christoval de ARMAS y ARCILA and Maria AMIRAUD [AMIRAULT] DUPLESSIS. Christoval Guillermo was confirmed in the St. Louis Cathedral of New Orleans on November 13, 1801. He later received a state pension for his service in the war. His father, Christoval, was born in the Canary Islands and was a merchant during the Spanish period and a notary and a clerk of court during the American period. His mother, Maria, died on October 2, 1832 and his father a few years earlier on June 4, 1828. I-A, lix; I-E, 4; II-A; II-B; III-E, 10, IV-B, 147; V-Ba, 144; VII-B, 61; IX-Pb, 101.

ARMAS, Michel de   Carabiniers
Michel de ARMAS was the son of Christoval de ARMAS Y ARCILA and Maria AMIRAUD [AMIRAULT] DUPLESSIS. Michel resided at 46 Chartres St. in New Orleans and had his office at 46 Royal St., where he conducted his business as notary public and as practicing lawyer. He established a law firm with J. T. PRESTON and later with Henry R. DENIS. Michel was also one of the editors of the newspaper *Les Amis de Lois.* He served in the Louisiana militia during the Territorial period, for in 1809 he was the quartermaster of the First Regiment. In 1816 he was elected state representative to the General Assembly from Orleans Parish, and in 1818 he ran for a seat in the state senate, but was narrowly defeated by Bernard MARIGNY. Michel died on October 12, 1833.

The muster roll in the appendix and that of Powell A. Casey place Michel de ARMAS in Jean Baptiste PLAUCHE's Battalion, but Mrs. J. B. Pelletier, Pierson and Marie Cruzat De Verges place him in DEJAN's Louisiana Militia. It is probable that the person could have been another Michel, for there was a Michel de ARMAS who in 1806 was appointed second lieutenant in the Fifth Regiment [German Coast] of Militia. Also, there was a Michel Théodore de ARMAS who was born in New Orleans on November 9, 1783, and died on September 6, 1823. I-A, lix; I-E, 4; II-A; III-A, 172; III-C, 185; III-E, 10; V-Ba, 144; VI-Ca, 664; VIII-A, 172; VIII-B, July 5, 1816; December 27, 1816; January 23, 1818; July 10, 1818; IX-G, 25.

ARMITAGE, James   Blues
James ARMITAGE was born in New York in 1776 or 1778. He was the son of James ARMITAGE and Abigail LOYAL. James Jr. came to New Orleans, where he married Emilie GUIDRY, from which union several children were born. One of them was Anthony ARMITAGE, who was born in August 6, 1806. James ARMITAGE died on July 11, 1828 and his wife, Emilie, died on July 2, 1840 at the age of fifty-six or sixty-five. I-Bd; II-A; II-B.

ARMSTRONG, John [Andrew]   Blues
One muster roll cites a John while another cites an Andrew ARMSTRONG. It is possible that the person may have been John Andrew ARMSTRONG or Andrew John ARMSTRONG.

In the 1820's there was a John ARMSTRONG who was a grocer residing at 35 Common St. in New Orleans and later moved his store to 52 Levée, while his home residence was at 105 Dauphin St. He was born in Baltimore, Maryland, and married to Emilie VALLET. He died on July 22, 1832 at the age of thirty-eight.

There was also an Andrew ARMSTRONG who was living in the vicinity of New Orleans, for correspondence arrived for him as early as 1811. This person could possibly have been A. ARMSTRONG who was the sheriff of Assumption Parish in 1816 who had placed a notice in the local papers announcing that he had captured a runaway slave named Jefferson. Also, there was an Andrew C. ARMSTRONG whose wife, Eliza Rosetta died in New Orleans in 1841. lxi; 1xi; I-D, 13; I-E, 4; III-E, 4; III-G, 18; V-Ba, 146; VIII-B, October 2, 1811; January 31, 1816.

ARNAUD [See ROBERT, Arnaud]

ARNAULT [See GERVAIS ARNAULT, Pierre]

ARNAULT, J. Louis Dragoons*
J. Louis ARNAULT is cited only by Pelletier as having served under PLAUCHE, but the writer was unable to identify him with any certainty for there were too many people living during the period with similar names who could possibly have been the soldier cited. It could have been a J. ARNAULD, who was a member of the Chamber of Representatives of the Legislative Council, or a Joseph ARNAUD, a lawyer residing at 63 St. Ann Street in New Orleans, or a Jean ARNOUS [ARNAUD?] who was a butcher living in New Orleans on Champs-Elysées, or a Louis ARNAUD, a native of Foulon, France, who died in New Orleans on February 18, 1825, at the age of sixty-four. I-D, 8; II-A; II-B; III-D, 5; III-F; III-H, 9; VI-Ca, 650; IX-G, 63.

AUDIGE [See ANDIGE, Bernard]

AVART, Erasme Robert Dragoons
Erasme Robert AVART was born on December 4, 1786. He was the son of Valentin Robert AVART and Julie Françoise ALLAIN. Erasme came from a large family, for he had a brother named Louis Robert who was married to Eugénie DELASSIZE; François Robert married to Amélie DELASSIZE; Célestin Robert, Eusebio, native of Pointe Coupee, Sosthénes, Valery, and a sister named

(4)

Marie Aurore who was married to Maurice BOURGEOIS. Erasme Robert died in New Orleans on October 8, 1818, eight months after the death of his mother, who died on April 19, 1818. I-A, lix; I-C, 24; I-D, 9; I-E, 5; II-A; IV—Ac, 544-559; V-Ba, 143.

AVART, Valery Robert [See AVART, Erasme] Carabiniers
Valery Robert AVART was born September 15, 1785. He was the brother of Erasme Robert AVART. Valery had his residence along Bayou St. John in New Orleans and his profession was listed as a gentleman. When his mother, Julie ALLAIN, died, he was appointed curator of the sizeable estate. He died on November 12, 1825, at the age of thirty-nine. I-A, lix; I-D, 6; I-E, 5; II-A; III-E, 4; V-Ac, 554-59; V-Ba, 141; VIII-A, November 1, 1825; VIII-B, August 3, 1818.

AYOT (AILLOT), Etienne Louis Francs
Etienne Louis AILLOT was born in 1783 in Marseille des Bouche, France. He married Rose LOMBARD, from which union several children were born. He was a baker who had his shop at 25 Maine St. and lived on 95 Royal St. in New Orleans. He died in New Orleans on August 2, 1833, at the age of fifty. I-A, lx; I-C, 24; I-E, 5; II-A; III-E, 4; VIII-B, September 13, 1816; July 15, 1817.

AZERETO (AZERETTE), Jean Baptiste Carabiniers
There were two Jean Baptiste AZERETTE who were living in New Orleans during the early nineteenth century. One was a grocer who had his store on 8 Jefferson St. and lived on 48 Levée St. He settled his business accounts in 1829 and shortly thereafter left the country.

The second Jean Baptiste AZERETTE was a turner who had his shop on 160 St. Peter Street in New Orleans. He most probably was the one who was married to Eugénie GLAISSEAU, from which union one of the children born was named Eugéne. Jean Baptiste died in 1843 and his wife, a native of St. Domingue

[Haiti], died in New Orleans on November 2, 1867 at the age of seventy-five. I-A, lxi; I-Ba; I-D, 4; I-E, 5; II-A; III-E, 4; III-G, 19; V-Ba, 146; VIII-A, July 4, 1829; VIII-B, May 3, 1813; March 25, 1816; July 15, 1818.

B

BACAS, Barthelemy   Carabiniers
Barthelemy BACAS was born in New Orleans on August 15, 1780. He was the son of Jean Baptiste Manuel BACAS, a native of St. Domingue [Haiti], and Catherine LANDRONY. Barthelemy was a carpenter, cabinet maker and a joiner who resided on St. Louis Street in New Orleans. One of his slaves named Cécile who helped him in his shop ran away in 1813 and he posted a reward for the runaway. Barthelemy had two other brothers whose names were Leon and Jean David BACAS. When his father, Manuel, died in 1816, Barthelemy became the testamentary executor of the will. Barthelemy died on August 29, 1858. I-A, lix; I-D, 6; I-E, 5; II-A; III-A, 19; III-D, 7; III-E, 4; III-G, 20; V-Ac, 51-52; VIII-B, October 22, 1813.

BADIGEE (BRANDEGEE), Therence   Dragoons
The writer was unable to locate in the records anyone with the surname of BADIGEE. The only person whom the writer located with a similar surname was Jacob BRANDEGEE, who was a merchant in New Orleans residing at 26 Chartes St. in 1810. By 1816 there also was a John BRANDEGEE who was also a merchant in New Orleans, and most probably related to Jacob, but the writer was unable to determine the relationship. The soldier with the surname of BADIGEE is cited only in the compilation in the appendix and by Pelletier. I-D, 10; III-D, 8; VIII-B, September 14, 1810; July 31, 1811.

BADIN (BAUDIN), Georges   Dragoons
Georges BADIN (BAUDIN) lived in New Orleans at 55 Bienville St. His widow continued to live at the same address after he died on November 1, 1832. I-D, 10; II-A; III-H, 13; III-J, 2.

BALLIX, Adolphe [See BALLIX, François]

BALLIX, François   Chasseurs*
Adolphe BALLIX is cited by Pelletier as a soldier in the Blues, while Casey cites an F. [François] BALLIX in the Chasseurs. The writer was unable to locate in the records anyone with the name of Adolphe BALLIX.

François BALLIX was born in 1797. He was the son of Michel BALLIX and Anne BOULAIS. His father, Michel, was a collector of revenues in New Orleans and the family resided at 253 Burgundy St. François died on May 13, 1822, at the age of twenty-five. I-A, lix; I-D, 16; I-E, 6; II-A; III-F.

BAPTISTE, Charles   Chasseurs
The writer only was able to locate a Charles BAPTISTE who lived in New Orleans and died on January 19, 1874, and a Charles Jean Baptiste who died in September 4, 1873. The compilation in the appendix cites only the surname, while Pelletier cites the soldier as Charles BAPTISTE. Casey and Pierson do not cite any person with the surname of BAPTISTE as having served under PLAUCHE. I-D, 15; II-A; II-B.

BAPTISTE, Jean   Dragoons*
Jean BAPTISTE is cited only by Pelletier as having served in the Dragoons. There were too many persons for the writer to have been able to determine with any certainty his identity. In 1805 there was a Jean who was a barber living at 7 Levée North in New Orleans, and by 1811 had moved his address to Conti St. A second possibility was the Jean BAPTISTE who was a butcher living in New Orleans in 1818. I-D, 9; III-A, 19; III-D, 6; III-H, 13; III-K, 3; VIII-B, July 15, 1818.

BARBERET, Théon   Dragoons
Théon BARBERET was living in New Orleans in 1813, where he and his brother established a gunsmith and goldsmith shop. In

1817 he moved his shop to 42 Toulouse St., in a house belonging to Monsieur BORE. In 1846 Théon received a state pension of seven dollars per month for service rendered during the war, and in 1850 his pension was renewed and increased to eight dollars per month. I-A, lx; III-E, 4; III-F; VI-Gr, 165; VI-Gu, 247; VIII-B, March 5, 1813; May 1, 1816; September 13, 1816; September 8, 1817; March 2, 1818.

BARBARIN, Etienne Louis Chasseurs
Etienne Louis BARBARIN was born in Baltimore, Maryland, on December 26, 1793, the son of Jean Louis BARBARIN and Eliza CORBET. Etienne was married to Madeleine NORRA and later to Marie RAMIREZ. Etienne, like his father, lived in New Orleans where he was a merchant-tailor. Etienne died on August 15-16, 1824 and his wife, Marie, on March 23, 1835. I-A, lxi; I-D, 15; I-E, 6; II-A; II-B; VIII-B, August 3, 1818.

BARBARIN, Jean Louis Antoine Carabiniers
Jean Louis Antoine BARBARIN was born in Marseille, France, on November 13, 1755. He was married to Eliza CORBET, from which union several children were born. Two of them were Etienne Louis and Joseph. Jean Louis was a merchant-tailor residing on the corner of Royal St. and St. Louis Street in New Orleans, but later moved to 68 Chartres St. He died in New Orleans on October 11, 1844 [1848?]. I-**A**, lix; I-D, 6; I-E, 6; II-B; III-C, 211; III-D, 7; III-E, 4; III-H, 14; III-J, 1; IV-C, 79; V-Bb, 252.

BARBOT, Pierre Victor Dragoons*
Pierre Victor BARBOT is cited only by Pelletier. Very little information was located on him, except that he drafted his will in 1828 in New Orleans. The writer also located a Louis BARBOT who was married to Jeanne MARTIN. It is possible that Louis was the father of Pierre, but the writer was unable to verify the relationship. I-D, 10; II-A; IV-Bb, 242.

BARRE, Jean Carabiniers*
There were two persons with the name of Jean BARRE who were living during the period, a Jean Louis BARRE and a Jean Jules BARRE. Jean Louis was born in 1780-1781 in Toulouse, France. He was married to Catherine DASTUGUE, from which union several children were born. Two of them were Jean Baptiste and Rose Joseph. Jean Louis died in New Orleans on December 5, 1836, at the age of fifty.

Jean Jules BARRE died in New Orleans on December 5, 1836, at the age of thirty-six. It is probable that he may have been the son of Jean Louis BARRE, but the writer was unable to verify it. One of the two Jeans was a tailor residing at 233 Bourbon St. in New Orleans. I-D, 7; II-A; II-B; III-F, 6; V-Bb, 247.

BART, Jean Carabiniers
The writer was unable to determine the identity of the soldier with the name of Jean BART with any certainty, for there were four persons living during the period with similar names. The first was J.M. BART, a teacher who lived in New Orleans at 56 Toulouse St., but later moved to Bourbon St. He died on April 25, 1870. The second was Jean Antoine BART who drafted his will in New Orleans in 1812. The third was Jean Baptiste JEANBART, who was an inspector in the Custom House at Fort St. John in New Orleans, and a sergeant-major of the *Garde d'Orléans* Company in 1829. He died on January 25, 1848. The fourth was Engle BART, who received a pension for service rendered during the War of 1812. He died on January 17, 1879, at the age of eighty. None of the compilers cite a soldier with the name of Engle BART, thus making it possible that "Engle" may have been one of the given names for Jean BART. I-A, lix; I-D, 6; I-E, 7; II-B; II-C, III-A, 19; III-B, 77; III-F, 6; III-H, 194; VBa, 150; VII-B, 61; VIII-A, January 21, 1829; VIII-B, January 5, 1816; April 1, 1816; July 15, 1816.

BARTHELEMY, Desiré   Dragoons
The soldier with the surname of BARTHELEMY is cited by Pelletier as Desiré BARTHELEMY, but the writer was unable to locate anyone with that name in the records. It is possible, however, that Desiré may have been one of the given names of two of the persons with the surname of BARTHELEMY the writer located in the records as having lived during the period. The first was Jean BARTHELEMY, who was born in 1775 in France, and married to Françoise FERRAUD, a native of St. Domingue [Haiti]. He was a baker residing at 29 Dauphine St. in New Orleans. He died on May 4, 1821. His widow continued the bakery business until her death in 1835. The second was Bienvú BARTHELEMY, a shoemaker, who lived at 47 Royal St. in New Orleans in 1811.
I-D, 9; I-E, 7; II-A; II-B; III-A, 19; III-D, 8; III-E, 4; V-Bb, 239; VIII-B, February 10, 1813; August 30, 1816.

BARTHELEMY, Jean François   Carabiniers
Jean François BARTHELEMY was married to Marie Claire CATOIRE, a native of New Orleans, and daughter of Pierre Antoine CATOIRE and Marie Thérèse CASTELBER. Jean François and his brother owned about ten arpents of land in the vicinity of New Orleans, which land grant was recognized by the federal government on the grounds that they had possession of it since 1790. Jean François later received a state pension for services rendered during the war. Marie Claire, the wife, died on December 27, 1834, and her husband much later. I-A, lix; I-D, 7; I-E, 7; II-B; VI-Ae, 905; VII-Da, 1.

BASSINET [See CASSINET, Théodule]

BAYARD, René Julien   Francs
René Julien BAYARD was a native of St. Domingue [Haiti]. He lived in the suburb "La Course" in New Orleans, where some members of his family owned a grocery and sausage-making business on Tchoupitoulas St. He died on February 22, 1815,

while he was still in the service. I-A, lx; I-Bb; I-E, 11; I-E, 8; II-A; III-D, 5; III-E, 4; VIII-B, November 15, 1813; November 25, 1814.

BARNET (BARNETT), Maurice [Sr.] Dragoons
Maurice BARNETT [Sr.] was born in 1776. He was married to Marie TRAHAN, a native of West Baton Rouge Parish who was born in August, 1789. Maurice and Marie had several children, three whose names were Maurice, Adolphe, and Caroline, who was married to Joseph SOLOMON, son of Aaron SOLOMON and Rebecca MYERS. Maurice was a merchant and trader who lived in West Baton Rouge, but later moved to New Orleans and established his residence on Rampart St. Maurice died in New Orleans on September 26, 1865, at the age of eighty-nine, having survived his wife, Marie, who died on January 17, 1850. I-A, lx; I-D, 9; I-E, 7; II-A; III-E, 4; III-G, 23; III-H, 15; III-K, 2; IV-C, 161; VIII-B, May 31, 1816; May 12, 1817; January 14, 1818.

BAUDIN [See BADIN, Georges]

BEANS, Ellis POLK Blues
Ellis POLK BEANS visited New Orleans between 1816-1817, for correspondence would arrive for him at the post office. He may have been the person cited in the records living in the Choctaw Indian Reservation in Oklahoma, for in 1834 a woman named Nelly BEANS, widow BEANS, claimed 160 acres of land from the federal government based on the Choctaw Treaty in existence. She lived in a household composed of seven members, and two were males over sixteen years of age. I-A, lxi; I-D, 13; I-E, 8; VI-Af, 65, 105, 123; VIII-B, January 3, 1816; July 15, 1816; December 31, 1817.

BEAU [See LEBEAU, Charles]

BEBEE, John Blues*
The writer was unable to locate in the records any person with the name of John BEBEE, although he found several persons with the

surname of BEBEE living in New Orleans during the period. The first one located was Henry BEBEE, who was a coach and harness maker in 1811. In the 1820's there was a Charles and Levi BEBEE, a coach maker and merchant respectively. It is possible the name of "John" may have been one of the given names of the persons mentioned, but the writer was unable to verify it. The only other person the writer located in the records with a similar surname was a Jean Baptiste BOUBEE [BEBEE?], a native of Bayonne, France, who died in New Orleans on November 16, 1834 at the age of sixty. I-A, lxi; I-Bd; II-A; II-B; III-D, 9; III-F, 2; III-H, 18.

BEL [See BELAUME, Jacques]

BELAUME, Dominique Chasseurs
Dominique BELAUME was a native of Havana, Cuba, born on September 30, 1794. He was married to Suzanne Victoire GERVAIS, who was born in St. Domingue [Haiti], from which union several children were born. One of them was Marie Arsène Clara, who was born July 9, 1816. Dominique was the keeper of the city prisons in New Orleans. He died on July 7, 1824, and his widow, Suzanne, later married Pierre MARCHAND, son of Simon MARCHAND and Antoinette CHAPUS. Suzanne died on February 3, 1864. I-A, lxi; I-Be; I-D, 15; I-E, 9; II-A; III-E, 4; III-F, 9; III-J, 3; IV-C, 28; V-Bb, 241.

BELAUME, Jacques Corporal Carabiniers
The writer was able to find very little information on Jacques BELAUME. He was living in New Orleans or vicinity in 1816, for he was receiving his correspondence at the post office. He may have died before 1834, for the writer located in the records two widows with the surname of BELAUME living in New Orleans, one on Bayou Road, and the other, a candy maker, on Orleans St. I-A, lix; I-D, 15; I-E, 9; III-H, 19.

BELIZE, J. Blues
The appendix compilation cites the name of the soldier as J. BELIZE, while Pelletier cites him as Mathews BELISE. The writer was unable to locate any of them in the records. The only persons with a similar surname whom the writer located living during the period was an M. BALIZE, who was a resident of Orleans Parish in 1810, and a Jordin [Jordan?] BALIZE in 1830; also there was a Francisco BALIZE, a native of Spain, who was living in New Orleans and died on April 22, 1828. I-D, 14; II-A; III-I, 7; III-K, 4; V-Bb, 242.

BELOT, Charles Quartermaster Dragoons
Charles BELOT is cited in the appendix compilation as a private, but the other compilers cite him as a sergeant and quartermaster in the Dragoons. André Charles Victor Joseph BELOT was born in St. Domingue [Haiti] in 1785-86. He was a carpenter, builder, and undertaker living on Rampart St. in New Orleans. He had a daughter named Marie Antoinette, who was married to Pierre DUCONGE in 1836. Charles died on November 24, 1846 at the age of sixty-one. I-A, lx; I-D, 8; I-E, 9; II-B; III-E, 4; III-G, 26; III-H, 20; IV-C, 99; VIII-B, November 25, 1814; August 29, 1817.

BELTREMIEUX, Félix Carabiniers*
Félix [Louis] BELTREMIEUX is cited only by Pelletier as the soldier who served in the Carabiniers, while other compilers do not cite anyone with the surname of BELTREMIEUX as having served in any unit during the war. The only person with the surname the writer located was Félix [Louis] BELTREMIEUX, who was married to Ann FREMONT. He was a commission broker in New Orleans, but he died in 1812 and his widow in 1828. I-D, 7; III-D; VAa, 325-26; VBa, 149; V-Bb, 242.

BENETAUD, François DeMOULIN 2nd Lt. Dragoons
François DeMOULIN BENETAUD was born in 1782-83. He was a merchant, whose store was located on Toulouse St. and his resi-

(14)

dence on Hospital St. in New Orleans. Later he moved to 19 Rail Road St. He served as an alderman for the Fifth Ward of New Orleans. He died on January 2, 1836 at the age of fifty-four. I-A, lix; I-D, 8; I-E, 9; II-A; III-E, 4; III-F, 8; III-H, 20; VIII-B, November 1, 1816; August 3, 1818.

BENITE (BENITEZ), Manuel Dragoons*
Manuel BENITE (BENITEZ) is cited only by Pelletier as having served in the Dragoons, while the other compilers cite other persons with the surname of BENITE as having served in the 2nd Regiment under CAVELIER.
Manuel BENITEZ was born in Granada, Spain. He lived in New Orleans on Casa-Calvo St. in the suburb Marigny, where he kept his shop of making ropes. He was also an amateur actor, for in 1816 he portrayed the role of Pierre-Luc in the play "The Count of Comminges" which was performed at the St. Philip Street Theatre, and the following year a benefit in his honor was performed at the same theatre. He died on September 24, 1819. I-D, 10; II-A; III-D, 10; V-Bb, 239; VIII-B, September 2, 1816; December 6, 1816; February 7, 1817.

BERLUCHAUX (BERLUCHEAU), A. [Antoine?] Carabiniers
The soldier with the surname of BERLUCHAUX (BERLUCHEAU) is cited by Pelletier as Pognon and by Pierson as A. [Antoine?] BERLUCHEAU. The writer was unable to locate in the records anyone with the name of Pognon, but found an Antoine who may have been the soldier cited by Pierson.
Antoine BERLUCHEAU was a bricklayer living in New Orleans at 107 Carondelet St. Most of the members of his family, Joseph and two by the name of Pierre, were in the construction trades. I-A, lix; I-D, 6; I-E, 10; III-E, 4; III-J, 3; III-K, 4.

BERLUCHAUX (BERLUCHEAU), Joseph Carabiniers
Joseph Jacques BERLUCHEAU was the son of Simon BERLUCHEAU and Charlotte BROYARD, the daughter of Etienne BROYARD and Louise BOUQUOI. Joseph was a bricklayer living

at 121 Carondelet St. in New Orleans. He died on June 1, 1833, a few months before his mother, who had married Valentin DAUBLIN, after the death of her first husband. I-A, lxi; I-D, 16; I-E, 11; II-A; III-E, 4; V-Bb, 244.

BERLUCHAUX (BERLUCHEAU), P. [Pierre?] L. Dragoons*
P. [Pierre?] L. BERLUCHEAU is cited by Pelletier as a soldier in the Dragoons. Pierson cites two persons with the name of Pierre BERLUCHEAU who served in the 4th Regiment under Morgan and in CHAUDURIER's Company.
One of the Pierre BERLUCHEAU was a carpenter and the other a bricklayer living at 41 Burgundy St. in New Orleans. One of them was married to Justine TONNELIER, from which union several children were born. Two of them were Matilde and Naissant. I-D, 10; I-E, 10; II-A; III-E, 4; III-H, 21; V-Bb, 252.

BERTEL, Etienne   2nd Lt.   Francs
Etienne BERTEL was a cabinet maker who lived in New Orleans on the corner of Toulouse and Chartes Sts. Later he moved his shop and residence to Rampart St., and he must have retired, for he was cited as a gentleman. During the war he was the immediate in command of the Sixth Battery, which was under the overall command of Brigadier General Joseph GARRIGUE FLAUJAC. Etienne was a member and officer of various Masonic Lodges, such as Senior Warden and Grand Master of *L'Etoile Polaire*. He ran for the seat of city councilman of the First District in New Orleans, but was narrowly defeated by M. GORDON and J. T. PRESTON. Etienne and other veterans were the prime organizers of a parade to celebrate the first anniversary of the Battle of New Orleans in 1816. He died in New Orleans in 1836. I-A, lx; I-D, 11; I-E, 10; III-D, 7; III-E, 4; III-G, 27; III-H, 22, 255, 257, 262; IV-D, 74; V-Bb, 247; VIII-A, April 7, 1829; VIII-B, January 5, 1816; IX-L, 148.

BIBARD [See RIBARD, Pierre]

BIBLE (BILLEY), Jean Pierre   Sergeant-Quartermaster   Francs
Jean Pierre BILLEY (dit DAMPIERRE) was born in Dole, France. He lived in New Orleans on Levée St. in the suburb Marigny, where he and his family had a blacksmith shop. Jean Pierre was wounded during the Battle of 28 December 1814 by a British howitzer, and he died a few days later on January 3, 1815. The howitzer which killed Jean Pierre, was destroyed by a howitzer in the company. I-A, lx; I-Bb; I-D, 11; I-E, 11; II-A; III-D, 5.

BICOMBELLE (COMBELLE), Bernard   Dragoons
Pelletier cites the name of the soldier as Bernard COMBELLE, while the other compilers cite only the surname. The writer located a Bernard COMBELLE who was one of the signers of a petition addressed to General Andrew Jackson asking him to spare the lives of the two soldiers named HARDEN and BRUMFIELD who had been sentenced to death for having been absent during the campaign at Chef Menteur. Bernard lived in New Orleans or its vicinity, and he may have died before 1830, for the census of that year lists only a widow COMBELLE. I-A, lx; I-D, 9; I-E, 28; III-K, 11; VI-Dc, February 27, 1815.

BILLEY [See BIBLE, Jean Pierre]

BILLY, William   Dragoons*
The writer was unable to locate in the records any information on William BILLY. The only person whom he located in the records and living during the period with the surname was a Jean BILLY, a free Black man, who was married to Sally LUITANA (alias Jeanne Sally). I-A, lx; I-Bb; I-E, 11; II-A.

BISE (BRIZE), S? J?   Dragoons
The writer was unable to determine the identity of the soldier with the surname of BISE, which he originally signed as BRIZE. His first name initial was either an "S" or "J" but the writer was

unable to make it out. Pelletier, on the other hand, cites him as A.B. BISE. The writer located in the records several persons with similar surnames who were living and of age during the period and could possibly have been the soldier in the Dragoons.

There were a J. BRISET [BRIZE?] who was a joiner living in 1811 at 30 Quartier [Barracks St.] in New Orleans, and a Geme [James?] BISSET, a butcher living on Champ Elysées St. A third possibility was Antoine BESSET (dit LYONAIS), a victualler and maker of sausages living on Barracks St. in 1824. Antoine was a native of Lyon, France, and married to Emilie MOREAU. He died on July 6, 1826. A fourth and final possibility was an A. BRISSET who was listed as a resident of Natchitoches in 1820. I-A, lx; I-Bb; I-D, 9; I-E, 10; II-A; III-D, 9; III-F; III-J, 5.

BLANCHARD, Jean B. Chasseurs
Jean BAILLY BLANCHARD lived in New Orleans on the corner of Conti and Bourgogne [Burgundy] Sts. in 1811. He, like the other members of his family were well-established merchants dealing in dry goods and other commodities. He died in New Orleans on October 18, 1818. I-A, lxi; I-D, 16; I-E, 12; III-D, 6; III-F; VIII-A, October 18, 1818.

BOEFFARD [See BOUFFART, Laurent]

BOETA, José Maria [See PORTE, François] Dragoons*
Casey cites a Jos. BOETA, Jr. as well as a senior as having served in the Dragoons. The writer was unable to locate any information except that a José Maria BOETA was living in New Orleans in 1834 at 193 Dauphine St. I-A, lx; I-Bb; III-H, 26.

BOLENCE (BERLENO), Robert Francs
The soldier with the surname of BOLENCE is cited by Pelletier as Robert BERLENO as well as BORLENA, but Pierson and Casey do not cite anyone with the surname. The writer was unable to

locate anyone in the records with the surname of BERLENO, BORLENA, or BOLENCE. It is possible that it may have been Rolland BOULLEMET, cited by Casey and Pierson as the corporal in the Francs but not cited by Pelletier or in the compilation in the appendix. I-D, 12; I-G, 66.

BOULLEMET, Rolland   Corporal   Francs
Rolland BOULLEMET is cited by Pierson and Casey as a corporal in the Francs, while Pelletier cites him as George BOULLEMET and as a private in the Francs.

Rolland BOULLEMET was born in Paris, France, in 1780. He was married to Elizabeth LECAMP, from which union several children were born. One of them whose name was Milland was born in 1816. Rolland lived in New Orleans or its vicinity, for his correspondence was sent to him in care of G. [George] VIDAL. Rolland died in New Orleans on September 28, 1825, at the age of forty-five. I-A, lx; I-Bc; I-E, 16; II-A; VIII-B, May 1, 1816; November 1, 1816.

BONABEL, [Antoine Jean]   Chasseurs
The soldier with the surname of BONABEL is cited by Pelletier as Denis BONABEL, while Pierson cites only a J. BONABEL as having served in the 2nd Regiment under CAVELIER. The writer was unable to locate anyone with the name of Denis BONABEL, and the only one with the surname of BONABEL who was of age whom the writer located was Antoine Jean BONABEL. Antoine Jean BONABEL was the son of Antoine BONABEL and Céleste MARATEAU. Antoine Jean was a planter living at 111 Dauphine St. in New Orleans. He had two sisters and a younger brother. The sisters were Rosa Céleste, who was married to Jean Louis RABAND, and Amélie Rosalie, who was married to Pierre GODET. The younger brother was Marcellin, whose parents died when he was a minor and Antoine Jean became his guardian and tutor. Antoine died in New Orleans in 1841. I-D, 16; I-E, 13; II-A; III-F; III-J, 10; III-K, 13; V-Ab, 375-79; V-Ae, 109; V-Bb, 237-38, 241; VIII-B, September 2, 1816; IX-E, 36l.

BONAVENTURE, Michel Francs
Pelletier cites the name of the soldier as René BONAVENTURE, but both Pierson and Casey cite him as Michel BONNAVENTURE. The writer was unable to locate in the records anyone with the name of Denis BONNAVENTURE. Michel Benjamin BONNAVENTURE was born in 1764-65, a native of Nimes, Department of Gard, France. He came to New Orleans in 1809 and established his residence between New Levée St. and Tchoupitoulas St. He died on January 30, 1834, at the age of seventy. I-A, lx; I-D, 11; I-E, 13; II-A; III-G, 31; III-J, 4; VIII, November 25, 1814.

BONNEMAISON, [Jacques] Dragoons
The soldier with the surname of BONNEMAISON is cited by Pelletier as Jacques BONNEMAISON, while the other compilers cite only the surname. In the records, the writer was only able to locate a Constantin BONNEMAISON who was living in New Orleans between 1811-1813 at 52 Main St. Also there was an M. BONNE living in New Orleans in 1820, who could possibly have been the same person. The only other person with a similar surname whom the writer located was a Jacques MAISON who claimed some land in Lafourche. I-A, lx; I-D, 8; I-E, 13; III-D, 8; VI-Aa, 367; VIII-B, March 5, 1813.

BONNEVAL, Alexandre Sergeant: Quartermaster Dragoons
Alexandre BONNEVAL was born in 1778, a native of France. He was married to Marie Elizabeth DURAND De ST. ROMES, from which union several children were born. Two of them were Josephine and Pauline. He lived in New Orleans at 122 St. Louis Street, but later moved to Main St. In the house on Main St., there also lived a J.A. BONNEVAL, an accountant, and a C.W. BONNEVAL, a collector of revenues. They most probably were the sons of Alexandre, but the writer was unable to verify it. Alexandre died on August 18, 1834. I-A, lx; I-D, 8; I-E, 13; II-A; II-B; III-F; III-G; III-H, 28.

BORILLET (BOUILLET), Louis? Dragoons
The soldier with the surname of BORILLET is cited by Pelletier as Louis BORILLOT, and by Pierson and Casey only with the surname of BOUILLET.

The writer was unable to identify the soldier, and the only reference he located in the records to a person with the surname of BOUILLET was a notice in a local newspaper placed by the French Consul in New Orleans, Jean François A. GUILLEMIN, in 1818 in which he inquired from the church and civil authorities if they knew the whereabouts of a person named BOUILLET who was born in Bernay, France. I-A, lx; I-D, 8; I-E, 14; VIII-B, October 5, 1818.

BOUFFART (BOEFFARD), Laurent Francs*
The writer was unable to locate anything on Laurent BOUFFART (BOEFFARD), and the only person with the surname whom he located was a John BOEFFARD who was a maker and repairer of carts in New Orleans on Elmire St. during the 1830's. He may have been the same person as Laurent or related to him, but the writer was unable to verify it. I-A, lx; I-E, 16; III-H, 26.

BOUILLET [See BORILLET, Louis]

BOULLEMET [See BOLENCE, Rolland]

BOUNY, E. Pierre Corporal Chasseurs
E. Pierre GODOFRY BOUNY was born in 1777, a native of Blaye [et-Ste.-Luce], France, son of Nicolas BOUNY and Marie CANON. E. Pierre was married to Félicité BARBIER, from which union several children were born. He was a merchant and shopkeeper in New Orleans living on Mandeville St. He was a business partner of a Monsieur BORICHET. E. Pierre died in New Orleans on July 5, 1829. I-A, lxi; I-D, 15; I-E, 5; II-A; III-D, 10; III-J, 4; III-K, 6; V-Bb, 242; VIII-B, November 25, 1814; April 11, 1817; December 9, 1818.

BOURGEOIS [See BOURGEOIS, Joseph] Dragoons*
Casey cites a soldier with the surname of BOURGEOIS who served in the Dragoons, but Pelletier and the compilation in the appendix cite only a Joseph BOURGEOIS who served in the Francs. It is possible that he may be the same soldier who perhaps changed companies. I-A, lx; I-E, 15.

BOURGEOIS, Joseph Francs
Although there were several persons with the name of Joseph BOURGEOIS living throughout the state during the period, it most probably was the Joseph who was a corporal in the Cabanohocy militia, which also included St. James Parish in 1800. By 1817 he was a resident of New Orleans. He was married to Magdeline HAYDEL, from which union several children were born. One was Louis, who was married to Mathilde DROUET. Joseph was living by 1830 in St. James and most probably died there. Louis, his son, settled in New Orleans and died there on January 17, 1843 at the age of fifty-two. I-A, lx; I-D, 11; I-E, 15; II-A; III-I, 4; III-K, 6; V-Ac, 339-40; VI-Ab, 590; IX-J, 235.

BOURGUE (BOURG, BOURQ), L. J. Chasseurs
The soldier with the surname of BOURGUE is cited by Casey as L. J. BOURQ and by Pierson only with the surname of BOURG. Pelletier cites him as Cyprien BOURKE. With so many possible variations of the spelling of the surname, the writer was unable to identify the soldier who served under PLAUCHE. I-A, lxi; I-D, 16; I-E, 15.

BOURNOS, Joseph TAUSIA [Jr.] Chasseurs
Joseph TAUSIA BOURNOS [Jr.] was born in 1790. He was married to Adèle GARDETTE, a native of Bourdeaux, France, from which union several children were born. Four of them were Philip, Félix, Laure, and Ernestine. Joseph was a teacher who lived at 37 Bourbon St. in New Orleans, but later moved his residence and academy to Burgundy St. He died in 1859 and his wife on

March 29, 1871. I-A, lxi; I-D, 16; I-E, 15; II-A, III-E, 6; III-G, 32; III-H, 30; III-K, 6; VIII-B, August 29, 1817; November 5, 1818.

BOURNOS, [Joseph TAUSIA] [Sr.] Chasseurs
The writer was unable to definitely identify the senior BOURNOS, but it is possible that he may have been a Joseph TAUSIA BOURNOS, for the writer located two of them living in New Orleans in 1830. Both the senior and the junior BOURNOS were discharged from the service on February 20, 1815. I-A, lxi; I-Be; I-E, 15; III-K, 6.

BOZANT, Baptiste Carabiniers
Jean Baptiste BOZANT was married to Marie Anne GALBERT, from which union several children were born. Two of them were Auguste and Josephine. Jean Baptiste was a cooper who lived at 51 Camp St. in New Orleans, but later moved his shop to Old Levée St. He died on August 7, 1874, and his wife much earlier in 1833. I-A, lix; I-E, 8; II-A; III-E, 6; III-G, 33; II-H, 30; III-I, 10; V-Bb, 244; VIII-B, May 3, 1818.

BOZANT, Jean Carabiniers
Jean BOZANT was married to Josephine CARTRE (CENTRE?), from which union several children were born. One of them was Anne Cécile, who was married to Xavier LAMBERT. Jean was an inspector of beef and pork in New Orleans and had his office at 22 Julia St., and his residence at 138 Magazine St.. I-A, lix; I-D, 6; I-E, 8; III-E, 6; III-F; III-G, 33; III-H, 23l; III-K, 7; IV-D, 168; VIII-B, August 2, 1816; January 1, 1817.

BRAVAXT (BRAVAT), Jacques Musician Carabiniers*
Jacques BRAVAT was born in 1775, a native of Auch, France, and son of Jean BRAVAT and Perrine THOMAS. Jacques was married to Marie Lucie TOMACHICHI, from which union several children were born. He was a cigar maker living at 4 Poydras St.

in New Orleans, but later moving to 48 Main St. He was one of the signers of the petition addressed to General Andrew JACKSON asking for an early discharge of Lt. William A. AUDEBERT, who was in the 2nd Regiment under Colonel CAVELIER, so that he could resume his duties as a teacher to instruct the children of New Orleans. Jacques died on November 9, 1828. I-A, lix; I-E, 17; II-A; III-D, 6; III-F; III-K, 7; VI-Da, January 21, 1815; VIII-B, October 28, 1813.

BRELET, Jean Baptiste Quartermaster Dragoons
Jean Baptiste François BRELET is cited in the compilation in the appendix as a private, but the other compilers cite him as a corporal and quartermaster.

Jean Baptiste was married to Marie Victoire De LABOSTORIE, from which union several children were born. One of them was Jean Baptiste Auguste, who was born on November 20, 1801, and died on April 15, 1840. Jean Baptiste François lived in New Orleans at 41 Marigny. He died before 1820, for the census of that year cites only his widow. I-A, lx; I-D, 8; I-E, 17; I-G, 16; II-A; III-A, 20; III-D, 10; III-E, 6; III-J, 5.

BRIZE [See BISE, S? J?]

BRONSEN (BROWNSON), J. Alexander Blues
Pelletier cites the name of the soldier as Edgard BROMSON, while Casey and Pierson cite him as Alexander BROWNSON. The writer was unable to locate anyone with the name of Edgard BROMSON or BROWNSON in the records and the only information he located on J. [John?] Alexander BROWNSON was that he was living or visiting New Orleans often for he was receiving his correspondence at the post office between 1814-1816. After that, the only other listing was in the census of 1830, which cited a John BROWNSON

who lived in the Parish of St. Mary, and a John BROWNSEN who lived in Lafayette. I-A, lxi; I-D, 13; I-E, 18; III-K, 8; VIII-B, November 25, 1814; February 5, 1816; May 3l, 1816.

BROUET, Jean Jacques Achille   Chasseurs
Jean Jacques Achille BROUET was born in 1794. He was married to Elizabeth Antoinette ROUX, from which union several children were born. He was an officer of the Mechanic and Trader's Bank of New Orleans. During the war, Jean Jacques was dispatched on several occasions to assist in the office of printer LECLERC. Jean died on August 1, 1858, and his wife, Elizabeth, in 1836. It is possible that Jean may have married again after the death of Elizabeth, for a widow Achille BROUET later received a state pension for services rendered during the war by her husband. I-A, lxi; I-E, 18; II-B; III-H, 32, 239; VII-B, 61; VIII-B, November 1, 1816; August 29, 1817.

BROWNSON [See BRONSEN, J. Alexander]

BUJAC, Mathew Jules   Carabiniers
Mathew Jules BUJAC was born in 1773-1774, a native of Philadelphia. He was a merchant and businessman living in New Orleans on the corner of Royal St. and St. Louis Street. He was a business partner with John DAVID. Mathew had served as a 2nd Lt. in the 1st Regiment, 2nd Battalion of the Territorial Militia, thus he had some military training by the time he served in the Carabiniers. During the Territorial Period, he was active in community and political affairs, for in 1810, he and the senior and junior François DUPLESSIS wrote a letter to John GRAHAM of the State Department recommending that Martin DURALDE, Jr., be appointed marshal for the District of Orleans, upon the resignation of Major [Michel] FORTIER. Mathew died in New Orleans on January 14, 1823. I-A, lix; I-E, 19; II-A; III-D, 6, 58; VI-Cb, 900; VIII-B, July 20, 1810; October 2, 1811.

BURIAU [See DURIO, Pierre Laurent]

BUSQUET, Alphonse — Dragoons*

Alphonse BUSQUET is cited only by Pelletier as a soldier having served in the Dragoons, but other compilers cite only a Louis BUQUET as a corporal in the 2nd Regiment under Louis D'AQUIN. The writer was unable to locate in the records anyone with the name of Alphonse BUSQUET, but located four persons living during the period with similar surnames who could possibly have been the soldier cited by Pelletier.

First there was Grégoire BUSQUET, a native of St. Domingue [Haiti], married to Carlota Anna DUCAS. He was a joiner living in New Orleans in 1811 at 30 Quartier St. [Barracks St.]. The second was Antonio BUSQUET, a trader who was living in New Orleans in 1834 on St. Peter St. The third person was Jean E. DEBOUSQUET, a practicing physician who lived in 1824 on Rampart St. in New Orleans; and the fourth person was Félix BOUSQUET who lived in New Orleans in 1834 on the corner of Hospital St. and Rampart St. I-D, 10; I-E, 19; II-A; III-D, 9; III-F; III-H, 35; III-K, 8.

(26)

C

CADION (DeGLAPION), Christophe DUMINY Dragoons
Christophe DUMINY DeGLAPION lived in New Orleans at 158 Bienville St. He received a state pension for service rendered during the war. He died on June 26, 1855. The writer also located in the records a Denis Christophe DUMINY DeGLAPION, who was married to Jeanne Sophie LALANDE FERRIER. They most probably were the parents of Christophe, but the writer was unable to verify the fact. I-A, lx; I-Bb; II-A; II-B; III-H, 91; VII-Db, 14.

CALABOUR (CALALOU), Joseph? Dragoons
The compilers cite only the surname of MARCENAT, MATENAS, or MASSENAS, while Pelletier cites him as Joseph MARCENAT. The writer was unable to locate in the records anyone with the name of Joseph MARCENAT living during the period, and the only one with the surname he found was Jean MARCENAT (alias CALALOU).

Jean MARCENAT (alias CALALOU) was born in 1773. He was married to Marie SAVANT, daughter of Pierre SAVANT and Françoise MANUEL. Jean lived at 18 St. Charles Street in the suburb St. Mary in New Orleans. He was delinquent in paying his taxes to repair and maintain the levee, that the mayor and city council had to publish a reminder in 1810. He died on June 20, 1833, and his wife a few years earlier on January 23, 1830. I-A, lx; I-D, 8; I-E, 80; II-A; III, 26; III-D, 36; VIII-B, November 16, 1810; August 2, 1816.

CALOGNE, François Chasseurs*
François CALOGNE is cited only by Pelletier, while the other compilers do not cite anyone with the surname as having served

in any unit during the war. The writer was unable to locate anyone with the name of François CALOGNE, and the only person with the surname he found was Paul CALOGNE, who lived in New Orleans and was an officer of the Masonic Lodge *La Persévérance.* I-D, 17; III-H, 255; III-K, 8.

CAMAS (CAMUS), François   Dragoons
Two soldiers with the surname of CAMUS are cited by Pierson as having served during the war. One was François CAMUS, who served in the 2nd Regiment under Zénon CAVELIER, and the other a soldier with the name of CANNES, who originally signed his name as CAMUS, who served under PLAUCHE.

The writer located two persons with the name of François CAMUS, but was unable to determine in which respective unit each served. First there was François CAMUS who was a native of France and lived in New Orleans. He died on October 8, 1829. The second was François Louis Auguste Timoté CAMUS, a native of France, son of Pierre François CAMUS and Marie Julie DULEATRE. François died in New Orleans on August 16, 1827. One of the François was married to Margarita BEDOUIN, a native of Marseille, and daughter of Joseph BEDOUIN and Maria CANNAU [which maiden name perhaps indicates why one of the soldiers with the name of CAMUS was listed as CANNES], and was a grocer living at 30 Bayou Road in New Orleans, but the writer was unable to determine which of the two. I-A, lx; I-D, 90; I-E, 20-2l; II-A; III-E, 7.

CANNES [See CAMUS, François]

CANY, [Jean Louis]   Musician*
The writer was able to locate in the records only one person with the surname of CANY. He was Jean Louis CANY, a coach maker living at 45 Royal St. in New Orleans in 1811. In 1817, he placed an advertisement in the newspaper announcing that he had for sale a used stage coach and offered his facilities for the storage of

(28)

coaches and chairs. He was still living in New Orleans in 1830, but the writer was unable to locate any other information on him. [See F. C. CARRY, for the compilation in the appendix and Pelletier cite him as the musician, while Casey and Pierson cite the musician as CANY]. I-A, lxi; I-Bf; I-E, 21; III-D, 14; III-K, 9; VIII-B, November 28, 1817.

CAPONY (CAPONI), Jean Musician
Jean CAPONI was born in 1795-96. He served in the Battalion of Orleans as one of the musicians, earning nine dollars per month. He lived at 28 St. Louis Street in New Orleans, where he owned a hat store, but later moved his business to Chartres St. He died on January 10, 1836. I-A, lix; I-D, 5; I-E, 21; II-B; III-D, 13; III-E, 7; III-I, 25; III-K, 9.

CARMACK [See CORNICO, David Daniel]

CARRABY, Etienne Chasseurs
Two soldiers with the name of Etienne CARRABY are cited as having served during the war, one in the 1st Regiment under DEJAN, and the other under PLAUCHE. The writer was unable to determine in which respective unit each served.

One Etienne CARRABY was married to Marie Anne COURCELLE (alias Aspasie), daughter of Joachim COURCELLE and Eulalie LEMAIRE. One of the Etiennes was a merchant residing on Chartres St. in New Orleans in 1807, while the other, or perhaps the same one, was cited as a gentleman living on Bourbon St. in 1822. Furthermore, one of them was an attorney who had served as a syndic in 1810 and elected as a state representative in 1818, and by 1824 was the vice-president of the Board of Health in New Orleans. During the war, the two Etiennes had signed the petition addressed to General Andrew JACKSON to spare the lives of the two soldiers named HARDEN and BRUMFIELD who had been sentenced to death for having been absent during the campaign at

Chef Menteur. I-D, 16; I-E, 22; II-A; III-B, 77; III-E, 7; III-F; III-H, 39; III-K, 9; IV-D, 7, 53,69; V-Bd, 6l; VI-Dc, February 27, 1815; VIII-B, October 3, 1810; August 2, 1816; May 5, 1817; June 24, 1818; July 10, 1818.

CARRY, F. C. [See CANY, Jean Louis]   Musician
The musician with the surname of CARRY cited in the compilation in the appendix is cited by Pelletier as F. C. CARRY, while Casey and Pierson cite only the person with the surname of CANY as the musician under PLAUCHE.

In examining the records, the writer was able to locate persons with similar surnames. One was Félix CARRE, a merchant living in New Orleans on Levée St. in 1822, and a Hinsley E. CARY (CURRY), a carpenter and officer of the custom house in New Orleans. Furthermore, in examining the pensions granted by the state, the writer discovered that a Thomas CURRY and a Dory CARRY received pensions, but none of them is cited by Pierson as having served in any unit during the war. I-D, 5; II-A; III-E, 7; VIII-B, 61; VII-D, 2; VIII-B, February 3, 1813; August 2, 1813.

CASSADY, Daniel   Chasseurs*
Daniel CASSADY is cited only by Casey as the soldier who served in the Chasseurs. The writer was unable to locate any information on him, and the only person with a similar surname who was located in the records was Alexander CASSEDY who was cited as living in East Baton Rouge Parish in 1820. It is possible that Alexander may be the same person or related to Daniel CASSADY, but the writer was unable to verify it. I-A, lx; III-J, 6.

CASSINET, Théodule?   Chasseurs
The soldier with the surname of CASSINET is cited by Pelletier as Théodule CASSINET, while Casey and Pierson cite him with only the surname of BASSINET. The writer was unable to locate in the records any person with the names cited above. The only

persons the writer located with similar surnames were a Pierre CASSANATE, who died in 1811, but the probate records mentions only that Jean Marie LaPEYRE was the curator of the estate, and a Baptiste BAZINET (BASSINET?), who lived in New Orleans and drafted a will in 1807. The writer was unable to locate the original will in the archives of the New Orleans Public Library. I-A, lxi; I-D, 16; I-E, 7; V-Aa, 49; V-Ba, 148.

CASSOU (CASSON), John Dragoons*
Pelletier cites the name of the soldier in the Dragoons as Bien-aimé CASSON, while Pierson cites him as Jn. [John] CASSON (CASSOU). Casey cites only the surname of CASSOU. Although there were several persons living during the period with the name of John CASSON living throughout the state of Louisiana, the writer located a John CASSOU who was living in New Orleans in 1811 and was sued by Bernard GOUX in city court to recover two slaves, whom Sheriff B. CENAS sold to satisfy the debt. I-A, lx; I-D, 10; I-E, 23; III-J, 6; III-K, 9; VI-C, 600, 639; VIII-B, September 30, 1811.

CAVAILLE, Pierre Corporal: Quartermaster Dragoons
Pierre CAVAILLE lived in New Orleans at 39 Foucher St., below St. Joseph St. He died in 1821 and his widow much later. I-A, lxi; I-D, 15; I-E, 24; III-E, 7; V-Bd, 60; VIII-B, January 10, 1816; March 13, 1816.

CAUVIN, Henry? [Jean] Francs*
Henry CAUVIN is cited only by Pelletier as having served in the Francs, while Pierson cites only one person with the surname as having served in the war. He was Jean CAUVIN, who served in the 2nd Regiment under Zénon CAVELIER. The writer was unable to locate anyone with the name of Henry CAUVIN in the records, and it is possible that Jean CAUVIN, cited by Pierson, may have transferred to the Francs.

Jean CAUVIN was born in 1787-88. He was a native of Bordeaux, France, and married to Dame FRETTE, from which union several children were born. He was a gunsmith living in New Orleans, and he died on June 16, 1833. I-D, 12; I-E, 24; II-A; III-J, 6; V-Bd, 59; VII-B, November 1, 1816.

CERESOL (CERESSOLES), François   Dragoons
François CERESSOLES was born in 1791-92, the son of Jean CERESSOLES and Marianne LAMBERT. François was a ship carpenter who lived at 30 Marigny St. in New Orleans, but later moved to 220 Levée St. He died on February 17, 1830 at the age of thirty-eight. I-A, lx; I-D, 9; I-E, 24; II-A; III-E, 25; III-F; V-Bd, 57.

CHAIGNEAU, P. B.   Chasseurs*
P. B. CHAIGNEAU is cited only by Pelletier as a soldier in the Chasseurs, while Pierson cites only a person with the surname of CHAIGNEAU who served under DEJAN, and a Pierre CHAIGNEAU who served under COLSSON. The writer was unable to locate any given information on any of the persons cited above. I-D, 17; I-E, 24.

CHALMETTE, Ignacio DELINO [See CHAUMET, J.] Carabiniers*
Ignacio DELINO CHALMETTE is cited by Pelletier and De Verges as having served in the Carabiniers, while Casey cites only a J. CHAUMET and Pierson a person with the surname of CHAMUTE. Pierson also cites a soldier with the name of CHALUMETTE who served in the 2nd Regiment under CAVELIER.
Ignacio DELINO CHALMETTE was born in 1774, the son of Louis Xavier DELINO CHALMETTE and Magdalena BROUTIN. Ignacio was married to Victoria VAUGINE in 1775. He was a military officer in the service of Spain, rising to the rank of captain, and fought in the campaign against Mobile in 1780 during the American Revolution. He died on February 11, 1815. I-A, lix; I-D, 7; I-E, 24-25; II-A; IV-B, 88; 100; IX-G, 20-22; IX-J, 101; IX-K, 318-20; IX-Pb, 142.

CHAMEAU, Denis Chasseurs*
Denis CHAMEAU is cited only by Pelletier as having served in the Chasseurs. The writer was unable to locate anyone with the name of Denis CHAMEAU in the records. The only persons with the surname the writer located living during the period were Pierre CHAMEAU, Sr. who was a broker living in New Orleans in 1811, and a Pierre CHAMBEAU, Jr. who was living at 91 Orleans St. in New Orleans in 1834. I-D, 17; III-D, 12; III-H, 43; III-K, 9; V-Bc, 368; VIII-B, July 10, 1810; July 16, 1810; August 3, 1818.

CHAMEAU, Desiré [See CHAMEAU, Denis] Francs*
Desiré CHAMEAU is cited only by Pelletier as having served in the Francs. I-D, 12.

CHARLEVILLE Dragoons
The soldier with the surname of CHARLEVILLE is cited by Pelletier as Vincent CHARLEVILLE, while other compilers cite only the surname. The writer was unable to locate any person named Vincent CHARLEVILLE in the records.

The writer located only two persons living during the period with the surname of CHARLEVILLE. The first one was Joseph CHARLEVILLE, who lived in New Orleans in suburb La Course in 1805. He was married to Antonia CLARISENG. In 1810 he was reminded by the mayor and city council that he was delinquent in paying his taxes for the maintenance of the levee. The second person the writer located with the surname was John B. CHARLEVILLE who was listed in the census of 1830 as a resident of Natchitoches. I-A, lx; I-D, 9; I-E, 25; II-A; III-A, 21; III-K, 10; VIII-B, November 16, 1810.

CHASSAGNE, Urbain? Dragoons
The soldier with the surname of CHASSAGNE is cited by Pelletier as Urbain CHASSAGNE, while other compilers cite only the sur-

name. The writer was unable to locate anyone in the records as cited by Pelletier, although he found three persons living during the period who could possibly been the soldier cited.

The first one located was Fouconet CASSAIGNE [CHASSAGNE] who was a baker living in New Orleans at 26 Conde St. The second was François CHASSAGNE who lived in New Orleans and died in 1829; and the third was Aimé CHASSAGNE, an architect living at 365 Bourbon St. in New Orleans in 1834. I-A, lx; I-D, 9; I-E, 7; III-H, 43; III-J, 7; V-Bd, 57; VI-Db, February 27, 1815; VIII-B, February 27, 1813.

CHASTANT, Jean Baptiste   Carabiniers
Jean Baptiste CHASTANT was married to Céleste AMANT, from which union several children were born. One was Jean, who was married to Aglaé Aimée FUSELIER. Jean Baptiste lived in St. James Parish. He died sometime before 1835, for in that year, the state legislature ordered payment of six hundred dollars to his widow for compensation of two slaves named Sylvia and Eliza who were condemned to death by state. I-A, lix; I-D, 6; I-E, 25; VI-Gj, 229-230; VIII-B, August 2, 1813; October 28, 1816.

CHAUMETTE, J. [See CHALMETTE, I. DELINO]   Carabiniers
The soldier with the surname of CHAUMETTE is listed by Casey as J. CHAUMETTE and by Pierson only as CHAMUTE. Pelletier and De Verges cite a soldier in the Carabiniers as Ignacio DELINO CHALMETTE, but most probably he was the soldier who served in the 2nd Regiment under CAVELIER, and later transferred and served under PLAUCHE.

The writer was unable to locate in the records anyone with the name cited by Casey, and the only one with the surname who was of age during the period was Gabriel CHAUMETTE (CHAUMETE), who lived in New Orleans. Gabriel was born in 1771-1772, and married to Marie GUILLOT. He was a collector of revenues for the city, living at 28 Poydras St., but later moving to Apollon St. He died on October 15, 1836, at the age of sixty-four, and his wife two years earlier on April 15, 1834. I-A, lix; I-D, 7; I-E, 25; II-A; II-B; III-D, 11; III-E, 7; III-G, 43; III-H, 44; III-K, 10; V-Bd, 61; VIII-B, November 25, 1811; August 2, 1816; July 15, 1818; IX-G, 20-22.

CHAUVEAU, Louis Carabiniers*
Louis CHAUVEAU is cited only by Pelletier as having served in the Carabiniers, while Pierson and other compilers cite only a John CHAUVEAU, a captain of cavalry in the militia, while LACARRIERE LATOUR cites him as a lieutenant.

Louis was born on September 20, 1790, the son of Jean CHAUVEAU and Marie Elizabeth BORDES. Louis may have been a native of Cadillac, France, for one of his younger brothers, Mauricio, was born there. Louis was married to Marianne MASCEY, widow of Joseph ANTHONY. Louis lived in New Orleans on Bienville St., for in 1824 he was authorized by the state legislature to organize a lottery to sell his house. He died on May 27, 1830. I-D, 6; I-E, 25; II-A; III-H, 44; VI-Gf, 120.

CHAZAL, Jacques Chasseurs
Jacques CHAZAL was discharged from the service on February 10, 1815. He lived in New Orleans at 169 Bayou Road in the 1830's with the widow CHAZAL, who most probably was his mother. He or his father may have been sailors, for in 1816 correspondence was arriving at the post office addressed to a CASAL [CHAZAL] who was a sailor aboard the ship "La Linote." The widow CHAZAL died in New Orleans on January 20, 1846, but the writer was unable to trace the place of death for the men. I-A, lxi; I-Be; I-E, 26; II-B; III-G, 43; III-H, 43; VIII-B, January 10, 1816; December 2, 1816; August 29, 1817.

CHEMINARD, Jean Chasseurs
The writer was unable to locate any vital information on Jean CHEMINARD, except that he was wounded in action on December

23, 1814, and that he lived in New Orleans or its vicinity for he was receiving his correspondence at the post office between 1813-1816. The only other person whom the writer located in the records with a similar name was Jean MICHINARD, who was married to Dame BARBOT. Jean lived in New Orleans and died on October 16, 1836, at the age of forty-three. I-A, lxi; I-Be; I-E, 26; II-B; V-Bm, 147; VIII-B, March 5, 1813; January 10, 1816.

CHEVALON (CHEVALLON), Charles   Sergeant   Francs
Pelletier cites the soldier as A. CHEVALON, while Casey and Pierson cite him as Charles CHEVALON. The writer located in the records a Charles CHEVALLON who lived in New Orleans in 1822 at 123 Royal St. Also the writer located a Black man whose name was Charles Alexandre CHEVALON who lived in New Orleans and was married to Elizabeth HOUARD. It is probable that he may be the same CHEVALLON who lived on Royal St., but the writer was unable to verify it. I-A, lx; I-D, 11; I-E, 26; II-A; III-E, 7; IV-D, 114; V-Bd, 57.

CHOPPIN, Alexandre   Sergeant   Carabiniers
Alexandre CHOPPIN was a merchant who travelled throughout Louisiana. Before 1820, he was very active in New Orleans. In 1807 he and his son were living in an apartment on the *Place d'Armes* [Jackson Square], and often stayed at the home of P. CENAS or other friends. He served as an examiner for the Charitable Society for the 3rd District of New Orleans, a member of a jury in a civil suit in which Laurent MILLAUDON, another veteran, was the foreman, and elected councilman for the 2nd Ward of New Orleans. He also served as a director of the State Bank of Louisiana. His business activities were varied, for he sold many types of dry goods when he came to New Orleans on business trips, and was the agent for a boating line which carried passengers and cargo between New Orleans and Natchez. I-A, lix; I-D, 5; I-E, 26; III-B, 77; III-J, 7; III-K, 10; VI-H, June 22,

1814; VIII-B, July 14, 1810; November 30, 1810; November 29, 1811; May 19, 1813; May 1, 1816; August 14, 1816; June 22, 1818.

CLAIRVAUX, J. L.   Dragoons
The soldier with the surname of CLAIRVAUX in the compilation in the appendix is cited by Pelletier as J. L. CLAIRVAUX, while the other compilers do not cite him. The writer was unable to locate anyone in the records with the surname, and the only person living during the period with a similar surname was Antoine CLAIREAU, who was living in St. James Parish in 1820. I-D, 9; III-J, 7.

CLERMONT   Dragoons*
The soldier with the surname of CLERMONT is cited by both Casey and Pierson, but the writer was unable to identify the soldier for lack of having found his first name or initial with which to identify him. The writer located four persons living during the period who were of age and possibly could have been the soldier cited.

First there was Paul Louis François CLERMONT, who was married to Lisette HOYO. He lived in New Orleans and died on September 30, 1817. One of his heirs was Joseph BOURGEOIS, another veteran under PLAUCHE; the second person was Joseph CLERMONT who lived in the suburb La Course in New Orleans and died in 1816; third there was Nicholas CLERMONT who lived in St. John the Baptist Parish in 1820; and fourth there was Etienne CLERMONT, a tinsmith who lived in New Orleans in 1832 on Conde St. I-A, lx; I-E, 27; II-A; III-G, 45; III-J, 7; V-Ab. 212-13; V-Ac, 339-41; V-Bc, 366.

CIBILOT [See SIBILOT, François]

CIBILOT [See SIBILOT, Joseph]

CIBILOT [See SIBILOT, Louis]

COEUR DE ROY, Dominique   1st Lt.   Carabiniers
Dominique C. COEUR DE ROY lived in New Orleans with his wife and children at 119 Bourbon St. One of his daughters was named B. Syndalis, who was born on November 23, 1814. Dominique was one of the prime organizers along with Auguste GUIBERT, Etienne BERTEL, and Henry De ST. GEME of a parade to celebrate the first anniversary of the Battle of New Orleans in 1816. Dominique had the misfortune of having a serious accident when he fell from the terrace of the Orleans Theatre. A vocal and instrumental concert was performed for his benefit at the Conde Ball Room in 1816 to help him financially while he was unable to work. He died in 1819. I-A, lix; I-D, 5; I-E, 29; II-A; III-E, 8; III-H, 47; III-J, 8; III-K, 11; IV-Bc, 368; VIII-B, January 5, 1816; January 22, 1816; October 31, 1818.

COHN   Carabiniers
The soldier with the surname of COHN is cited only in the appendix compilation as having served in the Carabiniers. The writer was unable to identify the soldier for lack of having located his first name or initials, but he located five persons living during the period who could possibly have been the soldier cited in the roster.

First there was John COHN who lived in New Orleans and died in 1835. Second, there was Joachim KOHN, a merchant who lived at 58 Royal St. in New Orleans in 1822. Third, there was a Solomon COHN, a businessman who was given by the legislature the privilege of building a turnpike road in New Orleans in 1847. Fourth, there was a Samuel KHONE (KUHN), a tavern keeper in New Orleans in 1811, but later became a merchant whose shop was located at 11 Toulouse St. Fifth, there was a George H. KUHN, a commission merchant who lived in New Orleans at 6 Bienville St. in 1822. III-D, 30; III-E, 16; III-G, 99; III-H, 47; III-J, 8; V-Bd, 61; VI-Gs, 159-60; VIII-B, May 3, 1813.

COHN (COHEN), Simon M.   Sergeant-Quartermaster   Dragoons
Simon M. COHEN is cited in the compilation in the appendix as

a private, but the other compilers cite him as a sergeant and quartermaster in the Dragoons.

Simon was born in 1785-1786. He lived in New Orleans where he had a cigar manufacturing business located at 10 Conti St., while his residence was at 17 Conde St. In the 1830's he must have retired from the business, for he was listed as a gentleman living in a house on the corner of St. Philip and Burgundy Streets. He continued his military career, for he was a sergeant-major in 1829 and a 2nd Lieutenant of the 1st Company of Artillery of the 1st Batallion of the Louisiana Legion by 1832. He died on August 20, 1836, at the age of fifty. I-A, lx; I-D, 8; I-E, 28; II-B; III-E, 8; III-G, 99; III-H, 47; III-K, 11; VIII-A, January 21, 1829; VIII-B, December 2, 1816; August 29, 1817; December 14, 1818.

COIGNARD, Lucien? Carabiniers
The soldier with the surname of COIGNARD is cited by Pelletier as Lucien COIGNARD and by Casey as COIGNARD COLLINS, but the writer was unable to locate anyone in the records with the names cited. However, he discovered that the BROUET and COIGNARD families were related, for they share the same tomb in the St. Louis Cemetery of New Orleans.

From other records, the writer located two persons who were of age and living during the period with the surname who possibly could have been the soldier cited. One was Louis COIGNARD, a merchant living in New Orleans in 1817, and the second was Charles COIGNARD, who was married to Louise Irma CAREL. I-A, lix; I-D, 6; I-E, 28; II-A; VIII-B, September 2, 1816; July 30, 1817; August 29, 1817.

COLLINS, Jean Carabiniers*
The writer was unable to identify the soldier John COLLINS who served in the Carabiniers. Casey cites him as John COLLINS while Pelletier cites him as Jean L. COLLINS. Pierson cites only

the surname. To complicate matters, Pierson cites at least two soldiers with the name of John COLLINS, each a captain in the 4th Regiment under DECLOUET, and a private in the 10th and 20th Consolidated Regiment.

The writer located various persons with the name of John COLLINS living in the New Orleans vicinity and outlying parishes during the period. In New Orleans there was a John COLLENS [COLLINS?] who was married to Marie Louise De ARCE. She was a native of Havana, Cuba, and died in New Orleans on May 31, 1833. A second person with the name in New Orleans was John COLLINS, a physician, and a third was a John COLLINS who was a sailor who had deserted his ship, "The General Brown" in 1825 and was placed in jail until the ship sailed. Finally, there was another John COLLINS who ran a boarding house on Ursuline St. in 1832.

Outside of the New Orleans area, there was a John P. COLLINS from St. Tammany Parish who received a state pension for service rendered during the war, and a John P. COLLINS, who may have been the same person, who was cited as living in East Baton Rouge Parish in 1830. I-A, lix; I-D, 6; I-E, 28; II-A; III-C, 11; III-G, 46; III-K, ii; V-Bc, 368; VI-Gb, 48; VI-Gu, 223; VI-I. January 24, 1825; VII-Da, 2; VIII-B, July 16, 1813; August 2, 1816.

COMBELLE [See BICOMBELLE, Bernard]

CONRAD [See KONRAD, Karl]

CONSOLOT (CONSOLAT), Pierre   Francs*
Pierre CONSOLOT (CONSOLAT) is cited by Pelletier as having served in the Francs, but other compilers cite only a Joseph CONSOLAT who served in the 4th Regiment under MORGAN during the war. The writer was unable to locate anyone with the

(40)

name of Pierre CONSOLOT or CONSOLAT in the records and living during the period.

The only persons with the surname whom he located living during the period was a François CONSOLAT who was a baker living in New Orleans in 1813, and Charles Joseph CONSOLAT, who may have been the soldier cited by Pierson, who was married to Rosalie BOUSQUET [BOURQUET]. Charles Joseph lived in New Orleans at 28 Poydras St. in 1811. He died on March 17, 1816, at the age of thirty-five. I-D, 12; I-E, 29; II-A; III-D, 11; III-H, 49; V-Ac, 459-60; V-Bc, 368; VIII-B, February 10, 1813.

CORDEVIOLLE, Etienne Dragoons*
The writer was unable to locate much information on Etienne CORDEVIOLLE except that he was a merchant living in New Orleans at 253 Bourbon St., but later moved his store to the corner of Main St. and Bourbon St., at which time he opened a shoe store. I-A, lx; III-F; III-H, 50; III-K, 11.

CORNICO (CARMACK), Daniel David Francs
The soldier cited in the appendix compilation as CORNICO is cited by Pelletier as David CONNICK. The writer was unable to locate anyone as cited in the records, but he suspects that it may have been Major Daniel David CARMACK, U.S.M.C., who, according to Major General Wilburt S. Brown, served under PLAUCHE in the action of December 28, 1814, in which he was wounded.

David Daniel CARMACK was born in 1773, a native of Philadelphia. He was married to Margarita COWPERTHWAIT, daughter of Santiago COWPERTHWAIT and Carlota O'BRIAN. David Daniel was a major in the service and head of the marine corps stationed in New Orleans in 1811. He died in New Orleans on November 7, 1816, at the age of forty-three. I-D, 13; II-A; III-D, 12; III-K, 11; IX-A, 119; IX-L, 121; IX-Pb, 97-98.

CORREJOLES, François [Jr.]   Dragoons
François CORREJOLES was the son of François CORREJOLES [Sr.] and Marie Cécile GUERLET (GRELET), a native of St. Domingue [Haiti], and daughter of Joseph GRELET and Marie Isabel FOURNAT. François [Jr.] was married to Lise PASCAL, from which union several children were born. The writer was unable to determine with any certainty which of the François was the one who continued his military career and was a 1st lieutenant of Chasseurs in the 2nd Battalion of the Louisiana Legion in 1832, and an officer of the Masonic Lodges *Les Amis Reunis* and *Les Trinosophes* in New Orleans. François [Jr.] received a state pension for service rendered during the war. He died in New Orleans on July 2, 1864, and his father a few years earlier on January 21, 1843. I-A, lx; I-D, 9; I-E, 30; I-F, 65; II-B; III-G, 218; III-H, 59; III-J, 8; IV-B, 61; IV-Da, 2; IX-G, 24.

CORREJOLES, Gabriel [Sr.]   Dragoons
Gabriel CORREJOLES, Sr. was born in 1780, a native of Ft. Dauphine, St. Domingue [Haiti], the son of François CORREJOLES and Marie Cécile GUERLET (GRELET). Gabriel was married to Elizabeth PRADINES, a native of Jérémie, St. Domingue, from which union several children were born. One of them was Félix, who was married to Magdeleine MEUNIER, daughter of Etienne MEUNIER and Rosalie DERUZE. Gabriel left Haiti during the slave revolt, and went to Cuba, but the conditions there were not suitable. He and other refugees signed a petition addressed to President James MADISON asking him to give him and the others permission to clear a vessel through New Orleans on its way to some port in France. Gabriel, however, decided to remain in New Orleans and established his residence at 71 Conti St., but later moved it to 176 Levée. Gabriel died on October 12, 1842, at the age of sixty-two. I-A, lx; I-D, 9; I-E, 30; II-B; III-D, 12; III-G, 48; III-H, 59; III-J, 11; IV-D, 155; V-Ae, 181; V-Bd, 64-65; VI-Fd, 418.

COTTON (COTTEN) Blues
The soldier with the surname of COTTON is cited only in the compilation in the appendix, but Vincent NOLTE, a merchant, writer and one of the veterans in the Carabiniers, confirms that there was a soldier named COTTEN who was an editor of the Louisiana *Gazette* and served under PLAUCHE. Casey and Pierson do not cite anyone with the surname as having served under PLAUCHE, but cite a G. B. [Godwin B.] COTTEN who was a corporal-sergeant and a J. COTTON in the 4th Regiment under MORGAN, and a James COTTON in the 12th and 13th Consolidated Regiment. It is possible that one of those cited by Pierson and Casey may have been the soldier who may have served by transferring units to the Blues.

The writer feels that the soldier who served in the Blues may have been Godwin B. COTTEN, for he lived in the Felicianas in 1812, but moved to New Orleans and was cited in 1824 as a printer and collector of marine intelligence. It could also have been a G. R. COTTEN who worked in the news room of a local newspaper in New Orleans and resided at 7 Camp St. in 1824. I-E, 29; III-F; VI-Ca, 1009-1012; VIII-B, December 2, 1816; IX-Q, 227.

COURCELLE, Hilaire Carabiniers*
Hilaire COURCELLE is cited only by Pelletier as having served in the Carabiniers, while PIERSON cites only a Joncin COURCEL who served under Captain CHAUVEAU, and a Léon COURCELLO who served in the 4th Regiment under MORGAN.

Hilaire COURCELLE was born on October 30, 1783. He lived in New Orleans in a house located on the corner of Rampart and Dumaine Sts., where he had a goldsmith shop, but later moved it to 163 St. Claude Street. He died on May 21, 1852. I-D, 7; I-E, 30; II-A; III-D, 12; III-F; III-J, 8; III-K, 11.

COUVERTIE, Jean Baptiste [Sr.] Sergeant Chasseurs
Casey cites the name of the soldier as Louis Baptiste COUVERTIE, Sr., while Pelletier cites him as Jean Baptiste COUVERTIE, Sr. The writer was able to locate in the records only a Jean Baptiste, but it is possible that his full name may have been Louis Jean Baptiste COUVERTIE.

Jean Baptiste COURVERTIE was a native of St. Domingue [Haiti]. He was a jeweler and goldsmith, like Louis Gabriel COUVERTIE, who, most probably was his brother. Jean lived in New Orleans for awhile, but by 1816 he placed a notice in a local newspaper informing his clients and creditors to settle all accounts, for he was about to depart from the country. He left shortly thereafter, for the writer was unable to locate him after 1816. I-A, lxi; I-D, 15; I-E, 30; VIII-B, January 13, 1813; March 13, 1816; March 29, 1816.

COUVERTIE, Louis Gabriel [Jr.] Sergeant Chasseurs
Louis Gabriel COUVERTIE was born in 1779-1780, a native of St. Marc, St. Domingue [Haiti]. He was a goldsmith living in New Orleans at 29 St. Peter Street, but later moved his business to the corner of Royal St. and St. Peter Street. He died in June, 1844, at the age of sixty-five. I-A, lxi; I-D, 15; I-E, 30; II-B; III-E, 8; III-F; III-G, 49; III-J, 8; V-Bd, 65; VIII-B, November 15, 1816; July 30, 1817.

CREMONA [See CRONIN, Peter]

CRICHCRAFT [See KRICHCRAFT, Frederick]

CRONIN (CREMONA), [Peter] Musician Battalion
The musician cited in the compilation in the appendix as CRONIN is cited by both Casey and Pierson as CREMONA, while Pelletier cites him as Thomas CRONIN. The only person whom the writer was able to locate in the records who was associated with other people in the music business was Peter CREMONA.

Peter CREMONA lived in New Orleans in a house on St. Ann Street belonging to Salvador CONSTANTIN. Peter died on August 12, 1817, and José Antonio BONIQUET, a Spaniard who had been one of the owners of the public dance hall and theatre in New Orleans during the Spanish period, became the testamentary executor. José declared to Judge James PITOT in the court of probates that Peter had only about one hundred dollars worth of personal property. I-A, lix; I-D, 5; I-E, 30; V-Ab, 423-424; V-Ac, August 21, 1817; V-Bc, 367; VIII-B, February 5, 1816; IX-Pa, 44-45.

CRUZEL, Jean Baptiste   Musician   Battalion
Jean Baptiste CRUZEL was born in 1793. He was married to Caroline TOSSIE, a native of St. Domingue [Haiti], from which union several children were born. Two of the children were Julie, who died in 1823, and Charles Joseph, who died in 1824. Jean Baptiste was granted a state pension for service rendered during the war. He died in New Orleans on November 14, 1833, at the age of forty. I-A, lix; I-D, 5; I-E, 30; II-A, III-K, 12; V-Bd, 60; VII-Da, 3; VIII-B, June 26, 1813.

CRUZEL, Jean François   Dragoons
Jean François CRUZEL was married to Marie Thérèse FERNANDEZ, from which union several children were born. One was Marie Emma, who was married to Monsieur BLINEAU, but later divorced him and married Antoine CARRIERE. Jean François also divorced his wife, Marie Thérèse, in 1825 and later married Jeanne Manuelle NAUTRE. Jean François was a cigar maker living in New Orleans at 126 Casa-Calvo St. He later received a pension for service rendered during the war. I-A, lx; I-D, 9; I-E, 30; III-G, 50; III-K, 12; IV-D, 38, 109; VI-Gf, 100; VII-Da, 3; VIII-B, February 5, 1816.

CUVILLIER, Jacques   [See CAVAILLE, Pierre]   Francs
The soldier with the surname of CUVILLIER cited in the compilation in the appendix is listed by Pelletier as Jacques CUVIL-

LIER, while Casey cites him as Pierre CAVAILLE, a corporal and quartermaster in the Chasseurs, and Pierson cites him only with the surname of CAVELIER as a corporal under PLAUCHE. The only person whom the writer located in the records who may have been the soldier cited by Pelletier was an M.J.A.A. CUVILLIER who lived in New Orleans and died in 1843.

Pierson cites six soldiers with the surname of CUVILLIER who served in other units during the war, and it is possible that one of them may have transferred and served under PLAUCHE. The soldiers cited by Pierson are as follows: In the 4th Regiment there was P.A. [Pierre Ambroise] CUVILLIER, a lawyer and state senate interpreter who lived in New Orleans. In the 5th Regiment under LABRANCHE there were two persons with the name of Joseph living in New Orleans, one who was a notary and the other a carpenter; a Pierre who was a gentleman living at 149 St. Charles [Ave.] in New Orleans; and an Antoine who was a resident of Assumption Parish in 1830. In the 7th Regiment under LeBEUF there was a Henry CUVILLIER. I-D, 11; I-E, 31; III-E, 9; III-F; III-G, 51; III-K, 12; V-Bd, 60; VI-Gb, 110.

(46)

Print of the Battle of New Orleans on January 8, 1815 by J. W. Steel.

Portrait of Bernard Duchamp, a veteran of the Battalion of Orleans.

(48)

D

DABNOUR [See DUBANOIS, Hypolite FORT]

DAMERON, Christopher   Blues
The soldier with the surname of DAMERON is cited by Casey as Christopher, by Pelletier as Charles, and by Pierson as Christian. It is possible that the soldier may have had all those names cited, but the writer was unable to confirm it.

The only information the writer located on Christopher DAMERON was that he lived in New Orleans or visited often, for he would receive correspondence at the post office. He was also one of the signers of the petition addressed to General Andrew JACKSON to spare the lives of the two soldiers named HARDEN and BRUMFIELD who were sentenced to death for having been absent during the campaign at Chef Menteur. I-A, lxi; I-D, 13; I-E, 32; VI-Dc, February 27, 1815; VIII-B, July 30, 1817.

DAMPIERRE [See BIBLE, Jean Pierre]

DANSE   Dragoons
The soldier in the compilation in the appendix with the surname of DANSE is cited by Pelletier as Philip DORSE, while Casey and Pierson do not cite anyone with the surname in the Dragoons, and the only person cited with a similar name is Samuel DORSEY who served in the 10th and 20th Consolidated Regiments.

The only persons who were of age during the period whom the writer located in the records with similar surnames were George W. DORSEY who was a merchant and commissioner of the Louisiana Insurance Company. He lived in New Orleans and later received a state pension for service rendered during the war, yet Pierson cites only Samuel DORSEY as having served during the war. Also there was a Philip Henry DARCE who was the sheriff of Terrebonne Parish who died in 1845 or 1846. I-D, 9; I-E, 38; III-G, 64; III-J, 10; III-K, 12; VI-Gr, 165; VII-Da, 3; VIII-B, April 15, 1816.

DAPPREMONT   Carabiniers
The writer was unable to identify the soldier with the surname of DAPPREMONT for having been unable to locate his first name or initial for the purpose of identification. Pierson and other compilers cite two persons with the surname of DAPPREMONT as having served in the war, one under PLAUCHE, and the other in the 4th Regiment under MORGAN.

The writer located five persons living during the period with the surname who could possibly have been the soldiers cited by the compilers. The first was Jean Louis LALANDE DAPPREMONT who lived in New Orleans in 1805 at 12 Julia St. He was married to Maria BAURE [BORE] and he died on March 26, 1827, at the age of seventy-five. The second was Alexandre DAPPREMONT who lived at 189 Dauphine St. in New Orleans in 1832. He was married to Thérèse DELONNAY. The third was Emmanuel DAPPREMONT [DASPPREMONT] who lived at 38 Orleans St. in New Orleans. He died without any legitimate heirs, but with a natural child named Alexandrine DEVILLE who became the benefactor of his estate. The fourth and fifth were J. DAPPREMONT and Antoine Charles DAPPREMONT who were living in 1830 in the parishes of Orleans and Assumption respectively. I-A, lix; I-E, 32; II-A; III-A, 21; III-G, 52; III-K, 12; I-Cc, 7; V-Be, 118; VI-Ca, 635; VI-Gn, 81-82; VIII-B, November 16, 1810; March 2, 1818.

DARBOIS, Gabriel? Louis?   Musician   Chief of Drummers*
The musician with the surname of DARBOIS cited by Casey and

Pierson, signed only his surname in the original payroll sheet thus preventing the writer from determining his identity. The writer located only two persons living during the period with the surname of DARBOIS. The first was Gabriel DARBOIS who lived in New Orleans. He was married to Rose DUQUE from which union several children were born. One, whose name was Rose, was born in 1816. The second person with the surname was Louis DARBOIS who was married to Marie Carmelite BOURGEOIS, a native of Lafourche. She died in New Orleans on January 14, 1829. I-A, lix; I-Bf; I-E, 32; II-A.

DAUNOY, Louis FAVBRE Chasseurs
Louis Théodore FAVBRE DAUNOY was born in 1797 or 1800. He lived in New Orleans, where he was a city marshal for the city court, and his home was located at 49 St. Ann Street. He continued his military career, and in 1832 he was a 2nd lieutenant in the *Cazadores de Orleans*, in the 2nd Battalion of the Louisiana Legion. Louis died on November 1, 1833, at the age of thirty-three or thirty-six. I-A, lxi; I-D, 5; I-E, 33; II-B; III-G, 53, 218; V-Bf, 233; VIII-A, January 9, 1829.

DAUPHIN, Jules Dragoons*
Jules DAUPHIN is cited by Pelletier in the Dragoons, but none of the other compilers cite him under PLAUCHE. Pierson cites four soldiers with the surname of DAUPHIN, a J. B., a Joseph, and a Francis who served under DECLOUET and a Charles who served in the 2nd Regiment under CAVELIER. It is possible that the name of "Jules" may have been one of the given names of the soldiers cited, but the writer was unable to confirm it. The only information the writer located was that a person named J. DAUPHIN was receiving his correspondence in New Orleans in 1816. I-D, 10, I-E, 33; VIII-B, August 2, 1816.

DAVID Dragoons
The soldier with the surname of DAVID in the compilation in the appendix is listed only by his surname by other compilers.

(51)

The writer was unable to identify the soldier because there were too many people living during the period with the surname. I-A, lx; I-E, 33.

DAVIS, Jean Dragoons*
Pelletier cites the name of the soldier as Jean Baptiste DAVIS, while Casey cites him only as J. DAVIS. Pierson cites only the surname of the soldier who served under PLAUCHE, but also cites a John DAVIS who served in the company of artillery under Captain ALLEN.

The writer located several persons who were living in New Orleans during the period, but could not determine which of them may have been the soldier or soldiers cited. In 1811, there were a John DAVIS who was a shoemaker living at 24 Conti St., and a John DAVIS who was a tobacco manufacturer at 22 Conde St. In 1816 there was a John DAVIS, who may also have been one of the persons cited above, who was the proprietor of the *Orleans Theatre,* and in 1822 there was another John DAVIS who was the proprietor of a grocery store at 55 Tchoupitoulas St. One of the persons with the name of John DAVIS received a state pension for service rendered during the war. I-A, lx; I-D, 10; I-E, 33; III-D, 17; III-E, 10; III-F; III-G, 53; VII-Da, 3; VIII-B, January 6, 1813.

DeBUYS, Pierre Gaspard Carabiniers
Pierre Gaspard DeBUYS was born in 1790, the son of Gaspard DeBUYS and Eulalie DEJAN. Pierre was married in 1811 to Jeanne Clémence VIEL. Pierre, like his father who was a broker, continued in the business tradition, for he was a merchant living in New Orleans at 40 Levée. Pierre and William DeBUYS were in partnership, for they owned a cotton press on St. Charles [Avenue]. Jeanne Clémence, the wife of Pierre died in New Orleans on April 6, 1868, at the age of seventy-six, but the writer was unable to determine the time of death for Pierre. I-A, lx; I-E, 34; II-A; III-D, 16; III-E, 10; III-F; III-G, 54, 60; IX-G, 26.

(52)

DeBUYS, William (Guillaume) Carabiniers
William (Guillaume) DeBUYS was married to Corine ANDRY, from which union several children were born. One was Sophie, who was born in 1822. William was a merchant in partnership with P.F. DUBOURG and A. LONGER, at 121 Gravier St. in New Orleans, and later William and Pierre DeBUYS owned a cotton press on St. Charles St. William continued his military career, for in the 1830's he was the commandant of the *Escadron des Chasseurs a Cheval*. In the 1840's he became the state treasurer, for which office his wife was authorized to become his surety.
I-A, lix; I-D, 7; I-E, 34; II-A; III-F; III-G, 54; III-H, 250; IV-D, 91; VI-Gp, 25; VIII-B, September 8, 1813.

DeENDE, Henry Blues*
John Henry Am [Ambrose] DeENDE was a native of Germany. He was a merchant in New Orleans in partnership with his brother, Frederick William, in a company known as J.H. & F.W. DeENDE. Henry died in August, 1817, and his brother Frederick went before the probate court of James PITOT declaring that he would like to be appointed the administrator of the estate of his late brother, for he was the only living relative in the United States and that the only other living relative was another brother who was living in Hamburg, Germany. The court agreed to the petition made by Frederick. He died a few years later in 1835.
I-A, lxi; I-Bd; I-E, 34; V-Ab, 444-47; V-Ac, 157-60; V-Be, 120; V-Bf, 234.

DeFORES [See DESFORGES and DeTORRES, Fernando]
  Carabiniers
Casey cites a soldier with the surname of DeFORES in the Carabiniers, while Pierson cites an F. DeTORRES who served under PLAUCHE. The appendix compilation and Pelletier cite two soldiers with the surname of DESFORGES, one a musician [Louis HUS] and the other a private in the Carabiniers. The writer was unable to locate in the records any person living during the period with the surname of DeFORES or J. Jacques DES-

FORGES as cited by Pelletier, and the only one he located was a Fernando DeTORRES. I-A,, lix; I-D, 7; I-E, 36.

DeFOURGE [DeSOUGE), Jean Baptiste　　　　　　**Dragoons**
Jean Baptiste DeSOUGE was a turner living at 37 Rampart St. in New Orleans. He died in 1836. I-A, lx; I-D, 7; I-E, 36; III-G, 56; III-H, 61; III-K, 13; V-Bf, 235.

DeGLAPION [See CADION, Christophe DUMINY]

DeGRUY, DUFOUCHARD　　　　　　　　　　　　**Chasseurs**
Although there were several persons in the records of the period with the surname of DeGRUY DUFOUCHARD, the soldier who served in the Chasseurs most probably was the one who was cited in the records only as DeGRUY DUFOUCHARD, who was an accountant in New Orleans in 1822 living at 40 Dauphine St. He was also an officer of the Consolidated Association [bank] of the Planters of Louisiana. During his military service, he was one of the soldiers who signed the petition addressed to General Andrew JACKSON asking him to spare the lives of the two soldiers named HARDEN and BRUMFIELD who had been sentenced to death for having been absent during the campaign at Chef Menteur. I-A, lxi; I-E, 34; III-E, 10; III-G, viii; III-H, 67, 236; VI-Dc, February 27, 1815.

DeGRUY, [Pierre VERLOIN]　　　　　　　　　　**Chasseurs**
The appendix compilation cites a soldier with the surname of DeGRUY, and another with the surname of DUFOUCHARD. The writer was able to determine that the soldier cited as DU-FOUCHARD was known as DeGRUY DUFOUCHARD, but the only other person cited by other compilers with solely the surname of DeGRUY was Pierre VERLOIN DeGRUY who served in the 4th Regiment under MORGAN. It is very possible that Pierre may be the same soldier, if he had transferred to the Chasseurs, but the writer was unable to verify it.

Pierre VERLOIN DeGRUY was married to Amélie DUPART, from which union several children were born. One, whose name was Théophile, was born in 1818-1819. Pierre was a grocer living in New Orleans at New Levée in 1822. Later he received a state pension for service rendered during the war. I-E, 34; II-A; III-E, 10; VII-Da, 3.

DeLABOSTRIE [See LABOSTORIE, J. P.]

DeLARUE, [Jean Baptiste? René?]
The soldier with the surname of DeLARUE cited in the appendix compilation is listed by Pelletier as Célestin DeLARUE, and by Casey and Pierson only with the surname. The writer was unable to locate anyone in the records as cited by Pelletier, but located two persons with the surname who were of age and living during the period.
The first was Jean Baptiste DeLARUE, who was a goldsmith living in New Orleans in 1805 at 8 Public Place [Jackson Square], but later moved his residence to 94 Bourbon St. The second was René DeLARUE who was a merchant living in New Orleans in 1805 at 78 Dauphin St. I-A, lix; I-D, 7; I-E, 34; III-A, 21; III-E, 10; III-F; III-J, 9; III-K, 13; VIII-B, October 3, 1810.

DeLINO [See CHALMETTE, Ignacio DeLINO]

DELPEUCH [See LAVERGNE, Cadet]

DEMOURUELLE, Humbert   Dragoons*
The writer located in the records two persons with the name of Humbert DEMOURUELLE living in New Orleans, but could not determine whether they were father and son or even related. The first Humbert was married to Suzanne LAVERGNE. He died before 1820 in New Orleans for his widow died in that year at the age of eighty-six. The second, or perhaps the same person, was married to Louise NOGUIES, from which union several children were born. One was Emilie, who was married to Jean

(55)

Baptiste HENO and later to Thomas BLOIS. He also lived in New Orleans. I-A, lx; I-D, 10; I-E, 61; II-A; III-H, 61; III-J, 9; III-K, 13; V-Be, 116.

DENESSE [See DEVIZE, Ferdinand]

DENIS, R. S.   Musician   Battalion
The musician with the surname of DENIS is cited by Pelletier as R. S. DENIS, while the other compilers and the original payroll sheet cite only the surname. The writer was unable to locate anyone in the records as cited by Pelletier and was unable to identify the musician because there were too many with the surname living during the period. I-A, lix; I-Bf; I-D, 5; I-E, 35.

DENIZE   Dragoons*
Casey and Pierson cite a soldier with the surname of DENIZE as having served in the Dragoons. The only persons whom the writer located in the records with a similar surname were John DENICE and Jean DANOSSE who resided in the parishes of St. Tammany and Iberia respectively in 1820. The census of 1830 cites only a person with the surname of DENISE who was residing in Orleans Parish. I-A, lx; I-E, 35; III-J, 8-9; III-K, 13.

DERUSE, (DERUZE), Anthony?   Blues
The soldier with the surname of DERUSE (DERUZE) is cited only in the compilation in the appendix. The writer was able to locate only one person with the surname in the records who was living during the period and was of age. He was Anthony DERUZE who was a watch maker and a jeweler with his shop on Gravier St. and his home at 193 Bourbon St. in New Orleans in 1822. Two other persons with similar names were Jean Baptise DEROUSSE, a native of Canada, who was living in New Orleans and died on August 26, 1829, at the age of thirty-four, and an Etienne DEROUSE who was cited as a resident of Natchitoches in 1820. II-A; III-E, 10; III-F; III-J, 9; VIII-B, August 29, 1817.

DESBANS (DESBAN), Jos. [Joseph]   Francs
The soldier with the surname of DESBANS (DESBAN), is cited by Pelletier as Jean Louis DESBAN, while Casey and Pierson cite only the surname. The writer located in the Jackson Papers a soldier with the name of Jos. [Joseph] DESBAN who had signed a petition asking that the two soldiers named HARDEN and BRUMFIELD be spared from the death sentence for having been absent during the campaign at Chef Menteur.
The writer was unable to locate any information on the soldier cited by Pelletier or as he signed his name in the petition to Andrew JACKSON. The persons whom he located who could possibly had been the soldier was a Michel DESBAN who died in New Orleans on April 23, 1817, at the home of Justice of the Peace A. DUBOURG; a Charles J. DESBAN who was a builder at 78 Julia St. in New Orleans in 1834; and a John DESBAHEN who was cited in the census of 1830 as a resident in Orleans Parish. I-A, lx; I-D, 12; I-E, 33, 34, 36; III-H, 60; III-K, 3; V-Ac, 424-27; Vi-Dc, February 27, 1815.

DESDUNES, Jean Baptiste   Chasseurs*
Pelletier cites two soldiers with the surname of DESDUNES who served in the Chasseurs, a Jean Baptiste and a POINCY DESDUNES. Pierson and other compilers cite only one person named Jean Baptiste DESDUNES who served in the war, but in the 2nd Regiment under CAVELIER.
In the records there were a senior and a junior Jean Baptiste DESDUNES, and the writer was unable to determine which of the two may have been the soldier, for both were of age. Jean Baptiste [Jr.] was born in St. Domingue [Haiti] on October 13, 1788. He lived in New Orleans at 94 Victory St., while the senior Jean Baptiste lived at 18 Mandeville St. One of them was married to Renette BALTHAZARD and was appointed captain of the 3rd Regiment on February 20, 1806. One of the two was also a clerk and interpreter in the state house of representatives, treasurer of the Library Society of New Orleans, and received a state pension for service rendered during the war. Jean Baptiste

(57)

[Jr.] died in New Orleans on April 5, 1842. I-D, 16; I-E, 34; II-A; II-B; III-H, 60; IV-Be, 239; VI-Gb, 108; VII-Ca, 634; VII-Da, 3· VIII-B, October 12, 1813; December 29, 1817.

DESDUNES, POINCY [See DESDUNES, Jean B.]   Chasseurs*
Jean Baptiste ROSSIGNOL DESDUNES POINCY [Jr.] was born in 1789-1790, a native of St. Marc, St. Domingue [Haiti]. He was married several times after he had become a widower. His wives were Julie Elizabeth Althée MOREAU LISLET, Elizabeth Mathilde HATREL, and Marie Magdeleine BANCIO PIEMONT. He was a baker living in New Orleans at 59 Conde St, but later moved his shop to 25 Main St. He died on April 6, 1840, at the age of fifty. I-D, 16; II-A; III-F; III-H, 61; V-Be, 120; V-Bf, 237; VIII-B, February 10, 1817.

DESFORGES, J. Jacques? [See DeTORRES, F.]   Carabiniers
The compilation in the appendix cites two persons with the surname of DESFORGES, one a musician [Louis HUS] and the other a private in the Carabiniers. Pelletier is in agreement with the compilation, for she cites Louis HUS DEFORGES as the musician and J. Jacques DESFORGES as the private in the Carabiniers. The writer was unable to locate anyone with the name of J. Jacques DEFORGES in the records. To add to the confusion, Casey and Pierson cite only one soldier with the surname of DESFORGES, but in addition, Casey cites a soldier with the surname of DEFORES and Pierson one surnamed F. DeTORRES. The writer was unable to locate in the records any person with the surname of DEFORES living during the period, but he located a Fernando DeTORRES. I-A, lix; I-D, 7; I-E, 36.

DESFORGES, Louis Hus   Musician   Battalion
The appendix compilation and that by Pelletier cite two persons with the surname of DESFORGES, one a musician and the other a private in the Carabiniers. Casey and Pierson cite only one person with the surname of DESFORGES as a private in the Carabiniers, and a person with a similar surname, DEJONGE, as the sergeant

of music and chief musician. The writer located the original payroll, and it conforms to the entries made by Casey and Pierson.

Louis HUS DESFORGES was born in 1780 in Amiens, France, and was a native of Rochelle. He was married to Elizabeth Victoire DUPRE, from which union several children were born. He was a master musician living in New Orleans. He was one of the few musicians during the period with the ability to rearrange the composition for an orchestra. Louis was a 2nd lieutenant in the 1st Regiment in 1806, and later an assistant registering clerk at the custom house in New Orleans. In 1824, when General James WILKINSON was being entertained in New Orleans, Louis and others incited a small-scale brawl when the Anglo-American guests insisted on singing "Hail Columbia", while Louis and other Franco-Americans countered by singing *La Marseillaise*. Later Louis received a state pension for services rendered during the war, and, although he was made deaf during the war, he continued his musical career until his death on November 19, 1861. [The writer is indebted to George Sénac Rapier for providing him with some of the information on Louis HUS DESFORGES, one of his ancestors]. I-A, lix; I-D, 5; I-E, 34, 36; II-A; III-D, 19; III-E, 10; III-G, 56; III-H, 229; IV-D, 32; VI-Ca, 181, 633; VI-Gh, 24; VI-Gt, 121; VI-Gu, 247; VII-A, 170; VII-Da, January 21, 1815; VIII-B, December 23, 1816.

DESGRAIS (DESGRES), François Dragoons*
François DESGRAIS (DESGRES) is cited by Pelletier as having served in the Dragoons, but the other compilers place him in the 2nd Regiment under CAVELIER.
M. François DESGRES was born on August 5, 1782. He was a carpenter living in New Orleans on Plauché St., north of Bayou Road in 1834. He died on June 3, 1853. I-D, 10; I-E, 34; II-A; III-H, 61.

DESMARATES, Louis Carabiniers
The soldier with the surname of DESMARATES is cited by Pelletier as Louis DESMARATES, while the other compilers cite

only the surname. The person as cited by Pelletier whom the writer located in the records was Louis George DEMARATES [DESMARATES?] who had made a land claim of thirty arpents in the Côte Blanche area in Attakapas, based on a land grant signed by Govenor MIRO during the Spanish period. In the New Orleans area, there were several persons with the surname during the period. They were Charles DESMARATES BAUDOUIN who was receiving his mail at the post office in 1816, and an Auguste DESMARE living in New Orleans in 1820. I-A, lix; I-D, 7; I-E, 35, 36; III-H, 60; III-J, 9; VI-Ab, 127; VIII-B, June 26, 1813; August 30, 1816.

DESONGES, Jean Baptiste [See DESOUGE, J. B.]   Dragoons
The soldier with the surname of DESONGES in the compilation is cited by Pelletier as Jean Baptiste DESANGES, while the other compilers do not cite him as having served in any unit during the war. The census of 1820 lists a J. B. DESONGES who was a resident of New Orleans living in the suburb Marigny, but the writer believes that it may be a misspelling for the surname of DESOUGE, which is cited by both Casey and Pierson. I-D, 9; III-J, 9.

DESOUGE [See DeFOURGE, Jean Baptiste]

DESPORTEL (DESPORTES), Jean Baptiste   Dragoons*
Jean Baptiste DESPORTES lived in New Orleans. He was married to Catherine LACOSTE, from which union several children were born. He received a state pension for service rendered during the war. He died between 1815-1816, for shortly thereafter correspondence was addressed only to his widow. I-A, lx; I-D, 10; I-E, 36; VI-Gf, 90; VI-Gu, 247; VII-B, 61; VIII-B, August 2, 1816.

DESPREZ, Sylvain   Dragoons*
Sylvain DESPREZ is cited by Pelletier as having served in the Dragoons, but the writer was unable to locate him either in the records of people living during the period or cited by other com-

pilers as having served during the war. The only person whom the writer located with the surname was a Madame DUBOURG CLOUET DESPRES who was receiving her correspondence at the post office in New Orleans in 1816. It is also possible that she may have been related to the soldier cited, but the writer was unable to verify it. I-D, 8; VIII-B, September 13, 1816.

DESPUIS (DUPUY) Dragoons
The soldier with the surname of DESPUIS in the appendix compilation is cited by Pierson as DUPUY. The writer was unable to identify the soldier because the compilers cite about twenty people with the surname of DUPUY or DUPUIS who served during the war. I-D, 41.

DESTOUCHE (DESTOUCHES), Marin Dragoons
Marin DESTOUCHES was a baker who lived in New Orleans. He was in a partnership with Dame CHANCEREL in 1813, but later dissolved the partnership. Marin was an average baker, for he usually utilized about ten barrels of flour per month, in comparison to Philip LANAUX, who averaged about thirty-four barrels per month. I-A, lx; I-D, 8; I-E, 36; VIII-B, January 13, 1813; February 10, 1813.

DESVIGNES, Jean Sergeant Carabiniers
Jean DESVIGNES was born in 1785-1786, the son of Jacques DESVIGNES. Jean lived in New Orleans with his father, a merchant, at 10 Public Place [Jackson Square], but later moved to 10 St. Peter St. In 1816 he sold a lot located on Hospital St. [Governor Nicholls], which formerly belonged to Monsieur THIERY. Jean found a gold watch in Jackson Square, and attempted to return it to its rightful owner by placing a notice in the newspaper. Jean died on August 27, 1816, at the age of thirty, and his father, Jacques, on August 25, 1825, at the age of seventy-six. I-A, lix; I-D, 5; I-E, 36; II-A; III-A, 22; III-D, 18; VIII-B, July 28, 1813; February 5, 1816; April 15, 1816; June 17, 1816; August 30, 1816.

(61)

DETORRES, F. [Fernando]   Carabiniers*
Pierson cites the soldier as F. DETORRES, while Casey cites him or another soldier with the surname of DEFORES. The writer was unable to locate anyone in the records with the surname of DEFORES, but located a Fernando DETORRES who may have been the soldier cited by Pierson. Fernando was a native of the Iberian Peninsula. He lived in New Orleans where he owned a grocery store on Old Levée, and two slaves named Marie Antoinette and Valentin. The writer was unable to determine when the soldier died. I-A, lix; I-E, 36; II-A; II-B.

DETOUR, Michel   Carabiniers
The soldier with the surname of DETOUR in the compilation in the appendix is cited by Pelletier as Michel DETOUR, while the other compilers do not cite him as having served during the war. The writer was unable to locate anyone as cited by Pelletier in the records, and the only persons whom he located were a ship captain named DUTOUR who lived in New Orleans or vicinity in 1813, and a DETOUR DESTOCHAN who lived in Orleans Parish in 1820, and an A. B. DUTOUR, who may have been the one cited as a ship captain, living at 143 Mandeville St. in New Orleans in 1834. I-D, 6; III-H, 72; III-J, 9; VIII-B, February 3, 1813.

DEVAUT (DEVAUD)   Musician   Battalion
Casey, Pierson, and the original payroll sheet cite a person with the surname of DEVAUT [DEVAUD?] as one of the musicians who served under PLAUCHE. The writer was unable to verify the identity of the musician for having been unable to locate his first name or initial. The only persons with similar surnames whom he located in the records of people living during the period were an N. DEVANT who was a resident of Orleans Parish in 1820, an Amand DEVEAU who lived at 268 Dauphine St. in New Orleans in 1834, and a Richard DEVAUD, who had an infant son who died in New Orleans in 1849. I-A, lix; I-Bf; I-E, 36; II-B; III-H, 61; III-J, 9.

(62)

DEVIZE (DEVEZE), Ferdinand   Carabiniers
The soldier with the surname of DEVIZE in the compilation in the appendix is cited by Pelletier as Ferdinand DEVIZE, while Casey and Pierson cite a soldier with the name of N. DENESSE as having served in the Carabiniers. Pierson also cites a soldier with the name of Jean DEVEZE who served as a 1st lieutenant under Captain LAGAN. The writer was unable to locate the soldier as cited by Pelletier or Casey. The only persons with similar surnames whom he located in the records were Jean DEVEZE who lived or visited New Orleans often, for he was receiving his correspondence at the post office in 1816, and Raymond DEVEZE who was a physician living on Royal St. in New Orleans in 1826. I-A, lix; I-D, 7; I-E, 36,37; III-E, 10; III-F; V-Be, 118; VIII-B, January 10, 1816; June 11, 1817.

DICHARRY (DUCHARRY), Antoine   Francs*
Antoine DICHARRY (DUCHARRY) is cited by Pelletier as a soldier who served in the Francs, while the other compilers cite only a Paul DECARY, who originally signed his name as DEQUARY, as having served in the 2nd Battalion under PEIRE. The writer was unable to locate anyone as cited above in the records, and the only person with a similar surname was a DUCHARRY who was one of the three partners in a business enterprise with Bernard DUCHAMP and one named KENNEDY. I-D, 12; I-E, 34; III-E, 10.

DOBBS, Hector   Corporal   Blues
The soldier cited as R. DOBBS in the compilation in the appendix is listed by Pelletier as Ralph DOBBS, while Casey and Pierson cite him as Hector DOBBS and as a corporal rather then a private. The writer was unable to locate anyone in the records as cited by Pelletier, but located in 1807 an H. DOBBS who was living in New Orleans at 40 Chartres St. In 1809 there was a listing for a DOBBS who was a barber residing at 3 Bourbon St., and between 1811-1832, the listing appears for a Henry M. DOBBS who was a watch maker in New Orleans, as well as president of the New

Orleans Mechanical Society. In 1817 correspondence was arriving at the post office for an M. Hector DOBBS, which may have been the same person. The only other reference to a DOBBS was in the census of 1830 which lists a Henry H. DOBBS as a resident of West Feliciana Parish. I-A, lix; I-D, 13; I-E, 37; III-B, 78; III-C, 212; III-D, 16; III-E, 10; III-F; III-G, 210; III-K, 14; VI-Dc, February 27, 1815; VIII-B, May 14, 1817.

DOMINGON, Hilaire J.   Carabiniers*
Hilaire J. DOMINGON is cited only by Pelletier as having served in the Carabiniers, while the other compilers do not cite any one with the surname, except a José DOMINGO who served in the regiment under BAKER.
Hilaire was a constable for the city of New Orleans in 1811, and later opened an auction business at 25 Magazine St., but soon thereafter moved it to St. Louis Street, while his residence was located on Rail Road [St.]. He entered into a business partnership with a Monsieur DUCAYET, another veteran of the war. I-D, 6; I-E, 38; III-E, 38; III-F; III-H, 63; III-J, 10; III-K, 14; VIII-A, September 4, 1827; VIII-B, March 21, 1811; November 15, 1813; February 5, 1816.

DOMINGUE (DOMINGUEZ), Manuel   Plauche*
Manuel DOMINGUE (DOMINGUEZ) is cited only by Pierson as having served under PLAUCHE, but he also cites a second soldier with the same name who served in the 7th Regiment under LeBEUF. The writer located three persons with the name of Manuel DOMINGUEZ who lived in New Orleans, but they all had died before 1814. The only other person who may have been the soldier who was living during the period was a Manuel [Emanuel] DOMINGUEZ who was a resident of Assumption Parish between 1820-1830. I-E, 38; III-J, 10; III-K, 14.

DORIOCOURT [See DURICON, Pierre]

(64)

DOUCE, Auguste Carabiniers*
Auguste DOUCE was born in 1785, the son of Nicolas DOUCE and Célestine BLOUDEAU. Auguste was married to Marie Eléonore MIOTON, from which union several children were born. One of the children was named Françoise Clémence who was born on December 25, 1810. Auguste was a joiner and cabinet maker living in New Orleans on Royal St. He was a member and officer of several Masonic Lodges and was president of various chapters. He continued his military career in the militia, for by 1824 he was a captain of the *Tirailleurs Louisianais* in the 2nd Battalion of the Louisiana Legion, and later received a state pension for his military service during the war and after. He died on May 10, 1835. I-A, lix; I-D, 7; I-E, 38; II-B; III-F; III-G, 59, 218; III-H, 64, 252, 254; VII-Da, 3; VIII-B, July 15, 1816; March 1, 1818.

DREUX (DREAUX), Edmond Dragoons*
Edmond DREUX (DREAUX) is cited by Pelletier has having served in the Dragoons, while Pierson cites only a Gentilly and Guy DREAUX as having served in the 3rd Regiment under DeLARONDE and the 2nd Regiment under CAVELIER respectively. An Armand DREAUX received a state pension for service rendered during the war, but the writer was unable to determine which of those cited may have been Armand. Edmond died in New Orleans in 1817 or 1818, for an inventory of his succession was opened in probate court in 1818. I-D, 10; I-E, 39; V-Be, 115; VIII-Da, 3.

DREUX (DREAUX), Jules [See DREUX, Edmond] Dragoons*
Jules DREUX (DREAUX) is cited only by Pelletier as having served in the Dragoons. Jules DREAUX was born in 1789, the son of Guy DREAUX and Genevieve TRUDEAU. Jules lived in the vicinity of New Orleans and died on December 13, 1815, at the age of twenty-six, and his testamentary executor was Francis DREAUX. I-D, 10; I-E, 39; II-A; IV-Be, 113; VIII-B, February 26, 1816.

DROUET [See DOUCE, Auguste]   Carabiniers
The soldier with the surname of DROUET cited in the compilation in the appendix is not listed by any of the other compilers as having served under PLAUCHE. Although there were several soldiers with the surname who served in other units, the writer suspects that the soldier cited as DROUET under PLAUCHE may have been Auguste DOUCE who was cited by all the other compilers, except in the compliation in the appendix. There were several persons with the surname of DROUET living during the period in New Orleans and other areas. In the New Orleans area there were a Jean Baptiste DROUET (alias CADET), who was married to Marie Céleste SINDOS, and who claimed, in conjunction with Edmund BROUET, who was most probably his brother, three arpents of land from the federal government; an Ursain DROUET who was a resident of St. Tammany Parish in 1820. I-E, 39; II-A; III-E, 10; III-G, 59; III-K, 10; VI-Ab, 582.

DROUILLARD, Louis   Chasseurs*
Louis DROUILLARD is cited only by Pelletier as a soldier in the Chasseurs, while Pierson and other compilers cite a Pierre DROUILLARD as a sergeant under Captain SONGY. The writer was unable to locate any of the persons cited above in the records, and the only ones whom he located living during the period were Jean Vincent DROUILLARD, who was a commission merchant in New Orleans and died between 1815-1816; an V. A. DROUILLARD, a druggist, and an B. S. DROUILLARD who lived in New Orleans in 1834. I-D, 16; I-E, 39; III-G, 59; III-H, 73; V-Be, 115; VIII-B, July 31, 1811; January 6, 1813; November 1, 1816.

DUBANOIS (DABNOUR), Hypolite FORT   Francs
Hypolite FORT DABNOUR was born in 1792, a native of St. Domingue [Haiti]. He lived in New Orleans with various members of his family. He died on December 21, 1832, at the age of forty. I-A, lx; I-E, 31, II-A; VII-Bf, 233.

DUBIGNON, Louis [Jean]   Corporal   Dragoons
The soldier with the surname of DUBIGNON in the compilation in the appendix is cited by Pelletier as Louis DUBIGNON, while Casey and Pierson cite only the surname. The writer was unable to locate in the records anyone as cited by Pelletier, and the only person who was of age during the period whom he located was Jean DUBIGNON. It is possible that Louis and Jean may have been the same person, but the writer was unable to verify it.

Jean DUBIGNON was born in Normandie, France, the son of Francois DUBIGNON and Marie Francoise DEVEAU. Jean was married to Marguerite ADAM, widow WILPOLES, from which union several children were born. Jean was a goldsmith living in New Orleans at 207 Camp St., on the corner of Camp and Julia streets. He died on September 24, 1841. I-A, lx; I-D, 8; I-E, 39; II-A; III-D, 16; III-E, 10; III-H, 65; III-J, 10; IV-D, 31.

DUBOIS, Charles   Bass Drummer   Battalion*
Charles DUBOIS is cited only by Pelletier as the bass drummer in the battalion under PLAUCHE, while the other compilers do not cite anyone with the name as having served during the war, and the only one they cite who was the chief of drummers and musician with a similar surname is DARBOIS.

The writer located two persons living during the period with the name of Charles DUBOIS, but was unable to determine which of the two may have been the musician cited by Pelletier. The first was Charles Auguste DUBOIS who lived in New Orleans and died in 1818 or 1819, for an inventory of his estate was opened in probate court in 1819. The second was Charles DUBOIS who was a baker living at 54 Music St. in New Orleans in 1834. I-A, lix; I-Bf; I-E, 32; I-D, 5; III-H, 65; V-Be, 117.

DUBOIS, Francois   Dragoons*
Although the writer located two persons with the name of Francois DUBOIS living outside of New Orleans, one in Lafourche in 1820

and the other in Terrebonne in 1830, he also located two others with the same name living in New Orleans during the period. Of those living in New Orleans, the first was François DUBOIS who was born in Toulouse, France, and died on February 26, 1820, at the age of twenty-two; and the second was a watch maker living at 137 St. Peter Street in 1834, who died on October 14, 1874. One of the two persons cited was married to Josephine REZIO [REGGIO?], but the writer was unable to verify to which of the two. I-A, lx; II-A; III-H, 65; III-J, 10; III-K, 15.

DUBOIS, Pierre L. Dragoons*
Pelletier cites the name of the soldier in the Dragoons as Pierre L. DUBOIS, while Casey and Pierson cite only the surname. Pierson, in addition to the soldier in the Dragoons he cites, a Pierre DUBOIS who served in the 5th Regiment under LABRANCHE.

The writer was able to locate only one person with the name of Pierre DUBOIS who lived in New Orleans in 1822, for a child of his died in that year, and by 1830, the census lists only a Pierre W. DUBOIS as a resident of New Orleans. Most probably he was the same Pierre whose child died in 1822. The only other Pierre whom the writer located outside of New Orleans was the one who claimed from the federal government twelve arpents of land on the River Teche in the Attakapas area in the 1830's. It is possible that he may have been the same person who was living in New Orleans earlier, but the writer was unable to verify it. I-A, lx; I-D, 8; I-E, 39; II-A; III-K, 15; VI-Ab, 126.

DUBUC, Jean Dragoons*
The original muster roll and Pierson cite only the surname DUBUC as the soldier in the Dragoons, while Pelletier cites him as J. L. DUBUC and DeVerges cites him as Jean DUBUC. The writer was able to locate in the records only a Jean François DUBUC who lived in New Orleans. He was a native of Gaudens, France, and son of Bertrand DUBUC and Jeanne Marie ST. MARTORY. Jean was mar-

ried to Maria Joseph [Josepha?] DUCRON. He died on May 29, 1833, and his widow went to live at 42 Old Levée in the same household as Joseph DUBUC, a tinsmith, and Lucien DUBUC, an accountant, who most probably were her children, but the writer was unable to verify it. I-Bd; I-D, 9; I-E, 39; II-A; III-H, xxii, 65; III-J, 10; IX-G, 63.

DUCAYET, J. [Joachim Frederico]   Carabiniers
The soldier with the surname of DUCAYET in the appendix compilation is cited by Pelletier as J. B. DUCAYET and by Casey as Fs. [?] DUCAYET. In examining the original payroll and muster, as well as the Andrew JACKSON Papers, the writer located that the soldier who served in the Carabiniers and the one who served in the Chasseurs both signed their names as J. DUCAYET. In the records for the period, the writer located only two persons with the surname of DUCAYET who were of age. Most probably they were the soldiers cited, but the writer was unable to determine which of the two was the corporal and which was the private.

Joachim Frederico DUCAYET was born in 1791 in Port-Au-Prince, St. Domingue [Haiti], the son of Etienne Victor DUCAYET and Jeanne Adélaide JOUANEL. Either Joachim or his brother, Jean Marie, signed the petition addressed to General Andrew JACKSON asking him to spare the lives of the two soldiers with the surnames of HARDEN and BRUMFIELD, who had been sentenced to death for having been absent during the campaign at Chef Menteur. Joachim died in New Orleans on October 23, 1819, at the age of twenty-eight. I-A, lix; I-Ba; I-D, 6; I-E, 39; II-A; VI-Dc, February 27, 1815.

DUCAYET, Joseph [See DUCAYET, Joachim] Corporal Chasseurs
Jean Marie Joseph DUCAYET was born on April 5, 1788, in St. Domingue [Haiti], the son of Etienne Victor DUCAYET and **Jeanne Adelaide JOUANEL. Joseph [as he preferred to be called** rather than Jean Marie] was married to Flora Catherine RITTIER, from which union several children were born. Some of their names

were César, Philip, Pierre, Remi, Etienne, and Urten Frederico. Joseph was a merchant in New Orleans where he also owned an auctioneering business, which was located on Magazine St. He established a business partnership with Hilaire DOMINGON, but later dissolved it. Joseph died on February 27, 1828. I-A, lxi; I-Be; I-D, 15; I-E, 39; II-A; III-E, 10; III-F; III-H, 66; IV-D, 35; V-Be. 118; VI-Dc, February 27, 1815; VIII-A, September 4, 1827.

DUCHAMP, Bernard Chasseurs
Bernard DUCHAMP was born in 1790, a native of Bordeaux, France. He was married to Marie Théodore Basilice PEDESCLAUX [PITTICLAUX], widow TANGUY. Bernard was a merchant living in New Orleans on Toulouse St., and had established a three-way partnership with Antoine DUCHARRY and one named KENNEDY, but later DUCHARRY left the partnership. Bernard was also one of the directors and president of the Louisiana State Bank and was a member and officer of various Masonic Lodges such as treasurer of the *W. Lodge Triple Bienfaissance.* He died on November 7, 1832. I-A, lxi; I-E, 39; II-A; III-E, 10; III-F; III-H, 60, 198; V-Be, 120; IX-G, 38.

DUCHAMPT (DUCHAMP), Charles Chasseurs
Charles DUCHAMP was born in 1784-1785, a native of Bordeaux, France, and son of Pierre DUCHAMP and Marie ESTEVE. Charles was a shoemaker specializing in women's shoes who lived in New Orleans in a house located on the corner of Toulouse and Bourbon Streets. He died on March 15, 1827. I-A, lxi; I-E, 39; II-A; III-D, 17; III-E, 10; III-F.

DUCHARRY [See DICHARRY, Antoine]

DUCOIN (DUCOING), François Dragoons
François DUCOING was married to Catherine VERRETE (VERRET), from which union several children were born. François was wounded on January 1, 1815, from which time he was awarded a state pension.

He was a tinsmith in partnership with one named Monsieur DUBRIE, living in New Orleans in 1811 on Custom House St. In the 1820's, François was cited as a store keeper at 105 Tchoupitoulas St., but by 1834 he was employed as a machinist at the LEEDS Foundry. It is possible that the store keeper and the machinist may have been two different persons with the same name, but the writer was unable to verify it. Bernard died on June 17, 1874. I-A, lx; I-D, 8; I-E, 39; II-B; III-D, 16; III-E, 10; III-F; III-G, 60; III-H, 64; VI-Ge, 20-22; VI-Gh, 24; VI-Gu, 27; VII-Da, 3;VIII-B, August 2, 1816.

DUFILHO, H. [Jr.] Musician Battalion
The musician with the surname of DUFILHO in the appendix compilation is cited by Pelletier as H. DUFILHO, while the other compilers cite him as DUFILHO, Jr. The only other soldier with the surname cited by Pierson as having served during the war was Louis DUFILHO who served under LABRANCHE.

The only reference the writer located on H. DUFILHO was that he lived in New Orleans near the new Coffee-Exchange, and in 1810 he was the host to Jean Baptiste FAGET, another musician, who placed a notice in the newspaper that he was establishing a business as a commission merchant. The other soldier cited as Louis DUFILHO, may have been the same as H. DUFILHO, but the writer was unable to verify it. There were two persons living in New Orleans and vicinity with the same name, a Louis DUFILHO [Sr.] who was married to Délphine MARMILLON, and a Louis Joseph DUFILHO [Jr.], who was married to Adèle BECNEL, and was a druggist living in New Orleans. I-A, lix; I-D, 5; I-E, 39; II-A; III-A, 22; III-C, 214; III-D, 17; III-E, 10; III-F; III-H, 251; IV-B, 159; VIII-A, September 8, 1827; VIII-B, August 15, 1810; June 29, 1818.

DUFOUCHARD [See DeGRUY, DUFOUCHARD]

DUHIGS (O'DUHIGG), Louis [O.] Dragoons*
Pelletier cites a Louis O. DUHIGS, which should have been Louis O'DUHIGG, as having served in the Dragoons, while Pierson and

other compilers cite only one person with the surname of O'DUHIGG as having served during the war, but in the 4th Regiment under MORGAN. The writer was unable to locate anyone in the records as cited by Pelletier, but found several persons with the surname living during the period who may have been one of the soldiers cited. The first was a François O'DUHIGG who was appointed a captain of the 3rd Regiment of the Territorial Militia in 1806. The second was Eloy O'DUHIGG who lived in New Orleans and died in 1821, and the third was one surnamed only O'DUHIGG, who could have been either François or Louis, who was a cotton broker living in New Orleans in 1824 at 15 St. Louis Street. I-D, 10; I-E, 90; III-F; III-H, 157; B-Bo, 183; VI-Ca, 634.

DUHULQUOD [See DULCOT, Pierre Joseph]

DUHY, Charles W.   Chasseurs
Charles W. DUHY was a printer and one of the editors of the Louisiana *Gazette*. He lived in New Orleans at 17 Bienville St. in 1822. During the war his skills as a printer were needed often, thus he usually was excused from drills and sent to work in the office of the printer LECLERC. Charles was living in New Orleans between 1811-1822, but the writer was unable to determine what happened to him after those dates. I-A, lxi; I-Be; I-D, 15; I-E, 40; III-E, 10; VIII-B, September 2, 1811; November 15, 1813.

DULCOT (DUHULQUOD), [Pierre Joseph]   3rd Lt. Dragoons
The soldier with the surname of DULCOT (DUHULQUOD) in the compilation in the appendix is cited by Pelletier as L. DUHOLQUOD, while Casey and Pierson cite only the surname. The writer was unable to locate in the records anyone as cited by Pelletier, and the only person whom he located as living during the period was Pierre Joseph DUHULQUOD. He was married to Marthe VERASSONE, from which union several children were born. He was a watch maker living in New Orleans in 1811 in a house located on the corner of Bourbon and Orleans Streets. In 1816 he sued his creditors in the court of James PITOT. In 1818 he was involved in

another litigation in the same court, and the judge rendered a decision in favor of Marthe, his wife, declaring that she was entitled to the sum of three thousand dollars and separation of all goods, property, and effects. Pierre died before 1824 and his wife in 1844. I-A, lx; I-D, 8; I-E, 40; III-D, 18; III-F; V-Bf, 230; VIII-B, March 31, 1813; September 2, 1816; September 4, 1818.

DULLIE, Jn. C.   Drummer   Battalion
Pierson cites the name of the soldier as Jn. [Jean] C. DULLIE, a private, while Pelletier cites him a Cyprien DALIA, a drummer in the Battalion under PLAUCHE. The writer was unable to locate any vital information on the soldier except a reference to a person with the surname of DULUE [DULLIE? DALIA?] who was a resident of Orleans Parish in 1830. I-D, 5; I-E, 40; III-K, 15.

DUMINY [See CADION, Christophe DUMINY]

DUPERON (DUPERRON), Jean   Dragoons
The soldier with the surname of DUPERRON is cited by Pelletier as J. L. DUPERRON, while Casey and Pierson cite him only with the surname. In addition to the DUPERRON who served under PLAUCHE, Pierson cites a Louis DUPERRON who served in the Regiment under DECLOUET.
The writer located several persons living in New Orleans during the period with the name of Jean DUPERRON, but was not able to determine which of them may have been the soldier in the Dragoons. Jean DUPERRON was wounded on January 1, 1815, and shortly thereafter received a state pension for service rendered during the war. Of those persons living in New Orleans with the name of Jean DUPERRON, the first was John L. DUPERRON [Jr.] who was a teacher of languages and dancing in New Orleans. He lived at 22 St. Peter St. He was also an amateur actor, for in 1810 he performed the role of the "savage" in one of the theatres in New Orleans. The second was a Jean DUPERRON [Jr.], who may have been the same person, and was a broker living at 53 St. Ann Street in 1822; and the third was Jean DUPERRON [Sr.]

who owned a billiard parlor in 1811 at 10 Bourbon St. I-A, lx; I-D, 8; I-E, 40; II-A; II-B; III-A, 8; III-D, 17; III-E, 10; III-G, 62; III-H, 69; VI-Gh; 24; VIII-B, March 21, 1810; November 13, 1811; February 1, 1813; January 3, 1816.

DUPLANTIER Dragoons

The soldier with the surname of DUPLANTIER in the compilation in the appendix is cited by Casey as P. [?] DUPLANTIER and by Pelletier as Théodore DUPLANTIER. The writer was unable to locate anyone in the records as cited above, and although there were several persons with the surname living in the parishes of St. James, East Baton Rouge, St. Landry and other parishes, the writer located only one person with the name of Jean B. DUPLANTIER living in New Orleans during the period. He was the proprietor of a store in which sold mineral water located at 2 St. Louis Street in 1822. I-A, lx; I-D, 9; I-E, 40; III-E, 10; III-J, 10; III-K, 15.

DUPLESSIS, Elie AMIRAUD [See DUPLESSIS, F.] Carabiniers*

Casey cites an E. A. DUPLESSIS and Pierson an A. DUPLESSIS as having served in the Carabiniers. Pelletier and the compilation in the appendix cite an F. or François DUPLESSIS as the soldier in the Carabiniers, while Pierson and other compilers cite François DUPLESSIS as having served in the 1st Regiment under DEJAN. It is possible that both Elie and François DUPLESSIS may have served under PLAUCHE, for at one point many soldiers were transferring at an alarming rate to various other units, that Governor Claiborne had to issue orders to stop it, before the units became ineffective.

Elie AMIRAUD DUPLESSIS was born in 1788, the son of François AMIRAUD DUPLESSIS [Jr.] and Marie Anne ROUSSEAU. Elie and his father were merchants and businessmen, for in 1821 they received permission from the state legislature to establish a ferry service between Bayou Plaquemines in Iberville Parish and Bayou Cypre-Mort in the Attakapas. Elie died in New Orleans on October

15, 1825, at the age of thirty-seven. I-A, lix; I-D, 40; II-A; VI-Gc, 20.

DUPLESSIS, François AMIRAUD [Jr.]   Carabiniers
François AMIRAUD DUPLESSIS [Jr.] was born in 1752-1753, the son of François AMIRAUD DUPLESSIS [Sr.] and MARIE SAULIER. François [Jr.] was married to Marie Anne ROUSSEAU, from which union several children were born. Three of them were Elie, who died in 1825; Marie Anne, who was married to Louis PEPE and then remarried to Jean Claude GRILLON; and José, who was confirmed in the St. Louis Cathedral in 1800. François [Jr.] had served in the military during the Spanish period, having attained the rank of 2nd Lt. in 1792, and the rank of 1st Lt. in the Territorial Militia in 1809. He was a gentleman, merchant, businessman, and entrepreneur living in New Orleans on Conti St. in 1805, but later moved to 18 Toulouse by 1822. His business activities were numerous, for he was a commission merchant in partnership with John K. WEST, one of the managers of the Orleans Theatre, and one of the directors of the Bank of Louisiana. He was also active in politics, for he served as a councilman representing the 2nd Ward of New Orleans, representative of the Legislative Council, and treasurer of the Territorial government. He died on May 27, 1832, at the age of eighty. I-D, 6; II-A; III-A, 22; III-B, 78; III-C, 162, 199, 201; III-D, 57; III-E, 11; IV-B, 99; V-Be, 120; VI-Ca, 11; VI-Gc, 20; VII-A, 174; VIII-B, February 16, 1816; March 15, 1816; IX-G, 39; IX-J, 184.

DURAND [See DURAND, Jean Maurice]   Dragoons
The compilation in the appendix cites two soldiers with the surname of DURAND, one who is a junior, while Casey cites three soldiers with the surname, of whom one is cited a M. DURAND. Pelletier cites the name of the two soldiers under PLAUCHE as J. J. and Célestin DURAND, but the writer was unable to locate them in the records. The only one whom the writer was able to identify was Jean Maurice DURAND, because there were too many people living during the period with the surname of DURAND

and many of them call themselves only Jean DURAND. I-A, lx; I-D, 9-10; I-E, 41.

DURAND, Jean Maurice Dragoons
Jean Maurice DURAND was a native of Nantes, France. He was a brass founder living in New Orleans at 167 Levée [St.]. He died on September 12, 1829. I-A, lx; I-e, 41; II-A; III-E, 41; III-F; V-Be, 119.

DUPUY, Bernard Chasseurs
Bernard DUPUY was born in 1798, a native of Gros Morne, St. Domingue [Haiti]. He was married to Adèle D. CARRE, who was born in Paris, France. Bernard was a gunsmith whose shop was located at 80 Bourbon St. in New Orleans, on the corner of Bourbon St. and Orleans St. Later he retired and was cited as a gentleman living on Main St. In 1832 he gave some slaves as gifts to Bernard Neuville DUREL and other members of the DUREL family who were related to him by marriage. Bernard died on June 23, 1845. I-A, lxi; I-D, 15; I-E, 41; II-B; III-E, 11; III-G, 63; III-H, 70; IV-D, 37; VIII-B, August 21, 1818.

DUREL, Jean Baptsite [Sr.] Carabiniers
Jean Baptiste DUREL [Sr.] was a merchant living in New Orleans on Royal St. He received a state pension for service rendered during the war. He died in New Orleans and was buried in the St. Louis Cemetery No. 2. The writer was unable to determine the identity of the soldier and provide more information, because there were several people with the name of Jean Baptiste DUREL, who were living in New Orleans during the period. Two of them were Jean Baptiste Gustave DUREL who was married to Marie Louise Coralie FORSTALL, and a Jean Baptiste Zénon DUREL, who was the son of Jean Baptiste DUREL and Clara ANDRY. I-A, lix; I-D, 7; I-E, 4l; II-B; III-A, 22; III-B, 78; III-C, 209; VII-B, 6l; VII-D, 3; IX-G, 40.

DUREL, Jean Baptiste Neuville   Carabiniers
Jean Baptiste Neuville DUREL was born in New Orleans on January 5, 1792, the son of François DUREL and Marie Manette DEJEAN. Jean Baptiste was married to Louise Eugénie DUPUY, a native of Môle St. Nicolas, St. Domingue [Haiti], from which union several children were born. Some of them were Bernard Neuville, Bernard Armand, Eugéne, Aimée, Eugénie, Armentine, and others. With so many children of school age, most probably he was the DUREL who signed the petition to General Andrew JACKSON asking for the early release from military duty of Lt. William A. AUDEBERT, a teacher who was a soldier in the 2nd Regiment under CAVELIER. Jean Baptiste was a merchant living in New Orleans on Royal St., but later moved to Main St. He was a business partner of A. L. OGER, but in 1829 dissolved the partnership. Jean Baptiste received a state pension for service rendered during the war and he died on February 26, 1841. I-A lix; I-D, 7; I-E, 41; II-A; III-F; III-G, 64; III-H, 71; V-Bf, 235, 238; VI-Da, January 21, 1815; VIII-Da, 3; VIII-A, February 25, 1829.

DURET, Joseph   Blues*
Joseph DURET is cited by both Casey and Pierson, but the writer was unable to locate any information on him. There were several persons living during the period with the surname of DURET or DURETTE in Natchitoches and St. Tammany in 1820, but none of them was Joseph DURET. I-A, lxi; I-D, 41; III-J, 11.

DURICON (DORIOCOURT), Pierre [See DURIO, Pierre]   Francs
The soldier with the surname of DURICON in the appendix compilation is cited by Pelletier as Pierre DORIOCOURT as well as in the "Roster of the Orleans Battalion." Casey and Pierson do not cite anyone with the surname as having served under PLAUCHE, but Pierson cites three soldiers with the same surname of DURIOCOURT as having served in the 4th Regiment under MORGAN. The writer was unable to locate anyone with the name of Pierre DORIOCOURT in the records of the period, and the only

persons with the surname whom he located in the vicinity of New Orleans were a François who died in 1819; an Antoine who died in 1828; and an Ursin DORIOCOURT who died in 1830. It is also possible that the soldier cited a Pierre DORIOCOURT may have been the soldier cited by Casey and Pierson as Pierre LAURENT DURIO who served in the Francs. I-D, 12; I-E, 38; I-F, 66; V-Be, 115, 118, 119.

DURIEUX [See DURU, Jean Baptiste]

DURIO, Pierre LAURENT Francs*
Pierre LAURENT (dit DURIO) lived in New Orleans in the suburb La Course in 1810. He was delinquent in paying his taxes to repair the levee, and the mayor and city council had to publish a reminder to him in the local newspaper. He drafted his will in 1824 and was cited as still living in New Orleans in 1830. He received a state pension for service rendered during the war, and after he died his wife continued to receive the pension. I-A, lx; I-Bc; I-E, 4l; III-K, 28; V-Bj, 119; VII-B, 6l; VII-Da, 3; VIII-B, November 16, 1810; May 1, 1816.

DURIVE (DURRIVE), [Pierre MARTINEAU] Blues
The soldier with the surname of DURIVE (DURRIVE) was cited only in the compilation in the appendix. The writer was able to locate only two persons living during the period with the surname, an Honoré DURRIVE who was a resident of St. John the Baptist Parish in 1820, and a Pierre MARTINEAU DURRIVE who was living in New Orleans in 1813.

Pierre MARTINEAU DURRIVE was born in 1768, a native of Bergerac, France. He was married to Marie PAUTARD (POTARD), from which union several children were born. Pierre was a merchant living in New Orleans in a house located on the corner of Bienville and Dauphine Streets. He was one of the signers of a petition addressed to General Andrew JACKSON asking for the early release from military duty of Lt. William A. AUDEBERT, a teacher who was serving in the 2nd Regiment under CAVELIER. Pierre died on August 28, 1830, at the age of sixty-one. II-A; III-G, 64; III-H, 71; III-J, 11; VI-Da, January 21, 1815; VIII-B, May 31, 1816; November 6, 1816.

DURU (DURIEUX), Jean Baptiste   Sapper   Battalion*
Jean Baptiste DURU (DURIEUX) is cited only by Pelletier as a sapper [engineering-type work] in the battalion, while Pierson cites only a person with the surname of DURHU and Casey a Pierre L. BURIAU [DURIO] in the Francs and one surnamed DUSU in the Carabiniers.

Jean Baptiste DURIEAU was born on November 3, 1747. He was married to Catherine FONTAINE, from which union several children were born. One of them was Theresa, who was married to Monsieur THESIER [TESSIER]. Jean Baptiste died in New Orleans on October 11, 1829, at the age of eighty-one. I-A, lix, lx; I-D, 4; I-E, 4l; II-A; II-B.

DUSSAC, Victorin   Dragoons*
Victorin DUSSAC is cited only by Pelletier as having served in the Dragoons, while the other compilers do not cite him as having served in any unit during the war. The writer was unable to locate any information on the soldier, and the only person with the surname whom he located in the records was a DUSSAC who lived in the vicinity of New Orleans and was a merchant in partnership with Alphonse VITRAC, another soldier who served in the Dragoons cited by Pelletier. I-D, 10; VIII-B, December 2, 1816; June 2, 1817.

DUSU (DUZU)   Carabiniers*
The soldier with the surname of DUSU (DUZU) is cited by Casey and in the original muster roll. The writer could not identify the soldier for being unable to discover his first name or initials.

(79)

The only persons whom he located in the records with similar surnames were a Jean DUSE who lived in New Orleans and died on September 10, 1824, at the age of twenty-eight, and a person with the surname of DUSIN who was one of the signers of the petition addressed to General Andrew JACKSON asking for the early dismissal from military duty of Lt. William A. AUDEBERT, a teacher in the 2nd Regiment under CAVELIER. I-A, lix; I-Ba; II-A; VI-Da, January 21, 1815.

DUVILLAS, [Charles François]   Dragoons*
Casey, Pierson, and the original muster roll cite a soldier with the surname of DUVILLAS as having served in the Dragoons. The writer was unable to identify the soldier for being unable to discover his first name or initials. The only person whom he located with the surname was a Charles François JUMONVILLE De DUVILLIAS [DUVILLAS?] who was married to Justine BAUMONT GIROUDAIS. He was in the vicinity of New Orleans or lived there for awhile, for in 1816 an infant son of his died there. I-A, lx; I-E, 41; II-A.

E

ENARD, [Etienne]   Dragoons
The soldier with the surname of ENARD cited in the compilation in the appendix as having served in the Dragoons is not cited in any other compilation. Pierson cites only one person with a similar surname, A. ESNARD, as a soldier in the 8th Regiment under MERIAM. The writer was unable to locate any information on the soldier as cited by Pierson, but located two persons with the name of Etienne ENARD and Pierre Charles ENARD living in New Orleans during the period. It is possible that one of them may have been the soldier cited as ENARD.

The first was Etienne ENARD, a carpenter in New Orleans who lived in the suburb Marigny in 1811, but later moved to Barracks St. in 1822. He was a native of France and died on November 25, 1822, at the age of fifty-six. The second was Pierre Charles ENARD, a native of Nantes, France, who died in New Orleans on February 15, 1838, at the age of seventy. Most probably they were brothers, but the writer was unable to confirm it. I-E, 43; II-A; III-D, 21; III-E, 11; III-J, 11; V-Bf, 240; VIII-B, March 2, 1818; June 29, 1818.

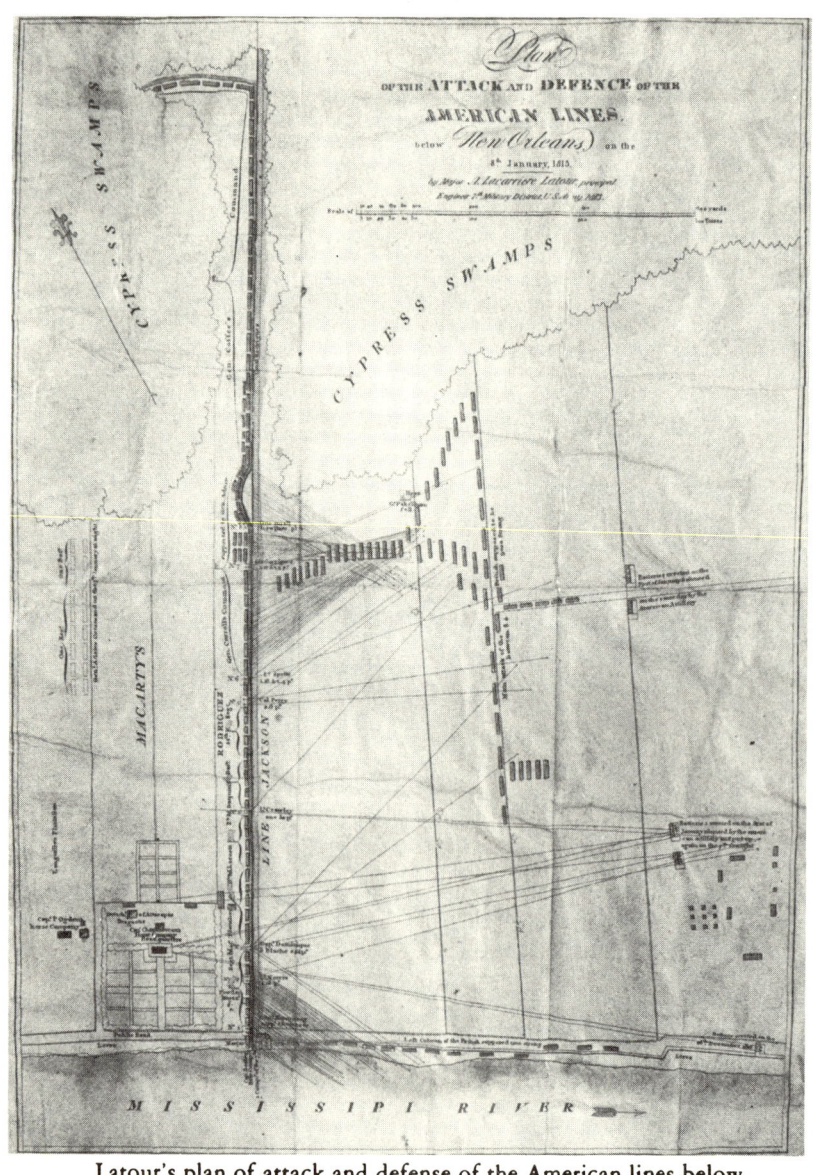

Latour's plan of attack and defense of the American lines below New Orleans on 8th January, 1815.

F

FAGOT, [See FAGOT, Jean Baptiste]   Carabiniers
The soldier with the surname of FAGOT in the compilation in the appendix is cited by Pelletier as Drousin FAGOT, while Pierson cites only the surname. Casey cites him as F. PAGOT, but the writer was unable to locate anyone as cited by Pelletier or Casey. The only other person who served during the war with the surname was Charles FAGOT, a sergeant in the 3rd Regiment under DeLARONDE. Charles was a justice of the peace in Plaquemines Parish. The only other persons whom the writer located with the surname of FAGOT in the records were Pierre FAGOT, a trader living at 92 Mandeville St., Neurise FAGOT, a turner living at 135 Victor St., and an Antoine FAGOT, a blacksmith living at 78 Spain St. in New Orleans in 1834. I-A, lix; I-D, 7; I-E, 43; III-H, 76; VIII-B, September 16, 1811; August 2, 1813.

FAGOT (FAGET), Jean   Musician   Battalion
DeVerges cites the name of the musician as Jean FAGET, while the other compilers cite him as J. B. [Jean Baptiste] FAGET. The writer was unable to positively identify the soldier for he located a Jean and Jean Baptiste FAGET living during the period.

Jean FAGET was born on July 8, 1749, in Mirande, France, the son of Jean FAGET and Françoise LAMOTHE. Jean was married to Marie NORMAND, daughter of Jean Joseph NORMAND and Louise PILIE. Jean (Jr.) died in New Orleans on December 6, 1819.

Jean Baptiste FAGET [Jr.] was married to Marguerite Antoinette LARAILLET, a native of Port-de-Paix, St. Domingue [Haiti], and daughter of Jean Charles LARAILLET and Elizabeth MORIN.

Jean Baptiste was a broker, merchant, and in the wholesale grocery business. In 1810 he opened his office as a broker in the house belonging to H. DUFILHO, another musician in New Orleans. Later Jean Baptiste moved his business to St. Louis St., while he established his residence on Main St., in the same house as the widow FAGET [most probably Marie NORMAND]. Jean Baptiste was also an officer in various Masonic Lodges, such as senior warden and president of various chapters. I-A, lix; I-D, 5; I-E, 43; II-A; III-F; III-G, 68; III-H, 255, 257; VIII-A, January 14, 1829; VIII-B, August 15, 1810; October 29, 1817.

FARGE, Maurice   Carabiniers
Maurice FARGE was born in 1792 in New Orleans, the son of Philibert FARGE and Marguerite Justin MONGET. Maurice was married twice, the first time to Marguerite OSTIN, daughter of Jean OSTIN and Marianne RIVARDE, and the second time, after the death of his first wife, to Camille BURAT [BURAS]. Maurice was a carpenter and cabinet maker living at 106 St. Claude St. in New Orleans, but moved to 40 Canal St. [near the corner of Carondelet St.]. Maurice had also been one of the signers of the petition to General Andrew JACKSON asking to spare the lives of the two soldiers named HARDEN and BRUMFIELD who had been sentenced to death for having been absent during the campaign at Chef Menteur. Maurice died on December 7, 1832, at the age of forty. I-A, lix; I-D, 7; I-E, 44; II-A; III-F; III-G, 68; VI-Dc, February 27, 1815; IX-Pa, 48.

FAUCHET [See FAUCHET, Edmond]   Musician Battalion*
The writer was unable to determine the identity of the musician with the surname of FAUCHET, for he was unable to locate his first name or initials. To complicate matters, the appendix compilation cites two musicians with the names of E. FAUCHET and one named FOUCHER, while Pelletier cites them as Edmond FAUCHET and Anthony FOUCHER. Casey and Pierson, who are usually the most accurate and reliable of the compilers, cite only the surnames as FAUCHET and FAUCHET, Jr. The writer

examined the original payroll sheet and confirms the transcriptions made by both Casey and Pierson. I-A, lix; I-Bf; I-D, 5; I-E, 44.

FAUCHET, Edmond [See FAUCHET] Musician Battalion
Edmond FAUCHET was a tailor living on Royal St. in New Orleans in 1824, but later moved his residence to Chartres St. He lived on the same street, and probably in the same house, as Joseph FAUCHET, another tailor, who most probably was related to Edmond, but the writer was unable to determine the family connection. I-D, 5; III-D, 22; III-E, 12; III-F; III-H, 77,83.

FAURE [See FORT] Chasseurs*
The writer was unable to identify the soldier with the surname of FAURE, for having been unable to locate his first name or initials. Casey, Pierson, and the original muster roll cite only the surname. Furthermore, there were four persons living during the period with the surname of FAURE, thus making it almost impossible for a definite identification of the soldier. I-A, lxi; I-Be; I-E, 44.

FAVBRE [See DAUNOY, Louis FAVBRE]

FE (FEE), Charles Francs
Charles FEE was born in France, the son of Jean FEE and Marie FERBRIER. Charles was married to Catherine LAURENT, widow of François DELATTE. Charles was an innkeeper in New Orleans at 36 Magazine St. in 1811, but later moved to Constance St., where he opened a grocery store. He was so delinquent in paying his taxes to repair the levee that the mayor and city council had to publish a reminder in the local newspaper. He died on July 10, 1827, and his wife on November 13, 1830, at the age of sixty. I-A, lx; I-D, 11; I-E, 44; II-A; III-D, 22; III-E, 12; VIII-B, November 10, 1810.

FERIET. [Louis] [See FERRER, T.] Dragoons
The soldier with the surname of FERIET is cited only in the appendix compilation. None of the other compilers cites anyone

(85)

with the surname as having served during the war, but it is possible that the soldier could have been T. FERRER cited by both Pierson and Casey as having served in the Dragoons.

The only person with the surname of FERIET whom the writer located in the records was Louis Baron de FERIET. Louis was born in 1776-1777. He lived in his plantation in Metairie in 1813, which was adjacent to the property belonging to a Monsieur ROUSSEAU. In 1822, he moved to the city of New Orleans, where he owned a rum distillery located at 289 Levée, in partnership with Monsieur SOMMEREAU. Louis was also a syndic for the lower suburbs of New Orleans. He died on May 8, 1845, at the age of sixty-nine. II-A; III-E, 12; III-F, 8; VIII-B, June 16, 1813; November 25, 1814; October 27, 1817.

FERNANDEZ, A. [Antoine]   Musician   Battalion
The writer was unable to definitely identify the musician with the name of A. or Antoine FERNANDEZ, because there were several persons with the name of Antoine or Anthony FERNANDEZ living during the period. To complicate matters, Pierson and DeVerges cite an Antoine FERNANDEZ who also served in the 2nd Regiment under CAVELIER. One of the persons with the name of Anthony FERNANDEZ received a state pension for service rendered during the war. The records indicate that there were several persons with the name of A. or Anthony or Antonio FERNANDEZ living in New Orleans and other areas during the period. The first was an A. FERNANDEZ who was an interpreter in West Florida in 1809. The second was Anthony FERNANDEZ who was a cabinet maker in partnership with Louis HOUDON. Anthony lived in New Orleans at 29 St. Ann Street in 1813. Of those persons with the name of Anthony or Antonio FERNANDEZ who died in New Orleans were Antonio FERNANDEZ who died in 1821-1822; Antonio FERNANDEZ, a native of Oviedo, Spain, who died on August 13, 1829, at the age of twenty-nine; and Anthony FERNANDEZ who died on July 10, 1873, at the age of eighty. I-A, lix; I-D, 5; I-E, 45; II-A; III-C,

205; III-G, 68; III-H, 78; V-Bg, 348; VII-Db, 42; VIII-B, July 14, 1810; November 22, 1813.

FERRAND, [J. L. ? Jean?] Dragoons
The soldier with the surname of FERRAND in the appendix compilation is cited by Pelletier as J. L. FERRAND, by Casey as Jean FERRAND, and by Pierson as Pierre FERRAND. Pierson also cites a second person under PLAUCHE with only the surname of FERRAND. The writer was unable to locate anyone with the name of Pierre FERRAND in the records, but located several people with the name of J. or Jean FERRAND living during the period in New Orleans. The first was Emmanuel Jean LAZARRE FERRANDO, a native of the Isle of Malta, who was born in 1799, and died on September 6, 1841; the second was L. J. FERRAND who was a butcher living at 41 Main St., but later moved to Dauphine St., where he opened a grocery store; and the third was a Jean FERRAND who was a merchant who in 1816 sued his creditors in civil court with the aid of his lawyer, Edward CAUCHIOX. I-A, lx; I-D, 10; I-E, 45; II-A; III-D, 23; III-G, 68; III-H, 79; VIII-B, November 6, 1816.

FERRER [See FERRERA, Jacques]

FERRER, T. [See FERIET, Louis] Dragoons*
The writer was unable to determine the identity of the soldier named T. FERRER cited by Casey and only with the surname by Pierson. It is possible that the soldier could have been cited as [Louis] FERIET in the compilation in the appendix, but the writer was unable to verify it. I-A, lx; I-E, 45.

FERRERA (FERRER), Jacques Carabiniers
The soldier with the surname of FERRERA in the appendix compilation, is cited by Pelletier as Jacques FERRERA, while Casey and Pierson cite only the surname but as FERRER. The only FERRERA whom the writer located in the records was a José FERRERA who died in New Orleans in 1832 or 1833, and a Manuel FERRERA who was living at 274 Magazine St. in New Orleans in 1834. There were also a J. FERRER who was

(87)

a merchant in partnership with E. ROUSSET in 1818 in New Orleans, and another J. FERRER, or perhaps the same one, who was in the grocery business at New Levée in 1834. I-A, lix; I-D, 6, I-E, 45; III-H, 79; V-Bg, 351; VIII-B, June 8, 1818.

FERRIER, P. [Pierre]   Dragoons*
There were two persons with the name of Pierre FERRIER living during the period in the vicinity of New Orleans, but the writer was unable to determine which of the two may have been the soldier in the Dragoons. The first was Jean Pierre [LALANDE] FERRIER, a native of Port-au-Prince, St. Domingue [Haiti], the son of Pierre FERRIER and Adélaide COUSSON. Jean Pierre was married to Aveline TEXIER DUPATY. He died on September 28, 1822, at the age of thirty-two. The second was Antoine Pierre De La FERRIER, who was married to Marguerite GAUDIN. She was a native of France, and died in New Orleans on August 8, 1825. I-A, lx; I-D, 9; I-E, 45; II-A; VIII-B, November 25, 1814.

FLAUJAC [See GARRIGUES FLAUJAC, Joseph]

FLEURY, Prosper   Dragoons*
Various members of the family with the surname of FLEURY lived in New Orleans and vicinity, but the only reference the writer located on Prosper FLEURY was that in 1810 he was the curator for the estate of the late Claude DUGAS and he was empowered by the court to sell a lot and building on Casa-Calvo St. for the sum of five hundred dollars. In 1811 there were several persons with the surname of FLEURY cited, and one with only the surname who owned a billiard parlor at 9 St. Philip Street, and by 1834 a B. P. FLEURY, who possibly could have been Prosper, was cited as a cigar maker at 383 Bourbon St. I-A, lx; I-D, 10; I-E, 45; III-D, 23, III-H, 81; VIII-B, July 30, 1810; September 3, 1810; March 14, 1817.

FONDERVIOLLE   [See CORDEVIOLLE, Etienne]

(88)

FORSTALL, Edmond J.　　　Corporal　　　Carabiniers
Edmond J. FORSTALL was born on November 17, 1794. He was married to Clara DUREL, from which union several children were born. One of them was named Mathilde. Edmond was a broker and merchant living in New Orleans. His office was located on Magazine St., while his residence was on Ursuline St., but later moved to Toulouse St. He was one of the directors of several banks such as the Louisiana State Bank, the Union Bank of Louisiana, and director of the Louisiana State [Marine and Fire] Insurance Company. He was also an officer in various Masonic Lodges such as Senior Warden of the W. Lodge Perfect Union. Later he received a state pension for service rendered during the war. He died in 1872 [November 17, 1873?] and his wife much earlier in 1824 or 1825. I-A, lix; I-D, 5; I-E, 46; II-A; II-B; III-A, 23; III-E, 13; III-F, 12, 15; III-G, 72, 198, 200, 203; III-H, 82, 237; IV-Bg, 349; VIII-B, February 14, 1818; IX-G, 45.

FORT [See FAURE]　　　Chasseurs
The soldier with the surname of FORT is cited only in the compilation in the appendix as having served in the Chasseurs. The other compilers cite four persons with the surname of FORT but as having served in other units. It is also possible that the soldier with the surname of FORT may have been the soldier cited as FAURE by the other compilers. I-E, 46-47.

FOUCHER [See FAUCHET and FAUCHET, Edmond]
　　　Musician　　　Battalion

FOUCHER, [P. Edmond? E. Pierre?]　　　Carabiniers
The soldier with the surname of FOUCHER in the Carabiniers is cited by Casey as P. E. FOUCHER, by Pelletier as P. Edmond FOUCHER, by Pierson as E. FOUCHER, and by DeVerges as E. Pierre FOUCHER. To complicate the matter of identifying the soldier, there were several persons living during the period with similar names.

E. Pierre FOUCHER, cited by DeVerges, was married to Louise METESSER. A second was Pierre Edmond FOUCHER [FOUCHE] who was born on July 17, 1796, the son of Antonio FOUCHER [Jr.] and Félicité BADON. Pierre Edmond was married to Louise Odile DESTREHAN. He was a merchant in New Orleans at 25 Conti St. He died on April 29, 1828. The third was Pierre FOUCHER, who was born on January 1, 1759, son of Antoine FOUCHER and Marguerite CARRIERE. He was a planter living at 43 Conde St. in New Orleans in 1822. He died on September 14, 1832. I-A, lix; I-D, 6; I-E, 45; II-A; III-E, 13; V-Bg, 349; VI-Ab, 581; VI-Ca, 11, 659-60; 838; VIII-B, July 18, 1810. IX-G, 49-50.

FOUCHET, Thomas [See TOUCHET, E.] Sergeant Francs
Thomas FOUCHET is cited by Casey as a sergeant in the Francs, while the compilation in the appendix cites an E. TOUCHET as a corporal, and Pelletier cites the soldier as Jean TAUCHET. The writer located a Thomas Nelson FOUCHE[T] who lived in New Orleans and received a state pension for service rendered during the war. He died on June 27, 1874. I-A, lx; I-D, 11; II-A; V-II-B, 61.

FOURCADE, Thomas Francs*
Thomas FOURCADE is cited only by Pelletier as having served in the Francs, while the other compilers do not cite him, although they cite other soldiers with the surname as having served in other units. The writer was unable to located any information on Thomas FOURCADE in the records. I-D, 11.

FOURNIER, A. B. [Alexis] Sapper Battalion*
A. B. FOURNIER is cited only by Pelletier as being a sapper [engineering-type work] under PLAUCHE, but the other compilers cite only an N. FOURNIER who served during the war in the Carabiniers. To complicate matters, the writer located a Mertile FOURNIER who received a state pension for service rendered during the war.

(90)

The only A. FOURNIER whom the writer located in the records was Alexis FOURNIER, who was born in 1788, a native of St. Maxent [-l'Ecole], France. He was married to Josephine MICHEL, from which union several children were born. One of them was Didier, who died in 1830. Alexis had a barber shop in New Orleans at 141 Chartres St., while his residence was located on Ursuline St. He died on December 26, 1848, at the age of sixty. I-A, lix; I-D, 4; I-E, 47; II-A; II-B; III-F; III-H, 84; VII-Db, 42.

FOURNIER, N. [Nicolas] Carabiniers*
N. [Nicolas] FOURNIER was from Provençal, France, and he had served under Napoleon in Egypt. He lived in New Orleans where he had established himself as a merchant dealing in glassware. He sold everything prior to the war and forwarded the money to France, but the war delayed his departure. Shortly after the war he left the country and returned to France. I-A, lix; I-E, 47; IX-Q, 239.

FOY, R. Prosper 1st Lt. and Adjutant Battalion
R. Prosper FOY [FOIX] was a sculptor, carver, marble cutter, and gilder living in New Orleans. He had two shops, one in the suburb Tremé and the other on the corner of Royal and St. Peter streets. In 1832 he moved his shop to Basin St. and later to Rampart St. He also owned a brick kiln which included seventeen slaves who helped him run it. Prosper offered to sell the kiln and slaves in 1817. He died in New Orleans, but the writer was unable to determine the date. His widow died on August 25, 1817. I-A, lix; I-D, 4; I-E, 46; II-B; III-G, 73; III-H, 84; VIII-B, June 30, 1817; October 22, 1817; July 24, 1818; August 28, 1818.

FREDERICK, Basil Francs
The soldier cited in the compilation in the appendix as B. FREDERICK, is cited by Pelletier as Bertrand FREDERICK, while Casey and the original payroll sheet cite him as Basil FREDERICK. Basil was a tailor living in New Orleans at 192 St. Ann Street in 1824, but was living on Terpischore St. in 1834. I-A, lx; I-Bc; I-D, 11; III-F; III-G, 74.

FREDERICK, Bastien Carabiniers*
Bastien FREDERICK is cited by Pelletier as having served in the Carabiniers, while Casey cites only the surname. The writer was unable to locate any information on Bastien, but suspects that the soldier may have been Ursin Célestin FREDERICK who received a state pension for service rendered during the war. Pierson cites only one soldier with the name of Ursin who served during the war, but there were an Ursin and an Ursin Célestin FREDERICK who received state pensions for service rendered during the war. Ursin Célestin was married to Eloise DUVERNAY. He was a bricklayer living in New Orleans on Terpsichore St. I-A, lix; I-E, 48; II-B; III-H, 84; VII-Db, 42.

FREDERICK, Ursin Dragoons
Ursin FREDERICK was born in New Orleans on August 1, 1792. He was a cabinet maker living in New Orleans in a house located on the corner of St. Philip and Rampart Streets, but later moved his shop to 21 Canal St., and his residence to 84 Casa-Calvo St. He received a state pension for service rendered during the war, and died on September 15, 1856. I-A, lx; I-D, 9; I-E, 48; II-B; III-E, 13; III-G, 73; III-H, 84; VII-Db, 14.

FREIDEN, J. Francs
J. FREIDEN is cited by Pelletier as Jacques FERALDIER, but the writer was unable to locate anyone as cited in the records of the period or by other compilers. I-D, 11.

FREMONT, Eustache 1st Lt. Francs
Eustache FREMONT was born in 1780, a native of Orbec, France, the son of Etienne FREMONT and Marie Elizabeth VEDIE. Eustache was married to Marguerite BENOIST, daughter of Nicolas Jean BENOIST and Hélen MONTONARY. Marguerite was also the widow of Manuel TOLEDANO. One of the children of Eustache and Marguerite was named Aurore, who died on February 12, 1819. Eustache lived in New Orleans. In 1813 he was appointed one of the commissioners to undertake an apprai-

sal of the property in order to allow the state to increase its revenues. Eustache died on June 6, 1826 and Marguerite on September 9, 1828. I-A, lx; I-D, 11; I-E, 48; II-A; V-Bg, 349; VIII-B, January 13, 1813; August 4, 1813; January 10, 1816; September 4, 1818.

FUNEL, [Jean Baptiste]   Carabiniers
The soldier with the surname of FUNEL is cited by Pelletier as Etienne FUNEL, while the other compilers cite only the surname. The writer was unable to locate anyone in the records as cited by Pelletier, and the only persons with the surname whom he located who was living during the period was Jean Baptiste Marie FUNEL, who was married to Mélanie CHAVANET. In 1818 he established a business partnership as brokers with Captain Jean HUDRY, the commanding officer of the Company of Francs. Jean Baptiste was also an inspector of peltries living at 37 Charles St. He died before 1834, because on that date, only the widow is cited in the directory. She died in 1841 or 1842, for an inventory of her estate was opened in probate court in 1842. I-A, lix; I-D, 7; I-E, 48; II-A; III-F; III-G, 87; V-Bg, 353; VIII-B, October 28, 1818.

G

GADOU, J. Louis [See GARGE, Jean] Francs*
J. Louis GADOU is cited only by Pelletier as having served in the Francs, while the other compilers do not cite anyone with the surname as having served in any unit during the war. The only person whom the writer located with a similar name was Jean GAUDEAU who lived in New Orleans and died on August 24, 1835, at the age of sixty-eight. I-D, 12; II-B.

GAIENNE [See GERVAIS, Jean]

GAILLIOT (GAILLOT), Jean Chasseurs
Jean GAILLOT was living in the vicinity of New Orleans around 1818, for correspondence was arriving for him at the post office. The only other definite reference to him was 1807 when a notice appeared in the local newspaper in New Orleans placed by Judge George KING of St. Landry Parish announcing that Jean GALIOT [GAILLIOT] who lived in New Orleans was an absent property owner in St. Landry and that he owed property taxes for 1807. By 1830, the census cites a Jean GALLOT and a J. T. GALLOT living in New Orleans, but the writer was unable to pinpoint the exact place. The writer also located that a Jean GALEAU [GAILLOT?], a native of Bordeaux, France, died in New Orleans on September 25, 1832, at the age of seventy-five, but was not able to determine whether it was the soldier cited. I-A, lxi; I-E, 49; II-A; III-K, 19; VIII-B, November 26, 1813; September 18, 1818.

GAIROIRD [See GUERONARD, Victor]

GANUCHAUX (GANUCHEAU), Séraphin   Carabiniers*
Séraphin GANUCHEAU is cited only by Pelletier as having served in the Carabiniers, while the other compilers do not cite anyone with the surname as having served during the war. The only persons whom the writer located in the records were living in New Orleans. The first was F. Joly V. GANUCHEAU who was sued in city court over the ownership of a slave named Babet in 1810. The second was Pierre F. GANUCHEAU who was a translator of languages living at 125 Grands Hommes St. He died in 1824-1825. The third was J. L. GANUCHEAU who lived on the area along Bayou St. John in 1834. I-D, 7; III-F; III-H, 87; III-J, 13; III-K, 19; V-Bh, 255; VIII-B, August 1, 1810; April 1, 1816.

GARCIA, Manuel   Carabiniers
The soldier with the surname of GARCIA cited in the appendix compilation is cited by Pelletier as Manuel GARCIA, while the other compilers cite three soldiers with the name of Manuel GARCIA but as having served in the 5th under LABRANCHE, the 11th under HICKEY, and a surgeon in the 2nd Battalion under D'AQUIN. One of the soldiers whose name was Manuel Joseph GARCIA received a state pension for service rendered during the war. Most probably the soldier who served in the Carabiniers lived in New Orleans or its immediate vicinity, and the writer located one person living there during the period. He was Manuel GARCIA, who was married to Amada MASSICOT. He lived in New Orleans as early at 1811, for that year he placed a notice in the newspaper announcing that he had lost a five hundred dollars bank note issued to the Louisiana State Bank which belonged to the captain of the Spanish schooner "Proserpine." Manuel died in New Orleans on May 28, 1828, at the age of fifty-four. I-D, 6; I-E, 49; II-B; III-I, 58; IV-B, 145; IV-C, 12, 15; V-Bh, 255; VII-D, 14; VIII-B, August 5, 1811; June 30, 1817.

GARGES, Jean   Francs*
Jean GARGES is cited as a soldier serving in the Francs by Casey, Pierson, and in the original payroll sheet. The writer was unable to definitely identify the soldier, but located several persons living

throughout Louisiana with similar surnames. The census of 1810 lists a Jean GRANGES who was a resident of Attakapas, and the census of 1820 cites him again but as Jean GRANJES. In the New Orleans area, there was a Jean GRONGES who was a native of Bordeaux, France, and who was a baker in partnership with a Monsieur LEMAIRE at 26 Conde St. in 1811. Jean died on February 24, 1823, at the age of seventy-eight. I-A, lx; I-Bc; I-E, 50; II-A; III-D, 25; III-F, 62; III-K, 20.

GARLICK, Jean**3rd Sergeant****Blues**
The soldier with the surname of GARLICK is cited by Pelletier as William GARLICK, while the other compilers do not cite him. The writer, however, located the name of a soldier with the name of John GARLICK who had signed a petition addressed to General Andrew JACKSON asking him to spare the lives of the soldiers named HARDEN and BRUMFIELD who had been sentenced to death for having been absent during the campaign at Chef Menteur.

John GARLICK lived or visited New Orleans between 1811-1813 for he was receiving his correspondence at the post office. There was a Joseph GARLICK living in New Orleans in 1820. He may have been the father or brother of John, for when Joseph died in 1823, John came to live in New Orleans and established himself as a blacksmith at 215 Magazine St. in 1824. He shortly thereafter left New Orleans and settled in the Parish of Iberia. I-D, 13; III-F; III-J, 13; III-K, 19; V-Bh, 254; VI-Dc, February 27, 1815; VIII-B, October 11, 1811; February 3, 1813.

GARRIDEL (GARIDEL), Louis [Ambroise]**Carabiniers**
Pelletier and DeVerges cite the name of the soldier as Louis GARIDEL, while Casey and Pierson cite him only as A.[Ambroise] GARIDEL. The writer located in the records an Ambroise as well as an L. A. [Louis Ambroise] GARIDEL, who most probably were father and son, but could not verify it with the records at hand.

Cerrier's print of the Battle of New Orleans on January 8, 1814 [1815].

Ambroise GARIDEL lived in New Orleans where he was a merchant and shop keeper on Levée. In 1813 he announced that he was moving his business, which was known as A. GARRIDEL & Son, to a house on St. Louis Street belonging to E. DEBON. Ambroise may have been the Juan Ambroise GARIDEL who was born in France in 1774 and died in New Orleans on February 11, 1823. By 1822, the records cite an L. A. [Louis Ambroise] GARIDEL who owned an auction business in New Orleans at 3 Conti St., while his residence was at 163 Royal St., but the writer was not able to determine whether it was the father or the son. I-A, lix; I-D, 6; I-E, 50; II-A; III-A, 23; III-B, 79; III-C, 209; III-D, 23; III-E, 13; III-H, 88; VIII-B, August 24, 1810; October 13, 1813; November 1, 1816; IX-G, 50-51.

GARRIGUES FLAUJAC, J. Secretary & Brigadier General Staff
Antoine Louis Joseph GARRIGUES FLAUJAC, a native of France, was the son of Jean Charles GARRIGUES FLAUJAC and Marie Jeanne LUBREJAEAN. Joseph, as Antoine Louis usually was addressed, was married to Marie Louise FONTENOT on August 7, 1805, from which union several children were born. One of them was Louise Irma, who was married to Louis Félix LASTRAPES. Joseph was secretary of the Staff of Governor Claiborne during the war and Brigadier General of the 4th Brigade of the 2nd Division when the militia was organized in 1805. During the battle of 8 January 1815, he was the overall commander of the 6th Battery, with Etienne BERTEL as the immediate in command. Joseph was a state senator from Opelousas in the General Assembly and served as director of the branch of the Louisiana State Bank in St. Martinville. Joseph died in Opelousas. I-A, 39, v; I-D, 4; I-E, 45; III-F, l; IV-Aa, 366; IV-Ab, 237; VI-Ab, 175, 580; IX-L, 133, 148.

GAUTHIER (GAUTIER), Jean Dragoons*
Jean GAUTHIER is cited by Casey and Pierson as having served in the Dragoons. The writer was unable to definitely determine the

identity of the soldier because he located several persons with the name living in New Orleans and vicinity during the period. The first was Juan [Jean] GAUTIER, who was a breveted captain in the Spanish service and sergeant major of the post in 1797. The second was Jean Jacques GAUTHIER, a native of France who died in New Orleans on November 17, 1867; and the third was Jean Baptiste GAUTIER who lived across the river from the city of New Orleans. I-A, lx; I-E, 50; II-A; IV-B, 73; VI-Aa, 329; VIII-A, September 8, 1827; VIII-B, September 13, 1816; October 5, 1818; IX-J, 123.

GAUTHIER, Sébastien   [See GAUTHIER, Jean]   Dragoons*
Sebastien GAUTHIER is cited only by Pelletier as having served in the Dragoons. The writer was unable to locate anyone in the records for the period nor listed by other compilers as having served during the war. It is possible that he may have been the Jean GAUTHIER cited by the other compilers who served in the Dragoons. I-D, 9.

GAUTIER (GAUTHIER), Michel [See GAUTHIER, J.] Dragoons
Michel GAUTIER (GAUTHIER) is cited only in the compilation in the appendix as a soldier in the Dragoons, but the writer was unable to locate anyone in the records with the name.

GAUTIER (GAUTHIER), Vincent?   1st Corporal   Dragoons
The soldier with the surname of GAUTIER cited in the compilation in the appendix is cited by Pelletier as Vincent GAUTIER, but the writer was unable to locate anyone with the name. It is possible that he may have been the ship captain of the "Hippolite" in 1817, but the records show only the surname. Casey cites only one soldier with the name of John GAUTHIER as having served under PLAUCHE, while Pierson cites two of them, a John as a

(99)

private, and one with only the surname as the corporal. I-A, lx; I-D, 8; I-E, 50; VIII-B, July 15, 1817.

GENATIE, Alexandre   Dragoons*
Alexandre GENATIE is cited only by Pelletier as having served in the Dragoons, while the other compilers do not cite anyone with the surname as having served in the war, and the only one with a similar name was Jean Auguste GENESTE who served in the 2nd Regiment under CAVELIER. Jean Auguste lived in New Orleans and received a state pension for service rendered during the war. The writer was unable to locate anyone as cited by Pelletier. I-D, 10; I-E, 51; III-I, 59; III-K, 19; VI-Gc, 32; VIII-B, August 14, 1816.

GENESTE [See GENATIE, Alexandre]

GENOIS, Bernard [Sr.]   Carabiniers
Bernard GENOIS [Sr.] was married to Catherine MORAN in 1789, from which union several children were born. Bernard was a merchant living in New Orleans on Levée South in the suburb St. Mary. He had been a corporal in the New Orleans Artillery Militia during the Spanish period. In 1804 he was one of the signers of a letter addressed to Congress in which he and other merchants in New Orleans protested that they were not being treated as American citizens for they were required to pay both import and export duties on their vessels, thus forcing them to retain their boats moored. The same year, Bernard was warned by Governor Claiborne that he must adhere to the ordinances issued by the city council and remove the obstruction which the road he built was causing on Bayou St. John. Bernard also owned some property in East Baton Rouge Parish in 1817, for that year a notice appeared in the local newspaper announcing that Sheriff Philemon THOMAS would confiscate the property if Bernard did not pay the back taxes owed. I-A, lix; I-E, 51; II-A; II-B, 79; III-C, 209;

III-D, 24; IV-C, 15; VI-Ca, 158; VI-Fb, 167; VI-Fe, 117; VIII-B, May 12, 1817.

GENOIS, Bernard [Jr.] Carabiniers*
Bernard GENOIS [Jr.] was the son of Bernard GENOIS and Catherine MORAN. Bernard [Jr.] was married to Azémie DORIOCOURT, from which union several children were born. Two of them were Adélaide and Bernard. Bernard [Jr.] lived in New Orleans, where he owned a brickyard located at 478 Tchoupitoulas St. [on the corner of Tchoupitoulas and Robin streets]. He died on October 26, 1821. I-A, lix; I-E, 51; II-A; III-E, 13; III-F; III-H, 89; V-Bh, 254.

GERVAIS, A. [ARNAULT? ARNOUD?] Corporal Carabiniers
The private cited in the compilation in the appendix as A. [ARNAULT or ARNOUD] GERVAIS is cited as corporal by Pierson. Casey cites only one soldier with the surname of GERVAIS, who most probably was Jean GERVAIS, as a private in the Chasseurs. Pelletier cites the name of the soldier as André GERVAIS, but the writer was unable to locate anyone with that name in the records. The only person whom the writer located who was of age during the period was Pierre GERVAIS ARNOULT who was married to Céleste Catherine LIVAUDAIS and to Rosa Hermina HALPHEN. He was a planter living in the vicinity of New Orleans on Metairie Road [Jefferson Parish]. He died on October 26, 1839. I-D, 7; I-E, 51; II-A; III-H, 90; VI-Af, 669, 904; IX-G, 63.

GERVAIS, [Jean? Joseph?] Chasseurs
The soldier with the surname of GERVAIS in the appendix compilation is cited by Pelletier as Sébastien GERVAIS, and by Casey as G. [?] GERVAIS. The writer was unable to determine the first name or initial of the soldier when he examined the original muster roll. He located two persons living during the period who may have been the soldier who served in the Chasseurs. The first was Jean GERVAIS who was born in 1795. He lived in St. Charles Parish in 1830, but later moved to New Orleans where he died on

December 31, 1879. He had received a state pension for service rendered during the war. The second was Joseph GERVAIS GAIENNE who served in the 6th Regiment under LANDRY. Joseph also received a state pension for service rendered during the war. I-A, lxi; I-Be; I-D, 16; I-E, 49; II-B; III-K, 19; VII-B, 61; VII-Db, 14.

GILLET, Christophe   Francs*
Christophe GILLET is cited by Pelletier as having served in the Francs, but the other compilers do not cite anyone with the surname as having served during the war. The writer was unable to locate in the records anyone as cited by Pelletier, but found three persons with the surname who could possibly had been the soldier. The first was Louis GILLET who was living in New Orleans in 1810, and by 1813 was staying at the City Hotel. In 1824 he moved to 27 St. Philip Street where he opened a brass foundry and metal turning shop. The second was F. GILLET who was a merchant living in New Orleans at 126 Canal St. in 1834; and the third was Edward GILLET who was a resident of Ascension Parish in 1830. I-D, 12; III-F; III-H, 90; III-I, 59; III-J, 13; VIII-B, August 2, 1813.

GILLY, Hypolite Jean Baptiste   Chasseurs
Hypolite Jean Baptiste GILLY was married to Juana PRIOR, from which union several children were born. One of them was Juan Joseph, who was born in 1811. Jean Baptiste, as Hypolite was usually addressed, was a commission merchant living in New Orleans on Gravier St. in 1822, but later moved to 51 Poydras St. He was one of the agents or manager of the Hancock College Lottery in 1818 to establish a college in Bay St. Louis, Mississippi. He was also one of the directors of the Louisiana State Bank elected by the stock holders rather than appointed by the state. He died in 1830 or 1831, for an inventory of his succession was opened in probate court in the latter year. I-A, lxi; I-D, 16; I-E, 52; II-A; III-E, 13; III-F; III-K, 20; IV-D, 10; V-Bh, 256; VIII-B, April 8, 1818; June 22, 1818.

(102)

GIOVANELLI (GIOVANOLI), Cora   Francs*
Cora GIOVANOLI is cited only by Pelletier as having served in the Francs, while the other compilers do not cite anyone with the surname as having served during the war. Cora GIOVANOLI was born in Switzerland, on April 3, 1798. He was a candy maker living in New Orleans at 170 Chartes St. He died on March 30, 1851. I-D, 12; II-B; III-H, 90; III-K, 20.

GIRAUDAU (GIRAUDEAU), Etienne   3rd Sergeant   Francs
Etienne GIRAUDEAU was married to Adélaide Délphine POMET, from which union several children were born. He was a blacksmith living in New Orleans on Rampart St. He died between 1817-1822, for after those years only his widow is listed in the records. The widow died in New Orleans on December 30, 1869. I-A, lx; I-E, 52; II-A; III-E, 13; VIII-B, April 1, 1816; June 29, 1817.

GIRAULT, Francis S.   1st Lt.   Blues
Although the GIRAULT family visited New Orleans between 1811-1818, and usually were the guests of Monsieur BLANCHET, Francis S. GIRAULT lived in Concordia Parish in 1830. The writer was unable to locate any other information on him and the rest of his family. I-A, lxi; I-D, 13; I-E, 52; III-K, 20; VIII-B, September 2, 1811; August 2, 1816; October 30, 1818.

GLAPION [See CADION, Christophe DUMINY]

GOFFORTH, William   2nd Corporal   Blues
William GOFFORTH was born in Connecticut, but later moved to Ohio. He was a physician and continued his practice when he came to Louisiana. During the war, he was usually detailed to hospital duty, where his services were more urgent. He lived in Lafourche Interior, where he owned fifty-five arpents of land. In 1808 he was appointed parish judge of Lafourche Interior, and in 1811 he served in the Constitutional Convention designed to draft the first constitution for the state of Louisiana. I-A, lxi; I-Bd; I-D, 13; I-E,

52; VI-Ab, 256; VI-Ca, 796, 835, 957; VIII-B, July 4, 1810; January 3, 1816; May 1, 1816.

GOLIS, Nicholas   Carabinier
The writer was able to locate only one person with the name of Nicholas GOLIS living during the period, but he was a Black man. It is possible that there may have been another person with the name, but the writer was unable to locate him. Nicholas (Nicolas) was married to Felicité FOUCHER, from which union several children were born. One was Desirée, who died in 1838 at the age of twenty-one. Nicholas was a merchant living in New Orleans at 24 Esplanade [Avenue] in the suburb Marigny. I-A, lix; I-D, 6; I-E, 52; II-A; III-E, 13; III-F; III-J, 14; VIII-B, September 13, 1816; December 31, 1817.

GORHAM, William T.   Sergeant: Quartermaster   Blues
The soldier cited in the compilation in the appendix as N. S. GORHAM, is cited by Pelletier as John GUERRONC, and by Casey and Pierson, who are the most accurate, as William T. GORHAM. The only information on William T. GORHAM which the writer located was that in 1830 he was a resident of St. James Parish. I-A, lxi; I-D, 13; I-E, 53; III-K, 20.

GOURSON (GOURJON), Jean [Jr.]   Chasseurs
Jean GOURJON was born in 1779, a native of Cap Français, St. Domingue [Haiti], the son of Jean Baptiste GOURJON and Dame AUGIER. Jean Baptiste [Jr.] was a merchant, commission broker, and accountant living in New Orleans on St. Louis Street. He was a business partner of one named Monsieur TANNERET. In 1808, Jean was appointed secretary-treasurer of the New Orleans Navigation Company, and in 1811 as justice of the peace for the 4th Ward of New Orleans. After the death of his father in 1821, he and his sister entered in a litigation over the ownership of some property which she claimed that her father had left her. Jean threatened to counter sue her if she did not cease making a spectacle of herself and prove that the property she claimed her father left

her was actually hers. Jean died in New Orleans on June 15, 1833.
I-A, lxi; I-D, 15; I-E, 53; II-A; III-C, 170; III-D, 23, 26; III-E, 13;
III-G, 81; V-Bh, 254, 257; VI-Ca, 789, 984; VIII-A, July 16, 1829;
VIII-B, July 18, 1810; August 5, 1811; September 30, 1811;
January 18, 1813.

GRANNIER (GRANIER) Chasseurs
Casey, Pierson and the original muster roll cite a soldier with the surname of GRANNIER (GRANIER), but the writer was unable to identify him for having been unable to locate his first name or initials. There were several persons living during the period in New Orleans and other parishes with the surname and possibly one of them could have been the soldier. In the New Orleans area there were several possibilities. First there was an Etienne GRANIER who died in 1816 and a Pierre GRANIER who died on January 6, 1836, at the age of thirty-four. It is possible that the latter may have been too young during the war. In the 1830's there were an Adolphe GRANIER who lived at 11 St. Philip Street, and a person with the surname of GRENIER [GRANIER?] who was a candy maker in partnership with Monsieur PETIE. The candy maker could have possibly been Pierre or Adolphe, but the writer was unable to determine it. Outside of the New Orleans area there were a C. GRENIER [GRANIER] who was a resident of Iberville Parish in 1810, and in 1830 there were a G. GRANIES [GRANIER?] and a Michel GRANIRE [GRANIER?] who lived in St. John the Baptist and East Baton Rouge Parishes respectively. I-A, lxi; I-E, 53; II-B; III-H, xxii, 94; III-I, 62-63; III-K, 20; V-Bh, 79.

GRASSET, Vincent? Joseph? Francs*
The soldier cited only with the surname of GRASSET by Casey, Pierson, and the original payroll, is cited by Pelletier as Vincent GROSSET. The writer was unable to locate anyone as cited by Pelletier, and the only person with the surname whom he found was Joseph GRASSET who was a trader who often visited or lived in New Orleans, for correspondence would arrive for him at the post office throughout 1816. The only other person with a similar

surname whom the writer located was a Jean GASSIOTE [GRASSET?] who was an innkeeper living in New Orleans on Bayou Road in 1811. It is possible that it may have been an incorrect spelling for the surname GRASSET, for the 1811 directory is not very accurate in spelling the surnames of the inhabitants of New Orleans. I-A, lx; I-Bc; I-D, 12; I-E, 53; III-D, 26; VIII-B, November 1, 1816.

GRAVIER, A. [See GRANNIER] Chasseurs*
The soldier with the surname of A. GRAVIER in the compilation in the appendix is cited by Pelletier as Antoine GRAVIER, while the other compilers cite only an Hambrose GRABIER [Ambroise GRAVIER?] as having served in the war in the 6th Regiment under LANDRY. It is also possible that the soldier may have been the soldier cited by Casey and Pierson as GRANNIER, but the writer was unable to verify it. Although there were several persons with the surname of GRAVIER living throughout Louisiana, the only two whom the writer located living in New Orleans were Nicholas GRAVIER, a goldsmith and maker of eyeglasses living on St. Louis St. in 1805, but moving to Bourbon St. by 1822, and a Jean GRAVIER who was a planter and owner of a brickyard on Poydras St. I-D, 16; I-E, 53; III-A, 24; III-E, 13; III-I, 62; III-J, 14; III-K, 20; V-Bh, 257; VII-Db, 14; VIII-B, September 14, 1810.

GREGOIRE, André Francs
André GREGOIRE was born in 1773-1774 in Marseille, France, the son of François and Rose GREGOIRE. André was married to Marguerite LAURENT (dit SAINTONGE) in New Orleans on November 5, 1817. He was a cordial distillerer and tobacconist living in New Orleans on Rampart St., but later moving to 303 Burgundy St. In 1818 he hired an attorney named E. CAUCHOIX and sued his creditors who were slow in paying their bills. André died on June 27, 1837. I-A, lx; I-E, 54; II-A; III-E, 13; III-H, 94; III-J, 14; VIII-B, November 25, 1814.

GRIMA, Barthelemy 2nd Lt. Carabiniers
Barthelemy GRIMA was living in New Orleans in 1822 where he owned a glass and china store on Chartres St. There was also another Barthelemy GRIMA (alias BERTHE) who was married to Marie Anne Filiosa TIMBALIER, and who owned a dry goods store on St. Anne St. in 1805. Most probably they were the mother and father of the first Barthelemy GRIMA cited, but the writer was unable to verify it. I-A, lix; I-D, 5; I-E, 54; II-A; II—B; III-A, 24; III-E, 13; III-H, 95; III-J, 14; III-K, 21; VIII-B, February 5, 1816; January 1, 1817; March 2, 1818; IX-G, 53.

GRIMDEN (GUIDON), Auguste Francs
The writer was unable to locate any vital information on Auguste GUIDON, except that he was cited as living in Orleans Parish in 1820. It is possible that he may be the one who was cited as August GULLON who lived in Avoyelles Parish in 1810. I-A, lx; I-Bc; I-D, 11; I-E, 55; III-I, 65; III-J, 14.

GUADIZ, Juan Diego 4th Sergeant Carabiniers
Juan Diego GUADIZ was a native of Cadiz, Spain. He was married to Marie Clémentine BOUQUOI, daughter of Juan Louis BOUQUOI and Felicité Perpétue BIJOT. Juan and Marie had several children, one of whose name was Juan Hipolito Thomas who was born in 1809. Juan lived in New Orleans, where he practiced his profession of barber, bleeder, and dentist. By 1822 he confined himself to only being a dentist when he moved to Chartres St. He was the curator for the minor Marguerite Carmelite CONSTANT in 1810, and he was empowered to sell some of her property. He was also an officer of various Masonic Orders, such being Captain General of the Order of Indivisible Friends of Encampment of Knight Templars. His wife died on July 16, 1842, but the writer was unable to find the date of his death; however, he is buried in the St. Louis Cemetery No. 1. I-A, lix; I-D, 5; I-E, 54; II-A; II-B; III-D, 23; III-E, 23; III-F; III-G, 83; III-H, 95; VIII-B, November 5, 1810; October 30, 1818.

GUERIN, Jean   4th Corporal   Francs
The writer was unable to determine the identity of the soldier named Jean GUERIN, for he located three persons with similar names who lived during the period in New Orleans and Plaquemines parishes. The only thing definite about Jean was that he received a state pension for service rendered during the war. There was a Jean Baptiste GUERIN, who was cited as a gentleman living on Esplanade [Avenue] in 1822. A second was Jean Jules GUERIN of Plaquemines Parish who was married to Thérèze Josephine ROSSIGNOL DESDUNES. And a third was Jean Baptiste GUERIN who was married to Henriette Catherine RAPP. It is possible that the last Jean Baptiste may have been the same one who was cited as a gentleman, but the writer was unable to verify it. I-A, lx; I-D, 11; I-E, 54; II-B; III-E, 14; III-G, 83; LV-D, 54, 84; VI-Ae, 675; VII-Db, 14; VIII-A, September 3, 1829; VIII-B, October 30, 1818.

GUERIN, [Louis]   Chasseurs
Pelletier cites the name of the soldier in the Chasseurs as Alexandre GUERIN, while Casey and Pierson cite only the surname. The writer located a person with the name of Louis GUERIN, who received a state pension for service rendered during the war. Pierson, however, does not cite a Louis, so it is probable that the soldier he and Casey cite only by the surname is Louis GUERIN. The writer, however, located two persons with the name of Louis who could have possibly been the soldier. One was Jean Louis Alexandre, a native of Cap Français, St. Domingue [Haiti], who lived in the vicinity of New Orleans or Plaquemines. He placed a notice, in 1813, offering a reward for the return of a dog he had trained and sold to a Monsieur SIGUR. Jean Louis died on January 11, 1821, and was buried in New Orleans. The other possibility was a Louis GUERIN who was cited in the census of 1830 as living in Plaquemines Parish. I-A, lxi; I-D, 16; I-E, 54; II-A; III-K, 21; VII-Db, 14; VIII-B, August 4, 1813.

GUERONARD (GAIROIRD), Victor   1st Sergeant   Chasseurs
Victor GAIROIRD lived in New Orleans at 37 Bourbon St., where he practiced his trade of cigar maker. After 1820, the writer was unable to locate Victor in the documents. I-A, lxi; I-D, 15; I-E, 49; III-D, 23; III-I, 57; III-J, 14; VIII-B, March 13, 1816; November 1, 1816; March 2, 1818.

GUESNARD (GUESNON), Etienne   5th Corporal   Carabiniers
Although the compilation in the appendix cites a person with the surname of GUESNARD as the corporal, Casey and Pierson, who are more accurate in their transcriptions, cite him as Etienne GUESNON. There was a Louis GUESNARD in the war, but he served in the 2nd Regiment under CAVELIER, and a Millien GUENARD who served under DeCLOUET.

Etienne GUESNON was born in New Orleans on March 22, 1792, the son of Jacques GUESNON and Marie Louise CARRABY. Etienne was married to Victoire Alexandrine DUCAYET, from which union several children were born. The names of three of them were Carlos, Elodie, and Marie Louise. Etienne lived in New Orleans at 276 Bayou Road. He received a state pension for services rendered during the war. He died on April 12, 1835 [1844?]. I-A, lix; I-E, 54; II-A; II-B; III-G, 83; III-H, 96; V-Bi, 261; VII-Db, 14; VIII-B, September 13, 1816; October 30, 1818.

GUESNON [See GUESNARD, Etienne]

GUIBERT, Auguste   Captain   Chasseurs
Jean Jacques Auguste GUIBERT was born in 1777-1778, a native of Port-au-Prince, St. Domingue [Haiti]. He was the son of Gabriel GUIBERT and Jeanne OSSONE De VERRIERE. Auguste was married to Marie Coralie BEAUVAIS, from which union several children were born. In 1804 Auguste was the master of the brig "Sally" which brought into New Orleans 150 slaves for sale. Eventually he settled in West Feliciana Parish. He was appointed an officer [cashier] for the branch of the Louisiana State Bank in

St. Francisville in 1818. He was also an officer of the Masonic Order *La Charité*. He died in New Orleans on March 24, 1832, at the age of fifty-four. I-A, lxi; I-D, 15; I-E, 55; II-A; II-B; II-D, 42; III-C, 96; III-J, 14; VI-Ca, 172; VIII-B, November 30, 1810; January 5, 1816; March 29, 1816; June 26, 1817; October 21, 1818.

GUICHARD, [Norbert]   Dragoons*
Casey and Pierson cite only the surname of the soldier, while Pelletier cites him as Norbert GUICHARD. The writer was unable to locate any person with the name of Norbert GUICHARD, and the only person cited was in the census of 1820 which lists a GUICHARD who lived in St. Tammany and a Jacques GUICHARRY who lived in St. James. By 1830, the only citings were for a Magloire GUECHARD [GUICHARD], who lived in St. Bernard and an M. GUICHARD who lived in New Orleans. I-A, lx; I-D, 8; I-E, 55; III-J, 14, III-K, 21.

GUICHARD, Robert [See GUICHARD, Norbert]   Francs*
Robert GUICHARD is cited only by Pelletier. Pierson and Casey cite only one person with the surname, but as having served in the Dragoons. I-D, 11.

GUIGNAN, [Edouard? Philip?]   Dragoons
Edouard GUIGNAN is cited as the soldier in the Dragoons by Pelletier, while Pierson and Casey cite only the surname. The writer was unable to locate any person living during the period with the name of Edouard GUIGNAN. Perhaps it was Edèlmore GUIGNAN, who lived in New Orleans and died in 1831, or Etienne GUIGNAND, who lived in New Orleans in 1820. The first persons with the surname whom the writer located in New Orleans from 1813-1822 were Philip GUIGNAN, a sea captain living along Bayou St. John, and married to Josephine GOISLOU, and François GUIGNAN, a merchant, who died in 1817-1818. I-A, lx; I-D, 9; I-E, 55; II-A; III-E, 14; III-J, 14; V-Bh, 253, 256; VIII-B, December 27, 1813; August 14, 1816; October 14, 1816.

(110)

GUILLEMIN [GUILLEMAIN? GUILLERMAIN?], AntoineFrancs The only information the writer was able to locate was that Antoine GUILLEMAIN was living in New Orleans in 1830. It is also possible, since the compilation in the appendix and Pelletier cite the surname as GUILLEMIN instead of GUILLERMAIN as Casey and Pierson cite, that the soldier could have been a T. A. GUILLEMIN who was married to Hortense ARNAULT, or Jean François A. GUILLEMIN, the French Consul in New Orleans, who was married to Caroline de PIERAY. I-A, lx; I-D, 12; I-E, 55; II-A; III-E, 14; III-G, 84; III-K, 21; V-Dh, 256, 257.

GUILLERMAIN [See GUILLEMIN, Antoine]

GUINDON [See GRIMDEN, Auguste]

H

HACHARD [ACART], Pierre　　　　　　　　　Chasseurs
The writer was unable to locate any information on the soldier with the surname ACART or HACHARD. The only person located with a similar name was Pierre HACHE, cited as living in Lafourche in 1810. I-A, lxi; I-F, 67; III-I, 65;

HACHER (HACKER), J. B.　　4th Corporal　　Dragoons
The compilation in the appendix cites the name of the soldier as J. B. HACHER (HACKER), and by Pelletier as J. J. HACKER. Casey and Pierson cite only the surname, but the former cites him as a private, while the latter as a corporal. The writer was unable to locate in the records any person with the name of J. B. or J. J. HACKER. The only person with a similar name the writer located was Jean Baptiste HACHA (HACHE), who lived in Lafourche and served under DeCLOUET.

The only person with the surname of HACKER the writer located as living and of age during the period was Pierre HACKER, a merchant-tailor living in New Orleans on St. Peter Street. He was born in 1781-1782, the son of Jorge HACKER and Ann DENIS. Pierre was married twice --- his first wife was Josephine MAHE DESPORTES, who died in 1821, and his second wife was Catherine LACOSTE, widow of Jean DESPORTEL and of Pierre LAPORTE. Pierre HACKER died in New Orleans on April 14, 1835. I-A, lx; I-D, 8; I-E, 56; II-B; III-E, 14; III-G, 85; III-H, 98; III-I, 65; III-K, 2; IV-D, 177; V-Bh, 362, 365.

HAGAN, John Blues
John HAGAN was a commission merchant and businessman who lived in New Orleans. His business office was located on Levée St. while his residence was on Canal St. He was a business partner with [Thomas] MELLON. John was involved in many business activities, for he was the director of the Branch Bank of the U.S. in 1824, and agent for a boat named "COOSA" which made trips from New Orleans to Bayou Sarah, Baton Rouge, and Port Hickey. Also, John was a member of the Mississippi Fire Engine Company No. 2 in 1834. I-A, lxi; I-D, 13; I-E, 56; III-D, 27; III-E, 14; III-F, 11; III-G, 85; III-H, 98; IV-D, 34; VIII-A, January 14, 1829.

HALL, James [See HULL, John] Blues*
James HALL is cited by Pelletier in the Blues, but Pierson and other compilers cite two persons with the name of James HALL under DeCLOUET and in the 12th and 13th Consolidated Regiment. James HALL was cited in the census of 1810 and of 1820 as living in Attakapas and in 1830 in Lafourche Parish. It is possible that Pelletier may have confused the soldier in the Blues with John HULL. I-D, 13; I-E, 56; III-I, 65; III-J, 15; III-K, 21.

HALLER, John Francs
The writer was unable to locate any information on John HALLER. The only reference to a person with the surname was Jacob HALLER, a mail contractor from New York, Virginia, who was to forward mail to New Orleans in 1803. I-A, lx; I-D, 12; I-E, 56; VI-Ca, 58.

HANBERT, [See DEMOURUELLE, HUMBERT] Dragoons
The soldier cited in the compilation in the appendix as HANBERT is cited by Pelletier as Cyrille HOMBERT, and by Casey as HUMBERT DEMOURUELLE. Pierson cites two soldiers with the surname of HUMBERT who served under PLAUCHE and in the 1st Regiment under DEJAN. The only persons with the surname of HUMBERT the writer located in the records were an A. HUM--

BERT who was a watch maker living at 130 Chartres St., and a Célestin HUMBERT living at 62 Toulouse St. in 1834 in New Orleans. I-A, lx; I-D, 10; I-E, 61; III-H, 107.

HARANG, Alphonse?   Chasseurs*
Alphonse HARANG is cited only by Pelletier as a soldier in the Chasseurs. Pierson and other compilers cite only two persons with the surname, an A. L. HARANG, a captain and a HARANG, [Jr.], a private, both in the 4th Regiment under MORGAN. Furthermore, the writer was unable to locate in the records an Alphonse HARANG as cited by Pelletier. I-D, 16; I-E, 57.

HARDY, Julien   Carabiniers*
Julien HARDY is cited as a soldier in the Carabiniers, while Pierson and other compilers do not cite anyone with the name of Julien HARDY as having served in any unit during the war, although there were several persons with the surname who served in other units. The only reference to a potential Julien HARDY the writer located was a J. HARDY who was a captain of a coasting vessel in 1816 in the New Orleans vicinity. It could also have stood for Joachim HARDY, who in 1822 was a seller of prepared foods [Victualler] in New Orleans. I-D, 7; I-E, 57; III-E, 14; VIII-B, August 30, 1816.

HART, Jacob   Carabiniers
Jacob HART lived in New Orleans, where he was a merchant and owner of a cotton press and warehouse on Common Street. By 1834 he had retired and was cited as a gentleman living on the corner of Rampart and Ursuline. There was also another Jacob HART [Jr.?] who lived at the same address and who was a lieutenant of the City Guard of New Orleans. It could have been his son, but the writer was not able to verify it from the records at hand. Jacob HART [Sr.] died on May 25, 1836. I-A, lix; I-D, 7; I-E, 57; II-C; III-C, 209; III-E, 14; III-F; III-G, 87; III-H, 100, 228; VIII-B, September 3, 1810; March 21, 1811; August 3, 1818.

HAYS, William H.   Corporal   Blues
William H. HAYS is cited as a corporal by both Casey and Pierson, while the compilation in the appendix and Pelletier cite him as a private. He was one of the soldiers who signed the petition to General Andrew JACKSON to spare the lives of the two soldiers named HARDEN and BRUMFIELD who were sentenced to death for having been absent during the Chef Mengaur Campaign. William died in New Orleans in 1828, and Justin WILLIAMS became the curator of his estate. I-A, lxi; I-D, 13; I-E, 58; V-Bi. 263; VI-Dc, February 27, 1815; VIII-A, February 25, 1829.

HENO, Jean Baptiste   Chasseurs*
Jean Baptiste HENO was married to Emilie DEMORUELLE, daughter of Humbert DEMORUELLE and Louise NOGUIES. Jean and Emilie had several children, two of whom were named Yrma and Pauline. Jean died in New Orleans in 1830, and his widow remarried in 1832 to Thomas BLOIS, widower of Dorothea BAYET. I-A, lxi; I-B; I-E, 58; II-A; IV-D, 30-31; V-Bh, 263.

HENO, Pierre [Jr.]   Dragoons*
Pierre HENO [Jr.] was the son of Pierre HENO [Sr.] and Marguerite TONNELLIER, daughter of Santiago TONNELLIER and Margarita LEYER. Pierre [Jr.] had several brothers and sisters, some of whom were named Ursin, who was married to Emilie BROU, and Maria Clara, who was confirmed in 1801. Pierre [Jr.] lived in New Orleans where he practiced his profession of commission merchant on Baronne St., but later moved to the corner of St. Paul and Common Streets. He did not follow the trade of butcher, which his father practiced in New Orleans. Pierre [Jr.] later received a pension for service rendered during the war. I-A, lx; I-D, 10; I-E, 58; II-A; III-D, 27; III-F; III-G, 88; III-H, 102; IV-B, 43; IV-D, 87; VII-Db, 43; VIII-B, July 14, 1813; March 14, 1817.

HENRY, Pierre Desiré Francs
The writer located two persons with the name of Pierre Desiré HENRY, but was not able to determine the family relationship. Both of the Pierres lived in New Orleans in 1822. One was a gunsmith living on Tchoupitoulas St. who later moved to St. Ann St. The other was a victualler living at 54 St. Philip Street. Furthermore, one of the Pierres was a commissary of police for the 5th ward in 1832, and he was also the agent for Louis ALLEN to issue licenses to all peddlers who travelled throughout the state selling their wares. One of the Pierres was married to Catherine Aimée LABADIE, and the other to Susana STERLINS (STERLINGS?). I-A, lx; I-D, 12; I-E, 58; II-A; III-E, 15; III-F; III-G, 89; III-H, 229; III-K, 23; VIII-A, January 10, 1828; May 15, 1828.

HIRIART, Sébastien Chasseurs
Sébastien HIRIART was discharged from service on December 30, 1814. He was from Iberville, for in 1834 he became state senator of the district. Also, he and some of his associates from the area, including Baton Rouge, such as Armand DUPLANTIER, Antoine BLANC, Thomas B. ROBERTSON, and Fulwar SKIPWITH, received permission from the legislature in 1827 to organize a corporation entitled the "Agricultural Society of Baton Rouge." I-A, lxi; I-Be; I-D, 16; I-E, 62; III-H, 223; VI-Gh, 44-48; VIII-B, May 1, 1816.

HOFFMAN, Pascal Francs
The compilation in the appendix cites two persons with the name of P. HOFFMAN as having served in the Francs, while Pelletier cites only one --- a Paul HOFFMAN. The writer was unable to locate any person with the name of Paul HOFFMAN in the records. Casey and Pierson, who are the two most reliable of the compilers, cite only one person with the surname of HOFFMAN as having served in the Francs and a Robert HUFFMAN who served in the 16th Regiment under THOMPSON. The only information the writer located on Pascal HOFFMAN was that he was

married to Eugénie LeGRAND, from which union a child named Francisco and another named José were born. Both of the children died in New Orleans on May 2, 1815 and November 24, 1816 respectively. I-A, lx; I-D, 12; I-E, 60; II-A.

HOLLANDER, Edward R. Carabiniers*
Pelletier cites Edward R. HOLLANDER as Ludoisky HOLLANDER, but the writer was unable to locate a Ludoisky or determine whether it may have been an alias or a former name for Edward R. HOLLANDER, as cited by Casey and Pierson.

Edward R. HOLLANDER was born on November 20, 1786, in Riga, Russia. He lived in New Orleans, where he was a merchant and businessman at 79 Canal St., but later moved to Custom House St. Edward was one of the directors of the Louisiana State Bank and the New Orleans Insurance Company. He was also the Russian consul in New Orleans. In addition, he was the business partner of Vincent NOLTE, who related in his memoirs that HOLLANDER was a very outspoken person and that he was going to be court martialled for being disrespectful to Major DAVEZAC, but that NOLTE had put up the bail of $2,000 on his behalf. The war ended and HOLLANDER was pardoned. HOLLANDER died on September 14, 1841. I-A, lix; I-D, 7; I-E, 60; II-B; III-F, 5, 12, 15; III-H, 105; V-Bi, 367; IX-Q, 230-31.

HUARD, J. Carabiniers*
J. HUARD is cited only by Pelletier as having served in the Carabiniers, while Casey does not cite him and Pierson does not even have him listed as having served in the war. The writer was unable to determine the identity of J. HUARD. The earliest person with the surname the writer located for the period was Louis HUARD, who lived in New Orleans on Ursuline St. in 1822. In in the 1830's the writer located a Jules J. HUARD, an accountant living on the corner of Esplanade [Avenue] and Casa-Calvo

St. in New Orleans and a J. J. HUARD, a carpenter living at 305 Dauphine St. Jules HUARD was married to Louise Hélene CHAPDU. She died in 1833. There was also a Jean SEVERIN HUARD who died in New Orleans in 1843 or 1844, for an inventory of his succession was undertaken in 1844. I-D, 5; III-E, 16; III-G, 91, 93; III-H, 106; III-K, 24; V-Bi. 364. 368.

HUBBARD, James   Blues
Casey cites the soldier as James HUBBARD, while Pelletier as Edmunds, and Pierson lists only the surname. The writer was not able to locate in the records any person with the name of Edmunds HUBBARD.

James HUBBARD lived in New Orleans. He was a captain of a boat around 1816-1817, but settled down and opened a billiard parlor at 26 Burgundy St. in 1822. Later he moved his address to Camp St. and then to Circus St. He died on May 7, 1875. I-A, lxi; I-D, 13; I-E, 61; II-B; III-E, 16; III-F; III-G, 92; III-K, 24; VIII-B, July 15, 1816; November 1, 1816; May 14, 1817.

HUDRY, Jean Claude   Captain   Francs
Jean Claude HUDRY was a merchant, broker, and entrepreneur living around New Orleans but constantly moving to other parts of the state and out of state. In 1818 he returned to New Orleans and was living on Jefferson St., but placed an announcement in the paper that he was seeking to rent an apartment in the vicinity of the public square [Jackson Square]. The same year he entered into a business partnership with Jean Baptiste Marie FUNEL as brokers, for each of the men had their own separate businesses. In 1833 the state legislature awarded HUDRY the sum of two hundred dollars, plus an additional fifty dollars pension for life for his services rendered during the war, as well as for having purchased from his own money arms, ammunition, uni-

forms and other materials for his men in the company. The same or similar claim was submitted to Congress in 1835, but Powell A. Casey, who has been researching the life of Jean HUDRY, claims that he died shortly thereafter. I-A, lx; I-D, 11; I-E, 61; VI-B, 144; VI-Gi, 113-14; VIII-B, August 6, 1813; January 21, 1818; October 28. 1818.

HUET, J. P. 4th Lt. Dragoons
Pelletier cites the name of the soldier as J. P. HUET, while Casey and Pierson cite only the surname of the soldier. The only persons with similar initials the writer located in the records was a P. [Pierre?] HUET, who died in New Orleans on September 29, 1833. Two other persons with the surname who were also of age during the period and not cited in other units were Louis HUET, a watch maker living at 223 Poydras in New Orleans in 1822, and a Charles HUET who died in New Orleans in 1845-1846. I-A, lx; I-D, 8; I-E, 61; II-A; III-E, 16; V-Bi, 369.

HUGOT, C. J. [Claude Joseph] Francs
The appendix compilation cites the name of the soldier as L. HUGOT, while Pelletier cites him as L. AGOT. Casey and Pierson cite him as C. J. HUGOT. The writer was unable to locate in the records any person with the name of L. HUGOT or L. AGOT. The only C. J. HUGOT the writer located in the records was Claude Joseph HUGOT who lived in New Orleans. He was married to Louisa Augustina CHEVALLON, from which union several children were born. Three of the children were Arcena, Carlos Francisco, and Jeanne Lucille, who was married to Victor WILTZ. A second possibility could be a Charles HUGOT who lived in St. Tammany Parish in 1820, but moved to New Orleans by 1830. I-A, lx; I-D, 11; I-E, 61; II-A; III-I, 71; III-G, 16; III-K, 24.

HULL, John   Blues
The writer located two persons with the name of John HULL in the records. One served in the Blues and the other in the 6th Regiment under LANDRY. The writer was not able to determine with absolute certainty which of the two served in which unit and whether or not they were related. The John HULL who served in the Blues most probably was the one who was living in Orleans Parish in 1820 and who was the overseer of the slave compound in New Orleans on the corner of Melpomene St. and Dryades in the 1830's. The compound was managed by John L. HALL, a merchant in New Orleans. The other John HULL, most probably the one who served in the 6th Regiment, lived in Iberville Parish in 1810 and was appointed justice of the peace in 1811. I-A, lxi; I-D, 13; I-E, 61; III-E, 16; III-G, 85; III-H, 106; III-I, 71; III-J, 16; VI-Ca, 984.

HUMBERT [See DEMOURUELLE, Humbert]

HUTCHINS (HUTCHINGS), [David]   Blues
The compilers cite two persons with the name of HUTCHINS (HUTCHINGS) who served in the War of 1812; one was William HUTCHINGS who served under DECLOUET and the other with only the surname who served under PLAUCHE. The writer located a soldier with the name of D. [David] HUTCHINS (HUTCHINGS) as a signer of the petition to General Andrew JACKSON to spare the lives of the two soldiers named HARDEN and BRUMFIELD who had been sentenced to death for having been absent during the campaign at Chef Menteur. David HUTCHINGS lived in New Orleans in 1811, where he and Jacob HUTCHINGS were listed as chair manufacturers on Conti St. I-A, lxi; I-Bd; I-E, 61; III-D, 27; VI-Dc, February 21, 1815.

I

ISNARD, [Jean]   7th Corporal   Carabiniers

The soldier with the surname of ISNARD is cited in the appendix compilation as a corporal in the Carabiniers. Other compilers cite three persons with the surname, but in other units. Pierson cites a Jean ISNARD in the artillery under Captain COLSSON and one with only the surname in the 2nd Regiment under CAVELIER. Casey cites a third, a Jean ISNARD, under Dominique YOUX.

The writer located three persons living in New Orleans with the name of Jean ISNARD, but was unable to determine which one served in the Carabiniers. The first was Jean Louis ISNARD, who was born on January 6, 1764, in France, and was married to Maria Anna DUFRASIA MARCHAND. He died on November 18, 1815. A second was Jean ISNARD, a grocer, who died in New Orleans in 1822. A third was Jean Jacques ISNARD, who was born on June 28, 1798. He was a gilder and stone cutter living on St. Claude Street in New Orleans. He died on August 15, 1824. I-A, lxxi; I-E, 62; II-A; III-A, 24; III-A, 16; III-F; III-G, 93; V-Bi, 369; VIII-B, October 10, 1817; February 8, 1818; March 13, 1818.

J

JEROME, [J. L.?]   Dragoons
The soldier with the surname of JEROME cited in the appendix is cited by Pelletier as J. L. JEROME and not cited at all by Pierson as having served in any unit during the war. The writer was unable to locate in the records any person with the name of J. L. JEROME, although he was able to locate three persons with the surname of JEROME who lived during the period in New Orleans. Two of the persons were Black, but the third was not determined by the writer. In 1805 the writer found an Etienne JEROME who lived at 41 Orleans St. and a Gabriel JEROME who lived at 4 Levée North. Gabriel, a Black, was married to Françoise FOISE MORIN (alias FANCHON). He died in 1835 and she died on October 21, 1840. A third was Charles Gabriel JEROME, Black, who was married to Adélaide JONAU. One of the persons with the surname of JEROME was an engineer. I-D, 10; II-A; III-A, 24; V-Bj, 109-110; VIII-B, November 1810; April 1, 1816; November 1, 1816; I-X, J, 243.

JONES, J.   Blues
Pelletier cites a C. Ralph JONES, while CASEY, who is the most reliable of the compilers, cites a J. JONES as the soldier who served in the Blues. The writer was not able to locate any person with the name of C. Ralph JONES. There were too many persons living during the period who also served in the war with the names of John, Jesse, Jacob and others for the writer to be able to identify the soldier in the Blues. I-A, lxi; I-D, 13; I-E, 64.

JOUBLANC, Jean Baptiste   Sgt.-1st Quartermaster   Dragoons
The writer located in the records two persons with the name of

Jean Baptiste JOUBLANC living in New Orleans. One of them was Black, while the other most probably was white. The Black Jean Baptiste JOUBLANC was born in 1778, a native of St. Domingue [Haiti]. He was the son of Juan Bautista JOUBLANC and Marie Marguerite AUBARET. Jean lived on Dauphine St. in New Orleans and died on November 3, 1816, leaving Pierre Charles ENARD as testamentary executor and property valued over $1,500. The other Jean Baptiste JOUBLANC was married to Felicité LAYE. A-I, lx; I-D, 8;I-E, 64; II-A; III-A, 24; III-K,17; IV-D, 93; V-Ac, 10-12.

JOURDAIN, L. T. [See JOURDAN, J. Louis] Carabiniers
The soldier with the surname of JOURDAIN in the compilation in the appendix is cited by Pelletier as L. T. JOURDAIN as having served in the Carabiniers. The writer was unable to identify the soldier.

JOURDAIN, Victor Carabiniers
Elie Victor JOURDAIN was married in 1803 to Marie Magdeleine Aspasie PEYTAVIN, daughter of Henry François DUPRELON PEYTAVIN and Bernarde MARMET. Elie Victor and Marie had several children; some of them were Elias Thomas, Elie, Estéphanie, Lemida, Paul Elie, Elizabeth Charichée who was married to Jean Ursin [Ursain] LAVILLEBUEVRE, and other children. Elie Victor was a cooper living in New Orleans on Common St. Later he moved to Bourbon St. in 1832. During the war he was one of the signers of the petition to General Andrew JACKSON asking for the early release of William A. AUDEBERT, a teacher, so that he could continue the instruction of the children. Marie Magdeleine, the wife, died on January 16, 1825 and Elie Victor much later. I-D, 7; I-G, 16; II-A; III-E, 16; III-F; III-G, 97; III-J, 17; IV-C, 17; IV-D, 49,55; VIII-B, December 30, 1816; January 1, 1817.

JOURDAN, [JORDAN], Daniel Blues
The writer was only able to determine that Daniel JOURDAN

(123)

was receiving correspondence in New Orleans in 1816. It is possible he may have been the Caleb D. [Daniel?] JORDAN who died in New Orleans in 1830-1831, but the writer was unable to verify it. I-A, lxi; I-D, 13; I-E, 64; V-Bj, 108; VIII-B, April 1, 1816; April 15, 1816.

JOURDAN, J. Louis Chasseurs*
J. Louis JOURDAN is cited only by Pelletier as having served in the Chasseurs. The writer was unable to determine the identity of the soldier with the records available, for there were several possibilities. There was a John Joseph JOURDAN who lived in New Orleans in 1805 at 51 St. Pierre Street. He died in 1832. A second possibility was Jean JOURDAN, a native of France, who lived in New Orleans and who died on September 12, 1822 at the age of twenty-five. A third possibility was a James JORDAN who died on March 4, 1831 in New Orleans. A fourth possibility was Louis JOURDAN, a carpenter in New Orleans in 1834. I-D, 16; II-A; II-B; III-A, 24; III-F; III-H, 113.

JOYCE, G. [Guillaume?] Dragoons
Casey cites a G. JOYCE as a soldier in the Dragoons, but the writer was only able to locate a person with the name William [Guillaume] JOYCE, a commissioner of public roads in West Baton Rouge Parish in 1827, and a John JOYCE who was living in New Orleans in 1812. I-A, lx; V-Bi, 370; VI-Gh, 180.

JUETTE (JOUET), Jean Baptiste Dragoons
Jean Baptiste JUETTE (JOUET) was married to Isabel SAUTERON, from which union several children were born. One of them was Maria Juana who was married to Pedro RIVERY. Jean Baptiste was a cooper in New Orleans at 10 Casa-Calvo St., but later moved to St. Philip Street and established a dry goods store. He died on September 19, 1849. I-D, 9; II-A; II-B; III-E, 16; III-G, 98; III-H, 113.

K

KONRAD (CONRAD), Karl   Francs*
Karl KONRAD (Carl CONRAD) is cited only by Pelletier as a soldier in the Francs. The writer was unable to locate any person with that name in the records. I-D, 12.

KRICHRAFT, Frédéric   Blues*
Frédéric KRICHRAFT is cited only by Pelletier as a soldier in the Blues, but the writer was unable to locate anyone with that name in the records for the period. I-D, 14.

L

LABARRE, [Louis]   Carabiniers
Pelletier cites Paul LABARRE as the soldier in the Carabiniers, while Casey, Pierson and the compilation in the appendix cite only the surname. The writer was unable to locate in the records any person living during the period with the name of Paul LABARRE. Furthermore, since Pierson cites three other persons with their full names who served in the 4th Regiment under MORGAN, the writer was able to determine that the soldier named Louis GRETAIS (GLETRAY) LABARRE, who received a state pension, most probably was the soldier who served in the Carabiniers.

Louis GRETAIS (GLETRAY) LABARRE was born in Poitiers, France, on October 30, 1770, the son of Edouard LABARRE and Marie DUPUY. Louis was married to Jeanne Thérèse FEUILLATRE, a native of St. Domingue [Haiti]. Louis was a cooper and tinsmith in New Orleans at 4 Conti St. He died on November 13, 1828, and his widow died on July 2, 1876. I-A, lix; I-D, 6; I-E, 67; II-A; III-E, 16; III-H, 117; IV-Bj, 120; VII-B, 62; VII-Db, 15.

LABARRIERE (LABARRURE), [Bertrand?]   Dragoons
Casey, Pierson and the compilation in the appendix cite only the surname LABARRURE as the soldier in the Dragoons, while Pelletier cites him as Bertrand LABARRURE. The writer was unable to locate any person in the records with the name cited by Pelletier. The only one the writer located with the surname was a Pierre Guillaume LABARRURE who lived in New Orleans and was married to Marie Julie SMITH. He died in 1840 or

1841, for an inventory of his succession was undertaken in 1841. I-A, lx; I-D, 9; I-E, 67; III-J, 17; V-Bk, 351; VIII-B, February 5, 1816; May 14, 1817; March 2, 1818.

LABARRURE [See LABARRIERE, Bertrand]

LABORDE, [Etienne] Carabiniers
Pelletier cites the soldier as Etienne LABORDE, while other compilers cite only the surname. LABORDE was killed in action on December 28, 1814. Vincent NOLTE narrates that he was from France and a hat maker in New Orleans. Also, NOLTE states that LABORDE was killed by the British Battery which was firing heavy fire. The shot that killed LABORDE would have killed another soldier named Philip PEDESCLAUX, but, when Philip bent over to light his cigar from John ST. AVID, the shot missed him and killed LABORDE. I-A, lix; I-D, 6; I-E, 67; III-A, 25; IX-Q, 218.

LABOSTORIE (LABOSTRIE), J. P. Dragoons*
J. P. LABOSTORIE is cited by Pelletier as a soldier in the Dragoons. The other compilers cite only Captain François DELABOSTORIE in the 2nd Regiment under DECLOUET as the soldier who served in the war with that surname. The writer located a J. DELABOSTRIE as a merchant in New Orleans in 1811 at 13 Toulouse St., which property was owned by François GODARD DELABOSTRIE. It is possible that J. and François DELABOSTRIE were father and son, but the writer was unable to verify it. I-D, 10; I-E, 34; III-D, 17; VIII-B, July 23, 1810.

LACAN, Hippolite Francs*
Hippolite LACAN is cited only by Pelletier as having served in the Francs, while the other compilers do not cite him as having served in any other unit during the war. The writer located only a letter forwarded to New Orleans in 1817 to Hippolite LACAN, a merchant, but in the other records he located only a Louis

Auguste LACAN, a druggist, who may have been related to Hippolite LACAN. Louis was a native of Augers, France, and died in New Orleans on August 20, 1833, at the age of fifty-six. I-D, 12; II-A; III-F; III-J, 18; III-K, 26; VIII-B, March 25, 1816; July 30, 1817.

LACROIX, Jean Baptiste   Musician   Battalion
Jean Baptiste LACROIX is cited as a comedian [actor, musician] living in New Orleans in 1822 at 86 Main St., but later moved to Dauphine St. He was married to Louise ROUX and then to Marie Délphine Angelique LANAUX. Jean Baptiste served as the cornet in the *Lanciers d'Orléans* in 1832. He was active in the theatre, for a benefit was given on his behalf in 1816 at the Orleans Theatre, and the following year he played various roles such as the "Jailkeeper" in the presentation of "The Deserters" at the Olympic Circus. I-A, lix, I-Bf; I-D, 5; I-E, 68; III-E, 16; III-G, 101; IV-D, 45, 51; VIII-B, April 15, 1816; March 14, 1817; April 11, 1817; June 29, 1818.

LAFARGUE, [J. B. François?]   Dragoons*
Pelletier cites a J. B. LAFARGUE, while DeVerges cites a François LAFARGUE, as the soldier who served under PLAUCHE. Casey and Pierson do not cite anyone with the surname of LAFARGUE as having served under PLAUCHE, but the latter cites a Fs. [François] LAFARGUE as a sergeant in the 1st Regiment under DEJAN.

The census lists a Jean LAFARGUIS [LAFARGUE] who lived in Plaquemines Parish in 1820 and a J. LAFARGUE in New Orleans in 1830. François LAFARGUE, cited by DeVerges, was born in Jamaica in 1783 and was married to Rosalie Jacques NICOLAS. He lived in New Orleans where he was a tinsmith and inspector of weights and measures. He died on July 7, 1863. I-D, 10; I-E, 68; III-F; III-J, 18; III-K, 26; IX-G, 60.

Nineteenth-century painting of the Lafitte brothers.

LAFFERANDRIE (LAFFERANDERIE), Lucien   Chasseurs
Pelletier and DeVerges cite the name of the soldier as Lucien LAFFERANDERIE, but Casey, Pierson and the compilation in the appendix only list the surname. According to DeVerges, Lucien LAFFERANDERIE was born in Bordeaux, France, on February 22, 1792. He was married to Marianne DELILLE DUPART, from St. John the Baptist Parish, on May 10, 1820. He died in New Orleans on September 29, 1850. The writer also located another person with the surname of LAFFERANDERIE who was a physician in New Orleans in 1811 on the corner of Mandeville St. and Moreau St. He died before 1820, but the writer was unable to determine whether he died before the war or after. I-A, lxi; I-D, 16; III-J, 18; III-K, 26; V-Bk, 351; VIII-B, June 24, 1813; IX-G, 60.

LAFITTE, Louis   Francs
Louis LAFITTE, according to one writer, was a privateer who came to New Orleans in 1804 in his ship *La Soeur Chérie*, which was armed in St. Domingue [Haiti] under orders from General BRUNET. It was stopped by orders of Governor CLAIBORNE, and Captain LAFITTE was allowed to make repairs. He may be the same one who eventually settled in Natchitoches Parish during the same year in the neutral area known as *Las Ormegas* [Las Hormegas] where, in 1826, he and Césare LAFITTE claimed six square leagues of land on the grounds that they had lived there for over twenty years. It is also possible that the soldier may have been the L. A. LAFITTE who lived in New Orleans in 1830. I-A, lx; I-D, 12; I-E, 68; III-J, 18; III-K, 26; VI-Ac, 65, 75; VI-Cb, 234; VI-Fb, 97-98.

LAHENS, (LAHEUS), [See LATTENS, J. B.]

LAHULLIERE, René   Dragoons*
René LAHULLIERE is cited only by Pelletier as a soldier in the Dragoons, while the other compilers do not cite him as having served in any unit during the war. The writer was unable to locate anyone with the surname in the records. I-D, 10.

LAIDLAW, Peter [Sr.]　　　　　　　　　　　　　　　Blues
Peter LAIDLAW was born in Scotland in 1794-1795. He was a merchant and businessman in New Orleans, as well as the consul for the Netherlands. His business and other activities were varied, for he was president of the Louisiana Insurance Company and secretary of the Louisiana Insurance Commission, one of the directors of the New Orleans Canal & Banking Company, as well as of the New Orleans S. Carrollton Railroad Company and many others. He was also an officer in the administration of the Charity Hospital of New Orleans and the Asylum of Destitute Orphan Boys. He later received a pension for service rendered during the war. He died in New Orleans on March 1, 1848. I-A, lxi; I-Bd; I-E, 68; II-C; III-E, 16; III-F, 15; III-G, 102, 204, 210; III-H, 119, 238, 242, 244, 248; VI-B, 275; VIII-B, January 20, 1817; June 22, 1818.

LAMAIGNER, Henry　　　　　　　　　　　　　　　Dragoons*
Henry LAMAIGNER is cited only by Pelletier as having served in the Dragoons, but the writer was unable to locate any information on him, although there were several persons with the surname living in New Orleans during the period. I-D, 10.

LAMBERT, Jeremiah　　　　　　　　　　　　　　　Blues
The writer was unable to locate any solid information on Jeremiah LAMBERT, except that he lived in New Orleans or the vicinity between 1813-1817, for he was receiving correspondence at the post office. I-A, lxi; I-D, 13; I-E, 69; VIII-B, June 26, 1813; May 1, 1816; May 14, 1817.

LAMBERT, Pierre　　　　　　　　　　　　　　　Dragoons
Pierre LAMBERT is cited by Pelletier as the soldier in the Dragoons, while the other compilers cite only the surname. Pierson also cites another Peter LAMBERT, a surgeon living in New Orleans, as having served in the 2nd Battalion under PEIRE. The writer located in the records two other persons with the name of Pierre LAMBERT who were living in New Orleans during the period.

One was a gunsmith who lived on St. Peter Street in 1807-1834, and the other was a baker who lived on Bayou Road in 1822. One of the Pierres, whose complete name was Pierre Valery LAMBERT, received a state pension for services rendered during the war. I-A, lx; I-D, 9; I-E, 69; II-A; II-B; III-C, 80; III-D, 32; III-E, 16; III-H, 120; VII-Db, 15.

LAMBERT [Richard] Chasseurs
Pelletier cites the soldier in the Chasseurs as Onésime LAMBERT, while other compilers cite only the surname. The writer was unable to locate anyone with the name in the records. It is possible that the soldier may have been Richard LAMBERT who lived in New Orleans, for he, and later his widow, received a state pension for services rendered during the war. Pierson cites ten persons with the surname of LAMBERT who served in the war, but two are cited only by surnames, and he does not account for Richard LAMBERT, which leads the writer to suspect that he may have been one of the two who served under PLAUCHE. I-A, lxi; I-D, 16; I-E, 69; III-J, 18; III-K, 26; VII-B, 62; VII-Db, 15.

LAMERENS, Richard Chasseurs*
Richard LAMERENS is cited only by Pelletier. The writer was unable to locate anyone with the surname in the records at hand. I-D, 17.

LAMOTHE, François Chasseurs
François LAMOTHE is cited by Pelletier and Pierson as having served in the Battalion of Orleans. The writer was unable to locate much vital information on François, but later found that he was living in New Orleans between 1816-1817, for correspondence addressed to him was arriving at the post office. One of his guests at his home was a Robert LAMOTHE. I-D, 16; I-E, 34; VIII-B, March 25, 1816; January 1, 1817.

LAMOTHE, J. S. [Sr.] Chasseurs*
J. S. LAMOTHE is cited by Pelletier as the soldier in the Chasseurs,

(132)

but the other compilers cite only the surname. The writer was unable to determine the identity of the soldier. In the records he located a Jacques LAMOTHE who was cited as a gentleman living in 1822 in New Orleans at 52 Main St., and a second Jacques LAMOTHE who owned a dry goods and shoe store in the 1830's. It is also possible that it could have been a Jean LAMOTHE who was married to Juana RAMONDE and died [Jean] in New Orleans on September 13, 1818, at the age of forty-six. I-A, lxi; I-D, 16; I-E, 69; II-A; III-E, 16; III-G, 103; III-H, 120.

LAMOTHE, Jean Baptiste [Jr.]   Sergeant   Chasseurs
The writer was unable to determine the identity of the soldier, for he located what appeared to be two persons with the name of Jean Baptiste LAMOTHE who were married to two different women. It is possible, however, that they may have been the same person, for one of the wives died early in the period. One Jean Baptiste LAMOTHE was married to Eloise (Louise) CLAVIE, daughter of André CLAVIE and Dame DEMOURUELLE. Eloise died on April 5, 1826 at the age of twenty-one in New Orleans. The other Jean Baptiste [perhaps the same one] was married in 1830 to Eulalie Elmire PELLERIN, daughter of Jean Baptiste PELLERIN and Eulalie CHESNE. Jean Baptiste LAMOTHE was a goldsmith in New Orleans, whose store was located on Royal St., but he later moved it to Chartres St. He was wounded during the war and received a state pension. He died [one Jean Baptiste] on November 13, 1874 at the age of seventy-four. I-A, lxi; I-Be; I-D, 15; I-E, 69; II-A; II-B; III-E, 16; III-F; III-G, 103; IV-D, 1; VI-Gt, 151; VI-Gu, 247; VII-B, 61; VII-Db, 175.

LANAUX, Antoine Philippe [Sr.]   Sergeant   Carabiniers
Antoine Philippe LANAUX was born on November 1, 1790. He was married to Marie Délphine TREME, from which union several children were born. He was a baker in New Orleans, then he was appointed inspector of flour. He was one of the signers of the petition to General Andrew JACKSON, asking him to

spare the lives of the two soldiers named HARDEN and BRUMFIELD who were sentenced to death for being absent during the campaign at Chef Menteur. Antoine Philippe died in New Orleans on October 10, 1863 and his wife in 1855. I-A, lix; I-D, 5; I-E, 69; II-A; III-D, 32; III-F; III-G, 103, 195, 218; III-H, 120; VI-Dc, February 27, 1815; VIII-B, May 1, 1816.

LANAUX, Charles   Carabiniers*
Charles Julien LANAUX, according to DeVerges, was born in New Orleans on March 14, 1792. He was married to Aimée Aglaé ROUSSEL, from which union several children were born. One was Angela, who died in New Orleans on July 17, 1825. He died in Havana, Cuba, on June 26, 1826. The writer located a Charles LANAUX, a baker whose shop was located at 16 Conti St. in 1822, and a Charles LANAUX who was a deputy clerk in the District Court of Joshua LEWIS. In 1816 he was elected as a state representative of the State General Assembly, but the writer was not able to determine if he was the same person as the first Charles LANAUX cited or two separate people. I-A, lix; I-D, 7; I-E, 69; II-A; III-F; V-Bj, 119; VIII-B, November 18, 1814; January 3, 1816; July 5, 1816; IX-G, 60.

LANAUX, Philippe   Corporal   Chasseurs
Philippe LANAUX is cited as a private in the rosters except by Pierson who cites him as a corporal. According to DeVerges, Philippe LANAUX was born in Nantes, France in 1752, the son of Pierre LANAUX and Jeanne JIRAUD (GIRAUD). Philippe was married to Angela BOZONIER de MARMILLON, daughter of Antoine BOZONIER and Lorenza GACHET. Philippe was a baker in New Orleans. He was one of the signers of a petition to General Andrew JACKSON, asking to spare the lives of the two soldiers named HARDEN and BRUMFIELD who had been sentenced to death for having been absent during the campaign at Chef Menteur. Philippe received a state pension for service rendered during the war. He died in New Orleans on January 3, 1816. The writer also located another person with the name of

Antoine Philippe LANAUX, who was also a baker and inspector of flour in New Orleans, but was not able to determine whether or not there was a family relationship between Philippe LANAUX and Antoine Philippe LANAUX. I-A, lix; I-D,7; I-E, 69; II-A; III-C, 212; III-E, 17; III-F, 8; III-H, 120; V-Bj, 116; VI-Aa, 314; VI-Dc, February 27, 1815; VII-Db, 16; VIII-B, February 10, 1813; January 5, 1816; IX-G, 62

LANDREAUX, Jean   Francs*
Casey and Pierson cite a Jean LANDRAUX (LANDREAUX) as a soldier in the Francs, while Pelletier and the compilation in the appendix cite a P. or Pierre LANDREAUX. The writer located in the records a Jean LANDREAUX who was curator of the estate of the late Théodore COUSIN in New Orleans in 1810. Jean was a bricklayer in New Orleans and lived at 23 St. Ann Street in 1811, but the writer was unable to trace him any further in the records. I-A, lx; I-D, 12; I-E, 69; III-D, 33; VIII-B, November 30, 1810.

LANDREAUX, Joseph   Plauche*
Joseph LANDREAUX, who was living in St. Landry Parish in 1820 and 1830, filed a claim to receive a state pension for his services during the war. He claimed that he served under PLAUCHE, but none of the other compilers cite him. VIII-C.

LANDREAUX, Pierre   Francs
Pierre LANDREAUX is cited only by Pelletier and in the compilation in the appendix. The writer located two persons living in New Orleans with the name of Pierre LANDREAUX, but was unable to determine which of the two may have been the soldier in the Francs. The first was Pierre LANDREAUX, a native of Nantes, France, who died on May 10, 1822. The second was Pierre LANDREAUX, an attorney and recorder of mortgages, living in 1832 on Toulouse St., but who later moved to St. Louis Street in New Orleans. I-D, 12; II-A; III-G, 103; III-H, 121, 237.

LAPORTE, Jean Baptiste   Chasseurs*
Jean Baptiste LAPORTE is cited only by Pelletier as having served in the Chasseurs during the War of 1812. Jean Baptiste LAPORTE lived in New Orleans where, in 1811, he was a chancellor in the French Consulate and, by 1834, he was cited as a gentleman. He drafted a will in 1838, but the writer was unable to determine what happened to him after that date. I-D, 17; III-D, 33; III-H, 122; V-Bk, 349; VIII-B, May 1, 1816.

LAPUCE (LAPICE), Peter M.   Chasseurs
Peter M. LAPICE lived in New Orleans, where he practiced his trade of shoemaker on Burgundy St. He received a state pension for service rendered during the war. He died before 1822, and his widow continued the business, as well as having continued to receive the state pension granted to her late husband. I-A, lxi; I-D, 15; I-E, 70; III-E, 17; VII-B, 62; VII-Db, 16.

LARCHEVAULT, Jacques   Dragoons*
Jacques LARCHEVAULT (LARCHEVAUX) was cited by Pelletier as a soldier in the Dragoons, while the other compilers do not cite anyone with the surname as having served in the war. The writer located in the records only one person with the surname, Antoine LARCHEVAUX, but he died in 1811 in New Orleans. The only other person with a similar surname was Jacques LARCHEVEQUE, alias LARCHE, who was married to Maria GERVAIS. He died in New Orleans on March 14, 1833 at the age of eighty-five. I-D, 10; II-A; V-Bj, 117; V-Bk, 346; VIII-B, October 9, 1811.

LARIN (LAURIN), A. [François]   Dragoons
The compilation in the appendix cites the name of the soldier as A. LARIN (LAURIN), but Pierson cites him as Fois [François] LARIN. The writer was unable to locate an A. LARIN or LAURIN, but found a François J. LAURIN who was living in New Orleans in 1820-1830 and drafted a will in 1837. Nothing else was located on him. I-E, 71; III-J, 19; V-Bk, 349.

LATOUR, Jean Baptiste   Carabiniers*
Jean Baptiste LATOUR is cited only by Pelletier as the soldier in the Carabiniers. Jean Baptiste LATOUR was married to Marie Aline LANGE, a native of St. Jérémie, St. Domingue [Haiti], from which union several children were born. Jean Bapitste lived in New Orleans on Main Street. In 1829 he sued P. [Pierre] ROCHEFORT in the court of Judge Gallien PREVAL over the ownership of a diamond ring. Jean Baptiste died on March 19, 1847 and his wife died on August 4, 1841. I-E, 6; II-A; II-B; III-F; III-H, 123; VIII-A, April 7, 1829.

LATTENS (LAHENS, LAHEUS), Jean Baptiste [Sr.]   Sg.-QM
                                                                                                                         Dragoons
Jean Baptiste LAHENS, (LAHEUS), [Sr.] was living in New Orleans between 1811-1816, where he was a music master and instrument maker at 46 Ursuline St. in 1811. He owned other property, for in 1810 he sold two lots located on the corner of Spain St. and Victoire St. I-A, lx; I-D, 8; I-E, 68; III-D, 34; VIII-B, August 15, 1810; June 26, 1813; April 1, 1816.

LAURENT [See DURIO, Pierre LAURENT]

LAUZUN (LAUZON), [François? Louis?]   Dragoons
The soldier with the surname of LAUZUN (LAUZON) is cited by Pelletier as Charles LAUZUN who served in the Dragoons. Pierson cites only the soldiers François and Louis LAUZON, who served under Captain LAGAN. Pelletier may have cited the soldier as Charles LAUZUN, because his correct surname was CHAREST LAUZON. It is possible that François or Louis CHAREST LAUZON, cited by Pierson, may have changed units and served under PLAUCHE. The writer was able to locate information only on François CHAREST DeLAUZON who lived in New Orleans. He was a native of Quebec, Canada, and was married to Perrine Thérèse de GOURNAY. He died on February 2, 1819 at the age of eighty-six. I-D, 9; I-E, 71; II-A; III-A, 25; III-G, 106; VIII-B, February 5, 1816.

(137)

LAVAN Chasseurs
The writer was unable to identify the soldier with the surname of LAVAN, who is cited only in the compilation in the appendix: Pierson cites a Nicholas LAVAN and Eugéne LAVAN, but they served in other units. The only other person with the surname that the writer located during the period who lived in New Orleans was a Charles LAVAN who lived on Dauphine St. in 1816-1817. I-E, 71; VIII-B, May 31, 1816; August 29, 1817.

LAVERGNE, Cadet Dragoons*
Cadet LAVERGNE, alias Antoine DELPEUCH [DELPUECH] is cited only by Pelletier as having served in the Dragoons, while the other compilers do not cite him as having served in any unit during the war. The writer was only able to determine that Cadet lived in New Orleans or vicinity and that he died in 1835 or 1836, for an inventory of his succession was opened in Orleans Parish in 1836. I-D, 10; V-Bf, 235.

LAVINO, Xénophon Dragoons
Xénophon LAVINO is cited only by Pelletier, but the writer was unable to locate the person with the name in the records. The only person with a similar name located was a Juan LIVANO who lived in New Orleans in 1834 on the corner of Old Levée and St. Ann Street. I-D, 9; III-H, 132.

LEAUMONT, Gabriel Chasseurs*
Gabriel Henry LEAUMONT is cited only by Pelletier, while other compilers cite only a Jules LEAUMOND as having served in another unit during the war. Gabriel Henry was married to Antoinette DALLEST, from which union several children were born. He lived in New Orleans on Royal St. He was also an officer of the masonic lodge, "*The W. Lodge Persévérence, No. 4.*" When he died, before 1834, his widow moved to Burgundy St. I-D, 17; I-É, 72; II-A; II-B; III-F; III-H, 125; III-K, 28.

LEBEAU, Charles? Marin? Dragoons
Casey cites the name of the soldier as Charles BEAU, while Pelletier cites him as Marin LEBEAU. Pierson and the compilation cite only the surname. The writer was unable to locate in the records either a

(138)

Charles BEAU or Marin LEBEAU. The only one who was located with a similar surname was a Charles LAVEAUX who owned a' tavern at 102 Levée St. in 1832 in New Orleans and a C. LAVAUD who owned a livery stable on Royal St. I-A, lx ; I-D, 9; I-E, 8, 72; III-G, 106.

LEBON, [Joseph] Dragoons
The soldier with the surname of LEBON cited in the appendix is listed by Pelletier as Joseph LEBON, while none of the other compilers cite him. Pierson cites a Louis LEBON, but in the 5th Regiment under LABRANCHE. The writer was unable to locate anyone with the name of Joseph LEBON in the records. The only persons with the surname the writer located in the records living during the period were Louis LEBON, who lived in St. John the Baptist Parish and owned an inn called Grand Turk; a François LEBON, who lived five leagues below New Orleans on a plantation adjoining the one belonging to Monsieur FENERET in 1816; and a Hippolite and a Henry LEBON who lived in the vicinity of New Orleans between 1814 and 1816, for they were receiving correspondence at the post office. I-D, 9; I-E, 73; III-J, 4; III-K, 5; VI-Ab, 581; VIII-B, August 4, 1813; June 2, 1814; July 30, 1817.

LEBRUN [See POPOTTE]

LEBROS (LEGROS) Jacques Dragoons
The only information the writer was able to locate on Jacques LEGROS was that he received a state pension for service rendered during the war. It is possible that he was the S. [Santiago] LEGROS who was living in 1832 as a teacher on the corner of Dauphine and St. Philip Street in New Orleans, or the J. T. GROS who lived on Bayou Road in 1834. I-A, lx; I-D, 4; I-E, 74; III-G, 109; III-H, 95; VII-Db, 14.

LEFAUX, [Louis? Charles?] Carabiniers*
Pierson cites only the surname of the soldier while Casey cites him as Louis LEFAUX and Pelletier lists him as Charles LEFAUX. The

writer was only able to determine that Louis LEFAUX lived in the vicinity of New Orleans in 1816, for he was receiving correspondence at the post office. Nothing was located on Charles LEFAUX, but the writer located a Charles BORBOMME DEFAUX living in Plaquemines Parish, who was a merchant in New Orleans. He was a native of France and died on February 6, 1846 at the age of seventy-seven. I-A, lix; I-D, 6; I-E, 73; II-A; III-D, 17; III-J, 19; VIII-B, November 16, 1810; May 1, 1816.

LEFEVRE (LEFEBVRE), Clair Chasseurs
Clair LEFEBVRE was born in 1793-1794. He was the son of Modeste LEFEBVRE and Victoire MARATEAU. Clair died in New Orleans on April 10, 1823 at the age of twenty-nine. I-A, lxi; I-D, 15; I-E, 73; II-A.

LEFEVRE (LEFEBVRE), Vin Chasseurs
The writer was unable to locate any information on Vin. [Vincent] LEFEBVRE. Most probably he was the son of Modeste LEBEBVRE and the brother of Clair, but the writer was unable to verify it. I-A, lxi; I-D, 15; I-E, 73.

LEGENDRE, Théophile Carabiniers*
Théophile LEGENDRE is cited only by Pelletier as having served under PLAUCHE, while other compilers cite several persons with the surname of LEGENDRE, but as having served in other units. The writer was unable to locate any person with the name of Théophile LEGENDRE, although he came across a T. LEGENDRE who was a state representative from East Baton Rouge Parish in 1834, but could not determine whether the "T" was for Théophile, Thomas, or another. I-D, 7; I-E, 74; III-H, 224.

LEGRIS, Cyrile Drummer Battalion*
Cyrile LEGRIS is cited as one of the drummers of the Battalion, but the writer was unable to locate any information on him in the records. I-D, 5.

LELOUP, P. [Benjamin] Dragoons
Casey cites the name of the soldier as P. LELOUP, while Pelletier

(140)

lists him as Rodolphe LELOUP. The writer was unable to locate any of the two citations in the records. Pierson, on the other hand, cites only the surname of the soldier, who served under PLAUCHE, as well as a François LOUPE, the only other person with a similar surname, who served in the 2nd Regiment under PEIRE. The writer located a Benjamin LOUP, who is not cited by any compiler, but who received a state pension for service rendered during the war. He lived in New Orleans and was a native of England. He died on August 15, 1825 at the age of forty-four. It is possible that he may have been the soldier who served in the Dragoons. I-A, lx; I-D, 9; I-E, 74, 77; II-A; VII-Db, 16.

LEMAITRE, Charles   Dragoons
The writer located two persons living during the period with the name of Charles LEMAITRE, but was not able to determine which of the two may have been the soldier in the Dragoons. The first was Charles Maturin [Mathurin] LEMAITRE, who was married to Marie Andrea BISCOCHE, from which union several children were born. He was a grocer living in New Orleans on Moreau St., but later moved to Grands Hommes St. The second Charles LEMAITRE was married to Desirée DARDAINE, from which union several children were born. He lived in New Orleans on Orleans St. in 1822. One of the two Charles received from the state legislature the sum of 200 dollars for service rendered. I-A, lx; I-E, 74; II-A; III-E, 18; III-F, 109; III-G, 127; V-Bj, 119; VI-Go, 83-84; VIII-B, February 5, 1816; January 1, 1817.

LEMAITRE, Jean [See MAITREJEAN, Louis]   Francs
Jean LEMAITRE is cited only in the compilation in the appendix and by Pelletier as the soldier in the Francs. Possibly he could have been Louis MAITREJEAN, the soldier in the Francs cited by Casey.

Jean was married to Célestine COMPTESSE, from which union several children were born. One of them was Marie Elizabeth, who died in New Orleans on August 19, 1831. The writer was unable to locate any other information on Jean LEMAITRE. I-A, lx; I-D, 10; II-A; III-K, 29.

LEMOINE, [Sr.] Chasseurs
The writer was unable to identify the soldier with the surname of LEMOINE, for there were too many people living during the period with the same surname. Furthermore, the soldier LEMOINE in the Chasseurs is cited only in the appendix compilation.

LEMOINE, A. Carabiniers
A. LEMOINE is cited in the appendix compilation, but Pelletier cites him as Ambroise LEMOINE, while Casey and Pierson list only the surname. The writer was unable to locate in the records anyone with the name of Ambroise LEMOINE. The only two other possibilities the writer located were an Antoine and Auguste LEMOINE. Antoine lived in New Orleans at 11 Dauphine St. in 1805. He was a native of Normandie, France, and was married to Dame BALDESQUI. He died on September 11, 1817, at the age of fifty-four. The second was Louis Auguste LEMOINE, a builder who lived on Julia St. in New Orleans. He was married to Anne Catherine St. HILAIRE. She died on February 20, 1833 at the age of fifty-six. I-A, lix; I-D, 7; I-E, 74; II-A; III-A, 25; III-E, 18; III-F; III-G, 109; III-H, 127; V-Bk, 352; VIII-B, September 18, 1818.

LEMONNIER, Yves Surgeon Staff
Yves LEMONNIER was a native of Rennes, France, son of René LEMONNIER and Anne Marie VIEL. Yves was married to Marie Aimée Charlotte BEAUCHET St. MARTIN, daughter of Pierre BEAUCHET St. MARTIN and Genevieve DECOLOGNE. Yves and Marie had several children, two of whom were named Théotiste and Marie Aimée, who was married to John MACREADY. Yves was a physician-surgeon who lived in New Orleans on Royal St., as well as the surgeon in the militia in 1832. In 1824 he was a member of the Board of Medical Examiners and in 1829 was elected as alderman for the 2nd District of New Orleans. He was a member of a masonic order and Deputy Grand Marshal of the Grand Lodge of the State of Louisiana. He died on June 8, 1832. I-A, lxi; I-D, 4; I-E, 74; II-A; III-E, 21; III-F, 17; III-G, 109. IV-D, 64; V-Bk, 346; VIII-B, April 7, 1829; IX-G. 65.

LENRUMET, Louis Drummer Battalion*
Louis LENRUMET is cited only by Pelletier as one of the drummers in the Battalion, but the writer was unable to locate any information on anyone with that name. I-D, 5.

LEPORT, Joseph Chasseurs*
Joseph LEPORT is cited only by Pelletier as the soldier who served in the Chasseurs, while the other compilers do not cite him as having served in any unit during the war. The writer was unable to locate in the records anyone with the name of Joseph LEPORT or LAPORTE. I-D, 16.

LEPRETRE, Jean Baptiste Chasseurs
Jean Baptiste Emile LEPRETRE was born in 1800. He was married to Marie Sophie ANDRY, from which union several children were born. He was a merchant and businessman who lived in New Orleans on Levée St. Later he moved to St. Louis Street. He established a business partnership with Louis LANOIX in 1813 and with M. T. HUBERT in 1818. Jean was one of the directors and stockholders of the Louisiana State Bank, President of the Levee Steam Cotton Press, director of the New Orleans Architect Company and others. He was also an officer in the masonic order, such as treasurer of the W. Lodge Union. He died in New Orleans on August 7, 1871 and his wife the following year in July 17, 1872. I-A, lxi; I-D, 15; I-E, 74; II-A, II-B; III-E, 19; III-F, 12; III-G, 109, 198, 207; III-H, 128, 240, 246; IV-D, 112; VIII-B, March 5, 1813; March 9, 1818; IX-G, 66.

LEROY Dragoons*
The soldier with the surname of LEROY is cited by Casey and Pierson as having served under PLAUCHE, but the writer was unable to identify him, because there were several persons with the surname living during the period. I-A, lx; I-E, 71.

LESCONFLAIR, Urbain? [Antoine] Chasseurs
Pelletier cites the name of the soldier as Urbain LESCONFLAIR, while the other compilers cite only the surname. The writer was unable to locate anyone in the records with the name of Urbain

LESCONFLAIR. The only person with the surname and of age during the period whom the writer located was Antoine Nicolas LESCONFLAIR, who was born in 1790-1791, a native of St. Jérémie, St. Domingue [Haiti], the son of Nicolas LESCONFLAIR and Julienne BRISSON. Antoine was married to Louise Adéline BLACHE. Antoine lived in New Orleans and died there on April 4, 1831 at the age of forty. I-A, lxi; I-D, 15; II-A; V-Ac, 335-337; V-Bj, 116; V-Bk, 346.

LESSASSIER, Vincent   Carabiniers
Vincent LESSASSIER was born on March 19, 1749, the son of Jean Charles LESSASSIER and Genevieve Marie GALLARD [dit CAHAMILLY]. Vincent was married to Modesta Marie CORBIN, from which union two children were born. One was named Vincent, who was married to Josephine Marie DUPUY, and the other Alexo-León, who lived in New Orleans. Vincent was living in New Orleans in the 1830's, but he moved around the state. He was one of the signers of the petition to General Andrew JACKSON to spare the lives of the two soldiers named HARDEN and BRUMFIELD who had been sentenced to death for having been absent during the campaign at Chef Menteur. Vincent also had served in the militia during the Spanish period and in his later years received a state pension for his services during the War of 1812. [The writer is indebted to Collin B. Hamer, Jr., for providing some of the genealogical material pertaining to Vincent LESSASSIER, who is one of his ancestors.] I-A, lix; I-E, 74; III-G, 110; III-H, 129; III-K, 29; IV-Ac, 510-12; VI-Dc, February 27, 1815; VI-Gu, 89; VIII-B, January 18, 1813; January 10, 1816; IX-J, 202.

LEVASSEUR, Laurent   Francs*
Laurent LEVASSEUR is cited only by Pelletier as the soldier who served in the Francs. The only person the writer located in the records who could possibly have been the soldier was an L. L. AUBIN LEVASSEUR, who died in New Orleans in the 1820's, for an inventory of his succession was opened in 1823. There was also a LEVASSEUR who was the second in command of the vessel "La Minerve", who was receiving his correspondence in New Orleans between 1816-1817. It is possible that he may have

been the same person as L. L. AUBIN LEVASSEUR, but the writer was unable to verify it. Another possiblity could have been Alexander LEVASSEUR, who was granted a state pension for services rendered during the war, but he was not cited by Pierson as having served during the war. I-D, 12; I-E, 75; IV-Bj, 119; VI-Gm, 16; VIII-B, April 1, 1816; June 2, 1817.

LIAUTAUD, Augustin   1st Corporal   Carabiniers
Augustin LIAUTAUD lived in New Orleans, where he was a merchant at 36 Levée St., but later moved to Royal St. He served in the militia before the war and was appointed 2nd Lt. in 1809 in the 2nd Regiment. He was one of the signers of the petition to General Andrew JACKSON asking him to spare the lives of the two soldiers named HARDEN and BRUMFIELD, who had been sentenced to death for having been absent during the campaign at Chef Menteur. Augustin was a member of the masonic order and secretary of the chapter Rose Cross Recompense of Virtue. I-A, lix; I-E, 75; III-D, 58; III-E, 19; III-F; III-G, 112; III-H, 130; V-Bj, 118; V-Bl, 89; VI-Dc, February 27, 1815; VII-A, 174.

LIBERAL, [Nicholas]   Carabiniers
The soldier with the surname of LIBERAL cited in the appendix compilation is cited by Pelletier as Nicolas LIBERAL, but the writer was unable to locate him in the records. The only two persons with the surname the writer located was Raymond LIBERAL, who was a grocer in New Orleans in 1811 on the corner of Dauphine St. and Hospital St. [Governor Nicholls St.], and an Auguste LIBERAL, who lived in or visited New Orleans often, for he was receiving correspondence at the post office between 1813-1818. I-D, 7; III-D, 34; VIII-B, October 25, 1813; April 11, 1816; September 18, 1818; December 14, 1818.

LONGPRE, Jean Baptiste   Chasseurs*
Jean Baptiste LONGPRE is cited only by Pelletier as a soldier in the Chasseurs, while Pierson does not cite him at all as having served in the War of 1812. Furthermore, Pelletier lists him as PONGPRE, rather than LONGPRE. Jean was a commission merchant living in New Orleans at 18 Conti St. He was one of the directors of the New Orleans Navigation Company and a member of the Board of

Administration of the Charity Hospital. In 1813 he was a business partner of Charles PAPET, another veteran of the war, and in 1829 was in partnership with François DUTILLET. Jean speculated in real estate, for in 1817 he purchased several tracts of land in East Baton Rouge Parish for the taxes owed. He died in New Orleans in the 1830's, for an inventory of his succession was undertaken in 1832. I-D, 16; III-F, 17; III-H, 132; V-Bk, 346; VIII-A, February 26, 1829; April 16, 1829; VIII-G, November 5, 1813; February 7, 1816; August 8, 1817; December 14, 1818.

LUCAS, Jean   Carabiniers
Pelletier cites the soldier with the surname as Jean LUCAS, while Pierson cites a LUCAS who served under PLAUCHE and a Jean LUCAS, who served in the company under Captain LAGAN. The writer located several persons with the name of Jean LUCAS in the records who were of age during the period, thus making it impossible to identify the soldier who served in the Carabiniers. The first was Jean LUCAS, a native of Bordeaux, France, who was a gold or silversmith in New Orleans in 1811. He died on September 24, 1822 at the age of twenty-three. The second was Jean LUCAS, who most probably was the father of the first cited, for he was also a native of Bordeaux. He was born on January 2, 1786 and was a marble engraver in New Orleans. He died on April 28, 1831. A third was a John LUCAS who was arrested in 1826 and sentenced in the Court of Judge ROFFIGNAC for being a suspicious character and having failed to give an account of how he earned his livelihood. I-A, lix; I-D, 6; I-E, 77; II-A; III-D, 34; III-E, 19; III-F; VI-I, February 28, 1826.

Scaki's print of the Battle of New Orleans and the death of Gen. Packenham.

Sketch by Hyacinthe Laclotte of the battlefield on January 8, 1815.

M

MACEY [See MASCEY, John A.]

MACOIN, Jean   Chasseurs
Jean MACOIN is cited by Pierson as a corporal, but a private by the other compilers. Jean was born in St. Domingue [Haiti] in 1790-1791. He was married twice, first to Emilie GALLON, a native of St. Domingue, who was the daughter of Louis GALLON and Louise Genevieve GALLON. Emilie died in 1819 and Jean married his second wife, Julie Desirée LAURENT (alias DURIO), daughter of Jean LAURENT and Emilie BROYARD in 1830. Jean lived in New Orleans on Carondelet St., but later moved to St. Ann Street. In 1825 he was brought before the court of Mayor Joseph ROFFIGNAC and fined the sum of five dollars for having violated the ordinance of throwing dirty water in the street in front of his home. He died on July 13, 1849 and his widow on May 27, 1859. I-A, lxi; I-D, 15; I-E, 77; II-A; II-B; III-G, 117; III-H, 137; IV-D, 13; VI-I, April 11, 1825.

MADA [NADA, Jean?]   Carabiniers*
Casey cites a soldier with the surname of MADA as having served in the Carabiniers, but the writer was unable to identify the soldier. The only person whom he located with a similar surname who may have been the soldier was Jean NADA, who was listed as a gentleman living at 94 Victory St. in New Orleans in 1824. I-A, lix; III-F.

MAGNOL, Michel   Dragoons*
Michel MAGNOL is cited by Pelletier in the Dragoons, but Pierson and other compilers cite him as a 1st Lt. in the 2nd Regiment under CAVELIER. Gilbert Michel MAGNOL was born in 1773-1774, a native of France. He was married to Céleste VINET, daughter of François VINET and Marie Joseph LAFRANCE, from which union several children were born. Michel lived in New Orleans, where he owned a shop which made candy and pastry goods on Chartes St.

He was active in community affairs, for in 1814 he served as a juror in Parish Court in a civil case. He died on August 3, 1816, and his widow then married André LACOUTRE. I-D, 10; I-E, 78; II-A; III-D, 38; IV-D, 57; V-Ab, 74-76; V-B1, 92; VII-H, June 22, 1814.

MAHE, Jean
Chasseurs

Jean MAHE was born in 1775-1776, a native of France. He lived in New Orleans, where he was a shopkeeper on the corner of St. Louis and Bourbon Streets. He died on June 11, 1827 at the age of fifty-two. Pierson cites only one person with the surname of MAHE as having served during the War of 1812, but the writer located a George MAHE who received a state pension for services rendered during the war. It is possible that Jean and George may have been the same person, but the writer was unable to verify it. I-A, lxi; I-D, 15; I-E, 78; II-A; III-D, 38; VII-Db, 16; VIII-B, May 3, 1813; February 5, 1816.

MAISON ROUGE
Chasseurs

The soldier cited in the compilation with the surname of MAISON ROUGE is listed by Pelletier as Célestin MAISON ROUGE, while Casey and Pierson cite only the surname. The writer was unable to locate anyone as cited by Pelletier and eliminated the possibility of the soldier being the Marquis of MAISON ROUGE, for he died in 1799. Perhaps one of his children may have been the soldier, but the writer was unable to verify it. The writer located in the records a Joseph ROUGE who was married to Magdeleine GERS, from which union a son named Louis Alexis was born in 1804-1805. It is possible that Joseph may have been the soldier, but the writer was unable to verify it. The only other reference to a person with the surname of MAISON ROUGE was that correspondence was arriving for him in New Orleans in 1817, in care of an M. R. BESSI [MAISON ROUGE, Bessie?]. I-A, lxi; I-D, 16; I-E, 78; II-A; VIII-B, May 14, 1817.

MAITREJEAN, Louis [See LeMAITRE, Jean] Francs
Louis MAITREJEAN was born in 1780-81. He was married to Mathilde JOURDAIN, from which union several children were born. Two of them were Joseph, who was born in 1831, and Estélle Marie, who was born in 1837. Louis lived in New Orleans at 368 Magazine St. He died on March 21, 1859. I-A, lx; I-Bc; I-E, 63; II-A; III-H, 137.

MAJOR, John Corporal Blues
John MAJOR [Jr.] is cited in the appendix compilation and by Pelletier as a private, but Casey and Pierson cite him as a corporal. John was born on March 9, 1792, in Frankfort, Kentucky. Shortly after the last battle of the war, he was sent to work in the hospital, until he was discharged. He lived in New Orleans and died on February 12, 1818. I-A, lxi; I-D, 13; I-E, 78; II-A; V-Bm, 138; VIII-B, December 1, 1813.

MARANS (MARANT), Claude Dragoons
Pelletier cites the name of the soldier in the Dragoons as Claude MARANT, while the compilers cite only the surname. The writer was unable to locate anyone in the records with the name cited by Pelletier, and the only person located who was of age during the period was Tranquil MARANT, who may have been the soldier.
Tranquil MARANT was born in 1793-94, a native of New York, and the son of Jean Baptiste MARANT and Jeanne MAGNAN. Tranquil was an engineer living in New Orleans on Marigny St. in 1822. He died on March 4, 1831, at the age of thirty-seven. I-A, lx; I-D, 9; I-E, 78; II-A; II-B; III-19.

MARAT (MORET), Simon Dragoons
The soldier cited in the appendix compilation as S. MARAT is cited by Pelletier as Simon MORET and by Pierson and Casey only by the surname. The writer was unable to locate any vital information on the soldier, except that he may have

lived near New Orleans or visited often, for he was receiving his correspondence at the post office in 1817. I-A, lx; I-D, 10; I-E, 86; VIII-B, May 1, 1816.

MARCENAT [See CALALOU, Joseph]

MARCHAND, Eugéne　　　　　　　　　　　　Carabiniers
Jean Eugéne MARCHAND was born on July 4, 1768, the son of Pierre MARCHAND and Catherine BERNARD. Jean Eugéne was married to Marie Anne BELUCHE, from which union several children were born. Three of their children were Eugenio, Joseph Eugéne, and Renée. Jean Eugéne was a captain of a vessel, but later retired and became a collector for the Port of New Orleans, as well as an inspector for the New Orleans Insurance Company. He lived at 282 Levée St. in New Orleans. He died on October 8, 1829, and his widow and some of the children moved to Montegut St. I-A, lix; I-D, 7; I-E, 79; II-A; III-E, 19; III-F, 8, 14, 98; III-G, 119; III-H, 138; V-Bm, 142; VIII-B, February 5, 1816.

MARCHAND, Simon　　2nd Corporal　　Carabiniers
The soldier with the name of MARCHAND is cited by Pelletier as T. B. MARCHAND and by Casey and Pierson as S. [Simon] MARCHAND. The writer was unable to locate anyone as cited by Pelletier. To complicate matters, the writer located two people with the name of Simon MARCHAND, but was unable to determine which of the two may have been the soldier in the Carabiniers.

The first Simon MARCHAND was born in 1765-66. He was married to Constance PERTHUIT [PERTUIS?], daughter of Nicolas PERTHUIT and Marianne DUROCHER. Constance died on October 24, 1807. The second Simon MARCHAND was married to Anne CHAPUS, from which union several children were born. One of them was Pierre, who was married to Victorine GERVAIS, widow of Dominique BELAUME. One of the two Simons, most probably the first one cited, was a sergeant in 1792 in the New Orleans Militia, and by 1809 was a captain in the 2nd Regiment of the Territorial Militia, while the other was a 2nd Lt. in the same regiment. Finally, one of them was a goldsmith living in New Orleans on Main St., but later moved to the corner of Grands Hommes and French St. I-A, lix; I-D, 5; I-E, 79; II-A; III-F; III-H, 138; IV-B, 142; IV-D, 28; VI-Fd, 384; VI-Ff, 199-200; VII-A, 174; IX-J, 204.

MARIN, Richard   Dragoons
Richard MARIN was born in 1774, a native of Les Cayes, St. Domingue [Haiti]. He lived in New Orleans, where he practiced his trade as a carpenter. He lived at 96 Bagatelle St. He died on November 10, 1834. I-A, lx; I-Bb; I-E, 79; II-B; III-G, 120.

MARIOT (MAIROT), Jean Claude   Chasseurs
Jean Claude MAIROT was born in 1772, a native of Paris, France, and son of Jean C. MAIROT and Catherine Elizabeth GEOTIN. Jean Claude was married to Pamela Melanie GALLA, from which union several children were born. One was Elizabeth Pamela, who was born in 1826. Jean Claude lived in St. Domingue [Haiti] before arriving in Louisiana, for he was one of the signers of a petition in 1809, asking President James MADISON to grant permission to allow a ship to be cleared at the Port of New Orleans, where he opened a goldsmith shop at 192 Royal St. In 1833 he received a state pension for services rendered during the war, and in 1839 the pension was increased to twenty dollars per month. He died on November 1, 1842, having survived his wife who died in 1834. I-A, lxi; I-Be; I-E, 78; II-A; III-F; III-G, 118; V-Bm, 146; V-Bn, 78; VII-Fd, 418; VII-Gi, 113-114; VII-Gm, 16; VIII-B, December 31, 1817.

MARQUERIE, [James]   2nd Lt.   Plauche*
The soldier with the surname of MARQUERIE is cited only by Pierson as having served as a 2nd Lt. under PLAUCHE. The other compilers do not cite anyone with the surname as having

served in the battalion. The only person with a similar surname whom the writer located in the records was a James MAQUERY [MARQUERIE], who was a resident of Orleans Parish in 1830. I-E, 79; III-K, 30.

MARQUETTE, François   Plauche*
François MARQUETTE is cited only by Pierson as having served under PLAUCHE, but the writer was unable to locate any information on him in the records, although he encountered several persons living in New Orleans in the 1830's with the surname of MARQUETTE. I-E, 79; III-G, 120; III-H, 139; III-K, 30, 31.

MARY, Joseph   Dragoons
The writer located two persons who could possibly have been the soldier living in New Orleans, but was not able to determine which of the two, if any, was the soldier in the Dragoons. One was José MARIA, who was born in 1787-88, and lived in New Orleans. He died on June 27, 1833. The other was a Joseph Claude MARY, who drafted his will in 1841 in New Orleans, but no other information on him was located. One of the two was married to Sébastienne MORALES, but the writer was unable to determine which of them. I-A, lx; I-Bb; I-E, 79; II-A; V-Bn, 77.

MASCEY, John A.   Carabiniers*
John A. MASCEY was born in 1785-1786, a native of Martinique, and son of John MASCEY and Elizabeth FOURAGE. John was married in New Orleans on June 2, 1814, to Rose TASSIER [FOSSIER], from which union several children were born. He was a builder and architect living in New Orleans on Esplanade [Avenue]. He died on October 25, 1834 and his wife died on February 14, 1859. I-A, lix; I-E, 77; II-B; III-G, 121; III-H, 136; V-Bm, 146.

MASSON, Nicholas Chasseurs*
Nicholas MASSON is cited only by Pelletier as having served in the Chasseurs, but the other compilers do not cite him as having served in any unit during the war. The only information the writer located on Nicholas MASSON is that he was receiving his correspondence in New Orleans in 1817, but nothing else was found on him. I-D, 6; VIII-B, May 14, 1817.

MAURIAN, Charles Chasseurs
Charles MAURIAN was a native of St. Domingue [Haiti]. He was married to Lasthénie PEYCHAUD, daughter of Louis PEYCHAUD and Rosalie MATHIEU. Charles was an attorney living in New Orleans at 121 St. Peter Street, as well as a member of the state house of representatives, and later became parish judge of Orleans Parish. He was also an officer of various masonic organizations, such as secretary of the Order of Indivisible Friends of the Encampment of Knight Templars, and Grand Master of *La Parfaite Union* No. l. I-A, lxi; I-D, 16; I-E, 80, 87; II-A; II-B; III-F, 1; III-G, 122, 192, 216; III-H, 226, 255.

MAURICE, F. Musician
Casey cites an F. [François] MAURICE as the musician. The writer examined the original signature on the payroll, and it conforms with the transcription made by Casey. There were two persons living in New Orleans during the period with the name of François MAURICE, who could possibly have been the musician cited as F. MAURICE. The first François was a ship carpenter living at 116 Grands Hommes in 1832, and the second was a grocer living at the corner of Dauphine and Toulouse Streets in 1834. The first François cited was a native of Italy and died on May 31, 1833 at the age of fifty. To add to the confusion, the writer also located a Pierre MAURICE living during the period, who was a teacher of languages and a musician. He was living in 1813 in the house on Main St. belonging to Jean Baptiste FAGET, another musician. Pierre died in 1818. The writer was unable to verify whether or not François

may have been part of Pierre's name, but he is the most likely candidate to have been the musician cited as F. MAURICE. I-A, lix; I-Bf; I-E, 80; II-A; III-E, 19; III-G, 122; III-H, 142; V-Bm, 138, 145; VIII-B, December 29, 1813; February 16, 1816; February 19, 1817; October 19, 1817.

MAYER, Charles Francs
Charles MAYER was a carpenter living in New Orleans at 69 Julia St., but later moved to a residence at 16 Carondelet St. He was an absentee landlord in Rapides Parish, for Justice of the Peace R. CLAIBORNE placed an advertisement in the newspaper that Charles was delinquent in paying his property taxes. I-A, lx; I-D, 11; I-E, 84; III-G, 123; III-H, 59; VIII-B, July 5, 1813; February 5, 1816; April 29, 1817.

MAYOUX, Norbert Francs*
Norbert MAYOUX is cited only by Pelletier as a soldier in the Francs. The only other person with a similar surname cited by Pierson as having served during the war was Louis MAYOU, a sergeant in the 2nd Regiment under CAVELIER. The writer was unable to locate any information on either of the soldiers. I-D, 12; I-E, 81.

McCALL, Henry Carabiniers
The writer was unable to determine whether or not there was only one person with the name Henry McCALL, for one was married to Céleste McCALL and the other, or perhaps the same Henry, was married to Lise JONES. Céleste died in New Orleans on May 2, 1815, and Lise died in Ascension Parish on February 25, 1825.

Henry was a merchant living in New Orleans on Bourbon St. in 1822, while his business establishment was located at 7 Chartres St. He established a business partnership known as Duncan, Winter and McCall. Henry was one of the directors of the Louisiana State Bank in 1831. He owned 7 arpents of land in the vicinity of New Orleans and made a claim to some property in Pensacola on behalf of his wife, Lise JONES, which was in conflict with a claim made by Bernard MARIGNY on behalf of his sons, Gustave and Prospère. I-A, lix; I-D, 6; I-E, 81; II-A; III-E, 19; V-B1, 92; VI-Ac, 128-29; VI-Ae, 909; VIII-B, April 5, 1816; June 22, 1831; IX-O, 61; IX-Q, 106.

McCLARAN, John J. Chasseurs*
John J. McCLARAN, also cited as James W. McCLARAN, was wounded on January 1, 1815. The only information the writer located on John was that he was living in or visiting New Orleans through the summer of 1816, for he was receiving his correspondence at the post office. I-A, lxi; I-Be; VIII-B, August 2, 1816.

McCLARAN, William Chasseurs*
The writer was unable to locate any information on William McCLARAN. I-A, lix; I-Be.

McCLELLAND, Auguste Chasseurs
The soldier with the surname of McClelland in the compilation in the appendix who served in the Chasseurs is cited by Pelletier as Auguste McCLELLAND, but the writer was unable to locate anyone in the records with the name Auguste. I-D, 15.

McCLELLAND, John Blues
The soldier listed as McCLELLAND in the compilation in the appendix is cited by Pelletier as John McCLELLAND, while Pierson cites a soldier with the name of John McCLELLAND as having served in the 16th Regiment under THOMPSON. The writer was unable to determine the identity of the soldier cited as John McCLELLAND, because he located several of them. Between 1806-1813, there was a John McCLELLAND who was a 1st Lt. in the 8th. Regiment. A second was cited as a private in the 3rd Regiment in 1813, and a third as a captain in the army. In 1822 there was a John McCLELLAND living in New Orleans

who was an accountant at 48 Common St., and finally, there were two persons with the name of John cited as residents of St. Landry Parish in 1830. I-D, 13; I-E, 83; III-C, 187; III-E, 19; III-K, 32; VI-Ca, 560; VII-A, 173; VIII-B, January 13, 1813; June 26, 1813; May 1, 1816; October 4, 1816.

McCLELLAND, Robert   Blues*
Robert McCLELLAND is cited by Casey and Pierson as the soldier who served in the Blues. Furthermore, Casey cites him as the only soldier with the surname who served under PLAUCHE, while Pierson cites him, as well as another soldier, with the same surname under PLAUCHE. The only information the writer located on Robert McCLELLAND was that he was a merchant living in New Orleans at 51 Poydras St. between 1809-1824. He most probably died in New Orleans, but the writer was not able to verify it. I-A, lxi; I-E, 81; III-C, 187; III-F; VIII-B, August 29, 1817.

McCLELLAND, William   Blues
The soldier cited in the compilation in the appendix as W. McCLELLAND is cited by Pelletier as William McCLELLAND. The writer located a William McCLELLAND who was living in the Feliciana area in 1812. He was one of the signers of a petition addressed to Congress, along with G. B. COTTEN, another soldier under PLAUCHE, objecting to the Orleans area organizing a state government which would exclude the other areas of the state. A second William McCLELLAND, or perhaps the same one, was a captain in the army and wrote a letter to Colonel Return J. MEIGS, asking him to recommend him to the State Department for the appointment of Indian agent for the Cherokee nation. I-D, 13; VI-Ca, 1012; VI-Cb, 251; VIII-B, November 25, 1814.

McCONACHO, John   Blues*
John McCONACHO was one of the signers of the petition addressed to General Andrew JACKSON to spare the lives of the

two soldiers named HARDEN and BRUMFIELD who had been sentenced to death for having been absent during the campaign at Chef Menteur. The only other information the writer located on John was that he was associated with the New London Company. I-A, lxi; I-Bd; VI-Dc, February 27, 1815.

McCRACKEN, Ralph Blues*
Ralph McCRACKEN is cited only by Pelletier as the soldier who served in the Blues, while the other compilers do not cite him as having served during the war in any unit. The writer was unable to locate anyone as cited by Pelletier, and the only person whom he located was a Samuel McCRACKEN, who was married to Eliza McCRACKEN. He lived in New Orleans and died on September 10, 1863, at the age of sixty-seven. I-D, 14; II-D; VIII-B, May 1, 1816.

McFARLAND, Richard Blues
The only Richard McFARLAND the writer was able to locate was the one who was living in New Orleans and got into trouble for having committed a second degree murder. He was sentenced to five years in the penitentiary but was pardoned in 1811 by Governor CLAIBORNE. Richard may have died before 1822, for the writer was only able to locate a listing for a widow Margaret McFARLAND who was living at 117 Poydras St. in New Orleans. I-A, lxi; I-E, 82; III-E, 19; VI-Ca, 983; VI-Ff, 166; VIII-B, November 5, 1810; April 11, 1817.

McNAB, Lucker Blues*
Lucker McNAB is cited only by Pelletier, while the other compilers do not cite anyone with the surname as having served during the war. The writer was unable to locate any information on the soldier. I-D, 14.

MEILLEUR, Michel Chasseurs
The writer encountered possibly three persons with the name of Michel MEILLEUR who were living in New Orleans, but was not

able to determine who of the three may have been the soldier who served in the Chasseurs. The more probable of the three would be the Michel MEILLEUR who was a grocer living in New Orleans in 1832 in a house located on the corner of Main St. and Rampart St. He was either the son of Michel MEILLEUR and Maria Francisca LAVIGNON (SAVIGNON) or Michel MEILLEUR and Margarita PICOU, but the writer was unable to verify it. I-A, lxi; I-D, 15; I-E, 83; II-A; III-C, 212; III-G, 124; III-H, 143; IX-J, 250.

MELLON [See MILLON, Thomas]

MENARD [See MENARD, Rocheville]   Chasseurs*
Pelletier cites two soldiers with the name of Rocheville MENARD as having served under PLAUCHE, one in the Dragoons and the other in the Chasseurs, while Casey and Pierson cite only one with the surname as having served in the Dragoons. It is possible that the soldier may have been Jean MENARD, for Pierson does not cite him as having served during the war, yet Jean received a state pension for services rendered during the war and later his widow received the benefits. I-D, 17; I-E, 84; VII-B, 62; VII-Db, 16.

MENARD, Rocheville   Dragoons
The soldier with the surname of MENARD is cited by Pelletier as Rocheville MENARD, while the other compilers cite only the surname. The only information the writer located on Rocheville was that he visited or lived in the vicinity of New Orleans between 1813-1816, for he was receiving correspondence at the post office. I-A, lx; I-D, 9; I-E, 84; VIII-B, March 5, 1813; January 10, 1816.

MENNIER (MEUNIER), Etienne   Chasseurs
Etienne MEUNIER was born on December 2, 1796. He was married to Adine [Rosalie] DERUZE, from which union several children were born. One was Magdeleine, who was

married to Félix CORREJOLES, son of Gabriel CORREJOLES and Elizabeth PRADINES. Etienne was a victualler living in New Orleans on Ursuline St. Later he received a state pension for services rendered during the war. He died on November 17, 1867. I-A, lxi; I-E, 84; II-B; III-G, 125; III-H, 144; IV-D, 155; VII-B, 61; VII-Db, 16; IX-G, 24, 73.

MERCIER, Henry   Carabiniers
Henry MERCIER was born in 1781-82, a native of France, and son of Simon MERCIER and Marie VALTON. Henry was a cooper living in New Orleans on St. Louis Street, but he later moved to Conti. He died on March 30, 1823 at the age of forty-one. I-A, lix; I-D, 7; I-E, 84; II-A; III-D, 39; III—E, 20; III-F; V-Bm, 140; VIII-B, April 15, 1816; May 14, 1817.

MERCIER, Jean Baptiste   Dragoons
Jean Baptiste MERCIER was born in 1780, son of Jean Baptiste MERCIER and Françoise RADEGONDE MAYEAU. Jean Baptiste [Jr.] was married to Marie Héloise LEDUC, from which union several children were born. Three of them were Jean Jacques Philip, who was married to Leontine BOULIGNY; Placide Jules Armand, who was married to Henriette Antoinette SMITH; and a third named Edouard. Jean Baptiste was a brick maker living in New Orleans in the suburb LaCourse in 1811. He died on June 1, 1832, and his wife much later. I-D, 8; I-E, 84; II-A; III-D, 36; IV-D, 23; IV-D, 130; V-Bm, 147; VIII-B, March 21, 1810; October 31, 1810; IX-N, 3.

MERIDIER, H.   Chasseurs*
H. MERIDIER is cited only by Pelletier as having served in the Chasseurs, while the other compilers do not cite anyone with the surname as having served during the war. The writer was unable to locate anyone in the records as cited by Pelletier, and the only

persons whom he located with the surname were an Antoine MERIDIER, who lived in or visited New Orleans between 1817-1818, and a Louis MERIDIER, who lived in New Orleans and drafted a will in 1841. I-D, 17; V-Bn, 77; VIII-B, May 14, 1817; September 18, 1818.

MICHAULT (MICHOUD), Js. Chasseurs
The soldier cited in the compilation in the appendix with the surname of MICHAULT is cited by Pelletier as Alexandre MICHAULT, by Casey as Js. MICHOUD, and by Pierson only as MICHAUD. The writer was unable to locate any information on the soldier as cited in the various compilations. The only persons with the surname located were an Antoine MICHOUD, a merchant living in New Orleans in 1824 and a Jean Baptiste MICHAUD, who lived on the corner of Main St. and Treme St. in 1834. A third possibility would be Jacques MICHOT (MICHOUD?), who was married to Marie Elizabeth BLACHE. He lived in New Orleans during the period. I-A, lxi; I-D, 15; I-E, 84; II-A, III-F; III-G, 145.

MICHEL, Constant Dragoons
Constant MICHEL was born in 1781-82, a native of Port-au-Prince, St. Domingue [Haiti]. He was a tailor living in New Orleans at 56 Casa-Calvo St., but later he moved to Craps St. He died on August 15, 1839. I-A, lx; I-D, 9; I-E, 84; II-A; III-E, 20; III-G, 125; III-H, 145.

MICHEL, Marius? Dragoons*
The soldier cited only by the surname of MICHEL by almost all of the compilers is cited as Marius MICHEL by Pelletier. The writer was unable to locate anyone with the name as cited by Pelletier in the records. The only one with a similar name whom he located was Marulain MICHEL, who was a maker of hats living in New Orleans. He was married to Marie FISHER, from which union several children were born. One was Rose, who was married to Thomas WILSON. I-A, lx; I-D, 9; I-E, 84; III-E, 20; III-G, 125; VIII-B, October 3, 1810.

MICHINARD [See CHEMINARD, Jean]

MILLAUDON, Laurent   Carabiniers
Laurent MILLAUDON was born in 1784-1785. He was married to Marie Marthe Elmire MONTREUIL, from which union several children were born. One of them was Antoinette Estélle, who was married to Dominique François Victor BURTHE. Laurent was a commission merchant and business entrepreneur living in New Orleans on St. Louis Street, but later moved to Royal St. and then to Bourbon St. His business activities were varied, for he owned a distillery, was one of the directors of the Mississippi Marine and Fire Insurance Company, the New Orleans Insurance Company, Orleans Navigation Company and others. He was also active in civic affairs, for in 1814 he served as a foreman of the jury in a civil court. He died on April 20, 1868 at the age of eighty-three. I-A, lix; I-E, 84; II-A; III-D, 37, 204; III-E, 20; III-F, 14, 16, 149; III-H, 146, 242, 244; III-J, 23; IV-D, 11, 113-114; VI-I, June 22, 1814; VIII-A, January 1, 1826; VIII-B, January 13, 1816; IX-Q, 206.

MILLBROUGH, Joshua   Blues*
Joshua MILLBROUGH is cited only by Pelletier as the soldier who served in the Blues, while the other compilers do not cite anyone with the surname as having served during the War of 1812. The only person whom the writer located in the records was a Benoit MILLBROUCK who lived in New Orleans. He most probably died before 1834, for in that year only a widow MILBROUX is cited as living on the corner of History and Grands Hommes Streets. I-D, 14; III-H, 146; V-Bm, 140.

MILLON (MELLON), Thomas   Blues
Thomas MELLON was a merchant living in New Orleans in partnership with John HAGAN, another veteran of the war, at 8 Levée. Later the partnership was dissolved, and Thomas moved his store to 51 Bienville St. The writer was unable to determine what happened to Thomas after 1824, whether he moved out and

settled somewhere else or died in New Orleans. I-A, lxi; I-E, 83; III-E, 14; III-F.

MILRENBERGER, Louis Christian   Surgeon   Plauche*
Louis Christian MILRENBERGER is cited by DeVerges as a surgeon attached to the batallion under PLAUCHE, but Pierson and other compilers cite him as a surgeon in the 1st Batallion under FORTIER. Louis Christian MILRENBERGER was married to Marie Aimée MERCIER. He lived in New Orleans in 1811 in a house located on the corner of Royal and Main Streets. He died in October, 1829. I-E, 85; III-D, 39; IX-G, 73.

MINICHE, Louis   Francs
Louis MINICHE was born in 1772 or 1778 in Germany. He and his wife, Marie Madeleine, had several children. One of them was Marie Gabriel [Gabrielle], who was married to Jean Baptiste ROUSSEVE. Louis lived in New Orleans and died on February 11, 1828 at the age of fifty. I-A, lx; I-E, 85; II-A; II-B; III-I, 105.

MIOTON, François Nicholas   Corporal   Dragoons
François Nicholas MIOTON was born in New Orleans on December 15, 1791. François was married to Marianne Emilie DARHAM (DARAM), from which union several children were born. Two of them were Marie Antoinette Celina, who was married to Adolphe TREME. François was a confectioner living in New Orleans on Chartres St. He continued his military career, for in 1832 he was a 1st Lieutenant on Grenadiers in the 2nd Battalion of the Louisiana Legion. He died on February 19, 1834. I-A, lx; I-D, 8; I-E, 85; II-A; II-B; III-E, 20; III-F; III-G, 127, 118; IV-D, 46, 128; V-Bm, 146; VIII-A, March 4, 1828; VIII-B, April 1, 1816; IX-G, 74.

MITCHEL, William   Carabiniers*
William MITCHEL is cited only by Pelletier as having served in the Carabiniers, while the other compilers do not cite anyone who served during the war, as cited by Pelletier. The writer was

(164)

unable to locate anyone with the name of William MITCHEL in the records, and the only one with a similar name was William MICHAEL, who was living in New Orleans in 1834 at 298 Grands Hommes St. I-D, 7; III-G, 60.

MOLE (MOLLAY), Nicolas   Francs
Nicolas MOLLAY was born on May 10, 1772, in St. Domingue [Haiti], the son of Santiago Francisco MOLLAY and Maria Ignes SAVARY. Nicolas lived in New Orleans, where he died on April 4, 1816. I-A, lx; I-E, 85; II-A.

MOLLAY [See MOLE, Nicolas]

MONNIER [See LEMONNIER, Yves]

MONTAMAT, Jean Gabriel [Sr.]   Chasseurs
Jean Gabriel MONTAMAT, Sr. was born in 1786 in Môle-St.-Nicolas, St. Domingue [Haiti]. He was married to Marguerite DEBAN [DEBON], from which union several children were born. Three of their names were Ives Armand, Félicité Coralie, and Louise Emilie. Jean Gabriel was an officer in the Bank of New Orleans and lived on Dauphine St. in 1822, but later moved his residence to St. Ann Street. He also owned a lumber yard on Basin St. in 1832 and by 1834 he was cited as a gentleman living at 55 Rail Road. He continued his military career and attained the rank of 2nd Lieutenant and Pay-Master of the 1st Division, 1st Brigade of the Louisiana Militia. He later received a state pension for service rendered during the war. He died on November 14, 1860. I-A, lxi; I-D, 15; I-E, 86; II-A; III-D, 39; III-E, 21; III-F; III-G, 128; III-H, 148; III-J, 22; VII-Dc, 125; VIII-B, January 1, 1817.

MOORE, L.   Blues
The soldier with the surname of MOORE cited in the appendix compilation is cited by Pelletier as Alfred MOORE and by Casey and Pierson as L. MOORE. The writer was unable to locate any-

one in the records as cited by Pelletier, and the only persons whom he located that may have been the soldier as cited by Casey and Pierson were an L. H. MOORE and a Louis MOORE who were residents of St. Tammany in 1820. L. H. Moore became a parish judge for St. Helena Parish by 1824. In 1820 there was also a Louis MOORE who was a resident of Attakapas. I-A, lxi; I-D, 13; I-E, 86; III-F, 3; III-J, 23.

MORCE (MORSE), [Nathaniel?] Carabiniers
The soldier with the surname of MORCE is cited in the appendix compilation, while the other compilers do not cite anyone with the surname as having served under PLAUCHE. Pierson cites a Nathan MORSE, who served under Captain OGDEN, and an Obediah MORSE, who served in the 2nd Battalion under PEIRE. The only person with the surname the writer located in the records of Célestin MORCE, who lived in New Orleans and died on October 16, 1829. There were three other persons living in New Orleans during the period with a similar surname. They were Nathaniel MORSE, a lawyer living at 7 Bourbon St. in 1822, an A. MORSE, a tavern keeper living at 4 Bienville St. in 1811, and a Jean DeMORSEY, a goldsmith in 1824. I-E, 87; III-D, 37; III-E, 22; III-F, 16-17; III-G, 121, 131; III-H, 152; III-J, 23; III-K, 23; V-Bm, 145; VIII-B, May 19, 1813; September 14, 1818.

MOREAU, Vincent Carabiniers*
Vincent MOREAU is cited only by Pelletier as having served in the Carabiniers, while Pierson does not cite anyone with the name as having served during the war. The writer was unable to locate any information on Vincent MOREAU, except that he lived in the vicinity of New Orleans, for he was receiving his correspondence in 1816 at the post office. I-D, 7; VIII–B, January 10, 1816.

MOREL, Pierre Louis Corporal Carabiniers
Pierre Louis MOREL is cited as a private in the appendix compilation, but Casey and Pierson cite him as a corporal. Pierre

Louis MOREL was born in France on May 16, 1776 [April, 1767?], the son of Louis MOREL and Louise LeBLOND. Pierre was married on June 21, 1806, to Victorine Marie Josepha DeARMAS, from which union several children were born. He was a lawyer in New Orleans with his office at 11 St. Ann Street and his home near the bridge on Bayou St. John. Pierre was elected as a representative to the general assembly in 1816 and in 1824 served as a member of the Board of Administration of the University of Orleans. He died in New Orleans on June 11 [May 11?], 1826. I-A, lix; I-D, 6; I-E, 86; II-A; III-E, 21; III-F; V-Bm, 141; VIII-B, July 5, 1816; IX-B, 74-75.

MORET [See MARAT, Simon]

MORIAN [See MAURIAN, Charles]

MORIN, Christophe   Chasseurs
The soldier with the surname of MORIN listed in the compilation in the appendix is cited by Pelletier as Christophe MORIN, while none of the other compilers cite anyone with the surname as having served in the Chasseurs. The writer located in the records one person living in New Orleans during the period who could possibly have been the soldier cited by Pelletier. He was C. A. MORIN who was an accountant living in 1834 at 278 Dauphine St. He was also a state director of the Union Bank of Louisiana and a liquidating commissioner of the Bank of Orleans. He asked and received permission from the legislature in 1846 for a leave of absence from his duties as a liquidating commissioner, for he had volunteered his services as a major in the Regiment of Infantry of the Louisiana Legion for him to participate in the campaign in Texas [Mexican-American War]. I-D, 16; III-H, 151; VI-Gr, 163.

MORIN, J. L.   Carabiniers
The soldier with the surname of MORIN in the appendix compilation is cited by Pelletier as J. L. MORIN, while Casey cites

only the surname and Pierson does not cite anyone with the surname as having served under PLAUCHE. Pierson, however, cites two soldiers with the names of Jean and Joseph MORIN in other units. The writer was unable to identify the soldier, although he located several persons who could have possibly been the soldier cited by Pelletier. The first was Jean MORIN, who was born in Cap Français, St. Domingue [Haiti]. He was married to Martine PITRE. He died in Plaquemines Parish on January 5, 1825, at the age of fifty-five and was buried in New Orleans. The second was a Joseph MORIN, who was a cabinet maker living in New Orleans in 1813. He later moved his shop to 277 Poydras St., where he was in business with a Laurent MORIN, who was most probably his brother. The third was Jean MORIN, who was a barber living in New Orleans in 1834 at 98 St. Ann Street. I-A, 1ix; I-D, 6; I-E, 87; II-B; III-H, 142; IV-C, 21; V-Bm, 140; VIII-B, August 24, 1810; May 31, 1813.

MORO, Sébastien   Carabiniers
The soldier with the surname of MORO in the appendix compilation is cited by Pelletier as Sébastien MORRO, while the other compilers cite only a François MORO, who served as a corporal in the 3rd Regiment under Colonel DeLaRONDE, and a George MORO (MOREAU), who served in the 1st Battalion under FORTIER. The writer was unable to locate anyone in the records as cited by Pelletier, and the only information he located on François [Francisco] MORO was that in 1825 he was granted a patent by the legislature for a method he invented for killing a weed then known as "grass nut." I-D, 7; I-E, 86-87; VI-Gg, 20-22.

MORSE [See MORCE, Nathaniel]

MORTIMER, Dionis   Francs
Dionis MOTIMER is cited by Pelletier as a soldier in the Francs, while the other compilers do not cite anyone with the surname as having served in any unit during the war. The only information

(168)

the writer located on a person who could possibly have been the soldier was that a D. MORTIMER was married to Emilie ZERINGUE and that she drafted a will in New Orleans in 1833, by which time her husband was already dead. I-D, 12; VI-Bm, 144.

MOULIN [See BENETAUD, François de MOULIN]

MOULINS, Alphonse   Chasseurs*
Alphonse MOULINS is cited by Pelletier only as having served in the Chasseurs, but the writer was unable to locate any information on him. I-D, 17.

MOUTON, Jean   Dragoons
The soldier with the surname of MOUTON in the compilation in the appendix is cited by Casey and Pelletier as Jean MOUTON, while Pierson cites only the surname. In addition to the soldier in the Dragoons, Pierson cites a Jean MOUTON, who was a sergeant in the company of artillery under Captain CHAUDURIER. It is possible that he may be the same soldier who served in the Dragoons, or two different persons, for there were both a senior and a junior Jean MOUTON who lived in what was then Lafayette Parish in 1820. Jean MOUTON, Sr. was a member of the state house of representatives representing St. Martin Parish in 1824. He also asked the legislature to grant him permission to subdivide his land near Bayou Vermillion to lay off a town to be called Vermillionville. Later Jean MONTON [MOUTON] received a pension for service rendered during the war. I-A, lxi; I-D, 9; I-E, 87; III-F, 2; III-J, 23; III-K, 34; VI-Gf, 16-18; VII-Dc, 125.

MUGGAT (MUGGAH), John   Blues
John MUGGAH was living in New Orleans between 1811-1813, where he and one named Monsieur PATTERSON had established a business partnership selling hardwares at 45 Levée. During the war he was one of the signers of the petition addressed to

General Andrew JACKSON to spare the lives of the two soldiers named HARDEN and BRUMFIELD, who had been sentenced to death for having been absent during the campaign at Chef Menteur. John was cited in the census index of 1820, but the writer was not able to locate him after that date. I-A, lxi; I-D, 13; I-E, 87; III-J, 23; VI-Dc, February 27, 1815.

MUROL Dragoons
The soldier with the surname of MUROL is cited by Pelletier as Jacques MOURELOT, but not cited by Pierson and Casey. The writer was unable to locate any information on the soldier. The only persons with a similar surname whom the writer located were a Joseph Antonio MOURAL and a Pierre MOURAL, who were residents of Assumption Parish in 1830. I-D, 10; I-K, 34.

MUSSON, Germain Carabiniers
Jean Baptiste Etienne Germain MUSSON was born on November 13, 1786, a native of Port-au-Prince, St. Domingue [Haiti]. He was married to Marie Céleste RILLIEUX, daughter of Vincent RILLIEUX and Marie IRONQUET, from which union several children were born. Germain, as he was addressed, was a businessman and merchant living in New Orleans. In 1804, he and Alexander GORDON purchased the Nashville and Mexican Gulf Railroad Company at Sheriff's sale, and by 1819 he assigned his commission business to B. BOUNY and Thomas F. TOWNSLEY. Germain served as a commissioner of voters for the 1st Ward in 1816 and earlier had served in the militia under Captain George T. ROSS. Germain died on May 10, 1853, and his wife died at a much earlier date on July 17, 1819. I-A, lix; I-D, 6; I-E, 87; I-F, 11; II-A; IV-D, 130, 139; Vi-Gr, 10; VIII-B, August 5, 1811; August 14, 1816; December 9, 1818; IV-Q, 206.

N

NADAUD, Jean   1st Corporal   Chasseurs
The soldier with the surname of NADAUD in the compilation is cited by Casey as Jn. [Jean] NADAUD, by Pelletier as Alexis NADAUD, and by Pierson only with the surname. The writer was unable to locate in the records anyone as cited by Pelletier. The writer located two persons with the name of Jean NADAUD, who were of age during the period. The first was [Jean] Jacques NADAUD, who was born in 1761-1762, a native of France. He was a broker living in New Orleans on Bourbon St. He died on July 5, 1822, at the age of sixty. His widow lived in the same house with a D. O. NADAUD, an accountant, who most probably was her son. The second was a Jean NADAUX [NADAUD], who was a tinsmith living in New Orleans in 1824 at 11 Common St.
I-A, lxi; I-D, 16; I-E, 88; II-A; III-B, 81; III-D, 41; III-F; III-G, 132; III-H, 153; III-J, 23; VIII-B, June 26, 1813; February 5, 1816.

NAGEL, Chrisphonte (Christophe)   Dragoons*
Christophe NAGEL is cited only by Pelletier as having served in the Dragoons, while the other compilers cite only a soldier with the surname of NAGEL as having served in the 2nd Regiment under CAVELIER.

Jean Christophe NAGEL was born on May 5, 1777, in Eppinger, Germany. He was married to Marie CAMINICHE, from which union several children were born. One of them was Angela, who was born in 1823. Christophe was a tailor and merchant living in New Orleans on St. Louis Street, but later moved to Rampart St. He may have retired, for by 1834 he was cited as a gentleman. He died on March 26, 1834 and his widow on November 26, 1850.
I-D, 10; I-E, 88; II-A; III-D, 41; III-F; III-H, 153; VIII-A, July 4,

1829; VIII-B, February 3, 1813; July 19, 1813; February 14, 1817.

NAVARRE, J. Louis   Chasseurs*
J. Louis NAVARRE is cited only by Pelletier as having served in the Chasseurs, while Pierson cites a Jean NAVARRE, who served in the 7th Regiment under LEBEUF. The writer located three persons, two in New Orleans and one in Lafourche, in the records with the name of Jean NAVARRE, but was unable to determine which of them may have been the soldier cited. One of them received a state pension for service rendered during the war. In the New Orleans area, the first was Jean NAVARRE, who was a native of Jérémie, St. Domingue [Haiti]. He was married to Marie Françoise CASSON, from which union several children were born. He died on July 9, 1825, at the age of thirty-nine. The second was Jean NAVARRE, a native of France, who died on September 30, 1824, at the age of thirty-six. One of the two was a grocer living on New Levée in 1824. The only other person living during the period was Jean M. NAVARRE, who was a resident of Lafourche in 1830. I-D, 17; I-E, 88; II-A; III-F; III-K, 34; VII-Dc, 125; VIII-B, August 1, 1810; May 14, 1817.

NICAUD, [Michel]   Chasseurs
The soldier with the surname of NICAUD is cited as Jacques C. NICAUD by Pelletier, while the other compilers cite only the surname. The writer was unable to locate anyone as cited by Pelletier, and the only person whom he located was Michel NICAUD. Michel Desiré NICAUD was born in St. Domingue [Haiti], in 1793, the son of Michel NICAUD and Marguerite RINCKER [REGNIER?]. Michel Desiré was married to Marguerite BURKE, from which union several children were born. Michel was a baker living in New Orleans on Conde St. He died on November 7, 1840. I-A, lxi; I-D, 16; I-E, 89; II-A; III-H, 155; V-Bn, 84; VIII-B, September 2, 1816; November 15, 1816.

(172)

NICE, [Michel]   Chasseurs
The soldier with the surname of NICE in the compilation is cited by Casey and Pierson only with the surname. The only other soldier who served during the war with the surname was Michel NICE, who served as an artificer under Captain CHAUDURIER. Most probably the soldier Michel NICE was the same soldier who also served in the Chasseurs. Michel was a tinsmith living in New Orleans in 1811 at 11 St. Peter Street. He left New Orleans and by 1820 was living in St. Landry Parish. He may have died before 1830, for the census of that year does not cite him. In the 1840's there was a child of Pierre Michel NICE and Célestine GAUDY who died in New Orleans. It is possible that Pierre Michel may have been the son of Michel NICE, but the writer was unable to verify it. I-A, 16; I-E, 89; I-F, 67; II-B; III-E, 41; III-J, 23.

NICHOLS (NICOLAS), [Joseph]   Blues
The soldier with the surname of NICHOLS cited in the compilation in the appendix is listed by Pelletier as Thadeus NICHOLS, but the writer was unable to locate anyone as cited in the records. The writer is of the opinion that the soldier may have been Joseph NICOLAS (NICHOLAS) who received a state pension for service rendered during the war, yet, he is not cited by any of the compilers as having served during the war. Joseph (NICHOLS, NICHOLAS) lived in New Orleans at 83 St. Louis Street in 1834, and he died the same year on November 18, 1834. The census of 1830 lists a Joseph NICHOLS, who was a resident of East Feliciana Parish, but the writer was unable to determine whether he was the same or a different person as the one cited as living in New Orleans. I-D, 13; II-B; III-H, 155; III-K, 35; VII-Dc, 125.

NICHOLS (NICHOLLS), Thomas C.   Blues
Pelletier and the compilation in the appendix cite the name of the soldier as J. C. NICHOLS, while Casey and Pierson cite him as Thomas NICHOLLS. Thomas C. NICHOLLS lived in Ascension Parish. He was a lawyer, and in 1811 he was appointed post-

master at the post of Lafourche, as well as Clerk of the 2nd Superior Court District. He was still living in Ascension Parish in 1830, but the writer was unable to determine when he died. I-A, lxi; I-D, 13; I-E, 89; VI-Ca, 952, 985; VIII-B, July 5, 1813; February 5, 1816.

NICOLAS [See NICHOLS, Joseph]

NICOLAS, Louis   Dragoons
The soldier cited in the compilation as L. NICOLAS is listed by Pelletier as Louis NICOLAS. The writer was unable to definitely identify the soldier, because he located two persons with the name of Louis NICOLAS living in New Orleans during the period. The first was Louis Jacques NICOLAS who was married to Constance MEILLEUR, daughter of Michel MEILLEUR and Marie Anne DAVIGNON. Constance was also the widow of François MEFFRE ROUZAN. The second was Jean Louis NICOLAS who was born in Rochelle, France, son of Jacques NICOLAS and Marianne DRAPEAU. Jean Louis died on December 30, 1819. One of the two persons cited as Louis was a shoemaker specializing in women's shoes, and the other was a baker. One of them was also commissary of police in the suburb Marigny. I-D, 9; II-A; III-C, 185, 212; III-D, 41; 57; III-E, 22; III-F; V-Bn, 81; VI-Ae, 907; VI-Ca, 633; VI-Da, January 21, 1815; VI-Fd, 383; VIII-B, February 26, 1816; May 1, 1816; June 11, 1817.

NICOLAS, Valery   Dragoons*
Louis Valery NICOLAS was the son of Jean Baptiste NICOLAS and Marguerite Magdeleine ADAM. Louis Valery was married to Marguerite BOISDORE, daughter of Louis BOISDORE and Marguerite DROUSSIN. Louis Valery and Marguerite had several children, one whose name was Valery was born in 1805 and died in 1816 at the age of eleven. Louis Valery was a gunsmith living in New Orleans at 19 Bourbon St. He died in 1829 and his wife a year earlier in 1828. I-D, 10; II-A; II-B; III-D, 41; V-Bn, 82; VIII-B, January 10, 1816; January 1, 1817; December 31, 1817.

NICOLAS, Zénon   Blues*
The only information the writer was able to locate on Zénon NICOLAS was that he was one of the signers of the petition addressed to General Andrew JACKSON to spare the lives of the two soldiers named HARDEN and BRUMFIELD who were sentenced to death for having been absent during the campaign at Chef Menteur. I-A, lxi; I-Bd; I-E, 89; VI-Dc, February 27, 1815.

NIPORT, J. B.   Dragoons
J. B. NIPORT cited in the compilation is listed by Pelletier as César NEPOTTE, while the other compilers do not cite anyone with even a similar surname as having served during the war. The writer was unable to locate any person with either the surname of NIPORT or NEPOTTE. I-D, 9.

NISBETT (NISBET), Robert   2nd Sergeant   Blues
Robert NISBET was a carpenter living in New Orleans at 109 Carondelet St. He may have died before 1830, but the writer was unable to pinpoint the date. I-A, lxi; I-E, 89; III-E, 22; III-J, 23; VIII-B, November 1, 1816.

NOLTE, Vincent   Carabiniers
Vincent NOLTE was born in Leghorn, Italy, on November 21, 1779, the son of John Henry NOLTE. He was a German citizen, world traveler and entrepreneur. He had an audience with Queen Victoria, was imprisoned in London, was confidential adviser to Austrian Premier VON KUEBECK, shipwrecked off the coast of Florida, and contracted yellow fever in New Orleans. He was an agent for European capitalists in the United States and merchant in New Orleans, as well as the Prussian and Hamburg Consul living at 39 Royal St., but later moved to 79 Canal St. In 1806 he had served as the captain of a company of militia in the territorial militia. He had a duel with the eldest son of one of the bankers named [Joseph] SAUL and was wounded when the ball from the pistol fell out before he could fire it. He returned to Germany and in 1854 he published his *Memoirs* which was

translated in 1934. I-A, lix; I-D, 7; I-E, 89; I-G, 1; III-E, 22; III-F; VI-Ca, 700; VIII-B, January 5, 1816; February 14, 1818; IX-D. 328; IX-I, 39-40; IX-Q, 184-234, 242-43, 306-339.

NOUCHE (NOUCHET), Seraphin?　　　　　　　　　Chasseurs*
Seraphin NOUCHE (NOUCHET) is cited only by Pelletier as having served in the Chasseurs, while Pierson cites only two soldiers with the surname as having served during the war. They were Gustave and Octave NOUCHET, who served in the 5th Regiment under LaBRANCHE. The writer was unable to locate anyone as cited by Pelletier, but located that Gustave NOUCHET was living on Grands Hommes St. in New Orleans in 1811, as well as an A. B. NOUCHET, who was living along Bayou St. John. One of the two cited above owned a billiard parlor on Peace St., but the writer was unable to determine which of the two. I-D, 16; I-E, 89; III-D, 41.

NOYE (NOYES)　　　　　　　　　　　　　　　　　　Dragoons
The soldier with the surname of NOYE (NOYES) in the compilation is cited by Pelletier as Denis NOYES and by Pierson as Dominique NOEVE. The writer was unable to locate anyone in the records, as cited by both Pelletier and Pierson. The only persons with the surname of NOYES whom the writer located between 1811-1817 in the New Orleans area were a Silas NOYES, J. M. NOYES, a boat captain, and a William B. NOYES. In 1834 there was also a listing for a Simon NOYES who lived at 102 Orleans St. I-D, 8; I-E, 89; III-H, 157; III-J, 23; VIII-B, August 5, 1811; May 1, 1816; August 29, 1817.

NUGENT, Thomas　　　　　　　　　　　　　　　　　Francs*
Thomas NUGENT is cited only by Pelletier as having served in the Francs, while the other compilers cite only an Isaac and John NUGENT as having served in the 17th, 18th, and 19th Consolidated Regiment. The writer was unable to locate a Thomas NUGENT, but located that Isaac NUGENT was living in Catahoula Parish in 1830. I-D, 12; I-E, 90; III-K, 90.

(176)

O

OBIGNON (OTTIGNON), [Claudis]   Carabiniers
The soldier with the surname of OBIGNON in the compilation is cited by Casey and Pierson only with the surname of OTTIGNON, while Pelletier cites him as Louis HOTTIGNON. The writer was unable to locate anyone, as cited by Pelletier, and the only person with the surname whom he located in the records was Claudius OTTIGNON, who was living in New Orleans or vicinity, for he was receiving correspondence at the post office between 1813-1816. I-A, lix; I-E, 6; I-E, 90; VIII-B, March 5, 1813; May 3, 1813; May 1, 1816.

O'DONNEL, Lynster   Blues*
Lynster O'DONNEL is cited only by Pelletier as having served in the Blues, while Pierson cites only a James O'DONNEL as having served in the 17th, 18th, and 19th Consolidated Regiment. The writer was unable to locate any information on any of them, and the only persons with the surname whom he located in the records living during the period were a Daniel, Anthony, and John O'DONNEL, who lived in New Orleans, and a Charles O'DONEL [O'DONNEL], who was a resident of the Felicianas in 1820. I-D, 14; I-E, 90; II-F; III-H, 64; III-J, 24; V-Bo, 183-184.

O'DUHIGG [See DUHIGS, Louis O.]

O'MEARA, Patrick   Blues*
Patrick O'MEARA is cited only by Pelletier as having served in the Blues, while the other compilers do not cite anyone with the surname as having served during the war. The writer was unable to locate anyone with the surname in the records. The only one with a similar name whom he located was a José OMIRIS

[O'MEARA], who was a resident of Orleans Parish in 1820. I-D, 14; I-J, 24.

O'NEAL, Arthur　　　　　　　　　　　　　　　　　　　Blues*
Arthur O'NEAL is cited by Pelletier as having served in the Blues, while Pierson cites him as having served under DeCLOUET. Arthur O'NEAL lived in New Orleans, where he died on November 28, 1834. I-D, 14; I-E, 90; II-B.

ORTEING (OSTIN), Jean　　　　　　　　　　　　　Carabiniers
Jean Joseph OSTIN was born on December 9, 1794, the son of Jean OSTIN and Marianne RIVARDE. Jean Joseph was married to Elaine RIVARDE, from which union several children were born. Jean Joseph had several brothers and sisters whose names were Marguerite, who was married to Maurice FARGE; Pierre Jean Baptiste, who was married to Claire RIVARDE; and Céleste and Marianne, who died when they were small children. Jean Joseph was a cabinet maker living in New Orleans on Rampart St., while his shop was located at 65 Bourbon St. He died on February 9, 1842. I-A, lix; I-Ba; I-D, 6; I-E, 5, 90; II-A; II-B; III-E, 22; V-Ab, 346-48.

OTTIGNON [See OBIGNON, Claudius]

P

PACKWOOD, Henry   Blues
Henry PACKWOOD lived in Plaquemines Parish, where he owned some land. In 1811 the Syndic Decoteaux SAUCIER ordered Henry to comply with the ordinance to build a levee in front of his property with a minimum base of twenty feet by six and one-half feet. Henry was still cited in the census of 1830, but the writer was unable to determine when he died. Some members of his family lived in New Orleans, for an L. PACKWOOD, who was a merchant on Levée South, was found in 1809, and there was also an S. W. PACKWOOD, a physician living at 4 Custom House St. in 1822. I-A, lxi; I-E, 91; III-C, 210; III-E, 22; III-K, 35; VIII-B, October 2, 1811; January 3, 1816; September 13, 1816.

PAGE, Valentine   Plauche*
Valentine PAGE is cited only by Pierson as having served under PLAUCHE. The writer was unable to locate anyone with the name in the records, as cited by Pierson, although he located several people with the surname living in Orleans and other parishes during the period. I-E, 91; III-D, 42; III-F; III-H, 160; III-J, 24; III-K, 35.

PAGEOT [See PAJAND, Pierre Auguste]

PAILLASON, Richard   Francs*
Richard PAILLASON is cited only by Pelletier as having served in the Francs, while other compilers do not cite anyone with the surname as having served during the war. The writer was unable to locate him in the records, and the only persons whom he located with similar surnames in New Orleans were Jean PAINSON, who was living on Craps St. in 1811 and G. PAPILLON, who was justice of the peace living on Bourbon St. in 1824. I-D, 12; III-D,

(179)

45; III-F; III-J, 24.

PAIRSON, Ambroise Dragoons*
Ambroise PAIRSON is cited only by Pelletier, but the other compilers do not cite him as having served in any unit during the war, although there were three soldiers with the surname of PEARSON who served. The writer was unable to locate any information on the person cited by Pelletier. I-D, 10.

PAJAND (PAJAUD), [Pierre Auguste] Carabiniers
The soldier cited in the compilation as PAJAND signed his name in the original as PAJAUD, but the original muster roll also cited him as PAGEOT. The writer was unable to distinguish the way the soldier signed his first name initial, for it appears as a "B", as well as a "P". In the records of the period the writer located a Pierre Auguste PAJAUD, who was born in 1779, a native of Jérémie, St. Domingue [Haiti]. He was married to Adélaide CAVALIER [CAVELIER?], from which union several children were born. He was a carpenter living in New Orleans at Toulouse St. He died on October 25, 1833, and his wife on April 21, 1869. I-A, 1ix; I-Ba; I-C, 64; I-E, 91; II-A; II-B; III-D, 43; III-F; III-K.

PALFREY, Henry William Blues
Henry William PALFREY was married twice, first to Sarah, who died on December 27, 1821, at the age of twenty, and second to Mary, who was born in New York and died on February 15, 1847. Henry was a merchant living in New Orleans on Camp Street. His company, known as Henry W. and George PALFREY, owned a cotton press and salt stores on Camp and Magazine Streets. He hired several German redemptioners to help him run his business, but they became runaways, and he offered a reward of ten dollars each for their apprehension and twenty dollars for a sailor named John MILLER, who enticed them to run away. Henry died in New Orleans at the age of sixty-eight and was buried in the Girod Cemetery. I-A, lxi; I-D, 14; I-E, 91; II-C; III-E, 22; III-F; III-G, 137; VIII-B, March 13, 1818; IX-G, 81.

PAPET, Charles Carabiniers
Charles PAPET was born in 1781. He was married to Charlotte Virginie LIVAUDAIS, from which union several children were born. He was a commission merchant and exchange broker living in New Orleans on St. Peter Street, but later moved to St. Louis Street, then to Royal St. He was in partnership with John LONGPRE in 1813, but later dissolved it. In 1817 his home was burglarized and some jewelry and other articles of value were taken. In 1818 he hired two lawyers, John R. GRYMES and J. F. CANNONGE, and sued his creditors in the court of James PITOT. Charles died on November 5, 1836, and his wife a few years earlier in 1817. I-A, lix; I-E, 91; II-B; III-F; III-G, 138; III-H, 160; V-Bo, 186; V-Bp, 236; VIII-B, November 5, 1813; March 13, 1816; October 6, 1817; October 16, 1817.

PARISIEN, Henry Chasseurs
The only information the writer located on the soldier cited as Henry PARISIEN was that there was a widow PARISIEN living in New Orleans between 1832-1834 on Terpsichore St., who may have been the wife of Henry PARISIEN, but the writer was unable to verify it. The writer is of the opinion that the soldier may have been Henry PARIZOT, who was born in 1791. He was a musicial instrument maker living in New Orleans on Royal St., but later moved to Rampart St. He died on August 17, 1836. I-A, lxi; I-D, 16; I-E, 91; II-B; III-F; III-G, 138; III-H, 161; IV-Bp, 236; VIII-A, August 18, 1829; VIII-B, May 14, 1814; June 2, 1817.

PASSAGE, Onésime Dragoons*
Onésime PASSAGE is cited only by Pelletier as having served in the Dragoons, but Pierson cites only a Louis PASSAGE as the only person with the surname who served during the war as a musician under Captain CHAUVEAU, and a John PASSIA [PASSAGE?] who served under PLAUCHE. The only person whom the writer located in the records with the surname was A. PASSAGE [Sr.], who was a musician living in New Orleans. In

(181)

1813 a benefit was performed on his behalf at the St. Philip Theatre, and he played the bassoon. He may have died before 1822 or left the state, for the writer was unable to locate him after 1816. I-D, 10; I-E, 91, 92; VIII-B, December 27, 1813; January 10, 1816.

PAXTON, Samuel　　　　　　　　　　　　　　　Carabiniers
Samuel PAXTON was a merchant living in New Orleans. His business place was located on Levée [St.], while his residence was on St. Charles Street, but later he moved to Custom House St. and to Cours des Tritons [St.]. In 1818 he was narrowly defeated [by six votes] in the election for director of the Louisiana State Bank, but the governor decided to appoint him as one of his selections to the state bank. In 1829 he ran for the seat of alderman for the 6th Ward, but he was defeated by Maunsel WHITE and J. P. FRERET. I-A, lix; I-D, 6; I-E, 92; III-E, 22; III-F; III-G, 129; VIII-A, April 7, 1829; VIII-B, June 22, 1818.

PEDESCLAUX, Etienne　　　　　　　　　　　　Carabiniers
Etienne PEDESCLAUX was married to Anne BOUMAY, from which union several children were born, one whose name was Joseph. Etienne served in the 1st Regiment of the Territorial Militia, for in 1806 he was appointed an ensign, and by 1809 he was a 2nd Lieutenant. He became ill after the war and went to Cuba to recuperate, but after spending some time there and realizing that he was becoming progressively worse, he decided to return home; however, he died aboard ship in 1818. I-A, lix; I-E, 92; III-C, 185; VI-Ca, 633; VIII-B, October 12, 1818; IX-O, 101.

PEDESCLAUX, Philip　　　　　　　　　　　　　Carabiniers
Philip PEDESCLAUX was born on April 27, 1791, the son of Pierre Antoine PEDESCLAUX and Marie LeDUC [LeDUGUE], daughter of Charles LeDUC [LeDUGUE] and Marie Josepha LeCOURT. During the war Philip was almost killed by a cannon ball, which just missed him, but hit Etienne LABORDE, who

was killed instantly. Philip lived in New Orleans where he was a lawyer and a notary public with his office on Royal St. and his home on Hospital St. [Govenor Nicholls St.]. He was appointed the director of the branch at Donaldsonville of the Louisiana State Bank. He was also an officer in the militia and member of various masonic lodges. He died on August 6, 1826. I-A, lix; I-E, 92; II-A; III-C, 185; III-F, 214; III-E, 22. 74-76; III-F; V-Bo, 190; VIII-B, August 14, 1816; October 21, 1818; IX-Pa, 18-19; IX-Q, 218.

PELLERIN, Barthelemy   Carabiniers
Barthelemy PELLERIN is cited as the soldier who served in the Carabiniers by DeVerges, but the other compilers cite only the surname of the soldier. Barthelemy was born in New Orleans on January 19, 1801. He died on October 17, 1855. I-A, lix; I-Ba; I-D, 6; I-E, 92; IX-G, 82.

PELLIER (SELLIER), [Pierre]   Dragoons
The soldier with the surname of PELLIER in the compilation is cited by Pelletier as Maximilien SELLIER, while Casey and Pierson cite only the surname. The writer was unable to locate anyone as cited by Pelletier in the records, and the only person with the surname whom he found was Pierre SELLIER, who was born in 1800 in France. He died in New Orleans on September 13, 1833. I-A, lx; I-D, 10; I-E, 107; II-A, III-K, 42; V-Br, 29.

PERIER, F [See FERRIER, P. and PERRIER, Charles] Dragoons
F. PERIER cited in the compilation in the appendix is listed by Pelletier as F. C. PELTIER, while the other compilers cite only a Charles PERRIER, but as a corporal in the Francs. It is also possible that the soldier may have been P. [Pierre] FERRIER, cited by both Casey and Pierson as a soldier in the Dragoons. The only persons with the surname of PERIER whom the writer located in the records were Jean and Joseph PERIER, who were living in 1805 at 5 Custom House St. and 5 Public Place respectively. I-A, lx; I-D, 9; I-E, 93; III-A, 27.

PERILLAT [PERILLIAT], Fulgence? Carabiniers*
Fulgence PERILLAT [PERILLIAT] is cited only by Pelletier as having served in the Carabiniers, while Pierson cites two soldiers with the name of François PERILLAT [PERILLIAT] as a 1st lieutenant in the 1st Regiment under DEJAN and a captain in the 2nd Regiment under CAVELIER, as well as a sergeant with only the surname in the 1st Regiment under DEJAN. The writer was unable to locate any information on the soldier cited by Pelletier. It is possible that one of the soldiers cited by Pierson may have also temporarily served under PLAUCHE, but the writer was unable to verify it. I-D, 7; I-E, 93.

PERRAULT, Jean Baptiste Private Chasseurs*
There were two persons with the name of Jean Baptiste PERRAULT who served under PLAUCHE, one as a sergeant-major on the staff, and the other as a private in the Chasseurs or Carabiniers. The writer was unable to determine whether these two men were father and son or even related. The first Jean Baptiste PERRAULT, who most probably was the elder of the two, was married to Anne Marie LeCANN, a native of Normandie, France. She died in New Orleans on January 15, 1845. The second Jean Baptiste PERRAULT was married to Justine Antoinette DUREL, daughter of François DUREL and Marie DEJAN. Justine was born in 1797 and died in New Orleans on February 8, 1842. One of the two Jeans was an officer at the Union Bank in 1834, and he lived at 21 Royal St. in New Orleans. I-A, lix; lxi; I-D, 7; I-E, 93; II-A; II-B, III-H, 164; III-J, 24; III-K, 36.

PERRIER [See SPERRIER, Charles]

PERRIER, J. B. [See SPERRIER, Charles Francs*
J. B. PERRIER is cited only by Pelletier as a private having served in the Francs, while Casey and Pierson cite a Charles PERRIER as a corporal in the unit. The writer was unable to identify the soldier as cited by Pelletier, and the only person whom he located in the records who may have been the soldier

was Jean PERRIE [PERRIER?], who was married to Ursula Jacob MAQUIN. They were living in New Orleans in 1816, for a child of theirs died that year. I-E, lx; I-D, 12; II-A.

PESSON (PESSOU), [Alphonse] 2nd Corporal Chasseurs
The soldier with the surname of PESSON in the compilation is cited by Casey as T. [?] PESSON, by Pierson only with the surname, and by Pelletier as Nicolas PESSOU. The writer was unable to definitely identify the soldier, for he located in the records both a T. J. PESSON, who was living in New Orleans in 1832 at 11 Conti St., and an Alphonse PESSOU, who was a gunsmith living at 40 Chartres St. in 1824. The writer is of the opinion that the soldier was Alphonse PESSOU, for he received a state pension for service rendered during the war, yet he was not cited by any of the compilers. I-A, lxi; I-D, 15; I-E, 93; III-F; III-G, 141; III-H, 165; III-K, 37; VII-Dc, 125.

PEYROUX, Sylvain Chasseurs
Jean Marie Sylvain PEYROUX was married to Rose Aglaé CANTRELLE, widow of Monsieur FABRE [FABVRE], and daughter of Michel CANTRELLE and Céleste ANDRY. Sylvain was a commission merchant and produce broker living in New Orleans on Toulouse St., with his office and warehouse on Burgundy St. He established a business partnership with G. M. PLICQUE in 1816, but the following year he dissolved it. Later he established another partnership with Achille RIVARDE in 1817 which lasted throughout the 1830's. Rose Aglaé died in New Orleans on August 27, 1840 and Sylvain much later. I-A, lxi; I-D, 16; I-E, 94; II-A; III-D, 44; III-E, 22; III-F; III-G, 142; III-H, 142; V-Bp, 238; VIII-B, January 5, 1816; January 8, 1817; August 8, 1817.

PHILIPS [PHILLIPS], John 1st Sergeant Blues
Although there were several persons with the name of John PHILIPS [PHILLIPS] living during the period in New Orleans and other parishes, which made it difficult for the writer to definitely identify the soldier in the Blues, the writer is of the

opinion that the soldier may have been one of the John PHILIPS [PHILLIPS] residing in Orleans or Ouachita Parishes in 1820. The one who lived in New Orleans was John L. PHILIPS [PHILLIPS], who was a merchant living at 19 Magazine St. He had sued his creditors in the Court of James PITOT to recover the sum of $456.50. He died on April 14, 1834. I-A, lxi; I-D, 13; I-E, 94; II-B, III-E, 22; III-H, 166; III-J, 25; III-K, 37; VI-H, June 25, 1814; VIII-B, November 5, 1813.

PICENA, Pierre   Carabiniers
Pierre PICENA was married to Eloise DELLOES, from which union several children were born. One of them was named Pierre, who was born in 1813 and died on September 10, 1815. Pierre [Sr.] was an undertaker living in New Orleans. He was an associate of Pierre HUARD, who together placed in court an injunction to prevent the sale of a house on Royal St. belonging to the late Solomon PREVOST, for the estate owed them the sum of $860. I-A, lix; I-D, 6; I-E, 94; II-A; VIII-B, April 21, 1813.

PIDOUX, Jean Vincent   Sergeant   Chasseurs
Jean Vincent PIDOUX was born in France in 1775. He was married to Jeanne Urbanie LAMOTHE, a native of St. Domingue [Haiti], and daughter of Jean LAMOTHE and Claudine DAMPUSE. Jean Vincent and Jeanne had several children, one whose name was Marie Uranie, who was born in 1810. Jean Vincent was a cigar maker living in New Orleans at 2 Levée South in 1811, but later became a gardener and moved his residence to Mandeville St. He died on May 7, 1829, and his wife a few years earlier on May 30, 1818. I-A, lxi; I-D, 15; I-E, 94; II-A; III-D, 41; III-E, 22; V-Bo, 190.

PIERRE, Nicolas Jean   Dragoons*
Nicolas Jean PIERRE is cited only by Pelletier as having served in the Dragoons during the war. Nicolas Jean PIERRE was married to Margaret VATELLE, from which union several children were born. Nicolas lived in New Orleans, where he owned a brickyard

located on St. Claude St. near the Bayou Gate [around the present-day Municipal Auditorium]. He also owned several lots and properties throughout the city. In 1813 he was sued by Jean L. ISNARD over the ownership of a lot located in the suburb Trémé, and Nicolas lost the judgment. Nicolas died on October 31, 1834, and his wife a few years earlier in 1813. I-D, 13; II-B; III-D, 42; VIII-B, July 4, 1810; February 8, 1813; February 10, 1813; August 14, 1816; August 11, 1818.

PILIE, Chery Chasseurs*
Chery PILIE is cited only by Pelletier as having served in the Chasseurs during the war, while the other compilers do not cite him as having served in any unit. The writer was unable to locate anyone, as cited, in the records. I-D, 17.

PILIE, Louis Philippe 2nd Lt. Chasseurs
Louis Philippe PILIE, a native of St. Domingue [Haiti], was married to Marie Louise ROSSIGNOL DESDUNES ARCUEIL [ARCUEL], from which union several children were born. Three of their children were Louis Bernard Armand, Jean Pierre Arthur, and Louis Joseph Auguste. Louis Philippe was a hatter and merchant living in New Orleans on Chartres St. and was one of the directors of the Louisiana State Bank appointed by the stockholders in 1834. In 1825 he was fined by Joseph ROFFIGNAC for allowing one of his slaves to attend an unauthorized slave reunion. Marie Louise died on April 19, 1836, and Louis a few years later. I-A, lxi; I-D, 15; I-E, 95; II-A; III-D, 43; III-E, 23; III-F; III-G, 144; III-H, 167, 234; VI-I, February 18, 1825; VIII-B, August 2, 1816.

PILLON, GERVAIS [See GERVAIS, A. and Jean] Chasseurs*
GERVAIS PILLON is cited only by Pelletier as having served in the Chasseurs, but Pierson does not cite anyone with the surname of PILLON as having served in any unit during the war. The writer was unable to locate anyone, as cited by Pelletier, and the only persons whom he located who were living during the period

(187)

were Thomas PILON, a hatter on Conde St. in New Orleans who died in 1833; a Richard PILONE, who died in New Orleans on May 15, 1834, at the age of forty-five; and a Siméon PILON, a Black man married to Adélaide LEFEVRE and living in New Orleans. I-D, 16; II-B; III-D, 44; V-Bo, 191; VIII-B, May 1, 1816; October 30, 1818.

PINEL, J. B. Carabiniers
J. B. Pinel is cited only by Pelletier as having served in the Carabiniers, while Pierson does not cite anyone with the surname as having served in any unit during the war. The writer was unable to locate anyone, as cited by Pelletier, in the records, and the only person living in New Orleans who may have been the soldier was Jacobo PINELL [PINEL], who died on June 8, 1883. I-D, 6; II-A.

PIQUERIN (PIQUERY), Pierre Dragoons
The soldier with the surname of PIQUERIN (PIQUERY) is cited by Pelletier as Pierre PIQUERY, while the other compilers cite only the surname. The writer located two persons with the name of Pierre PIQUERY living in New Orleans and was not able to determine which of the two may have been the soldier cited by Pelletier. The first Pierre PIQUERY was married to Marie ARCHIBALD, and the second was married to a Dame LeBLANC. One of the Pierres was a carpenter living on Thalia St., and the other was a dentist living on Delor St., but later moved to a residence located on the corner of Apollon and Terpsichore Streets. I-A, lx; I-D, 9; I-E, 94; II-A; III-B; III-E, 23; III-F; III-G, 144; III-H, 167.

PLAUCHE. Jean Baptiste Major Commandant of the Battalion
Jean Baptiste PLAUCHE was born in New Orleans on January 28, 1785. He was married in 1809 to Mathilde DASPIT ST. AMANT, a native of St. Charles Parish, and daughter of Antoine DASPIT ST. AMANT and Eulalie ZERINGUE. Jean Baptiste was a cotton broker, and commission merchant living in New Orleans on Magazine St., while his business office was located on Gravier and

(188)

Magazine Streets. He was also one of the directors of the Savings Bank, and an officer of various Masonic Lodges, such as the W. Lodge Perfect Union and *La Fraternité*, No. 35. He was politically involved, for he served in various offices at the local level and as lieutenant governor in 1850. He also continued his military career, for he was the brigadier general of the Louisiana Legion. He died on January 2, 1860, and his wife a few years earlier. I-A, lix; I-D, 4; I-E, 95; II-A; II-B; III-D, 57; III-E, 23; III-F, 17; III-G, 145, 202; III-H, 168, 249, 255; V-Bp, 239; VIII-B, August 14, 1816; IX-G, 83; IX-Q, 210.

POCHE, [See PORTE, François and BOETA, José]   Dragoons
The soldier with the surname of POCHE in the compilation is cited by Pelletier as Bertrand PORCHE, while the other compilers do not cite anyone with the surnames of POCHE as having served in the Dragoons. The writer was unable to locate any of the above cited in the records, and although there were seven or eight soldiers with the surname of POCHE in various other units, the writer is of the opinion that the soldier who served in the Dragoons may have been the soldier with the surname of BOETA or POETE, as cited by both Casey and Pierson as having served in the unit. I-D, 9; I-E, 95. I-D, 9; I-E, 95.

POETE [See PORTE, François and BOETA, José]

POINCY [See DESDUNES, POINCY]

POLITY (POLITE), Nicolas   Francs*
Nicholas POLITE was married to Magdeleine CUVILLIER, daughter of Joseph CUVILLIER and Dame VINICK. Nicolas and Magdeleine had several children, one whose name was Antoine, who was born in 1829 and died in New Orleans on August 9, 1832. Magdeleine died in New Orleans on August 9, 1832, but the writer was unable to determine when and where Nicolas may have died. I-A, lx; I-Bc; I-E, 95; II-A.

POLK [See BEANS, Ellis POLK]

POMMIER, C.   Chief Musician   Battalion
The writer was unable to locate any information on C. POMMIER, who was the chief musician of the battalion. The only information located was that as head of the musicians he earned eleven dollars per month while the others earned nine. The only two persons with the surname the writer located was Louis POMMIER, who served in the 17th., 18th., and 19th Consolidated Regiment and was a resident of St. Martin Parish in 1830; and an Etienne POMMIER, who was a native of St. Domingue [Haiti] and died in New Orleans on November 3, 1840, at the age of fifty. It is possible that either or both of the two persons cited may have been related to C. POMMIER, but the writer was unable to verify it. I-A, lix; I-Af; I-D, 5; I-E, 96; II-A, III-K, 37.

PONCET, Paul   Dragoons*
Paul PONCET is cited only by Pelletier as having served in the Dragoons, while the only person cited by Pierson with a similar surname as having served during the war was Michel PONCE, who served as a sergeant in the 2nd regiment under CAVELIER. It is possible that Paul and Michel PONCET [PONCE] may have been the same person, but the writer was unable to verify it. The writer located in the New Orleans area a Jean Paul PONTZ [PONCET], who was an exchange broker living on Toulouse St. in 1811 and a P. PONSET, who was a carpenter living on Amour St. in the suburb Marigny. I-D, 10; I-E, 96; III-D, 11.

PONS [John Baptiste]   Dragoons
The soldier with the surname of PONS cited in the compilation in the appendix is listed by Pelletier as J. François PONS, while the other compilers do not cite anyone with the surname as having served during the war. The writer was unable to locate in the records anyone as cited by Pelletier, and he located only a Jean Baptiste PONS, who most probably was the soldier. Jean Baptiste was born in 1786, a native of St. Domingue [Haiti], and he was the son of Marc Antoine PONS and Jeanne Agnés Augustine

(190)

GARCIA PIEMONT [PIEMONT]. Jean Baptiste was a carpenter living in New Orleans in the suburb Marigny. He has served in 1806-1807 in the New Orleans Territorial Militia in the company under Captain George POLLACK. Jean Baptiste died on April 22, 1818 at the age of thirty-two. I-D, 8; I-F, 65; I-G, 5; II-A; III-D, 45; V-Ab, 354-55; V-Bo, 186; VIII-B, November 16, 1810; February 5, 1816.

POPOTTE [See **LEBRUN**, Popotte] Drummer Dragoons*
The drummer in the Dragoons is cited by Casey and Pierson as POPOTTE, while Pelletier cited him as POPOTTE LEBRUN. The census of 1820 and 1830 cite various spellings of the surname POPOTTE as living in New Orleans, with one of them cited as Martine POUPOW. The writer also located a POPONE [POPOTTE?] GUIHART, who was living in New Orleans at 59 Rampart St. in 1824. The only person with the surname of LEBRUN, as cited by Pelletier, whom the writer located was a Jacques LEBRUN, who was an innkeeper in New Orleans living in a house on the corner of History and Amour Streets in 1811. He died in 1820. I-A, lx; I-D, 5; I-E, 96; III-D, 35; III-F; III-J, 25; III-K, 36; V-Bj, 118; VIII-B, December 31, 1817.

PORCHE (PUCHE), Joseph [Jr.] Carabiners
The only information the writer was able to locate on Joseph PUCHE was that he was married to Arcona ALACHE [LARCHE?], from which union a child named Joseph was born in 1813. The child died in New Orleans in September 22, 1815. I-A, lix; I-Ba; II-A.

PORTE (POETE), François? John? [Sr. and Jr.] Dragoons
Pierson states that the soldier with the surname of PORTE originally signed it as POETE. Casey cites a Jos. BOETA [Jr.] and a senior BOETA as the soldiers in the Dragoons, but he places a question mark to indicate uncertainty of the correct spelling. The writer viewed the original muster roll and interpreted the signature to be that of POETE.
In checking the records for the period, the writer was unable to

locate a Jos. POETE, only a José Maria BOETA [See BOETA, José]. He found only two persons, however, with the surname POETE who were living during the period in New Orleans. The first was François POETE, who was married to Jeanne GOURIER, from which union several children were born. One was Elizabeth Françoise, an infant of three months who died on July 3, 1815. The second person was John POETE, a native of Guadaloupe, who was the son of François POETE and Marie Ann SIRONDELLE [GIRONDELLE]. It is possible that François, the father of John, was also the father of François who was married to Jeanne GOURIER, but the writer was not able to verify it. I-A, lx; I-Bb; I-E, 96; II-A.

POYCOT (POYNOT), P. J. Carabiniers*
P. J. POYCOT (POYNOT) is cited only by Pelletier as having served in the Carabiniers, while the other compilers do not cite him or anyone with the surname as having served during the war. The only person with the surname whom the writer located in the records was Pierre POYNOT, who lived in New Orleans and was married to Genevieve Marie BREMONDY [BERMOUDY?] PIGALLES. Pierre and Genevieve had several children, some of whom were named Pierre Emile, Pierre, Azelie, Marie Marguerite and others. Pierre lived on Poétes St. and was a clerk working in the office of the mayor. I-D 6; II-A; III-F; III-J, 25; III-K, 38.

PRIEUR, Alexandre Carabiniers
Alexandre PRIEUR was the son of Prospère PRIEUR and Marie CASSANAVE. Alexandre was married to Marie Pauline LANUSSE, daughter of Paul LANUSSE and Céleste MACARTHY, from which union several children were born, one whose name was Félicité Pauline, who was born on August 24, 1831, but died seven months later. Alexandre was a commission merchant specializing in hardwares and ship chandlery, living in New Orleans on Royal St., the same address as Denis PRIEUR, who was mayor of New Orleans. Alexandre had established a business partnership with Pascal PRIEUR, and later with the firm of TOWNSLEY.

Alexandre continued serving in the militia, for he was a 1st Lieutenant of Grenadiers in the 2nd Battalion in 1834. Marie Pauline, his wife died on June 23, 1833, and Alexandre a few years later. I-A, lix; I-D, 7; I-E, 97; II-A; III-E, 23; III-F; III-G, 147; III-H, 172, 252; IV-B, 139; VIII-B, October 14, 1816; October 14, 1816; October 28, 1816; January 1, 1817.

PRIOR (PRYOR), James   Blues
The writer was unable to locate any information on the soldier James PRYOR. It is possible that he may have been the ship captain named PRIOR [PRYOR] who died in New Orleans on August 19, 1835, but the writer was unable to verify it. I-A, lxi; I-D, 13; I-E, 97; II-C.

PRUDIER, [Paul]   Dragoons*
The writer was unable to identify the soldier cited by Casey and Pierson as PRUDIER, due to having been unable to locate his first name or initial. The only person whom the writer located in the records was cited in the census of 1820 as Paul PRUCIER [PRUDIER], who was a resident of Orleans Parish. I-A, lx; I-E, 97; III-J, 26.

PUCHE [See PORCHE, Joseph]

PUECH [Jr.], [Jean]   Musician   Battalion
The musician cited as PUECH, Jr., in the compilation is cited by Pelletier as Ed. PUECH, by Pierson only with the surname of PUCHE, and by Casey and the original payroll as POUCHE. The writer was unable to locate anyone in the records as cited by Pelletier, but is of the opinion that the musician may have been Jean Baptiste PUECH, for a person with the name of Baptiste DELPENCH [DELPUECH] received a state pension for services rendered during the war, yet Pierson does not cite anyone with the surname of PUECH or DELPUECH as having served during the war. Jean Baptiste PUECH was a grocer living in New Orleans at 34 Barracks St., in 1805, but later moved to Levée St. in 1824.

(193)

He was married to Sophie BARRIERE, from which union several children were born. One of them was named Catherine, who was the widow of Jean CHAUTARD [CHOTARD]and wife of Louis MOREAU. Jean Baptiste died on July 23, 1833, at the age of sixty-four. I-A, lix; I-Bf; I-D, 5; I-E, 96; II-A; III-A, 28; III-F; VII-Da, 3; VIII-B, August 2, 1813.

Q

QUAYS, Joseph   Carabiniers*

Joseph QUAYS [O'QUAYS?] is cited only by Pelletier as having served in the Carabiniers, while Pierson cites only a Baptiste O'Quays as having served in the war in the 7th Regiment under LeBEUF. The only information the writer located on Joseph QUAYS was that he was living in New Orleans between 1811-1816. In 1813, Justice of the Peace R. CLAIBORNE of Rapides Parish placed a notice in the local newspaper of New Orleans, stating that Joseph QUAYS and his wife were both absentee property owners of the parish and their land would be confiscated, if they did not pay the delinquent taxes; and in 1816 he sold his house or a house he owned through a lottery drawing. The writer was unable to trace his whereabouts after 1816. I-D, 6; I-E, 90; VIII-B, September 2, 1811; July 5, 1813; July 15, 1816.

R

RABY, A.   Francs*
The soldier A. RABY is cited by Pierson, Casey, and the original payroll as having served in the Francs. In addition to him, Pierson cites an Antoine RABY who served in the 1st Battalion under FORTIER. The writer was unable to identify the soldier A. RABY, for there were an Antoine RABY, who was most probably the one who served under FORTIER, who was a tailor living in New Orleans on Dauphine St. in 1811 and an Anatole RABI [RABY], who lived in New Orleans and died on March 5, 1871. The census of 1830 cites an Antoine RABY living in St. Tammany, who most probably was the tailor who was living in New Orleans in 1811. I-A, lx; I-Bc; I-E, 98; II-B; III-D, 47; III-K, 38.

RAMEL, Henry   Dragoons
The soldier with the surname of RAMEL in the compilation in the appendix is cited by Pelletier as Henry RAMEL, while the other compilers cite only a soldier with the surname, but as having served in the 2nd Regiment under CAVELIER. The writer was unable to definitely identify the soldier, because there were two persons with the name of Henry RAMEL living in New Orleans during the period. The first was Henry J. L. RAMEL, who was married to Françoise TERRIER. He was a carpenter living in New Orleans at 94 Carondelet in 1822. He died in 1832 and his wife on June 29, 1876, at the age of eighty-nine. The second Henry RAMEL was a grocer living on Baronne St. in 1822. I-D, 9; I-E, 98; II-A; III-E, 24; III-G, 149; III-H, 173; III-K, 38; V-Bq, 342; VIII-B, September 18, 1818.

RAPALLO, Giovani [Jean]   Dragoons
Giovani [Jean] RAPALLO is cited only by Pelletier as having served in the Dragoons, while Pierson does not cite anyone with the surname as having served during the war. Giovani [Jean] RAPALLO

lived in New Orleans where he was an umbrella maker at 15 Conde St., but later moved to St. Peter Street and continued to make umbrellas, but branched out his business by listing himself as an oculist. He may have been the Estephen RAPALLO, who died in New Orleans in 1842 or 1843, for an inventory of his succession was opened in probate court in the latter year. I-D, 10; III-F; III-G, 174; V-Bq, 346.

RAULANT, Zénon Chasseurs*
Zénon RAULAND is cited only by Pelletier as having served in the Chasseurs, while the other compilers do not cite him as having served in any unit during the war. The writer was unable to locate anyone in the records as cited by Pelletier. The only two persons with similar surnames who served during the war were René RAULAND, who served in the 2nd Battalion under D'AQUIN and Jacques MEFFRE ROUZAN, who served in the 1st Regiment under DEJAN. I-D, 6; I-E, 99, 103, 104.

RAUX, J. F. Surgeon Mate: Staff Battalion
J. F. RAUX was the surgeon's mate of the battalion. The writer was unable to locate any information on him, except that in 1811 a Simon RIEUX [RAUX], a chemist, and one with only the surname, an apothecary, were living at 37 Toulouse St. in New Orleans. By 1820 the census cites only the widow RAUX, who was residing in New Orleans in the suburb Marigny. I-A, lix; I-Bg; I-E, 99; III-D, 47; III-H, 184; III-K, 26.

RAYMOND [See REYNAUD, Louis Melchior] Dragoons
The compilation in the appendix cites two soldiers with the surname of RAYMOND, who served in the Dragoons. Casey and Pierson cite only one soldier with the surname of RAYMOND in the Dragoons, but also cite a Louis Melchoir RAYMOND, who originally signed his name as L. M. REYNAUD, as a 1st Lieutenant and Adjutant Major of the Battalion. The second soldier with the surname of RAYMOND, who served in the Dragoons was most

(197)

probably Charles RAYMOND, who received a state pension for service rendered during the war, yet he is the only person with the surname of RAYMOND who is unaccounted for in Pierson's compilation. I-A, lix, lx; I-E, 98-99.

RAYMOND, [Charles]   Dragoons
The writer is of the opinion that the soldier with the surname of RAYMOND is Charles RAYMOND, who received a state pension for service rendered during the war. Pierson accounts for all the soldiers with the surname of RAYMOND, except for the one who served under PLAUCHE and cites him only with his surname. Charles was married to Adélaide ROCHEFORT, from which union several children were born. He was a bricklayer living in New Orleans at 50 St. Claude [Avenue], but later moved his residence to 95 Main St. I-A, lx; I-E, 99; I-A; III-F; III-H, 174; III-K, 38; VII-Dc, 126.

REGNAULT, Théodore?   Dragoons*
The soldier in the Dragoons cited by Casey with the surname of REGNAULT is cited by Pelletier as Théodore REGNAULT and by Pierson only with the surname of REYNAULT. The writer was unable to locate anyone in the records as cited by Pelletier and was, therefore, unable to identify the soldier, for there were too many variations in the possible spelling of the surname. I-A, lx; I-D, 9; I-E, 100.

REGRET [See SANSCHARGRIN, Joseph]

RESIGNON, Henry   Dragoons*
The only information the writer located on Henry C. B. RESIGNON was that he was an engineer working for the water works in New Orleans in 1834. He died in New Orleans in 1836 or 1837, for an inventory of his succession was opened in probate court in the latter year. I-A, lx; I-E, 100; I-H, 178; V-bq, 344.

REYNAUD, Louis Melchior   1st Lt. and Adjutant Major Battalion
Jean Louis Melchior REYNAUD was born in 1785. He was married to Eloise RILLIEUX, from which union several children were born. One was named Marie Laure, who was born on December 4, 1830. Jean Louis was a broker and a commission merchant living in New Orleans. He lived on Chartres St., but later moved to various other places. He also owned a cotton press located on Tchoupitoulas St. He was an officer of the Asylum for Destitute Orphan Boys and was elected as a representative in 1811 to the Territorial Convention. He received a state pension for service rendered during the war and died on September 20, 1835. I-A, lix; I-D, 4; I-E, 100; II-A; III-E, 25; III-F; III-G, 151; III-H, 176, 248; V-Bq, 343; VII-C; VII-Dc, 126; VIII-B, October 9, 1811; April 1, 1816.

REZAISON [See RESIGNON, Henry]

RIBARD (BIBARD), Pierre   Francs
Pierre BIBARD lived in New Orleans in the suburb "La Course." He was delinquent in paying his taxes to repair the levee, and the mayor and city council had to place a notice in the local paper reminding him and others who were delinquent. He died in New Orleans in 1818. I-A, lx; I-D, 11; I-E, 11; V-Bd, 238; VIII-B, November 16, 1810.

RICHARD, A.   Chasseurs
The soldier cited as A. RICHARD in the compilation is cited as Antoine RICHARD by Pelletier. Pierson cites three soldiers with the name of A. RICHARD, one who served in the Chasseurs. Also, he cites an Anaclet, Auguste, and Augustus RICHARD, who served in other units. The writer located an Alexandre Antoine RICHARD in the records who was the son of Pierre Richard and Constance LeBLANC. Alexandre Antoine was confirmed by Bishop Peñalver in St. James Parish in 1796. The only other person with the surname of RICHARD who lived in New Orleans during the period was Auguste RICHARD, a native of Bordeaux, France, who was

born in 1790. He was a tailor living on St. Louis Street in 1809. He died on September 17, 1825. I-A, lix; I-D, 16; I-E, 100; II-A; III-C, 213; III-J, 26; III-K, 39; IV-B, 10; V-Bp, 244; VII-C; VII-Dc, 126; VIII-B, December 27, 1813; September 18, 1818.

RIVARDE, Achille   Carabiners*
Achille RIVARDE is cited by Pelletier as having served in the Carabiners, while the other compilers place him in the 1st Regiment under DEJAN. Achille lived in New Orleans, where he was a merchant living at 9 Toulouse, but later moved to 119 Esplanade [Avenue]. He had formed a business partership with Silvain PEYROUX, another veteran of the war, but later dissolved the partnership. Achille died on March 28, 1848. I-D, 7; I-E, 101; II-A; II-B; III-F; III-G, 178; VIII-B, August 8, 1817.

RIVAUX, [RIVEAUX], Eugéne   Dragoons
The soldier cited with the surname of RIVAUX in the compilation is cited by Pelletier as Eugéne RIVAUX, while Casey and Pierson cite only the surname of RIVAUX. Pierson, in addition, cites a Eugéne RIVEAU (RIVAUX) as having served as a corporal in the 2nd Battalion under PLAUCHE, but the writer was unable to verify it. The only information the writer located on Eugéne RIVAUX was that he was a constable living in New Orleans at 54 St. Peter in 1822. I-A, lx; I-D, 9; I-E, 101; III-E, 25.

RIVIERE   Dragoons
The soldier with the surname of RIVIERE cited in the compilation in the appendix as having served in the Dragoons is listed by Pelletier as Drausin RIVIERE. The other compilers cite only a François RIVIERE as having served during the war in the artillery company under Captain CHAUDURIER. The writer was unable to locate anyone as cited by Pelletier, but located that an F. [François?] was living in the suburb Marigny in New Orleans in 1820, and a François RIVIERE, who was a resident of St. Landry Parish in 1830. The only three persons with the surname of RIVIERE living in New Orleans during the period were a Bernard RIVIERE, who

was married to Genevieve TOURNE, and who died on October 18, 1837, at the age of sixty; Jean RIVIERE, a grocer who died on January 9, 1870, at the age of seventy; and Jérôme RIVIERE, a wheelwright living at 43 Julia St. in 1824. I-D, 9; I-E, 101-102; II-A; III-F; III-H, 178; III-J, 27; III-K, 39.

ROBERT, Arnaud   4th Sergeant   Francs
Casey, Pierson and the original payroll sheet cite the 4th Sergeant as Arnaud ROBERT, while Pelletier cites him as Antoine ROBERT. Pierson cites Antoine ROBERT as a private who served in the 2nd Regiment under CAVELIER. Arnaud ROBERT was married to Louise VINOT, from which union several children were born. One of them was named Henriette Hélene, who was born in 1814. Arnaud was a shoemaker living in New Orleans in 1811 at 29 Orleans St. I-A, lx; I-Bc; I-D, 11; I-E, 102; II-A; III-D, 47.

ROBERTIN, Sébastien   Francs*
Sébastian ROBERTIN was cited only by Pelletier as having served in the Francs, while the other compilers do not cite anyone with the surname as having served during the war. The writer was unable to locate in the records anyone with the surname of ROBERTIN. I-D, 12.

ROBERTSON, Louis   3rd Corporal   Blues*
Louis ROBERTSON is cited only by Pelletier as the 3rd Corporal in the Blues, while the other compilers do not cite anyone with the name of Louis ROBERTSON as having served in the war. The only persons living in New Orleans during the period whom the writer located who could possibly have been the soldier cited was an L. [Louis?] ROBERTSON, who was an accountant living on the corner of Railroad and Levée Streets, and an R. L. ROBERTSON who was an inspector of the Louisiana Insurance Company and the Merchants Insurance Company in 1834. I-D, 13; III-G, 179, 242-243; III-K, 40.

ROBIN, André   Chasseurs*
André ROBIN is cited only by Pelletier as having served in the Chasseurs, while Pierson cites an Andrew ROBINE [ROBIN] as having served under DeCLOUET. In New Orleans there was only an André ROBIN, a native of France, and son of Lorenzo ROBIN and Marguerite BRO [BREAUX], who died on September 3, 1814. The only other André ROBIN was cited as a resident of St. Landry Parish in the census of 1820 and 1830. I-D, 16; I-E, 102; II-A; III-J, 27; III-K, 40; V-Bp, 242.

ROBLOMT, Lucien   Francs*
Lucien ROBLOMT is cited only by Pelletier as having served in the Francs, while the other compilers do not cite anyone with the surname as having served during the war. The writer was unable to locate anyone with the surname in the records. It is possible that the soldier may have been [Nicolas] ROBELOT, who was cited by Vincent NOLTE in his memoirs, yet he is not cited by Pierson. N. [Nicolas] ROBELOT was a physician and one of the administrators of the Charity Hospital of New Orleans in 1811. He lived at 44 Main St., but sold his house and shortly after the war went to France. I-D, 12; III-D, 47; VIII-B, October 9, 1811; July 5, 1813; IX-Q, 239.

ROCHE, Charles Marie   3rd Lt.   Carabiniers
Charles Marie ROCHE was born in 1768-1769, a native of Leon [Lyon?], France, and the son of Michel ROCHE and Micaëla BESSON. Charles was married to Eulalie SALANNE [LALANE?], from which union several children were born. One was named Oliver, who died on October 5, 1817, at the age of ten. Charles and his brother Pierre owned a book and stationery store in New Orleans in Royal St. He was active in community affairs, for in 1814 he served as a juror in a case in parish court. He received a state pension for service rendered during the war and died on August 21, 1819. I-A, lix; I-D, 5; I-E, 102; II-A; III-E, 25; V-Bp, 243; VI-H, June 23, 1814; VII-Dc, 126; IX-Q, 211.

ROCHE, Pierre F.   Captain   Carabiniers
Pierre F. ROCHE was born on August 13, 1790, the son of Michel ROCHE and Micaëla BESSON. Pierre was married to Dame HARDY, from which union several children were born. One was Elémore Roy, who died when he was less than a year old. Pierre and his brother Charles owned a book and stationery shop in New Orleans. Pierre was an experienced and outstanding officer, for Vincent NOLTE in his memoirs claims that he fought with Napoleon in the Egyptian Campaign and when Major Jean Baptiste PLAUCHE hesitated to order the battalion into combat because he did not want to risk the lives of so many fathers, Pierre calmed him and encouraged him to proceed into combat. Shortly after the war Pierre went to France to settle some business, but then returned to New Orleans. He was an officer of various Masonic Lodges, such as Grand Marshal of the Grand Lodge of New Orleans. He received a state pension for service rendered during the war, and he died on November 17, 1856, and his wife a few years earlier on February 26, 1848. I-A, lix; I-D, 5; I-E, 102; II-A; III-E, 25; III-F; VII-Da, 3; VIII-B, November 25, 1814; IX-G, 83; IX-L, 180; IX-Q, 205, 210, 244.

ROLAND [ROLLAND] [See ROLLAND, Vincent
The compilers cite four soldiers who served under PLAUCHE with the surname of ROLAND or ROLLAND. Two of them were cited as George ROLLAND and [Jean] Baptiste ROLLAND, while two others were cited only by their surnames. Pelletier, however, cites the ones with only the surnames as Simon ROLAND, who served in the Carabiniers, and Théophile ROLLAND, who served in the Chasseurs. The writer located only that Simon ROLAND was a corporal of the New Orleans Militia during the Spanish period in 1792, but was unable to locate a Théophile ROLLAND in the records. The only one with a similar name whom he located was a Théodule ROLAND [ROLLAND], who was living in New Orleans on the corner of Julia and Foucher Streets in 1834. The writer is of the opinion that the name of one of the soldiers cited by Pelle-

tier as either Simon and Théophile, may actually have been Vincent ROLLAND, who received a state pension for service rendered during the war, yet he is not accounted for by either Casey or Pierson. I-A, lix, lxi; I-D, 7, 16; I-E, 103; III-H, 181; IX-J, 254.

ROLLAND, George   Francs
George ROLLAND was married to Carmelite BOCOD [BOUQUOI], from which union several children were born. George was divorced from Carmelite in 1820. He lived in New Orleans on the corner of Jacobé and Tchoupitoulas Streets. I-A, lx; I-E, 103; III-H, 181; VI-Gb, 48.

ROLLAND [ROLAND], Jean Baptiste   Francs
Jean Baptiste ROLLAND [ROLAND] was born on January 1, 1794, the son of Jean Baptiste ROLLAND and Isabel Anne Barbara CAMBRE. Jean Baptsite [Jr.] was married to Victoire LABATUT, from which union several children were born. One was named Manuel Marceline, who was born in 1816. Jean died in New Orleans on December 29, 1827. I-A, lx; I-E, 103; II-A; III-D, 46; V-Ab, 362-75; V-Bp, 242.

ROLLAND (ROLANDO), Vincent [See ROLAND]
Vincent ROLLAND (ROLANDO) was born in 1790, a native of Italy. He received a state pension for service rendered during the war. He died in New Orleans on September 24, 1829. I-A, lix, lxi; I-E, 103; II-A; VII-Dc, 126.

ROMAN (ROMAIN), [Pierre]   Musician   Carabiniers*
Casey and Pierson cite the musician with only the surname of ROMAN as having served in the Carabiniers. In addition, Pierson cites seven other soldiers with the first names and surnames of ROMAN or ROMAIN, who served under DeCLOUET or in the 6th Regiment under LANDRY. The writer is of the opinion that the musician who served in the Carabiniers may have been Pierre ROMAN (ROMAIN), who was of age and living in New Orleans in

1811. He was a barber and later a merchant of perfumes living in Spain St., while his store was located on Chartres St. Later he established a company in partership with his son, Pierre Louis. I-A, lix; I-E, 103; III-D, 47; III-F; III-G, 155; III-H, 182; III-J, 27; III-K, 40; V-Br, 33.

RONDEAU, [François? Jean?] 8th Corporal Carabiniers
The writer was unable to determine in the original muster roll whether the first name initial of the soldier with the surname of RONDEAU was either a "J" or an "F". Casey cites him as X. E. RONDEAU, while Pierson and Pelletier cite only the surname. To complicate matters, the writer located both a François and a Jean RONDEAU living during the period in New Orleans. François RONDEAU was married to Marie Claudine MOUTAS, from which union a daughter named Marie Louise Uranie was born. Marie Louise was married to Jean Bernard BERTUS. The second was Jean RONDEAU, a merchant living in New Orleans on Tchoupitoulas St. between 1816-1822. He signed the petition addressed to General Andrew JACKSON to have Lt. William AUDEBERT, a teacher, released early from the service, so that he could continue to instruct the children. I-A, lix; I-Ba; I-D, 5; I-E, 103; II-A; III-E, 25; VI-Da, January 21, 1815; VIII-B, May 1, 1816; December 31, 1817.

ROSSIGNOL [See DESDUNES, POINCY]

ROUCHET, [Joseph] Dragoons
The soldier with the surname of ROUCHET in the compilation in the appendix is cited by Pelletier as S. L. ROUCHET, while Pierson does not cite anyone with the surname as having served during the war. The writer was unable to locate in the records anyone as cited by Pelletier, and the only person with the surname whom he located was Joseph ROUCHET, who was married to Catherine HARTERMANN. He was living in New Orleans, for a daughter named Marie Françoise was born on April 25, 1827 and died on January 30, 1830. A second possibility would be Dominique

ROUQUETTE, who was also not cited by Pierson as having served during the war. Dominique was a native of France and son of Bernard ROUQUETTE and Marianne St. ANTONINI. Dominique was married to Louise COUSSIN (COUSIN), from which union several children were born. He was a merchant living in New Orleans and had served as a 1st Lt. in the Territorial Militia. He died on March 16, 1819. I-D, 9; II-A; III-K, 40; V-Bp, 242; VI-Ca, 633; VIII-B, November 16, 1810.

ROUSSEAU, Pierre André   Dragoons*
DeVerges cites Pierre André ROUSSEAU as having served in the company of sharpshooters, while Pelletier cites him as Pierre ROUSSEAU, who served in the Francs. Casey and Pierson cite only the surname of the soldier, but Casey and the original payroll sheet cite the soldier in the Dragoons.

Pierre André [Antoine] ROUSSEAU was born on December 5, 1787, the son of Pierre George ROUSSEAU, a distinguished captain in the service during the Spanish period, and Marguerite Catherine MILHET, daughter of Joseph MILHET and Marguerite WILTZ. Pierre André was married in 1815 to Marie [Eulalie] Laure Félicité DREAUX, from which union several children were born. He lived in the suburb La Course in 1816 and was appointed syndic [justice of the peace] for the unincorporated suburbs of the upper precincts of New Orleans. He was also an officer of the Board of Health in New Orleans in 1824. He died on January 1 [14?], 1840. I-A, lx; I-Bb; I-D, 12; I-E, 104; II-A; III-F, 10; VIII-B, January 3, 1816; November 17, 1817; IX-G, 84-85.

ROY [See COEUR DE ROY, Dominique]

ROYER, Marcelin   Dragoons*
Marcelin ROYER [ROGER?] is cited only by Pelletier as having served in the Dragoons, while Pierson cites only a John ROYER who served under DeCLOUET. The writer was unable to locate anyone as cited by Pelletier in the records, and the only persons

(206)

whom he located were a Pierre ROYERRE, who was a baker in 1811 and Jean Baptiste ROYER [ROGER], who was a dryer and scourer living in New Orleans. Pierre died in 1842 or 1843, for an inventory of his succession was opened in probate court. Outside of New Orleans there was only a Charles ROYER, who lived in St. Charles Parish in 1830. I-D, 10; I-E, 105; III-D, 48; III-F; III-K, 40; V-Bq, 346; VIII-B, December 31, 1817; October 30, 1818.

RUFF, Daniel Peter Blues
Daniel Peter RUFF was born in 1781-1782, a native of Maryland. He died in New Orleans on March 1, 1849. I-A,, lxi; I-D, 13; I-E, 105; II-C.

S

SAGORY, Louis Mathurin　　　　　　　　Carabiniers

Louis Mathurin SAGORY was married to Eugénie Félicité TRICOU, from which union several children were born. Three of their names were Louis, Eugénie and Louise. Louis Mathurin was a merchant living in New Orleans at 22 St. Louis Street in 1811. He was sued in court in 1814, and Judge Jacques PITOT ordered that he pay the plaintiff the sum of $1,024. In 1816 someone burglarized his house and took some jewelry, including a gold watch. His wife died on June 9, 1822. The writer was not able to determine when Louis died. I-A, lix; I-D, 105; II-A; III-D, 49; VI-H, July 9, 1814; VIII-B, March 21, 1810; July 4, 1810; January 5, 1816.

SAINET, Emile　　　　　1st Lt. - Quartermaster Battalion

The writer was unable to determine the identity of the soldier, because he located two persons with the name of Emile SAINET living during the period. Most probably they were father and son, but the writer was unable to verify it. One of them had an alias of Jean François. One Emile was an accountant living in New Orleans at 113 Dauphine St., while the other was a merchant living at 17 St. Louis Street in 1822. Emile, the merchant, later moved his resident to St. Ann Street. One of them was a stockholder and director of the Louisiana State Bank, and one, most most probably the accountant, was associated with the firm of Andrew LOCKART [LOCKHART?] & Company. I-A, lix; I-D, 4; I-E, 105; III-E, 25; III-G, 162, 199; III-H, 185, 235; V-Bt, 38; VIII-B, July 18, 1810; September 9, 1811.

ST. ARMAND (St. AMANT, St. ARMANT) Carabiniers
The writer was unable to identify the soldier cited in the compilation in the appendix as St. AMANT and its variations in spelling. Pelletier cites him as Baptiste St. AMAND, but there were six or seven with the name of Baptiste or Jean Baptiste St. AMANT living during the period in Orleans, St. Charles, and Natchitoches Parishes. It is also possible that the soldier may have been either Victor St. AMAND or Marcel DASPIT St. ARMAND, who received state pensions for service rendered during the war, for neither of them is cited by Pierson with the names of Victor and Marcel as having served during the war. I-A, lix; I-D, 6; I-E, 111-112; VII-Dd, 147.

St. AVID, Jean Carabiniers
Jean Martin LASSERVE De St. AVID was born in Tulle, France, on July 13, 1778. He was an attorney and planter. In 1804 he was one of the guests at one of the public halls in New Orleans which was entertaining General James WILKINSON, when a small-scale brawl broke out, when the Americans demanded the band play *"Hail Columbia"*, while the Franco-Americans insisted on *La Marseillaise*. He was also the second of Vincente NOLTE, when Vincent was challenged to a duel with the eldest son of the banker [Joseph] SAUL. Jean died in New Orleans on June 27, 1847. I-A, lix; I-E, 112; II-B; VI-Ca, 181; VIII-B, May 19, 1813; January 31, 1817; July 23, 1817; IX-Q, 218, 242-43.

St. CYR, Joseph Private? Sergeant? Chasseurs? Carabiniers?
The writer was able to determine that Joseph and Stanislas Louis St. CYR were the two soldiers who served under PLAUCHE, but was unable to determine which one was the sergeant in the Chasseurs and which one the private in the Carabiniers. To complicate matters, the writer located three persons with the name of Joseph St. CYR living about the same time, and a third a little later. The first Joseph St. CYR lived in Pointe Coupée Parish in 1820 and 1830. The second Joseph St. CYR lived in New Orleans where he was a printer living at 46 Main St. in 1822, but later moved to

267 Bourbon St. The third Joseph St. CYR also lived in New Orleans and was a carpenter living on Plauche St. near Julia St. in 1834. One of the three Josephs, most probably the one who was the printer, was married to Léocadie BLACHE. The wife of the other Joseph living in New Orleans was named Aspasie, and he received a gift in 1827 from Joseph LeCARPENTIER and his wife Modesta BLACHE. The Joseph who served in the war received a state pension for service rendered during the war. He most probably was the one who died in New Orleans on March 28, 1869. I-A, lix, lxi; I-D, 7, 15; I-E, 112; II-B; III-E, 25; III-G, 57. 167; III-H, 195; III-J, 29; III-K, 43; IV-D, 85, 120; VII-B, 61; VII-Db, 147.

St. CYR, Stanislas Louis [See St. CYR, Joseph]

Stanislas Louis St. CYR was a gold and silversmith living in New Orleans at 25 St. Peter Street in 1822, but later moved to 201 Bourbon St. [on the corner of Bourbon and St. Ann Streets]. He continued his military career in the militia, having attained the rank of major of infantry in the 2nd Battalion of the Louisiana Legion. He later received a state pension for service rendered during and after the war. I-A, lix; lxi; I-D, 7, 15; I-E, 112; III-E, 27; III-G, 167, 218; III-H, 195, 251; VII-B, 61; VII-Dd, 147.

St. GEME, Henry   Captain   Dragoons

Henry Baron De St. GEME lived in New Orleans in a house located on the corner of Levée North and Barracks Streets. He was well-to-do, for he owned several houses in New Orleans. He was an experienced soldier, for he had been in the English service in Jamaica, according to Vincent NOLTE. Henry was in charge of the howitzer of Battery No. I during the battle of 8 January 1815. NOLTE also claims that Henry was the secret partner of Dominique

YOUX and the agent. Henry died before 1842, but the writer was unable to determine the exact date. I-A, lix, 30-32; I-D, 4; I-E, 105; III-D, 49; V-Bh, 260; VIII-B, January 5, 1816; November 26, 1816; IX-L, 147; IX-Q, 206, 208.

St. GERMAIN Francs

The soldier with the surname of St. GERMAIN in the compilation in the appendix is cited as Valere [Valery] St. GERMAIN by Pelletier, but the writer was unable to locate in the records anyone with the name of Valery. In addition to the St. GERMAIN who served under PLAUCHE, Pierson cites four others who served in other units and perhaps one of them may have transferred and served under PLAUCHE. The soldiers with the surname of St. GERMAIN cited by Pierson are F. [François?] St. JERMIN [GERMAIN] and M. [Manuel?] St. JERMIN [St. GERMAIN], who served in the 2nd Regiment under CAVELIER; and Martial St. GERMAIN and Pierre St. GERMAIN, who served in the 3rd Regiment under De LaRONDE and in the marines under Captain SONGY respectively. Manuel (Emmanuel) and later his widow [Dame DUROCHER] received a state pension. Manuel and Martial lived in Orleans Parish in 1820, but Martial was cited as living in Jefferson Parish by 1830. François St. GERMAIN, the son of Pierre St. GERMAIN and Dame BENJINAU, died in New Orleans

(211)

on September 7, 1822, at the age of thirty-nine; and Pierre St. GERMAIN lived in St. Bernard Parish in 1830. I-A, lxi; I-D, 11; I-E, 51, 113; II-A; II-B; III-J, 29; III-K, 43; V-Bq, 348; VIII-B, 61; VII-Dc, 3.

St. JEAN [See MAITREJEAN, Louis]   Dragoons
The private with the surname of St. JEAN cited in the compilation in the appendix is listed by Pelletier as Mathieu JEAN, while Pierson cites only the surname as JEAN. Casey does not cite a St. JEAN or JEAN as a private in the Dragoons, only the one who was the lieutenant. The writer was unable to locate in the records anyone with the name of Mathieu JEAN and could not identify the soldier with the surname, for there were too many of them living during the period. I-D, 9; I-E, 63.

St. JEAN, Jean   1st Lt.   Dragoons
Jean St. JEAN was a merchant living in New Orleans. He had established a business partnership with S. HUBERT, but he dissolved it in 1817. His wife died in New Orleans on November 12, 1878, at the age of seventy, but the writer was unable to determine the date of the death of the husband. I-A, lix; I-D, 8; I-E, 113; II-A; VIII-B, April 1, 1816; September 13, 1816; October 8, 1817.

St. PE, [Pierre De]   Carabiniers*
The soldier with the surname of St. PE is cited by both Casey and Pierson as having served in the Carabiniers. The writer is of the opinion that the soldier may have been Pierre De St. PE, who was the only person with the surname whom the writer located in the records as living during the period and of age. He was married to Marie Hortense VERLOIN DeGRUY, from which union several children were born. One of them was Elizabeth Délphine, who married William Auguste CLAIBORNE FARRAGUT. Marie Hortense died either in 1826 or 1827, for an inventory of her

(212)

succession was opened in probate court in the latter year, and her husband died before 1824. There was also an Etienne PE, who lived and died in New Orleans, for an inventory of his succession was opened in 1826. He may have been the same person as Pierre St. PE, but the writer was unable to verify it. I-A, lix; I-E, 113; IV-D, 89; V-Bo, 190; V-Br. 32.

St. ROMES, Joseph Charles　　　　1st Lt.　　　　Chasseurs
Joseph Charles De St. ROMES was born in 1790-1791 in Port-au-Prince, St. Domingue [Haiti]. He was married to Marie Thérèse Elizabeth VION, but had to obtain special permission from the legislature, because she was his niece. She was the daughter of Marie Elizabeth St. ROMES and Michel VION. Joseph Charles lived in New Orleans on Chartres St. He was one of the principal editors of the Louisiana *Courrier*, and by 1818 he became the official printer for the state. He received a state pension for service rendered during the war and died on August 21, 1843, and his wife much later. I-A, lxi; I-Be; I-D, 15; II-B; III-E, 10; III-F; III-G, 57; III-H, 61; IV-D, 78; V-Br, 38; VI-Gd, 82; VI-Gg, 154; VII-Da, 3; VIII-B, December 4, 1816; January 12, 1818; October 23, 1818; IX-Q, 206.

SANGLIER, [Adolphe]　　　　　　　　　　　　　Chasseurs
The writer was unable to identify the soldier with the surname of SANGLIER who served in the Chasseurs. The only persons whom he located with the surname were living in New Orleans. One was Adolphe SANGLIER, who died on September 26, 1876, and the other was Angelique Genevieve SANGELIER (SANGLIER), who died in New Orleans on August 13, 1835, at the age of seventy. She may have been the mother of Adolphe, but the writer was unable to verify it with the records at hand. I-A, lxi; I-Be; I-E, 106; II-B.

SANSCHAGRIN (SANSREGRET), Joseph   Francs
Joseph Louis SANSREGRET was born in 1779-1780 in Mole St. Nicholas, St. Domingue [Haiti]. He lived in New Orleans where he died on August 29, 1823. I-A, lx; I-Bc; I-D, 11; I-E, 106; I-F, 66; II-A; V-Bq, 350.

SAPHIA [SAFIA], François   Sergeant   Plauche*
François SAPHIA [SAFIA] is cited as a sergeant who served under PLAUCHE only by Pierson. The other compilers do not cite anyone with the surname as having served in the battalion. The writer was unable to locate any information on the soldier, except that he may have been the person cited in the census of 1820 as François SAFOU, who was a resident of Orleans Parish. I-E, 106; III-J, 27.

SAULET [SOULAY], Charles   Dragoons
Charles SAULET [SOULAY] lived in New Orleans at 291 Rampart St. in the 1830's. He and his wife owned a slave named Annette who died on May 25, 1858. Charles died on December 4, 1859. I-A, lx; I-E, 106, 111; II-A; II-B; III-G, 160; III-H, 187.

SCHARP (SHARP), John   Blues
John SHARP was born in 1787, a native of Sussex County, Delaware, and son of Thomas SHARP and Anne MELSON [NELSON]. John was married to Louise GENOIS, daughter of Bernard GENOIS and Catherine MORANT. John and Louise had several children. Five of their names were Jean Baptiste, Louise, Marie Elie, John, and Marie Adélaide, who was married to Elijah CANNON. John [Sr.] was a merchant-tailor living in New Orleans on Burgundy St., while his shop was located on Chartres St. In 1829 he brought suit against Louis A. LACAN and John MYERS, and Judge Gallien PREVAL ordered the marshal to sell some of the furniture belonging to the defendants to satisfy the debt. John died on December

11, 1837, and his wife a little earlier on June 11, 1833. I-A, lxi; I-D, 13; I-E, 108; II-A; III-E, 25; III-F; III-G, 162; III-H, 190; IV-D, 90; V-Br, 34; VIII-A, October 23, 1829; VIII-B, April 1, 1816.

SCHOMBERG, Siméon Philogéne   Chasseurs
Siméon Philogéne SCHOMBERG was born in 1791-1792, a native of Jérémie, St. Domingue [Haiti], and son of Jean Thomas SCHOMBERG and Marie PAICEAUD. Siméon Philogéne received a state pension for service rendered during the war. He died in New Orleans on August 24, 1823, and his widow died on December 16, 1869. I-A, lxi; I-E, 108; II-A; V-Br, 37; VII-Dd, 147; VIII-B, December 2, 1816; March 2, 1818.

SCOTT, John   1st Corporal   Blues
The soldier cited with the surname of SCOTT in the compilation in the appendix is cited by Casey as John G. SCOTT and by Pierson as I. [J.] S. SCOTT. However, they both cite him as a sergeant, instead of a corporal. To complicate matters, Pelletier cites the soldier as Daniel SCOTT. The writer was unable to identify the soldier who served in the Blues, because he located several persons with the name of John SCOTT living in New Orleans and other parishes, as well as a Daniel SCOTT as cited by Pelletier. A soldier with the name of John SCOTT received a state pension for service rendered during the war, but it could have been the John SCOTT who served under PLAUCHE or the John SCOTT who served under Captain LAGAN. I-A, lxi; I-D, 13; I-E, 107; VII-Dd, 147.

SCOUFFLEUR [SCOUFLEUR]   Corporal   Plauche*
The soldier with the surname of SCOUFFLEUR [SCOUFLEUR] is cited only by Pierson as having served as a corporal under PLAUCHE, while Casey does not cite him as having served in the battalion. The only reference the writer located on a person who may have been the soldier was that a person with the surname

(215)

of SOUFFLEUR was residing in Orleans Parish in 1820. I-E, 107; III-J, 28.

SEIGNOURET, [Joseph]   Carabiniers
The soldier with the surname of SEIGNOURET in the compilation in the appendix is cited by Casey as F. (?) SEIGNOURET, and by Pierson as F. SEIGNOURET. The writer examined the original muster roll and the citation appeared as J. SEIGNOURET. The writer located in the records a Joseph SEIGNOURET, who was of age during the period, as well as a François SEIGNOURET, who was living in New Orleans in 1832, but he was too young to have been the soldier. The writer is of the opinion that the soldier was Joseph SEIGNOURET, who was born in Bordeaux, France, on September 3, 1788. He was a merchant living in New Orleans on Royal St. in 1822. He owned an upholstery and furniture store. By 1832 he had moved his store and residence to 30 Main Street, while François, who most probably was his son, ran the furniture warehouse on Royal Street. Joseph died on May 3, 1856, I-A, lix; I-D, 6; I-E, 107; II-B; III-E, 25; III-F; III-G, 162; III-H, 188; VIII-B, October 9, 1818.

SEL, Jean Baptiste   Chasseurs
The soldier cited as J. B. SEL is cited by Pelletier as Jean Baptiste SEL, while Casey and Pierson cite only the surname of SEL. In addition, Pierson cites a J. B. SEL as having served in the 2nd Regiment under CAVELIER, but it is possible that he may be the same soldier who served in the Chasseurs, for at one time there was a large scale transferring of soldiers from one unit to another.

Jean Baptiste SEL was born in 1780-1781, a native of St. Domingue [Haiti]. He was a miniature and portrait painter living in New Orleans in 1811 at 33 Conde St., but later moved his residence to 43 Main St. He was also an amateur actor and dancer, for in 1817 a benefit to raise money was performed at the Conde Ball Room, and he was one of the principal dancers. He died on January 29, 1832, at the age of fifty-one. I-A, lxi; I-D, 16; I-E, 107; II-A; III-D, 50; III-E, 25; III-K, 42; VIII-B, February 16, 1816; March 6, 1816; February 7, 1817.

SELLIER [See PELLIER, Pierre]

SHARP [See SCHARP, John]

SHEPHERD, James Henry   Carabiniers
James Henry SHEPHERD was a commision merchant living in New Orleans in 1809 at 9 St. Louis Street, but later moved his business and residence to Royal St. [on the corner of Royal and Canal Streets]. He was a business associate of [Henry William? George?] PALFREY in 1805, but later dissolved the partnership. James was one of the directors of the New Orleans Insurance Company in 1824, as well as the Swedish Consul. He later received a state pension for service rendered during the war. He died in 1836 or 1837, for an inventory of his succession was conducted by the court of probate in the latter year. I-A, lix; I-D, 7; I-E, 103; II-C; III-A, 29; III-C, 211; III-E, 25; III-F, 14; III-G, 162; III-H, 190; V-Br, 36; VII-Dd, 147; IX-Q, 206.

SIBILOT (CIBILOT), François   Carabiniers
François CIBILOT was a tailor living in New Orleans on the corner of St. Ann and Royal Streets in 1811. The writer was unable to locate any other information on the soldier. I-A, lix; I-D, 6; I-E, 27; III-D, 12.

SIBILOT (CIBILOT), [Joseph]   Chasseurs

SIBILOT (CIBILOT), Louis
The compilation in the appendix cites two soldiers with the surname of SIBILOT (CIBILOT) who served in the Chasseurs, and one of them is cited as a senior. Casey, Pierson and the original muster

roll cite the soldier as Louis CIBILOT, Jr. and CIBILOT, Sr. The writer located that Louis CIBILOT (alias LALUNE) was a tin plate craftsman living in New Orleans in 1822 at 101 Grands Hommes St. He died in July 23, 1832. The writer was unable to locate a senior with the name of Louis or François, and the only other person with the surname whom he located was Joseph CIBILOT, who was a tailor like François CIBILOT, the other soldier who served in the Carabiniers. Joseph was living in New Orleans in 1822 in a residence located in the corner of Apollon and North Erato Streets. The writer was unable to determine whether or not there was a family relationship among all the persons with the surname of CIBILOT cited. I-A, lxi; I-Be; I-E, 27; II-A; III-E, 7; III-J, 29; III-K, 10; VIII-B, September 13, 1816.

SIFFLET, Jean Francs
Jean SIFFLET [Sr.] was a barber living in New Orleans in 1811 on Levée South, but later moved his shop and residence to 181 Tchoupitoulas St. His son, Jean SIFFLET [Jr.], was also a barber whose shop was located at 114 St. Joseph Street, and his residence was on Erato St. near Prytania St. in 1834. Jean [Sr.] was also a constable in 1811 in the suburb St. Mary. During the war he became ill and was confined to the hospital until he rejoined his unit on February 1, 1815. I-Bc; I-D, 11; I-E, 109; III-D, 48; III-G, 163, 165; III-H, 191; III-J, 28; VIII-B, August 5, 1811; January 3, 1816.

SIMILIEN Dragoons
The soldier with the surname of SIMILIEN cited in the compilation in the appendix is cited by Pelletier as Lubin SIMILIEN, while Casey and Pierson cite only the surname. In addition to the SIMILIEN who served in the Dragoons, Pierson cites another who served in the 2nd Battalion under D'AQUIN. The writer was unable to locate in the records anyone cited by Pelletier, but located several persons living in New Orleans during the period with the surname who could possibly have been the soldier in the

Dragoons. First there was a George SIMILIEN who sued his creditors in the court of James PITOT in 1816. The second was Jean Baptiste Paul SIMILIEN who was married to Josephine St. CYR. He most probably was the son of Paul SIMILIEN, a native of Venice who died on June 26, 1814 at the age of sixty. Jean Baptiste was a grocer living in New Orleans on Craps Street. The third was Joseph SIMILIEN who was a shoemaker living at 298 Dauphine Street in 1834. I-A, lx; I-D, 9; I-E, 109; II-A; III-D, 50; III-E, 26; III-H, 191; III-K, 42; V-Bq, 348; VIII-B, January 26, 1816.

SIMON, Lyonnel   Sapper   Battalion*
Lyonnel SIMON is cited as a sapper [engineering-type work] only by Pelletier, while the other compilers do not cite him as serving in any unit during the war. The writer was unable to locate anyone cited by Pelletier in the records. I-D, 4.

SISSET (CICETE), Pierre   Francs
The writer was unable to locate any vital Information on Pierre CICETE, except that he received a state pension for service rendered during the war. A Charles CISSET [CICETE] drafted a will in 1813 in New Orleans, but the writer was unable to determine the relationship. I-A, lx; I-Bc; V-Bc, 366; VII-B, 6l; VIII-B, November 13, 1811.

SMITH, R. [Raphaél]   Blues
The soldier with the surname of SMITH in the compilation in the appendix is cited by Pierson, Casey, and the original payroll as R. SMITH, while Pelletier cites him as William SMITH. There were too many people living during the period with the name of R. SMITH, as well as William Smith, for the writer to have been able to identify the soldier who served under PLAUCHE in the Blues. The writer is of the opinion that the soldier may have been Raphaél [Raphiel] SMITH, who was a resident of St. Landry Parish in 1820 and 1830, and in 1805-1806 he had been appointed captain in the 8th Regiment [in Attakapas and Opelousas] of the Territorial Militia. Pierson cites three Roberts, one Richard, and

an R. SMITH as having served during the war, but does not cite Raphaél SMITH who had military experience, was an officer in the Territorial Militia, and was living during the period. I-A, lxi; I-Bc; I-D, 13; I-E, 110; III-J, 29; III-K, 43; VII-A, 172.

SOUBERCAZE, Antoine   2nd Sergeant   Carabiniers
The soldier with the surname of SOUBERCAZE in the appendix compilation is cited by Casey and Pierson as Ant. [Antoine], and by Pelletier as P. [Pierre] SOUBERCAZE. The writer located both a Pierre and an Antoine SOUBERCAZE living during the period. Antoine SOUBERCAZE was a merchant living in New Orleans who had established in 1810-1811 a business partnership with Jean Baptiste FAGET, Jr. Their business establishment was located at 39 Chartres. Antoine left New Orleans and went to live in Ouachita Parish, for he was cited as living there in the census of 1820. Pierre SOUBERCAZE was born in 1782, a native of Arudy, France. He was married to Eugénie BADENS [BADINS], from which union several children were born. Pierre was a merchant living in New Orleans in 1809 on Levée [St.], but moved his establishment to 12 Toulouse St. by 1811. He died on November 20, 1834. I-A, lx; I-D, 5; I-E, 111; II-A; III-C, 211; III-D, 11, 49; III-J, 29; V-Br, 35; VIII-B, August 15, 1810; September 16, 1811.

SOUBERCAZE, Fleury [See SOUBERCAZE, J. P.] Carabiniers*

SOUBERCAZE, J. P.
Pelletier cites both a Fleury and a J. P. SOUBERCAZE as having served in the Carabiniers, while Casey and Pierson cite an F.[Fleury] and Fcs. [François] who were military secretary on the staff of Governor CLAIBORNE and a private in the 1st Regiment under DEJAN, respectively. The soldier cited by Casey, Pierson, and Pelletier may have been the same person, for the writer was only able to locate in the records a Fleury, Antoine, and Pierre SOUBER-CAZE who were living during the period. The only information the writer located on Fleury SOUBERCAZE was that he was

appointed as 2nd lieutenant in the 1st Regiment of the Territorial Militia in 1809 and that he was the curator for the estate of Monsieur NAVARINE in 1811. I-A, v; I-D, 7; I-E, 111; VI-F, 383; VII-A, 174; VII-B, September 30, 1811.

SOULAY [See SAULET, Charles]

SOULET, J. L. [See SAULET, Charles]   Dragoons
J. L. SOULET is cited by Pelletier as having served in the Dragoons, but the writer is of the opinion that she may have attempted to cite the soldier with the name of Charles SAULET [SOULAY], for he was the one cited by Casey and in the original payroll. I-D, 8.

SPERRIER, E. [Charles]   2nd Corporal   Francs
The soldier cited in the compilation in the appendix as E. SPERRIER, is cited by Pelletier as Eusébe SPERRIER, while Casey and Pierson cite him as Charles PERRIER. To complicate matters, the writer located in the records a Charles SPERRIER [SPERIER] who was living in New Orleans with his brother [Louis] in 1811 and were guardsmen living on Burgundy St. and also a Charles PERRIER, who was a resident of St. James Parish in 1820 and 1830. I-A, lx; I-D, 11; I-E, 93; III-D, 50; III-J, 25; III-K, 36.

STABLE, Richard   Dragoons*
Richard STABLE is cited only by Pelletier as having served in the Dragoons, while Pierson does not cite anyone with the surname as having served during the war. The writer was unable to locate in the records anyone cited by Pelletier, and the only person with the surname whom he located was F. STABLE, who was a gold and silversmith living at 40 Ursuline St. in New Orleans in 1811, but in 1813 was living on Royal St. in a house belonging to Madame DUPRE. I-D, 8; III-D, 48; VIII-B, July 30, 1813.

STERLIN (STERLING), [Lotrege] Plauche*
The soldier with the surname of STERLIN (STERLING) is cited only by Pierson as having served under PLAUCHE. In addition, Pierson cites also a Louis STERLING and a second soldier with only the surname who served in the 10th and 20th Consolidated Regiments. The writer is of the opinion that the soldier who served under PLAUCHE may have been Lotrege STERLING, who was a cabinet maker living in 1811 in New Orleans at 4 Ursuline St. He was cited in the census of 1820, but may have died before 1830, for he was not listed. I-E, 112; III-D, 50; III-J, 29.

STRINGER, Caleb Blues*
The writer located two persons with the name of Caleb STRINGER living during the period, but was unable to determine who was the senior or the junior. The first Caleb STRINGER was a carpenter a cabinet maker living in New Orleans in 1811 at Champs Elysées St., but later moved to Milicerte St. The second Caleb STRINGER was a grocer living in New Orleans in 1822 at 175 Custom House St., while his grocery was located on New Levée [St.]. One of the two Calebs, most probably the carpenter, had served in the Territorial Militia in 1806-1807 in the Company of Orleans Rangers under Captain George T. ROSS. I-A, lxi; I-E, 113; I-G, 12; III-D, 51; III-F; III-G, 168; III-K, 44; VIII-B, September 2, 1811; January 15, 1817.

STRINGER, Greenberg, R. Carabiniers
Greenberg R. STRINGER was a lawyer and notary public living in New Orleans at 44 Bienville St., while his office was located at 42 Chartres St. in 1822, but later he combined his office and home and established it on Royal St. He was one of the directors of the Louisiana State Bank in 1818, and a member of the Board of Health in 1822. He had established a legal firm known as G. R. STRINGER and [J. S.] KENNEDY, but later dissolved it. He died

on September 13, 1849. I-D, 6; I-E, 113; II-A; III-E, 27; III-F, 10; III-G, 168; III-H, 197; VIII-B, June 22, 1818.

STUART, S. Corporal Carabiniers*
The writer was unable to locate any information on the soldier cited as S. STUART by Casey, Pierson, and the original muster roll. The only person whom he located with the surname was Oliver N. C. STUART, who was living in New Orleans in 1818. I-A, lix; I-Ba; I-E, 113; V-Bq, 349.

SUISSE, Barthelemy Plauche*
Barthelemy SUISSE is cited only by Pierson as having served under PLAUCHE, while the other compilers do not cite anyone with the surname as having served in the battalion. Pierson also cites a Barthelemy SUIZA, who served in the company of artillery under Captain WALLACE. It is possible that he may have been the same soldier cited under PLAUCHE. The writer was unable to locate any information on the soldier. I-E, 113.

SYLER, Valentin Carabiniers
The soldier with the surname of SYLER in the compilation in the appendix is cited by Pelletier as Edward SYLER, by Casey as N. SAYLER(?), and by Pierson as V. SAYLER. The writer examined the original muster roll and the name appeared to him as cited by Pierson. V. [Valentin] SAYLER(SYLER) was a cooper living in New Orleans at 103 St. Charles Street, while his shop was located at 30 Camp St. He died in 1824. I-A, lix; I-Ba; I-D, 6; I-E, 107; III-F; V-Br, 32.

T

TESSIER [See TEXIER, François]

TESSIER, Auguste   Musician   Battalion
Auguste TESSIER was born in 1762, a native of Paris, France, and son of Antonio Nicolas TESSIER and Eléonore DELAUNEY. Auguste and his wife had several children, one whose name was Alfred later became an accountant. Auguste was a musician living in New Orleans on Bourbon St. In 1805 he rented from Bernardo COQUET the ballroom in the St. Philip Street Theatre in which two balls per week were performed. His plan was to invite free black women and white men. This, according to Kmen, was the beginning of the "Quadroon Balls." By 1810 Auguste became the manager of the theatre on Conde St., which belonged to Joseph Antoine BONIQUET. In 1817, Auguste played the role of corporal of grenadiers at the performance of "The Deserters" at the Olympic Circus Theatre. Auguste died on October 13, 1817, and his wife much later. I-A, lix; I-Bf; I-E, 115; II-A; III-D, 52; III-G, 170; III-H, 199; V-Br, 41; VIII-B, March 21, 1810; November 30, 1810; March 14, 1817; IX-H, 46-47, 66-67.

TETE, Auguste   Carabiniers
Auguste TETE was married to Marie Rose CLEMENT, from which union several children were born. One of them was Marie Louise who was born in 1814, but died at the age of ten months. Auguste lived in New Orleans where he was the proprietor of a dry goods store located on Levée [St.]. He was a syndic [justice of the peace] for a district in New Orleans. One of his primary duties was to sell at public auction property which had been confiscated by orders of the court. He later received a state pension for service rendered during the war. I-A, lix; I-D, 6; I-E, 115; II-A; III-E, 28; III-F; VII-Dd, 147; VIII-B, August 7, 1818; November 13, 1818.

TEXIER (TESSIER), François Dragoons*
François TEXIER (TESSIER) is cited only by Pelletier as having served in the Dragoons. François was a candy maker and seller living in New Orleans in 1824 at 63 Chartres St. The writer was unable to determine when he died or his family relationships. I-D, 10; III-F.

THEARD, René N. Dragoons*
René Nicholas THEARD was married to Marie Rose ROBERT, from which union several children were born; some of them were named Charles, Jean, and René. René N. was a carpenter, builder, and architect who lived on St. Philip Street in New Orleans, but later moved his residence to Bayou Road. He also owned property in the suburb Marigny, for he sold a lot to Samuel WINTER and Thomas HARMAN. He also sold a plantation in Lafourche which was located opposite the Attakapas Canal, next to the property belonging to Madame André MAYEAUX. René, Jr. did not follow his father's profession, for in 1827 he opened a jewelry and watch store at 187 Chartres St. in New Orleans. René [not certain whether the father or the son] died in New Orleans in 1835. I-A, lx; II-A; III-G, 171; III-H, 199; V-Bs, 11; VII-C; VIII-A, October 13, 1827; VIII-A, November 15, 1813; September 2, 1816; April 9, 1817; IX-M, 314.

THEON [See BARBERET, Théon]

THERCOUT, F. [François] Francs
F. [François] THERCOUT is cited only in the compilation in the appendix as having served in the Francs. The only other person with a similar surname who served in the war was cited by Pierson as Francis TURCUIT [TERCUIT], who served under DeCLOUET. The writer was unable to locate any information on the soldier, except that he may have lived in the parish of St. James, for the writer located a J. TERCUIT living there in 1830. I-E, 115; III-K, 44.

(225)

THEVENOT, François   Francs*
François THEVENOT is cited by both Casey and Pierson as having served in the Francs. He may have been the same soldier cited as François THAVENOT, who was a sergeant in the 2nd Regiment under CAVELIER. The writer was unable to locate any information on the soldier. I-A, 116; I-E, 115-116

THOLOZAN, J. S.   Carabiniers*
J. S. THOLOZAN is cited only by Pelletier as having served in the Carabiniers. Pierson cites only Victor THOLOZAN as having served during the war in the 1st Regiment under DEJAN. The writer was unable to locate any persons in the records as cited by Pelletier, and the only ones with the surname he located were Victor THOLOZAN, who died in New Orleans in 1820 or 1821, Auguste THOLOZAN, who lived on New Levée [St.] in 1834, and Garigue THOLOZAN, and Martin THOLOZAN, who were residents of Orleans Parish in 1830. I-D, 6; I-E, 116; III-H, 199; III-K, 44; V-Br, 41; VIII-B, January 1, 1817.

THOMAS, Mathieu   Francs
Mathieu THOMAS is cited by both Casey and Pierson, but the writer was unable to locate any information on him. I-A, lxi; I-E, 116.

THOMPSON, Nathan   2nd Lt.   Blues
The soldier cited in the compilation as N. THOMPSON is cited by Pelletier as Nicholls THOMPSON and by Casey and Pierson as Nathan THOMPSON. The writer was unable to locate in the records anyone as cited by Pelletier, and the only information he located on Nathan THOMPSON was that he may have lived in or visited New Orleans often, for he was receiving his correspondence at the post office between 1813-1817. I-A, lxi; I-D, 13; I-E, 116; VIII-B, November 5, 1813; July 30, 1817; December 31, 1817.

TOLEDANO, Christoval   Cpl. Q.M.   Francs
Christoval TOLEDANO is cited as a private in the compilation in the appendix, but Casey, Pierson and the original payroll cite him as a corporal and quartermaster. Christoval TOLEDANO was married to Bazilice BARBAY, from which union several children were born. Some of the children were Adolphe, Antoine, Arsène Christoval, Sosthénes, and others. Christoval was a broker and commission merchant living in New Orleans on Magazine St., while his business estabishment was located on Levée [St.]. He established a business partnership with Jean Baptiste HUDRY, but it was dissolved by 1811. Christoval was also one of the directors appointed by the legislature of the Louisiana State Bank. Christoval continued his military duties, for in 1832 he had the rank of captain of the cavalry unit of the New Orleans Dragoons and received a state pension for his military service.
I-A, lx; I-Bc; I-E, 117; II-A; II-B; III-F; III-G, 217; III-H, 201, 234; VII-Dd, 147; VIII-B, November 29, 1811.

TOLEDANO, Jérôme   Francs
Jérôme TOLEDANO was born in 1799-1800. He was married to Hyacinthe DROUET, daughter of Louis DROUET and Dame SAINET. Jérôme was a dray keeper living in New Orleans in 1832 in a house located on the corner of Tchoupitoulas and Benjamin Streets. He received a state pension for service rendered during the war, and he died on May 10, 1862. He may have remarried again, for his first wife, Hyacinthe, died on June 11, 1833, and the records show that his widow continued to receive a state pension after his death. The writer was unable to determine the name of his second wife, if that was the case.
I-A, lxi; I-Bc; I-E, 117; II-A; III-G, 173; V-Bs, 11; VII-B, 62; VII-Dd, 147.

TOLEDANO, Raphaél   Francs
Raphaél TOLEDANO was born on December 20, 1795. He was married to Aimée BEAUVAIS, from which union several children

were born. Two of them were Anne, who was born in 1819, and Fergus, who was born in 1841. Raphaél was a commission merchant and broker living in New Orleans on Conti St., while his business establishment was located on Levée St. He established a business partnership by 1834 with the brothers Henry and George LEGENDRE as commission brokers on St. Louis Street. Raphaél died on July 2, 1861, and his wife a few years later. I-A, lxi; I-Bc; I-D, ll; I-E, 117; II-A; III-E, 28; III-F; III-G, 173; III-H, 201.

TORRES [See DeTORRES, Fernando]

TOUCHET, E. [See FOUCHET, Thomas] Francs
The soldier is cited in the appendix as E. TOUCHET, while Pelletier cites him as Jean TAUCHET. Casey does not cite any person with the surname of TOUCHET or TAUCHET in the Battalion, but he does cite a Thomas FOUCHET as a sergeant in the Francs. The writer was unable to locate in the records any person with the names, but he found a Thomas TOUCHES [TAUCHET], who was living in New Orleans and was an innkeeper at 1 Levée North in the suburb Marigny. Thomas died on February 17, 1820 at the age of forty-five. I-A, lx; I-D, 11; II-A; III-D, 5l; VIII-B, May 1, 1816.

TOURLA, Angel 1st Sergeant Carabiniers
Angel TOURLA was a merchant living in New Orleans in 1811 on St. Peter Street. In 1817 he was sued in court by his creditors, thus he retained as his lawyer a Monsieur DePEYSER. The court rendered a decision against TOURLA and declared him an insolvent debtor, whereupon the creditors appointed Peter MASPERO as their representative to make their claims, and the court appointed the syndic, Auguste TETE, to accept all the claims made by the creditors of Angel TOURLA. Angel may have died shortly thereafter or left the area, for the writer was unable to locate him after 1818. I-A, lix; I-E, 117, 118; III-D, 52; VIII-B, March 28, 1817; April 11, 1817; April 18, 1817; August 7, 1818.

TOURNE, Jérôme   2nd Sergeant   Francs
Jèrôme TOURNE is cited as a 2nd sergeant in the compilation in the appendix and by Pelletier, while Casey and Pierson cite him as a 1st Sergeant. Jérôme was a victualler living in New Orleans at 49 Julia St. in the 1820's, but later opened a shoe store on the corner of Levée and St. Philip Streets, while his residence was located at 56 Hospital St. [Governor Nicholls St.]. Jérôme later received a state pension for service rendered during the war. I-A, lx; I-D, II; I-E, 117; III-E, 28; III-F; III-G, 173; III-H, 202; III-J, 30; VII-Dd, 147; VIII-B, August 2, 1816; May 14, 1817.

TREME [See TRIME, Edouard]   Musician   Battalion*
Casey, Pierson, and the original payroll sheet cite two musicians with the surname of TREME who served under PLAUCHE, one only as TREME, Sr. and the second as Edouard TREME, Jr. The compilation in the appendix cites only one person with the surname of TRIME as the musician, while Pelletier lists him as H. TRIME. The writer located an H. [Henry] TREME, who owned a brickyard and lived in the same household, below the city of New Orleans near a convent [Ursuline], with Edouard TREME, who was one of the musicians cited. Henry was also a 1st Lieutenant in the Chasseurs of St. Bernard by 1834. The writer is of the opinion that the musician under PLAUCHE may have been Benoit TREME, for he received a state pension for service rendered during the war and is the only person with the surname of TREME who is unaccounted for by Casey and Pierson in their compilations. The writer located in the records that Benoit TREME was a resident of St. Bernard Parish in 1830. He was married to Eliza BELLO, daughter of Maximilien BELLO and Jeanne DUPRE. A second person with the name of Benoit, or perhaps the same one, was also married to Silvanie DARCANTEL. It is possible that he may have been the same person who remarried after the death of his first wife, but the writer was unable to confirm it with the records at hand. I-A, lix; I-Bf; I-D, 5; I-E, 118; II-A; II-B; III-G, 174; III-H, 203, 250; VII-Dd, 148; VIII-B, October 3, 1810.

TREMOULET, Bernard   3rd Corporal   Carabiniers
L. P. Bernard C. TREMOULET was born on July 13, 1756, a native of Mirande, France, and son of Antoine TREMOULET and Catherine CATINAT. Bernard was married in 1795 to Marie Victoire SOUBIE, from which union several children were born. Three of them were Bernard, who died in 1815, Charles, and Cyprien. Bernard [Sr.] lived in New Orleans where he was a businessman and owner of a hotel. He lived in a house on Levée North in 1805, but later moved to 143 Bourbon St., where he was cited as a gentleman. He established a business partnership with Jean TURPIN, but he dissolved it by 1813. Bernard also used to manage the New Coffee Exchange which belonged to Peter MASPERO, but he had to give it up. The legislature occasionally used the hotel owned by Bernard to hold its convention, such as in 1816, when he charged them $750 for its use. Bernard died on November 21, 1828. I-A, lix; I-Ba; I-D, 5; I-E, 118; II-A; III-A, 23; III-D, 51; III-E, 28; III-H, 203; VI-Aa, 331; VI-Ga, 14; V-I, June 25, 1814; VIII-B, October 31, 1810; November 16, 1810; May 28, 1813; November 8, 1814; March 17, 1817; May 5, 1817; IX-G, 95.

TREMOULET, Charles   Carabiniers
Charles TREMOULET was born in New Orleans on November 4, 1796. He was married to Henriette Coralie ROCHE, from which union several children were born. Two of them were Louise Aimée and Charles. Charles lived in New Orleans, where he was a commission merchant and broker at 48 Main St. Charles died on September 9, 1843 in LeHavre, France, and his wife on December 9, 1867, in New Jersey. I-A, lix; I-E, 118; II-A; II-B; III-G, 174; III-D, 45.

TREPAGNIER, F.   Carabiniers
The soldier with the surname of TREPAGNIER in the compilation in the appendix is cited by Pelletier as Fulgence TREPAGNIER, while Casey, Pierson and the original muster roll cite the soldier only as F. TREPAGNIER. The only information the writer located

on Fulgence TREPAGNIER was that he visited or lived around New Orleans in 1816, for he was receiving his correspondence at the post office for that year. The census of 1820 cites only an F. B. TREPAYNER [TREPAGNIER], but it does not state in which parish he resided, but most probably it was in St. Charles Parish. There was also a François TREPAGNIER from St. Charles Parish, who was married to Louise LABRANCHE, but he may have been too old or dead. He was from St. Charles Parish and served in the German Militia during the Spanish period. I-A, lix; I-Ba; I-D, 7; I-E, 118; II-A; III-J, 31; VIII-B, August 2, 1816; October 14, 1816; IX-J, 257.

TRICOU, Pierre Joseph   Carabiniers
Pierre Joseph TRICOU was a native of Bordeaux, France. He was married in 1786 to Marie Anne (alias Manette) MARCHAND, daughter of Pierre MARCHAND and Catherine BERNARD. Joseph, as he usually was addressed, and Marie Anne had several children, some whose names were Joseph Adolphe, who was married to Eugénie DeBUYS, Marie, Pierre Joseph [Jr.], and others. Joseph [Sr.] was a merchant, broker, and businessman living in New Orleans on Royal St., but later moved to Rampart St. He was one of the directors of the New Orleans Navigation Company and in 1813 was appointed a commissioner by the state to reappraise the property, in order to allow the state to raise more revenues. Before the war, he had served in the 1st Regiment of the Territorial Militia as a 2nd lieutenant in 1806 and as a 1st lieutenant by 1809. Marie Anne died on July 30, 1842, and Joseph a few years earlier. I-A, lix; I-Ba; I-D, 6; I-E, 118; II-A; III-A, 29; III-B, 83; III-E, 185; III-D, 51; III-E, 28; III-F, 14; III-G, 174; III-H, 203; IV-C, 33; V-Bs, 11, 13; VI-Ca, 158, 579, 639; VII-A, 172, 173; VIII-B, March 21, 1810; November 10, 1810; August 4, 1813; May 12, 1817.

TRIME, Edouard [See TREME]   Musician   Battalion
Edouard TRIME (TREME) was a musician during the war whose pay scale was nine dollars per month. He lived in a two story brick

house located below the city of New Orleans near the convent [Ursuline]. He and H. [Henry] TREME, whose relationship the writer was unable to determine, were the owners of a brickyard. I-A, lix; I-Bf; I-E, 118; III-G, 174; III-H, 203, 250; VIII-B,, October 3, 1810.

TUDOR, Florent   Dragoons*
Florent TUDOR is cited only by Pelletier as having served in the Dragoons, while the other compilers do not cite anyone with the surname as having served during the war. The writer was unable to locate anyone in the records as cited by Pelletier, and the only person with a similar name whom he located was a J. JUDOR [TUDOR?], who in 1811 asked that his creditors present their claims against him at the house of James PITOT. I-D, 10; VIII-B, March 21, 1811.

TURPIN, Jacques   5th Sergeant   Carabiniers
Jacques TURPIN was married to Emilie OLIVIER, from which union several children were born. One of them was Desirée, who was born in 1818 and died when she was fifteen years of age. Jacques was living in Plaquemines Parish, but moved to New Orleans where in 1822 he opened a grocery store at 11 St. Peter Street. He died in New Orleans on October 14, 1844. I-A, lix; I-E, 119; II-A; II-B; III-E; III-J, 3l.

TURPIN, Jean Baptiste [Jr.]   Carabiniers
Jean Baptiste TURPIN was born on August 27, 1790, a native of Bordeaux, France, and son of Jean Baptiste TURPIN [Sr.] and Magdeleine Genevieve Amélie DOUCET. Jean Baptiste [Jr.] was married to Henriette TREMOULET, from which union several children were born. Jean Baptiste was a jeweler living in New Orleans at 8 St. Peter Street, but later moved to Chartres and then Main St. He had established a business partnership with Bernard TREMOULET but dissolved it by 1813. Jean Baptiste also was involved in other business activities, for in 1813 he

sponsored some balls at a local dance hall which he entitled the "Grand Hall of Terpsichore." In 1816 he became associated with the Navy Hotel and advertised that public baths would be offered along with a display of hydraulics to be conducted by Monsieur LeRICHE, the architect of the king of Westphalia. Jean Baptiste died on October 1, 1822 [November 24, 1823], and his wife a few years later. I-A, lix; I-D, 6; I-E, 118; II-A; III-A, 29; III-D, 52; III-G, 75; VIII-B, August 16, 1811; September 30, 1811; May 28, 1813; November 19, 1813; January 5, 1816; March 15, 1816.

V

VALENTINE [VALENTIN] Musician Battalion
The musician with the surname of VALENTINE (VALENTIN) is cited by Pelletier as S. VALENTIN, while the other compilers cite only the surname. The writer located several persons living during the period whose names were Samuel VALENTINE, a native of Philadelphia who died in New Orleans on October 17, 1832; Sallue VALENTINE who died in New Orleans on March 23, 1868, at the age of seventy-one; and Santiago [Jacques] VALENTINE who was married to Marie Catherine BARROSO [BARROSE], but he served in the 3rd Regiment under DeLaRONDE. The writer is of the opinion, in view of the citations made by Pelletier as being highly unreliable, that the soldier with the surname of VALENTINE may have been a François VALENTIN, who was a tailor living in New Orleans at 8 Bourbon St., or an F. VALENTIN who was also a tailor on St. Anthony Street in the suburb Marigny in 1811. Both of them were of age and living during the period in the New Orleans area, but of the eight persons cited by the compilers with the surname of VALENTINE or VALENTIN, none accounts for them as having served during the war. I-A, lix; I-D, 5; I-E, 119; II-A; II-C; III-D, 53; III-K, 205; III-J, 31; V-Bs, 16; VIII-B, January 10, 1816; February 5, 1816; March 13, 1816.

VALLE (VALLET), Amand Constant Chasseurs
The soldier cited in the compilation in the appendix as C. VALLE is cited by Casey, Pierson, and the original muster roll as A. VALLE. Pelletier cites him as Pierre VALLEE, but most probably it was P. R. VALLE who served in the 1st Regiment under DEJAN or the Pierre VALET who served in the mounted company under Captain HUBBARD.

(234)

Amand Constant VALLET was married to Clarisse BENARD, from which union several children were born. Amand lived in New Orleans in the suburb Marigny. He received a state pension for service rendered during the war, and in 1850 had it renewed by the legislature at eight dollars per month. His wife died in 1833, and Amand much later. I-A, lxi; I-Be; I-D, 16; I-E, 119; III-J, 31; III-K, 45; V-Bs, 17; VI-Gu, 109.

VANEL, [Joseph François]   Carabiniers
The soldier with the surname of VANEL cited in the compilation in the appendix is listed by Pelletier as Théodore VANNEL, while Casey, Pierson, and the original muster roll cite only the surname of VANEL. The writer was unable to locate in the records anyone as cited by Pelletier, but located a Joseph François VANEL, who was the only person with the surname who was of age and living during the period. Joseph was married to Emelette [Emilie] ADAN [ADAM], from which union several children were born. One of them was Emilie, who was born in 1812. Joseph was a tailor and broker living in the vicinity of New Orleans. He sold in 1813 a plantation belonging to Pierre PART, which was located one league above the Church [St. Louis Cathedral] in what was then called Cantrelle's Parish, and in 1816 sold several lots and buildings located on the corner of Clio and Erato Streets. He died before 1830, and his widow moved and went to live in the city at 156 Barracks St. I-A, lix; I-Ba; I-D, 6; I-E, 119; II-A; III-H, 106; III-K, 45; V-Bs, 17; VIII-B, March 31, 1816; July 5, 1813; January 5, 1816; February 5, 1816; August 1, 1816.

VASSEL (VASSELLE), Nicolas   3rd Cpl.   Francs
Nicolas VASSELLE was born in 1782, a native of Paris, France. He was married to Dame CIMELLE, the widow of Louis TAUNOU, a native of St. Charles Parish. Nicolas also lived in St. Charles Parish, but he died in New Orleans on September 30, 1828, while his widow remarried in St. Charles. I-A, lx; I-Bc; I-D, 11; I-E, 119; II-A; III-K, 45.

(235)

VEAU, Pierre   Chasseurs
Pierre VEAU was born in 1788-1789. He was married to Délphine GUENER, from which union several children were born. One of them was Marie Octavie, who was born in 1817. He was a wood merchant living in New Orleans at 127 Victory St. Pierre died on January 19, 1828, and his widow, who moved to 95 Marigny after his death, died much later. I-A, lxi; I-Be; I-D, 16; I-E, 120; II-A; III-E, 18; III-F; III-H, 207.

VERLOIN [See DeGRUY, Pierre VERLOIN]

VERRON (VERON), Jean Baptiste   Chasseurs
The soldier with the surname of VERRON cited in the compilation in the appendix is listed by Pelletier as Jean Baptiste VERON, while Casey and Pierson do not cite him at all. In addition, Pierson does not cite anyone with the surname of VERON as having served during the war, nor does he cite a François VARION who received a state pension for service rendered during the war. The writer located information on both Jean Baptiste VERON and François VARION, but was unable to determine with certainty which of the two, if any, served under PLAUCHE.

Jean Baptiste Grégoire VERON was born in 1776, a native of St. Domingue [Haiti]. He was married to Gertrude GRAMMONT, from which union several children were born. One of them was Cecilia Josephine, who was confirmed in the St. Louis Cathedral in 1813. He was a merchant living in New Orleans and established a partnership with a Monsieur MILHET in 1810. Jean was also an officer in the Masonic Order, such as secretary of the Grand Lodge of Louisiana. He died in New Orleans on July 20, 1828. Jean François VARION [VARIAN] was married to Claire LeFEURE, from which union several children were born. One of them was Louise, who was born in Cuba in 1807. Jean François lived in New Orleans and received a state pension for service rendered during the war. I-D, 16; II-A; IV-B, 62; VII-Dd, 148; VIII-B, August 15, 1810, January 6, 1813; March 17, 1813.

VIENNE, Philip Carabiniers*
Philip VIENNE is cited only by Pelletier as having served in the Carabiniers, while the other compilers cite only two persons with the name of Louis VIENNE as having served under Captain ALPUENTE and in the 4th Regiment under MORGAN. The writer was unable to locate anyone in the records as cited by Pelletier, although there were several persons with the surname living during the period in the parishes of Orleans, St. John, and Natchitoches. I-D, 7; I-E, 120; III-J, 31; III-K, 46.

VILLEMONT Dragoons*
The writer was unable to identify the soldier with the surname of VILLEMONT cited by Pierson and in the original muster roll. There were several people living during the period in New Orleans who were of age and could possibly have been the soldier cited. The first was Louis Célestin VILLEMONT, who was married to Marie Félicité DUREL. He lived in New Orleans where he was a cabinet maker at Craps St. in the suburb Marigny. The second was Emile VALMONT [VILLEMONT], who was an accountant living in New Orleans at 29 St. Peter Street in 1822. The third was a Charles VILLEMON [VILLEMONT], who was listed as a resident of Orleans Parish in 1820; and the fourth was an A. St. VILMON [VILLEMONT], who was cited as a resident of Orleans Parish in 1830. I-Bb; I-E, 120, 121; II-A; III-D, 54; III-E; III-G, 177; III-J, 31; III-K, 46.

VISINIER, Charles Félix Carabiniers
Charles Félix VISINIER was a merchant living in New Orleans on St. Peter Street. He established a business partnership in 1817 with John C. WEDERSTRANDT, but later dissolved it. Charles lived in the same household with Nicolas Victor VISINIER, a teacher, who was married to Clémentine PONS, but the writer was unable to determine the family relationship. It is possible that they may have been father and son or brothers. I-A, lix; I-D, 6; I-E, 121; I-G, 6; II-A; III-B, 83; III-C, 213; III-E, 28; III-F; VIII-B, April 9, 1817; August 3, 1818.

VITRAC, Alphonse   Dragoons*
Alphonse VITRAC is cited only by Pelletier as having served in the Dragoons, while Pierson does not cite anyone with the surname as having served during the war. The writer was unable to locate anyone as cited by Pelletier, but located a Hyppolite VITRAC, who was a merchant living in New Orleans between 1817-1824 at 302 Burgundy St. He had established a business partnership in 1817 with [Victorin] DUSSAC, another soldier cited by Pelletier. The only other persons whom the writer located with similar surnames were Charles VITRAE and P. VITRAE, who were residents of Orleans and Avoyelles Parishes in 1820. I-D, 10; III-F; III-J, 31; VIII-B, June 2, 1817.

VOISIN, Jean Baptiste   Carabiniers
Jean Baptiste DUFOURGET VOISIN was born in Louisiana on December 7, 1793, the son of Pierre VOISIN and Charlotte Céleste LESSASSIER. Jean Baptiste was married to Rosalie Uranie FAVIER, from which union several children were born. Four of them were Délphine, Pétronile, Jeanne Célestine, and Angeliae Claire, who was married to Cypriene DESFORGES, the son of the master musician Louis HUS DESFORGES and Elizabeth Victoire DUPRE. Jean lived in New Orleans on St. Joseph Street, and he was a discount clerk and later a first teller of the Bank of Orleans. He later received a state pension for service rendered during the war, and he died on May 2, 1877. [The writer is indebted to George Sénac Rapier for providing him with some of the information on Jean Baptiste VOISIN, one of his ancestors.] I-A, lix; I-Ba; I-D, 7; I-E, 121; II-A; II-B; III-E, 28; III-F; III-G, 178; III-H, 208; 236; IV-D, 125; VII-B, 61; VII-Dd, 148; VIII-B, February 5, 1816; September 18, 1818.

Print by J. Yeager of the Battle of New Orleans and the death of Gen. Packenham.

W

WACHFIELD, Eliphalet   Blues*
Eliphalet WACHFIELD is cited by Pelletier as having served in the Blues, while the other compilers do not cite anyone with the surname as having served in any unit during the war. The only person with a similar surname whom the writer located in the records was a C. A. WARFIELD, who was a resident of Orleans Parish in 1830. I-D, 14; III-K, 46.

WALE, Patrick   Carabiniers
Patrick WALE was born in 1741, a native of Ireland. He had several children, three of whom were named Patrick, Marie, the wife of Honoré COUVERTIE, and Patrick Alexander, who was a natural son. Patrick [Sr.] was a merchant who was residing in Rapides Parish in 1820. In 1813 he and C. D. DONALDSON became the testamentary executors of the late William DONALDSON. They offered to sell fifteen acres of sugar cane, which was harvested on the plantation belonging to the deceased DONALDSON. Patrick died in New Orleans on November 13, 1826, at the age of eighty-five. I-E, 121, 122; II-A; III-J, 31; IV-D, 115; VIII-B, December 27, 1813; December 29, 1813.

WHITE, Lee   Blues
The writer was unable to definitely indentify the soldier named Lee WHITE, except that he was living in New Orleans or vicinity in 1816, for he was receiving correspondence at the post office. The only other person whom the writer located in the records with the name of Lee WHITE was Thornley Lee WHITE, who was

married to Mathilde Feliciane SHAW. After Thornley Lee died, the widow remarried a James JONES in 1832. I-A, lxi; I-D, 13; I-E, 123; IV-D, 42; VIII-B, March 13, 1816; April 15, 1816.

WHITE, Maunsel   Captain   Blues
Maunsel WHITE was born in 1783, a native of Ireland. He came to New Orleans via Louisville, Kentucky, in the early 1800's and married firstly to Eliza Céleste DeLaRONDE and secondly to Héloise DeLaRONDE, daughters of Pierre Denis DeLaRONDE and Eulalie GUERBOIS. Maunsel was a merchant, banker, businessman, railroad promoter, councilman, owner of a plantation in Plaquemines Parish. He lived in New Orleans on St. Charles Street, while his business establishment was located on Gravier St. His business activities were varied, which included being director of various establishments, such as the Savings Bank, the U. S. Branch Bank, Mechanic's and Trader's Bank, the Louisiana Insurance Company, and others. He was also an inventor, for in 1837 the state legislature granted him a patent for settling sugar kettles. He continued his military service and by 1834 had attained the rank of colonel of the 4th Regiment. He died in 1863 and was buried in Cypress Grove Cemetery. I-A, lxi; I-D, 13; I-E, 123; II-A; III-E, 29; III-F; III-G, 180, 197, 202, 204; III-H, 211, 238, 239, 253; IV-D, 46-47; VI-Gl, 82; VIII-A, April 7, 1829; IX-D, 279, 333; IX-G, 100; IX-Pa, 137-138; IX-Q, 206.

WHITE, Richard   Blues*
Richard WHITE was a tailor living in New Orleans at 34 Gravier St., but by 1834 he had moved to 59 Hevia St. During the war Richard was one of the signers of a petition addressed to General Andrew JACKSON, asking him to spare the lives of two soldiers named HARDEN and BRUMFIELD who had been sentenced to death for having been absent during the campaign at Chef Menteur. I-A, lxi; I-E, 123; III-F; III-H, 211; III-J, 32; VI-Dc, February 27, 1815.

WIDNUY (WIDNEY), James Blues
James WIDNEY was married to Jane TOAS, from which union several children were born. One of them was Elizabeth, who was born on May 1, 1818. James lived in New Orleans, where he owned a grocery store in 1811 at 46 Levée South. In 1810 he sued Boag B. HUNTLEY in court over the possession of a slave named Abraham, and the court rendered a decision in favor of the plaintiff [James]. During the war, James was one of the signers of the petition addressed to General Andrew JACKSON, asking him to spare the lives of the two soldiers named HARDEN and BRUMFIELD who had been sentenced to death for having been absent during the campaign at Chef Menteur. James most probably died before 1822, but the writer was unable to verify the date. I-A, lxi; I-E, 124; II-A; III-D, 54; III-J, 32; VI-Dc, February 27, 1815; VII-B, November 30, 1810; July 15, 1816.

WILLIAMSON, J. Drummer Battalion*
J. WILLIAMSON is cited only by Pelletier as a drummer who served under PLAUCHE, while the other compilers cite two persons with the name of John WILLIAMSON, but as having served in the 10th and 13th Consolidated Regiment. The writer was unable to identify the musician, for he located, as living during the period, three persons with the names of John, James, and Joseph WILLIAMSON living throughout Louisiana. I-D, 5; I-E, 124.

WILLIGIE, John Carabiniers*
John WILLIGIE is cited only by Pelletier as having served in the Carabiniers, while the other compilers do not cite anyone with the name as having served in any unit during the war. The writer was unable to locate anyone with the surname in the records, and the only person whom he located with a similar surname was John WILLIE, who was one of the editors of the newspaper *Price Current,* and lived in the New Orleans on Magazine Street between 1816-1824. I-D, 7; III-F; VIII-B, July 15, 1816; January 1, 1817; December 31, 1817.

WINN, John   Blues*
John WINN is cited by Casey, Pierson, and in the original payroll sheet as having served in the Blues, but the writer was unable to locate any information on the soldier, although there were several persons with the surname of WINN living in New Orleans during the period. I-A, lxi; I-Bd; I-E, 125.

INDEX OF THE NAMES OF THE PERSONS ASSOCIATED WITH THE SOLDIERS OF THE BATTALION OF NEW ORLEANS

ADAM, Marguerite	See Louis DUBIGNON
ADAM, Marguerite M.	See Valery NICOLAS
ADAN [ADAM], Emilie	See Joseph F. VANEL
ALACHE, Arcona	See Joseph PORCHE (PUCHE)
ALLAIN, Julie Françoise	See Erasme Robert and Valery Robert AVART
ALLEN, Louis	See Pierre D. HENRY
ALVAREZ, S., Santiago, Simon D.,	See Philip ALVAREZ
AMANT, Céleste	See Jean B. CHASTANT
AMIRAULT DUPLESSIS, Maria	See Cristoval Guillermo and Michel de ARMAS
ANDRY, Céleste	See Sylvain PEYROUX
ANDRY, Clara	See Jean B. DUREL, Sr.
ANDRY, Corine	See William De BUYS
ANDRY, Marie Sophie	See Jean B. LEPRETRE
ANTHONY, Joseph	See Louis CHAVEAU
ARCHIBALD, Marie	See Pierre PIQUERIN (PIQUERY)
ARCILA, Christoval Guillermo	See Christoval Guillermo and Michel de ARMAS
ARCUEIL [ARCUEL], Marie L.	See Louis P. PILIE
ARMITAGE, Anthony James (Sr.)	See James ARMITAGE, Jr.

ARMSTRONG, Eliza Roseta, John	See Andrew ARMSTRONG
ARNAUD (ARNAULD), J. Joseph, Louis	See J. Louis ARNAULT
ARNAULT, Hortense	See Antoine GUILLEMIN
ARNAULT, Pierre	See A. GERVAIS
ARNOUS, Jean	See J. Louis ARNAULT
AUBARET, Marie Marguerite	See Jean. B. JOUBLANC
AUDEBERT, William A.	See J. B. Neuville DUREL
AUBIN LEVASSEUR, L. L.	See Laurent LEVASSEUR
AUDIGE, Guillaume Pierre	See Bernard ANDIGE
AUGIER, Madame	See Jean GOURSON
AVART, Célestin Robert	See Erasme Robert AVART
Eusebio	
François Robert	
Louis Robert	
Marie Aurore	
Sosthénes	
Valentin	
AZERETO, Eugéne	See Jean B. AZERETO
BACAS, Jean Baptiste	See Barthelemy BACAS
Jean David	
Léon	
BADENS, (BADINS), Eugénie	See Antoine SOUBERCAZE
BADON, Felicité	See P. Edmond FOUCHER
BAILLY, Jean	See Jean B. BLANCHARD
BALDESQUI, Madame	See A. LEMOINE
BALIZE, Francisco	See J. BELIZE
Jordin (Jordan)	
M.	
BALLIX, Michel	See François BALLIX
BALTHAZARD, Renétte	See Jean B. DESDUNES
BANCIO PIEMONT, Magdeleine	See POINCY DESDUNES
BARBARIN, Joseph	See Jean Louis BARBARIN
BARBAY, Bazilice	See Christoval TOLEDANO
BARBIER, Félicité	See E. Pierre BOUNY
BARBOT, Louis	See Pierre Victor BARBOT

BARBOT, Madame	See Jean CHEMINARD
BARNET, Adolphe	See Maurice BARNET, Sr.
Caroline	
BARRE, Rose Joseph	See Jean BARRE
BARRIERE, Sophie	See Jean PUECH
BARROSO [BARROSE], Marie	See VALENTINE
BART, Engle	See Jean BART
BARTHELEMY, Bienvú	See Desiré BARTHELEMY
Jean	
BAUMONT, Justine	See Charles F. DUVILLAS
BAURE, Maria	See DAPPREMONT
BAYET, Dorothéa	See Jean B. HENO
BAZINET, Baptiste	See Théodule CASSINATE
BEANS, Nelly	See Ellis Polk BEANS
BEAUCHET St. MARTIN, Marie, Pierre	See Yves LEMONNIER
BEAUVAIS, Aimée	See Raphaél TOLEDANO
BEAUVAIS, Marie Coralie	See Auguste GUIBERT
BEBEE, Charles	See John BEBEE
Henry	
Levi	
BEDOUIN, Joseph, Margarita	See François CAMAS
BELAUME, Dominique, Marie Arsène	See Simon MARCHAND
BELISE, Mathews	See J. BELIZE
BELLO, Eliza, Maximilien	See Benoit TREME
BELOT, André Charles, Marie Antoinette	See Charles BELOT
BELUCHE, Marie Anne	See Eugéne MARCHAND
BEMOUDY PIGALLES, Genevieve	See P. J. POYCOT
BENARD, Clarisse	See Amand C. VALLE
BENJINAU, Madame	See St. GERMAIN
BENOIST, Nicolas J.	See Eustache FREMONT
BERLENO, Robert	See Robert BOLENCE
BERLUCHAUX, Mathilde, Naissant	See P. L. BERLUCHAUX
BERLUCHAUX, Pognon	See A. BERLUCHAUX
BERLUCHAUX, Simon	See Joseph BERLUCHAUX

BERNARD, Catherine   See Eugéne MARCHAND and Pierre TRICOU
BERTUS, Jean Bernard   See François RONDEAU
BESSET, Antoine   See S. J. BISE
BESSI, M. R.   See MAISON ROUGE
BESSON, Micaële   See Charles M. ROCHE and Pierre ROCHE
BIJOT, Félicité P.   See Juan Diego GUADIZ
BILLY, Jean   See William BILLY
BISCOCHE, Marie A.   See Charles LEMAITRE
BISE, A. B.   See S. J. BISE
BLACHE, Léocadie, Modesta   See Joseph St. CYR
BLACHE, Louise A.   See Urbain LESCONFLAIR
BLACHE, Marie E.   See Js. MICHAULT
BLANC, Antoine   See Sébastien HIRIART
BLANCHET, Monsieur   See Francis S. GIRAULT
BLINEAU, Monsieur   See Jean F. CRUZEL
BLOIS, Thomas   See Humbert DEMOURUELLE and Jean B. HENO
BLOUDEAU, Célestine   See Auguste DOUCE
BOCOD, [BOUQUOI], Carmelite   See George ROLLAND
BOEFFARD, John   See Laurent BOUFFART
BOISDORE, Louis, Marguerite   See Valery NICOLAS
BONABEL, Amélie Rosalie Denis J. Marcellin Rosa Céleste   See Antoine Jean BONABLE
BONIQUET, José Antonio   See Peter CRONIN and Auguste TESSIER
BONNAVENTURE, René   See Michel BONNAVENTURE
BONNE, M.   See Jacques BONNEMAISON
BONNEMAISON, Constantin   See Jacques BONNEMAISON
BONNEVAL, C. W. J. A.   See Alexandre BONNEVAL

BONNEVAL (cont.)   See Alexandre BONNEVAL
    Josephine
    Pauline
BORBOMME DEFAUX, Charles   See Louis LEFAUX
BORDES, Marie   See Louis CHAVEAU
BORE, Monsieur   See Theón BARBERET
BORICHET, Monsieur   See E. Pierre BOUNY
BORILLOT, Louis   See Louis BORILLET
BOUBEE, Jean Baptiste   See John BEBEE
BOULAIS, Anne   See FrançoisBALLIX
BOULLEMET, Milland   See Rolland BOULLEMET
BOUMAY, Anne   See Etienne PEDESCLAUX
BOUNY, B.   See Germain MUSSON
BOUQUOI, Juan Luis   See Juan Diego GUADIZ
    Marie Clémentine
BOUQUOI, Carmelite   See George ROLLAND
BOUQUOI, Louise   See Joseph BERLUCHAUX
BOURGEOIS, Joseph   See CLERMONT
BOURGEOIS, Louis   See Joseph BOURGEOIS
BOURGEOIS, Marie C.   See Gabriel DARBOIS
BOURGEOIS, Maurice   See Erasme R. AVART
BOURKE, Cyprien   See L. J. BOURGUE
BOURNOS, Ernestine   See Joseph BOURNOS, Jr.
    Félix
    Laure
    Philip
BOURQ, L. J.   See L. J. BOURGUE
BOURQUET, Rosalie   See Pierre CONSOLOT
BOUSQUET, Félix   See Alphonse BUSQUET
BOUSQUET, Rosalie   See Pierre CONSOLOT
BOZANT, Auguste, Josephine   See Baptiste BOZANT
BOZANT, Anne Cécile   See Jean BOZANT
BOZONIER DeMARMILLON, Angela   See Philippe LANAUX
    Antoine
BRANDEGEE, Jacob, John   See Therence BADIGEE

BRAVAT, Jean	See Jacques BRAVAXT
BREAUX, Marguerite	See André ROBIN
BRELET, Jean B. Auguste	See Jean B. BRELET
BREMONDY PIGALLES, Genevieve	See P. J. POYCOT
BRISSET, A.,Géme, J.	See S. J. BISE
BRISSON, Julienne	See Urbain LESCONFLAIR
BROMSON, Edgard	See J. Alexander BRONSEN
BROU, Emilie	See Pierre HENO, Jr.
BROUET, Achille	See Jean Jacques BROUET
BROUTIN, Madalena	See Ignacio CHALMETTE
BROWNSEN, John	See J. Alexander BRONSEN
BROWNSON, Alexander	See J. Alexander BRONSEN
BROYARD, Charlotte Etienne	See Joseph BERLUCHAUX
BROYARD, Emilie	See Jean MACOIN
BUQUET, Louis	See Alphonse BUSQUET
BURAT, (BURAS), Camille	See Maurice FARGE
BURKE, Marguerite	See Michel NICAUD
BURTHE, Dominique F.	See Laurent MILLAUDON
BUSQUET, Antonio Grégoire Félix Jean E.	See Alphonse BUSQUET
CAHAMILLY, Genevieve Marie	See Vincent LESSASSIER
CALABOU, Jean	See Joseph CALABOUR
CALOGNE, Paul	See François CAMAS
CAMBRE, Isabel Anne	See George ROLLAND
CAMINICHE, Marie	See Chrisphonte NAGEL
CAMUS, Pierre	See François CAMAS
CANNAU, Maria	See François CAMAS
CANNON, Elijah	See John SCHARP
CANNONGE, J. F.	See Charles PAPET
CANON, Marie	See E. Pierre BOUNY
CANTRELLE, Michel, Rose Aglaé	See Sylvain PEYROUX
CAREL, Louise	See Lucien COIGNARD

CARMACK, Daniel David	See Daniel David CORNICO
CARRABY, Marie Louise	See Etinne GUESNARD
CARRE, Adéle D.	See Bernard DUPUY
CARRE, Félix	See F. C. CARRY
CARRIERE, Antoine	See Jean F. CRUZEL
CARRIERE, Marguerite	See P. Edmond FOUCHER
CARRY, Dory, Hinsley E.	See F. C. CARRY
CARTRE, Josephine	See Jean BOZANT
CASSAIGNE, Fouconet	See Urbain CHASSAGNE
CASSANATE, Pierre	See Théodule CASSINATE
CASSANAVE, Marie	See Alexandre PRIEUR
CASSEDY, Alexander	See Daniel CASSADY
CASSON, Bienaimé	See John CASSON
CASSON, François	See J. Louis NAVARRE
CASSOU, John	See John CASSON
CASTELBER, Marie Thérèze	See Jean François BARTHELEMY
CATINAT, Catherine	See Bernard REWMOULET
CATOIRE, Marie Claire	See Jean François BARTHELEMY
Pierre Antoine	
CAUCHOIX, E.	See André GREGOIRE
CAUVIN, Jean	See Henry CAUVIN
CAVAILLE, Pierre	See Jacques CUVILLIER
CAVALIER (CAVELIER), Adélaide	See Pierre A. PAJAND
CENAS, B.	See John CASSON
CENAS, P.	See Alexandre CHOPPIN
CERESSOLES, Jean	See François CERESOL
CENTRE, Josephine	See Jean BOZANT
CHAIGNEAU, Pierre	See P. B. CHAIGNEAU
CHAMEAU, Sr. Pierre	See Denis CHAMEAU
Jr. Pierre	
CHANCEREL, Madame	See Marin DESTOUCHE
CHAPDU, Louise H.	See J. HUARD
CHAPUS, Anne	See Simon MARCHAND
CHAPUS, Antoinette	See Dominique BELAUME
CHAREST DeLAUZON, François	See François LAUZUN
CHAUTARD (CHOTARD), Jean	See Jean PUECH

CHESNE, Eulalie	See Jean B. LAMOTHE, Jr.
CHARLEVILLE, John B. Joseph Vincent	See CHARLEVILLE
CHASSAGNE, Aimé, François	See Urbain CHASSAGNE
CHASTANT, Jean	See Jean B. CHASTANT
CHAUMETTE, Gabriel	See J. CHAUMETTE
CHAUVEAU, John, Mauricio	See Louis CHAUVEAU
CHAVANET, Mélanie	See Jean B. M. FUNEL
CHEVALON, A., Charles Alexandre	See Charles CHEVALON
CHEVALLON, Louisa	See Claude Joseh HUGOT
CIMELLE, Madame	See Nicolas VASSEL
CISSET, Charles	See Pierre SISSET
CLAIBORNE, R.	See Charles MAYER
CLAIRORNE FARRAGUT, William	See Pierre St. PE
CLAIREAU, Antoine	See J. L. CLAIRVAUX
CLARIZENG, Victoria	See CHARLEVILLE
CLAVIE, André Eloise (Louise)	See Jean B. LAMOTHE, Jr.
CLEMENT, Marie R.	See Auguste TETE
CLEMENT, Etienne Joseph Nicholas Paul Louis	See CLERMONT
COEUR DeROY, B. Syndalis	See Dominique COEUR DeROY
COIGNARD, Charles Louis	See Lucien COIGNARD
COLLENS, John	See John COLLINS
COLLINS, Jean L. John P.	See John COLLINS
COMPTESSE, Célestine	See Jean LEMAITRE
CONN, John	See COHN
CONNICK, Davis	See Daniel David CORNICO
CONSOLAT, Charles Joseph François	See Pierre CONSOLOT

CONSTANT, Marguerite	See Jean Diego GUADIZ
CONSTANTIN, Salvador	See Peter CRONIN
COQUET, Bernardo	See Auguste TESSIER
CORBET, Eliza	See Etienne Louis BARBARIN and Jean Louis BARBARIN
CORBIN, Modesta Marie	See Vincent LESSASSIER
CORREJOLES, Félix	See Gabriel CORREJOLES, Sr.
CORREJOLES, Félix, Gabriel	See Etienne MENNIER
COTTEN, B. G. R., Godwin B.	See COTTON
COTTEN, G. B.	See William McCLELLAND
COTTON, J.	See COTTON
COURCEL, Joncin	See Hilaire COURCELLE
COURCELLE, Joachim, Marie Anne	See Etienne COURCELLE
COURCELLO, León	See Hilaire COURCELLE
COUSIN, Théodore	See Jean LANDREAUX
COUSSIN (COUSIN), Louise	See S. L. ROUCHET
COUSSON, Adélaide	See P. FERRIER
COUVERTIE, Honoré	See Patrick WALE
COUVERTIE, Louis B. (Sr.)	See Jean B. COUVERTIE, Sr.
COWPERTHWAIT, Margarita, Santiago	See Daniel D. CORNICO
CREMONA, Peter	See Peter CRONIN
CRONIN, Thomas	See Peter CRONIN
CRUZEL, Charles Joseph, Julie	See Jean B. CRUZEL
CRUZEL, Marie Emma	See Jean François CRUZEL
CURRY, Hinsley E., Thomas	See F. C. CARRY

CUVILLIER, Henry
  Joseph
  M. J. A. A.
  Pierre
  Pierre Ambroise
	See Jacques CUVILLIER

CUVILLIER, Magdeleine	See Nicolas POLITY (POLITE)
DALIA, Cyprien	See Jn. C. DULLIE
DALLEST, Antoinette	See Gabriel LEAUMONT
DAMERON, Charles, Christian	See Christopher DAMERON
DAMPUSE, Claudine	See Jean V. PIDOUX

DANOSSE, Jean	See DENIZE
DAPPREMONT, Alexandre	See DAPPREMONT
Antoine Charles	
Emmanuel	
J.	
Jean Louis	
DARBOIS, Rose	See Gabriel DARBOIS
DARCANTEL, Silvanie	See TREME
DARCE, Philip Henry	See DANSE
DARDAINE, Desirée	See Charles LEMAITRE
DARHAM (DARAM), Marianne E.	See François MIOTON
DASPIT St. AMANT, Antoine, Mathilde	See Jean Baptiste PLAUCHE
DASPIT St. ARMAND, Marcel	See St. ARMAND
DASTUGUE, Catherine	See Jean BARRE
DAUBLING, Valentin	See Joseph BERLUCHAUX
DAUPHIN, Charles	See Jules DAUPHIN
Francis	
J.	
J. B.	
Joseph	
DAVEZAC, Major	See Edward R. HOLLANDER
DAVID, John	See Mathew (Matthew) BUJAC
DAVIS, J.	See Jean DAVIS
Jean Baptiste	
John	
DeARCE, Marie Louise	See John COLLINS
DeARMAS, Victorine	See Pierre Louis MOREL
DEBAN (DEBON), Marguerite	See Jean G. MONTAMAT, Sr.
DEBON, E.	See Louis GARRIDEL
DeBOUSQUET, Jean E.	See Alphonse BUSQUET
DeBUYS, Eugénie	See Pierre J. TRICOU
DeBUYS, Gaspard	See Pierre G. DeBUYS
DECARY, Paul	See Antoine DICHARRY

DECOLOGNE, Genevieve	See Yves LEMONNIER
DeENDE, Frederick	See Henry DeENDE
DEFAUX, Charles	See Louis LEFAUX
DeGLAPION, Christophe Denis	See Christophe CADION
DeGRUY, Marie Hortense	See Pierre St. PE
DeGRUY, Théophile	See Pierre G. DeGRUY
DEJAN, Eulalie	See Pierre G. DeBUYS
DEJAN, Marie	See Jan B. PERRAULT
DEJEAN, Marie	See Jean B. Neuville DUREL
De LABOSTORIE, François François GODARD	See J. P. LABOSTORIE
De LABOSTORIE, Marie Victoire	See Jean B. BRELET
De LARONDE, Eliza Héloise Pierre Denis	See Maunsel WHITE
DeLARUE, Célestin	See Jean B. DeLARUE
DELASSIZE, Amélie Eugénie	See Erasme Robert AVART
DELAUNEY, Eléonore	See Auguste TESSIER
DELILLE DUPART, Marianne	See Lucien LAFFERANDRIE
DELINO CHALMETTE, Ignacio	See Ignacio CHALMETTE
DELLOES, Eloise	See Pierre PICENA
DELPENCH (DELPUECH), Baptiste	See Jean PUECH
DELPEUCH, Antoine	See Cadet LAVERGNE
DEMARATES, Louis George	See Louis DESMARATES
DeMORSEY, Jean	See Nathaniel MORCE
DeMOULIN, François	See François BENETAUD
DEMOURUELLE, Humbert	See Jean B. HENO
DEMOURUELLE, Madame	See Jean B. LAMOTHE
DENICE, John	See DENIZE
DENIS, Ann	See J. B. HACHER
DENIS, Henry	See Michel de ARMAS
DePEYSER, Monsieur	See Angel TOURLA
DEROUSSE, Jean B.	See Anthony DERUSE

DERUZE, Adine R.	See Etienne MENNIER (MEUNIER)
DERUZE, Rosalie	See Gabriel CORREJOLES, Sr.
DESBAHEN, John	See Jos. DESBANS
DESBAN, Charles J.	See Jos. DESBANS
Jean Louis	
Michel	
DESFORGES, Cypriene	See Jean B. VOISIN
DESMARATES BAUDOUIN, Charles	See Louis DESMARATES
DESMARE, Auguste	See Louis DESMARATES
DESPORTES, Josephine	See J. B. HACHER
DESTREHAN, Louise	See P. Edmond FOUCHER
DESVIGNES, Jacques	See Jean DESVIGNES
DETOUR DESTOCHAN	See Michel DETOUR
DEVANT, N.	See DEVAUT
DEVAUD, Richard	See DEVAUT
DEVEAU, Marie Françoise	See Louis DUBIGNON
DEVEZE, Jean, Raymond	See Ferdinand DEVIZE
DeVILLE, Alexandrine	See DAPPREMONT
DOBBS, Henry H.	See Hector DOBBS
Henry M.	
M. Hector	
R.	
DOMINGO, José	See Hilaire DOMINGON
DOMINGON, Hillaire	See Joseph DUCAYET
DONALDSON, C. D., Willian	See Patrick WALE
DORIOCOURT, Antoine	See Pierre DURICON
François	
Ursin	
DORSE, Philip	See DANSE
DORSEY, George	See DANSE
Philip	
Samuel	
DOUCE, Auguste	See Auguste DOUCE
Françoise Clémence	
DOUCET, Magdeleine G.	See Jean B. TURPIN, Jr.

(256)

DOUFOURGET VOISIN, Jean B.	See Jean B. VOISIN
DREAUX, Francis, Guy	See Jules DREUX
DREAUX, Marie	See Pierre A. ROUSSEAU
DREUX, Armand	See Edmond DREAUX
Gentilly	
Guy	
DROUET, Antoine	See DROUET
Edmund (Edmond)	
Jean Baptiste	
Ursain	
DROUET, Hyacinthe	See Jérôme TOLEDANO
Louis	
DROUET, Mathilde	See Joseph BOURGEOIS
DROUILLARD, B. S.	See Louis DROUILLARD
Jean Vincent	
Pierre	
V. A.	
DROUSSIN, Marguerite	See Valery NICOLAS
DUBIGNON, François	See Louis DUBIGNON
Jean	
DUBOIS, Pierre W.	See Pierre DUBOIS
DUBOURG, A.	See Jos. DESBANS
DUBOURG, P. F.	See William DeBUYS
DUBOURG CLOUET DESPRES, Madame	See Sylvain DESPREZ
DUBRIE, Monsier	See François DUCOIN (DUCOING)
DUBUC, Bertrand	See Jean DUBUC
J. L.	
Jean François	
Joseph	
Lucien	
DUCAS, Carlotta	See Alphonse BUSQUET
DUCAYET, César	See Joseph DUCAYET
Etienne	
Etienne Victor	

DUCAYET (cont')   See Joseph DUCAYET
    Jean Marie
    Philip
    Pierre
    Urten
DUCAYET, Etienne Victor   See J. DUCAYET
    F. S.
    J. B.
    Jean Marie
    Joachim Frederico
DUCAYET, Victoire A.   See Etienne GUESNARD
DUCHAMP, Pierre   See Charles DUCHAMP
DUCHARRY, Antoine   See Bernard DUCHAMP
DUCONGE, Pierre   See Charles BELOT
DUCRON, Marie Joseph   See Jean DUBUC
DUFILHO, H.   See Jean FAGOT
DUFILHO, Louis   See H. DUFILHO
    Louis Joseph, Jr.
DUFRASIA, Maria Anna   See Jean ISNARD
DUGAS, Claude   See Prosper FLEURY
DUHULQUOD, L.   See Pierre J. DULCOT
DULEATRE, Marie Julie   See François CAMAS (CAMUS)
DUMINY, Christophe   See Christophe CADION
    Denis
DUPART, Amélie   See Pierre DeGRUY
DUPERRON, J. L.   See DUPERON
    Jean (Jr.)
    Jean (Sr.)
    John L.
DUPLANTIER, Armand   See Sébastien HIRIART
DUPLANTIER, Jean B.   See DUPLANTIER
    Théodore
DUPLESSIS, A.   See Elie A. DUPLESSIS
    E. A.
    François A. (Jr.)

DUPLESSIS, Elie (Sr.)	See François A. DUPLESSIS
François A.	
José	
Marie Anne	
DUPLESSIS, François (Jr.)	See Mathew (Matthew) BUJAC
DUPLESSIS, Maria AMIRAUD	See Christoval G. de ARMAS
DUPRE, Elizabeth V.	See Louis DESFORGES and Jean B. VOISIN
DUPRE, Jeanne	See TREME
DUPRE, Madame	See Richard STABLE
DUPUY, Josephine Marie	See Vincent LESSASSIER
DUPUY, Marie	See Louis LABARRE
DUQUE, Rose	See Gabriel DARBOIS
DURALDE, Martin (Jr.)	See Mathew (Matthew) BUJAC
DURAND, Célestin	See DURAND
J. M.	
Jean Maurice	
M.	
DURAND de St. ROMES, Marie E.	See Alexandre BONNEVAL
DUREL, Aimée	See Jean B. Neuville DUREL
Armand	
Armentine	
Bernard	
Eugéne	
Eugénie	
François	
DUREL, Clara	See Edmond J. FORSTALL
DUREL, François	See Jean B. PERRAULT
Justine	
DUREL, Jean B. Gustave	See Jean B. DUREL, Sr.
Jean B. Zénon	
DUREL, Marie F.	See VILLEMONT
DUREL, Neuville	See Bernard DUPUY
DURIO, Jean	See Jean MACOIN
Julie Desirée	

DUROCHER, Madame	See St. GERMAIN
DUROCHER, Marianne	See Simon MARCHAND
DURRIVE, Honoré	See Pierre DURIVE
Pierre	
DURU (DURIEUX), Theresa	See Jean B. DURU
DUSSAC, Victorin	See Alphonse VITRAC
DUTILLET, François	See Jean B. LONGPRE
DUTOUR, A. B.	See Michel DETOUR
DUVERNAY, Eloïse	See Bastien FREDERICK
ENARD, Pierre Charles	See Etienne ENARD and Jean B. JOUBLANC
ESNARD, A.	See Etienne ENARD
ESTEVE, Marie	See Charles DUCHAMP
FABRE (FABVRE), Monsieur	See Sylvain PEYROUX
FAGET, Jean Baptiste	See H. DUFILHO, Jr. F. MAURICE and Antoine SOUBERCAZE
FAGET, Widow	See Jean FAGOT
FAGOT, Antoine	See FAGOT
Charles	
Drousin	
Neurise	
Pierre	
FAGOT (FAGET), Jean	See FAGOT
Jean Baptiste (Jr.)	
FANCHON, Françoise	See J. L. JEROME
FARGE, Maurice	See Jean ORTEING (OSTIN)
FARGE, Philibert	See Maurice FARGE
FARRAGUT, William A.	See Pierre St. PE
FAUCHET, E.	See FAUCHET
Edmond	
FAUCHET, Joseph	See Edmond FAUCHET
FAVBRE, Louis	See Louis DAUNOY
FAVIER, Rosalie U.	See Jean B. VOISIN
FE (FEE), Jean	See Charles FE (FEE)

FENERET, Monsieur	See Joseph LEBON
FERALDIER, Jacques	See J. FREIDEN
FERNANDEZ, Marie	See Jean François CRUZEL
FERRAND, Pierre	See J. L. FERRAND
FERRANDO, Emmanuel Jean	See J. L. FERRAND
FERRAUD, Françoise	See Desirée BARTHELEMY
FERRER, T.	See Louis FERIET
FERRERA, José Manuel	See Jacques FERRERA
FERRIER, Antoine Pierre Jean Pierre	See P. FERRIER
FEUILLATRE, Jeanne T.	See Louis LABARRE
FISHER, Marie	See Marius MICHEL
FLEURY, B. P.	See Prosper FLEURY
FOISE MORIN, Françoise	See J. L. JEROME
FONTAINE, Catherine	See Jean B. DURU (DURIEUX)
FORSTALL, Marie Louise	See Jean B. DUREL, Sr.
FORSTALL, Mathilde	See Edmond J. FORSTALL
FORT DABNOUR, Hypolite	See Hypolite DABNOIS
FOSSIER, Rose	See Johan A. MASCEY
FOUCHE, Pierre Edmond	See P. Edmond FOUCHER
FOUCHER, Anthony	See FAUCHET
FOUCHER, Antoine Antonio (Jr.) E. Pierre P. E.	See P. Edmond FOUCHER
FOUCHER, Félicité	See Nicolas GOLIS
FOUNEE (FOUREE), Marie Thérése	See Bernard ANDIGE
FOURAGE, Elizabeth	See John A. MASCEY
FOURANT, Marie	See François CORREJOLES, Jr.
FOURNIER, Didier Mertile N.	See A. B. FOURNIER
FREDERICK, Bertrand	See Basil FREDERICK

(261)

FREDERICK, Ursin	See Bastien FREDERICK
Ursin Célestine	
FREMONT, Ann	See Félix BELTREMIEUX
FREMONT, Aurore	See Eustache FREMONT
Etienne	
FRERET, J.P.	See Samuel PAXTON
FRERET, Madame	See Henry CAUVIN
FUNEL, Etienne	Jean B. FUNEL
FUNEL, Jean Baptiste	See Jean B. HUDRY
FUSELIER, Aglaé Aimée	See Jean B. CHASTANT
GACHET, Lorenza	See Philippe LANAUX
GAINNE, Joseph GERVAIS	See Jean GERVAIS
GALBERT, Marie Anne	See Baptiste BOZANT
GALLA, Paméla M.	See Jean C. MARIOT
GALLARD, Genevieve	See Vincent LESSASSIER
GALLON, Emilie	See Jean MACOIN
Louis	
Louise Genevieve	
GALLOT, J. T.	See Jean GAILLOT
Jean	
GANUCHEAU, F. Joly V.	See Seraphin GANUCHAUX
J. L.	
Pierre F.	
GARCIA, Manuel Joseph	See Manuel GARCIA
GARCIA PIEMONT, Augustine	See Jean B. PONS
GARDETTE, Adéle	See Joseph BOURNOS, Jr.
GARIDEL, Ambroise	See Louis GARRIDEL
GARLICK, Joseph	See Jean GARLICK
William	
GARRIGUES FLAUJAC, Jean Charles	See Joseph GARRIGUES
Louise Irma	
GASSIOTE, Jean	See Jean GRASSET
GAUDEAU, Jean	See J. Louis GADOU
GAUDIN, Marguerite	See P. FERRIER

GAUDY, Célestine	See Michel NICE
GAUTHIER (GAUTIER), Jean Baptiste	See Jean GAUTHIER
Jean Jacques	
Juan	
GENESTE, Auguste	See Alexandre GENATIE
GENOIS, Adélaide	See Bernard GENOIS, Jr.
Bernard	
GENOIS, Bernard	See John SCHARP (SHARP)
Louise	
GEOTIN, Catherine E.	See Jean C. MARIOT
GERS, Magdeleine	See MAISON ROUGE
GERVAIS, André	See A. GERVAIS
Pierre	
GERVAIS, Joseph	See Jean GERVAIS
Sébastien	
GERVAIS, Maria	See Jacques LARCHEVAULT
GERVAIS, Suzanne Victoire	See Dominique BELAUME
GERVAIS, Victorine	See Simon MARCHAND
GILLET, Edward	See Christophe GILLET
F.	
Louis	
GILLY, Jean Joseph	See Hypolite GILLY
GIOVANOLI, Cora	See Cora GIOVANELLI
GIRAUD, Jeanne	See Philippe LANAUX
GIRAUDAIS, Justine	See Charles François DUVILLAS
GIRONDELLE, Marie Ann	See François PORTE (POETE)
GLAISSEAU, Eugénie	See Jean B. AZERETO
GODARD, François	See J. P. LABOSTORIE
GODET, Pierre	See Antoine Jean BONABEL
GODOFRY, E. Pierre	See E. Pierre BOUNY
GOISLOU, Josephine	See Edouard GUIGNAN
GOLIS, Desirée	See Nicholas GOLIS
GORDON, Alexander	See Germaine MUSSON
GORDON, M.	See Etienne BERTEL

GORHAM, N. S.	See William T. GORHAM
GOURIER, Jeanne	See François PORTE (POETE)
GOURJON, Jean Baptiste (Jr.)	See Jean GOURSON, Jr.
GOUX, Bernard	See Jean CASSON
GRAHAM, John	See Mathew (Matthew) BUJAC
GRAMMONT, Gertrude	See Jean B. VERRON
GRANGES, Jean	See Jean GARGES
GRANNIER (GRANIER), Adolphe	See GRANNIER (GRANIER)
C.	
Etienne	
G.	
Michel	
Pierre	
GRASSET, Joseph	See Vincent GRASSET
GRAVIER, Ambroise	See A. GRAVIER
Antoine	
Jean	
Nicholas	
GREGOIRE, François	See André GREGOIRE
Rose	
GRELET, Joseph	See François CORREJOLES, Jr.
Marie Cécile	Gabriel CORREJOLES, Sr.
GRILLON, Jean Claude	See François A. DUPLESSIS, Jr.
GRONGES, Jean	See Jean GARGES
GROS, J. T.	See Jacques LEBROS
GRYMES, John R.	See Charles PAPET
GUADIZ, Juan Hypolito	See Juan Diego GUADIZ
GUENER, Délphine	See Pierre VEAU
GUERBOIS, Eulalie	See Maunsel WHITE
GUERIN, Alexandre	See Louis GUERIN
Jean Louis	
GUERIN, Jean Baptiste	See Jean GUERIN
Jean Jules	
GUERLET, Joseph	See François CORREJOLES, Jr.
Marie Cécile	Gabriel CORREJOLES, Sr.

GUESNARD, Louis	See Etienne GUESNARD
Millien	
GUESNON, Carlos	See Etienne GUESNARD
Elodie	
Jacques	
Marie	
GUIBERT, Gabriel	See Auguste GUIBERT
GUICHARD, M.	See Norbert GUICHARD
Magloire	
GUICHARRY, Jacques	See Norbert GUICHARD
GUIDRY, Emilie	See James ARMITAGE
GUIGNAN, Edélmore	See Edouard GUIGNAN
Etienne	
François	
Philip	
GUIHART, Popone	See POPOTTE
GUILLEMIN, François A.	See Louis BORILLET
GUILLEMIN, Jean François	See Antoine GUILLEMIN
T. A.	
GUILLOT, Marie	See J. CHAUMETTE
GUINDON, Auguste	See Auguste GRIMDEN
HACHA, Jean Baptiste	See J. B. HACHER
HACKER, J. B.	See J. B. HACHER
J. J.	
Jorge (George)	
Pierre	
HAGAN, John	See Thomas MILLON (MELLON)
HALL, John L.	See John HULL
HALLER, Jacob	See John HALLER
HALPHEN, Rosa H.	See A. GERVAIS
HARANG, A. L.	See Alphonse HARANG
HARDY, J.	See Julien HARDY
Joachim	
HARDY, Madame	See Pierre F. ROCHE
HARMAN, Thomas	See René THEARD

HART, Jacob (Jr.)	See Jacob HART
HARTERMANN, Catherine	See Joseph ROUCHET
HATREL, Elizabeth	See POINCY DESDUNES
HAYDEL, Magdeleine	See Joseph BOURGEOIS
HENO, Jean Baptiste	See Humbert DEMOURUELLE
HENO, Maria Clara	See Pierre HENO, Jr.
Pierre (Sr.)	
Ursin	
HENO, Pauline	See Jean B. HENO
Yrma	
HILL, Stephen Robert	See François N. MIOTON
HOFFMAN, Francisco	See Pascal HOFFMAN
José	
Paul	
HOLLANDER, Ludoisky	See Edward R. HOLLANDER
HOMBERT, Cyrille	See HANBERT
HOTTIGNON, Louis	See Claudius OTTIGNON
HOUARD, Elizabeth	See Charles CHEVALON
HOUDON, Louis	See A. FERNANDEZ
HOYO, Lisette	See CLERMONT
HUARD, J. J.	See J. HUARD
Jean SEVERIN	
Jules	
Jules J.	
Louis	
HUARD, Pierre	See Pierre PICENA
HUBBARD, Edmunds	See James HUBBARD
HUBERT, M. T.	See Jean B. LEPRETRE
HUBERT, S.	See Jean St. JEAN
HUDRY, Jean Baptiste	See Jean B. FUNEL
	Christoval TOLEDANO
HUET, Charles	See J. P. HUET
Louis	
Pierre	
HUFFMAN, Robert	See Pascal HOFFMAN

HUGOT, Arcena   See Claude Joseph HUGOT
    Carlos
    Charles
    Francisco
    Jeanne Lucille
    L.
HUMBERT, A.   See HANBERT
    Célestin
HUNTLEY, Boag B.   See JAMES WIDNUY (WIDNEY)
HUTCHINGS, Jacob   See David HUTCHINS (HUTCHINGS)
    William
IRONQUET, Marie   See Germain MUSSON
ISNARD, Jean L.   See Nicolas J. PIERRE
JEAN, Mathieu   See St. JEAN
JEANBART, Jean Baptiste   See Jean BART
JEROME, Charles Gabriel   See J. L. JEROME
    Etienne
    Gabriel
JONAU, Adélaide   See J. L. JEROME
JONES, C. Ralph   See J. JONES
JONES, James   See Lee WHITE
JONES, Lise   See Henry McCALL
JORDAN, Caleb D.   See Daniel JOURDAN
JORDAN, James   See J. Louis JOURDAN
JOUET, Maria Juana   See Jean B. JUETTE
JOUNEL, Jeanne   See J. DUCAYET and
                                        Joseph DUCAYET
JOURDAIN, Elias Thomas   See Victor JOURDAIN
    Elie
    Elie Victor
    Elizabeth Charichée
    Estéphanie
    Lemida
    Paul

JOURDAIN, Mathilde	See Louis MAITREJEAN
JOURDAN, Jean John Joseph	See J. Louis JOURDAN
JOYCE, John William	See G. JOYCE
JUDOR (TUDOR), J.	See Florent TUDOR
JUMONVILLE, Charles François	See Charles François DUVILLAS
KENNEDY, J. S.	See Greenberg R. STRINGER
KENNEDY, Monsieur	See Bernard DUCHAMP
KHONE, Samuel	See COHN
KING, George	See Jean GAILLIOT (GAILLOT)
KOHN, Joachim Solomon	See COHN
KUHN, George H.	See COHN
LABADIE, Catherine	See Pierre D. HENRY
LABARRE, Edouard Louis GLETRAY Paul	See Louis LABARRE
LABARRURE, Pierre G.	See Bertrand LABARRIERE
LABAT, Marie Ann	See Barthelemy PELLERIN
LABATUT, Victoire	See George ROLLAND
LABORDE, Etienne	See Philip PEDESCLAUX
LABRANCHE, Louise	See F. TREPAGNIER
LACAN, Louis A.	See Hippolite LACAN John SCHARP (SHARP)
LACOSTE, Catherine	See Jean B. DESPORTEL J. B. HACHER
LACOUTURE, André	See Michel MAGNOL
LAFARGUE, François, J., Jean	See J. B. LAFARGUE
LAFITTE, Captain Césare L. A.	See Louis LAFITTE
LAFRANCE, Marie Joseph	See Michel MAGNOL
LALANDE, Jean Louis	See DAPPREMONT
LALANDE, Jean Pierre	See P. FERRIER

LALANDE FERRIER, Jeanne Sophie	See Christophe CADION
LALANE, Eulalie	See Charles ROCHE
LALUNE, Louis	See Louis SIBILOT
LAMBERT, Marianne	See François CERESOL
LAMBERT, Peter Pierre Valery	See Pierre LAMBERT
LAMBERT, Onésime	See Richard LAMBERT
LAMBERT, Xavier	See Jean BOZANT
LAMOTHE, Françoise	See Jean FAGOT
LAMOTHE, Jacques, Jean	See J. S. LAMOTHE, Sr.
LAMOTHE, Jean Jeanne Urbanie	See Jean V. PIDOUX
LAMOTHE, Robert	See François LAMOTHE
LANAUX, Angela	See Charles LANAUX
LANAUX, Antoine Philippe Pierre	See Philippe LANAUX
LANAUX, Marie Délphine	See Jean B. LACROIX
LANDREAUX, Pierre	See Jean LANDREAUX
LANDRONY, Catherine	See Barthelemy BACAS
LANGE, Marie A.	See Jean B. LATOUR
LANGLIER, Adolphe	See Adolphe SANGLIER
LANOIX, Louis	See Jean B. LEPRETRE
LANUSE, Marie Pauline Paul	See Alexandre PRIEUR
LaPEYRE, Jean Marie	See Théodule CASSINET
LAPICE, Peter M.	See Peter M. LAPUCE
LAPORTE, Pierre	See J. B. HACHER
LARAILLET, Marguerite Jean Charles	See Jean FAGOT
LARCHE, Jacques	See Jacques LARCHEVAULT
LARCHEVAUX, Antoine	See Jacques LARCHEVAULT
LARCHEVEQUE, Jacques	See Jacques LARCHEVAULT
LASSERVE De St. AVID, Jean	See Jean St. AVID
LASTRAPES, Louis F.	See Joseph GARRIGUES
LAURENT, Catherine	See Charles FE (FEE)

(269)

LAURENT, Jean	See Jean MACOIN
Julie Desirée	
LAURENT, Marguerite	See André GREGOIRE
LAURENT, Pierre	See Pierre DURIO
LAURIN, François	See A. LARIN
LAUZON, Charles Louis	See François LAUZIN
LAVAN, Charles Eugéne Nicholas	See LAVAN
LAVAUD, C.	See Charles LEBEAU
LAVEAUX, Charles	See Charles LEBEAU
LAVERGNE, Suzanne	See Humbert DEMOURUELLE
LAVIGNON (SAVIGNON), Maria F.	See Michel MEILLEUR
LAVILLEBUEVRE, Jean U.	See Victor JOURDAIN
LAYE, Félicité	See Jean B. JOUBLANC
LeBLANC, Constance	See Pierre RICHARD
LeBLANC, Madame	See Pierre PIQUERIN (PIQUERY)
LeBLOND, Louise	See Pierre L. MOREL
LeBON, François Henry Hippolite Louis	See Joseph LEBON
LEBRUN, Jacques	See POPOTTE
LeCAMP, Elizabeth	See Rolland BOULLEMET
LeCANN, Anne Marie	See Jean B. PERRAULT
LeCARPENTIER, Joseph	See Joseph St. CYR
LECLERC, Monsieur	See Jean Jacques BROUET
LeCOURT, Josepha	See Philip PEDESCLAUX
LeDUC (LeDUGUE), Charles Marie	See Philip PEDESCLAUX
LeDUC, Marie Héloise	See Jean B. MERCIER
LEFEBVRE, Modeste	See Clair LEFEVRE
LEFEVBRE, Adélaide	See Gervais PILLON
LeFEURE, Claire	See Jean B. VERRON

LEGENDRE, George	See Raphaël TOLEDANO
LEGENDRE, T.	See Théophile LEGENDRE
LeGRAND, Eugénie	See Pascal HOFFMAN
LEGROS, Santiago (Jacques)	See Jacques LEBROS
LELOUP, Rodolphe	See P. LELOUP
LEMAIRE, Eulalie	See Etienne CARRABY
LEMAIRE, Monsieur	See Jean GARGES
LEMAITRE, Charles Mathurin	See Charles LEMAITRE
LEMAITRE, Marie Elizabeth	See Jean LEMAITRE
LEMOINE, Antoine	See A. LEMOINE
Auguste	
Louis Auguste	
LEMONNIER, Marie Aimée	See Yves LEMMONIER
René	
Théotiste	
LeRICHE, Monsieur	See Jean B. TURPIN, Jr.
LESCONFLAIR, Antoine N.	See Urbain LESCONFLAIR
Nicolas	
LESSASSIER, Alexo-Léon	See Vincent LESSASSIER
Jean Charles	
Vincent (Jr.)	
LESSASSIER, Charlotte Céleste	See Jean B. VOISIN
LEUMOND, Jules	See Gabriel LEAUMONT
LEVASSEUR Alexander	See Laurent LEVASSEUR
LEWIS, Joshua	See Charles LANAUX
LEYER, Margarita	See Pierre HENO, Jr.
LIBERAL, Auguste	See Nicholas LIBERAL
Raymond	
LIVANO, Juan	See Xénophon LAVINO
LIVAUDAIS, Céleste	See A. GERVAIS
LIVAUDAIS, Charlotte	See Charles PAPET
LOCKHART, Andrew	See Emile SAINET
LOMBARD, Rose	See Etienne L. AYOT (AILLOT)
LONGER, A.	See William DeBUYS

LONGPRE, John	See Charles PAPET
LOUP, Benjamin	See P. LELOUP
LOUPE, François	See P. LELOUP
LOYAL, Abigail	See James ARMITAGE
LUBREJEAN	See Joseph GARRIGUES
LUITANA, Sally	See William BILLY
LYONAIS, Antoine	See S. J. BISE
MACARTHY, Céleste	See Alexandre PRIEUR
MACREADY, John	See Yves LEMONNIER
MAGNAN, Jeanne	See Claude MARANS
MAHE, George	See Jean MAHE
MAHE DESPORTES, Josephine Widow	See J. B. HACHER
MAIROT, Elizabeth Jean C.	See Jean Claude MARIOT
MAISON, Jacques	See Jacques BONNEMAISON
MAISON ROUGE, Bessi (Bessie) Marquis de	See MAISON ROUGE
MAITREJEAN, Estélle Marie Joseph	See Louis MAITREJEAN
MANUEL, Françoise	See Joseph CALABOUR
MAQUERY, James	See James MARQUERY
MAQUIN, Ursula J.	See J. B. PERRIER
MARANT, Jean Baptiste Tranquil	See Claude MARANS
MARATEAU, Céleste	See Antoine Jean BONABEL
MARATEAU, Victoire	See Clair LEFEVRE
MARCENAT, Jean Joseph	See Joseph CALABOUR
MARCHAND, Eugenio Joseph Eugéne Pierre Renée	See Eugéne MARCHAND
MARCHAND, Maria Anna	See Jean ISNARD

MARCHAND, Marie Anne Pierre	See Pierre J. TRICOU
MARCHAND, Pierre T. B.	See Simon MARCHAND
MARCHAND, Pierre Simon	See Dominique BELAUME
MARIA, José	See Joseph MARY
MARIGNY, Bernard	See Michel DeARMAS
MARIGNY, Bernard Gustave Prospére	See Henry McCALL
MARMET, Bernarde	See Victor JOURDAIN
MARMILLON, Délphine	See H. DUFILHO
MARTIN, Jeanne	See Pierre V. BARBOT
MARTINEAU, Pierre	See Pierre DURIVE
MASCEY, John	See John A. MASCEY
MASCEY, Marie Anne	See Louis CHAVEAU
MASPERO, Peter	See Angel TOURLA Bernard TREMOULET
MASSICOT, Amada	See Manuel GARCIA
MATHIEU, Rosalie	See Charles MAURIAN
MAURICE, François Pierre	See F. MAURICE
MAYEAUX, André (Madame)	See René THEARD
MAYOU, Louis	See Norbert MAYOUX
McCALL, Céleste	See Henry McCALL
McCLARAN, James W.	See John J. McCLARAN
McCRACKEN, Eliza	See Ralph McCRACKEN
McFARLAND, Margaret	See Richard McFARLAND
MEFFRE ROUZAN, François	See Louis NICOLAS
MEFFRE ROUZAN, Jacques	See Zénon ROULANT
MEIGS, Return J.	See William McCLELLAND
MEILLEUR, Constance Michel	See Louis NICOLAS
MELLON, Thomas	See John HAGAN

MELSON (NELSON), Anne	See John SCHARP (SHARP)
MENARD, Jean	See MENARD
MERCIER, Edouard	See Jean B. MERCIER
Jean Baptiste (Sr.)	
Jean Jacques Jules	
Placide Jules Armand	
Placide Jules Armand	
MERCIER, Marie Aimée	See Louis C. MILRENBERGER
MERCIER, Simon	See Henry MERCIER
MERIDIER, Antoine	See H. MERIDIER
Louis	
METESSER, Louise	See P. Edmond FOUCHER
MEUNIER, Etienne	See Gabriel CORREJOLES, Sr.
Magdeleine	
MEUNIER, Magdeleine	See Etienne MEUNIER (MEUNIER)
MICHAEL, William	See William MITCHEL
MICHAULT, Alexandre	See Js. MICHAULT
MICHEL, Josephine	See A. B. FOURNIER
MICHEL, Marulain	See Marius MICHEL
Rose	
MICHINARD, Jean	See Jean CHEMINARD
MICHOUD, Antoine	See Js. MICHAULT
Jacques	
Jean Baptiste	
MILHET, Joseph	See Pierre A. ROUSSEAU
Marguerite	
MILHET, Monsieur	See Jean B. VERRON
MILLAUDON, Antoinette Estélle	See Laurent MILLAUDON
MILLBROUCK, Benoit	See Joshua MILLBROUGH
MILLER, John	See Henry W. PALFREY
MINICHE, Marie Gabriel (Gabrielle)	See Louis MINICHE
Marie Madeleine	
MIOTON, Claire	See François N. MIOTON
Marie Antoinette	
MOLLAY, Santiago F.	See Nicolas MOLE (MOLLAY)

MONGET, Justine	See Maurice FARGE
MONTAMAT, Félicité	See Jean G. MONTAMAT, Sr.
Ives Armand	
Louise Emilie	
MONTONARY, Hélen	See Eustache FREMONT
MONTREUIL, Marie Marthe	See Laurent MILLAUDON
MOORE, Alfred	See L. MOORE
L. H.	
Louis	
MORALES, Sébastienne	See Joseph MARY
MORAN (MORANT), Catherine	See Bernard GENOIS, Sr.
	Bernard GENOIS, Jr.
	John SCHARP (SHARP)
MORCE, Célestin	See Nathaniel MORCE
MOREAU, Emilie	See S. J. BISE
MOREAU LISLET, Julie	See POINCY DESDUNES
MOREL, Louis	See Pierre L. MOREL
MORIN, C. A.	See Christophe MORIN
MORIN, Elizabeth	See Jean FAGOT
MORIN, Françoise	See J. L. JEROME
MORIN, Jean	See J. L. MORIN
Joseph	
Laurent	
MORO, François	See Sébastien MORO
George	
MORSE, A.	See Nathaniel MORCE (MORSE)
Nathaniel	
Obedia	
MOURAL, Joseph Antonio	See MUROL
Pierre	
MOURELOT, Jacques	See MUROL
MOUTAS, Marie	See François RONDEAU
MYERS, John	See John SCHARP (SHARP)
MYERS, Rebecca	See Maurice BARNET, Sr.
NADA, Jean	See Jean MADA

NADAUD, Alexis
    D. O.
    Jean Jacques
NAGEL, Angela
NAUTURE, Jeanne
NAVARINE, Monsieur

NAVARRE, Jean
    Jean M.
NELSON, Anne
NEPOTTE, César
NICAUD, Jacques C.
NICE, Pierre Michel
NICHOLAS, Joseph
NICHOLS, J. C.
NICHOLS, Thadeous
NICOLAS, Jacques
    Jean Jacques
    Jean Louis
NICOLAS, Jean Baptiste
    Valery
NICOLAS, Rosalie R.
NOGUIES, Louise
    Humbert
NOLTE, John Henry
NOLTE, Vincent

NORMAND, Jean Joseph
    Marie
NORRA, Madeleine

NOUCHET, A. B.
    Gustave
    Octave
NOYES, Denis
    J. M.

See Jean NADAUD

See Chrisphonte NAGEL
See Jean F. CRUZEL
See Fleury SOUBERCAZE
J. P. SOUBERCAZE
See J. Louis NAVARRE

See John SCHARP (SHARP)
See J. B. NIPORT
See Michel NICAUD
See Michel NICE
See Joseph NICHOLS
See Thomas C. NICHOLS
See Joseph NICHOLS
See Louis NICOLAS

See Valery NICOLAS

See J. B. LAGARGUE
See Jean B. HENO
DEMOURUELLE
See Vincent NOLTE
See Edward R. HOLLANDER
Lucien ROBLOMT
See Jean FAGOT

See Etienne L. BARBARIN

See Seraphin NOUCHE

See NOYE (NOYES)

NOYES (cont')	See NOYE (NOYES)
Silas	
Simon	
William B.	
NUGENT, Isaac	See Thomas NUGENT
John	
O'BRIAN, Carlota	See Daniel D. CORNICO
O'DONNEL, Anthony	See Lynster O'DONNEL
Charles	
Daniel	
James	
John	
O'DUHIGG, Eloy	See Louis DUHIGG
OLIVIER, Emilie	See Jacques TURPIN
OMIRIS [O'MEARA], José	See Patrick O'MEARA
O'QUAYS, Baptiste	See Joseph QUAYS
OSSONE DeVERRIERE, Jeanne	See Auguste GUIBERT
OSTIN, Céleste	See Jean ORTEING (OSTIN)
Marianne	
Marguerite	
Pierre Jean Baptiste	
OSTIN, Marguerite	See Maurice FARGE
Jean	
OTTIGNON, Claudius	See Claudius OBIGNON
PACKWOOD, L.	See Henry PACKWOOD
S. [Samuel] W.	
PAJAUD, Pierre	See Pierre A. PAJAND
PALFREY, George	See Henry W. PALFREY
Mary	
Sarah	
PALFREY, George	See James H. SHEPHERD
Henry William	
PAPET, Charles	See Jean B. LONGPRE
PAPILLON, G. [Gatien]	See Richard PAILLASON

PARISIEN, Widow	See Henry PARISIEN
PARIZOT, Henry	See Henry PARSIEN
PART, Pierre	See Joseph F. VANEL
PASCAL, Lise	See François CORREJOLES, Jr.
PASSAGE, A. Louis	See Onésime PASSAGE
PASSIA, John	See Onésime PASSAGE
PATTERSON, Monsieur	See John MUGGAT (MUGGAH)
PAUTARD, Marie	See Pierre DURIVE
PE, Etienne	See Pierre St. PE
PEDESCLAUX, Pierre A.	See Philip PEDESCLAUX
PELLERIN, Eulalie John Baptiste	See Jean B. LAMOTHE, Jr.
PELLIER, Maximillien	See Pierre PELLIER
PELTIER, F. C.	See F. PERIER
PEPE, Louis	See François A. DUPLESSIS, Jr.
PERILLAT, François	See Fulgence PERILLAT
PERRIE, Jean	See J. B. PERRIER
PERRIER, Charles Jean Joseph	See F. Perier
PERRIER, Eusébe	See E. [Charles] SPERRIER
PERTHUIT [PERTUIS], Constance	See Simon MARCHAND
PESSON (PESSOU), Nicholas T. J.	See Alphonse PESSON (PESSOU)
PETIT, Monsier	See GRANNIER
PEYCHAUD, Lasthénie	See Charles MAURIAN
PEYROUX, Silvain	See Achille RIVARDE
PEYTAVIN, Henry F. DUPRELON Marie Magdeleine	See Victor JOURDAIN
PAICEAUD, Marie	See Siméon P. SCHOMBERG
PAINSON, Jean	See Richard PAILLASON
PHILIPS, John L.	See John PHILIPS
PICENA, Pierre (Jr.)	See Pierre PICENA
PICOU, Margarita	See Michel MEILLEUR

(278)

PIDOUX, Marie Uranie	See Jean V. PIDOUX
PIERAY, Caroline	See Antoine GUILLEMIN
PILIE, Jean Pierre	See Louis Philippe PILIE
Louis Bernard	
Louis Joseph	
PILIE, Louise	See Jean FAGOT
PILON, Siméon	See Gervais PILLON
Thomas	
PILONE, Richard	See Gervais PILLON
PINELL (PINEL), Jacobo	See J. B. PINEL
PIQUERY, Pierre	See Pierre PIQUERIN
PITRE, Martine	See J. L. MORIN
PITTICLAUX, Marie	See Bernard DUCHAMP
POCHE, Bertrand	See POCHE
POETE, Elizabeth	See François PORTE(POETE)
POLITY (POLITE), Antoine	See Nicholas POLITY (POLITE)
POLLACK, George	See Jean B. PONS
POMET, Adélaide	See Etienne GIRAUDAU
PONCE, Michel	See Paul PONCET
PONS, Clémentine	See Charles F. VISINIER
PONS, Marc Antoine	See Jean B. PONS
PONSET, P.	See Paul PONCET
PONTZ, Jean Paul	See Paul PONCET
POTARD, Marie	See Pierre DURIVE
POUPOW, Martine	See POPOTTE
POYNOT, Azélie	See P. J. POYCOT
Marie Marguerite	
Pierre	
Pierre Emile	
PRADINES, Elizabeth	See Gabriel CORREJOLES, Sr.
	Etienne MENNIER (MEUNIER)
PRESTON, J. T.	See Michel de ARMAS
	Etienne BERTEL
PREVAL, Gallien	See Jean B. LATOUR

PREVOST, Solomon	See Pierre PICENA
PRIEUR, Denis	See Alexandre PRIEUR
Félicité Pauline	
Pascal	
Prospère	
PRIOR (PRYOR), Captain	See James PRIOR
PRIOR, Juana	See Hypolite GILLY
PRUCIER, Paul	See Paul PRUDIER
PUCHE, Joseph	See Joseph PORCHE (PUCHE)
PUECH, Catherine	See Jean PUECH
Ed.	
Jean Baptiste	
RABAND, Jean Louis	See Antoine Jean BONABEL
RABY, Anatole	See A. RABY
Antoine	
RADEGONDE MAYEAU, Françoise	See Jean B. MERCIER
RAMEL, Henry J. L.	See Henry RAMEL
RAMIREZ, Marie	See Etienne Louis BARBARIN
RAMONDE, Juana	See J. S. LAMOTHE, Sr.
RAPALLO, Estephen	See Giovani RAPALLO
RAPP, Henriette C.	See Jean GUERIN
RAULAND, René	See Zenón RAULANT
REGGIO, Josephine	See François DUBOIS
REYNAUD, Marie Laure	See Louis M. REYNAUD
REZIO, Josephine	See François DUBOIS
RICHARD, Alexandre Antoine	See A. RICHARD
Anaclet	
Antoine	
Auguste	
Augustus	
Pierre	
RIEUX[RAUX], Simon	See J. F. RAUX
RILLIEUX, Eloise	See Louis M. REYNAUD
RILLIEUX, Marie Céleste	See Germain MUSSON
Vincent	

RITTIER, Flora	See Joseph DUCAYET
RIVARDE, Achille	See Sylvain PEYROUX
RIVARDE, Claire	See Jean ORTEING (OSTIN)
Elaine	
Marianne	
RIVARDE, Marianne	See Maurice FARGE
RIVERY, Pedro	See Jean B. JUETTE
RIVIERE, Bernard	See RIVIERE
Drausin	
François	
Jean	
Jérôme	
ROBELOT, Nicolas	See Lucien ROBLOMT
ROBERT, Antoine	See Arnaud ROBERT
Henriette Hélene	
ROBERT, Marie Rose	See René N. THEARD
ROBERTSON, R. L.	See Louis ROBERTSON
ROBERTSON, Thomas B.	See Sébastien HIRIART
ROBIN, Lorenzo	See André ROBIN
ROBINE, Andrew	See André ROBIN
ROCHE, Elémore Roy	See Pierre F. ROCHE
ROCHE, Henriette C.	See Charles TREMOULET
ROCHE, Michel	See Charles M. ROCHE
Olivier	Pierre F. ROCHE
Pierre	
ROCHEFORT, Adélaide	See Charles RAYMOND
ROCHEFORT, Pierre	See Jean B. LATOUR
ROLAND (ROLLAND), Simon	See ROLAND
Théodule	
Théophile	
ROLLAND, Jean B. (Sr.)	See Jean B. ROLLAND
Manuel Marceline	
ROMAN (ROMAIN), Pierre Louis	See Pierre ROMAN
RONDEAU, Marie Louise	See François RONDEAU
ROSS, George T.	See Germain MUSSON

ROSSIGNOL DESDUNES, Thérèze	See Jean GUERIN
ROSSIGNOL DESDUNES ARCUEIL, Marie	See Louis P. PILIE
ROUCHET, S. L.	See Joseph ROUCHET
Marie Françoise	
ROUGE, Joseph	See MAISON ROUGE
Louis Alexis	
ROUQUETTE, Bernard	See Joseph ROUCHET
Dominique	
ROUSSE, E.	See Jacques FERRERA
ROUSSEAU, Marie Anne	See Elie A. DUPLESSIS
ROUSSEAU, Monsieur	See Louis FERIET
ROUSSEAU, Pierre George	See Pierre A. ROUSSEAU
ROUSSEL, Aimée A.	See Charles LANAUS
ROUSSEVE, Jean Baptiste	See Louis MINICHE
ROUZAN, François	See Louis NICOLAS
ROUX, Elizabeth	See Jean Jacques BROUET
ROUX, Louise	See Jean B. LACROIX
ROYER (ROYERRE), Charles	See Marcelin ROYER
Jean Baptiste	
John	
Pierre	
SAFOU, François	See François SAPHIA
SAGORY, Eugéne	See Louis M. SAGORY
Louis Mathurin	
Louise	
SAINET, Jean François	See Emile SAINET
SAINET, Madame	See Jérôme TOLEDANO
St. AMAND, Baptiste	See St. ARMAND
Jean Baptiste	
Marcel	
Victor DASPIT	
St. AMANT, Antoine	See Jean B. PLAUCHE
Mathilde	
St. ANTONINI, Marianne	See S. L. ROUCHET
St. CYR, Aspasie	See Joseph St. CYR

St. CYR, Josephine   See SIMILIEN
St. GERMAIN, François   See St. GERMAIN
    Manuel
    Martial
    Pierre
    Valery
St. HILAIRE, Anne C.   See A. LEMOINE
St. MARTORY, Jeanne Marie   See Jean DUBUC
St. PE, Elizabeth Délphine   See Pierre St. PE
St. ROMES, Marie Elizabeth   See Alexandre BONNEVAL
                                      Joseph C. St. ROMES
St. VILMON, A.   See VILLEMONT
SAINTONGE, Marguerite   See André GREGOIRE
SALANNE, Eulalie   See Charles M. ROCHE
SANGELIER (SANGLIER), Angelique   See Adolphe SANGLIER
SAUL, Joseph   See Jean St. AVID
                                           Vincent NOLTE
SAULIER, Marie   See François A. DUPLESSIS, Jr.
SAUTURON, Isabel   See Jean B. JUETTE
SAVANT, Marie   See Joseph CALABOUR
    Pierre
SAVARY, Maria Ignes   See Nicolas MOLE (MOLLAY)
SAVIGNON, Maria F.   See Michel MEILLEUR
SAVIGNON, Marie Anne   See Louis NICOLAS
SAYLER, N.   See Valentin SYLER
SCHOMBERG, Jean Thomas   See Siméon P. SCHOMBERG
SCOTT, Daniel   See John SCOTT
SEIGNOURET, François   See Joseph SEIGNOURET
SELLIER, Pierre   See Pierre PELLIER
SEVERIN HUARD, Jean   See J. HUARD
SHARP, Jean Baptiste   See John SCHARP (SHARP)
    John
    Louise
    Marie Adélaide
    Marie Elie
    Thomas

SHAW, Mathilda F.   See Lee WHITE
SIFFLET, Jean (Jr.)   See Jean SIFFLET
SIGUR, Monsieur   See Louis GUERIN
SIMILIEN, George   See SIMILIEN
    Jean Baptiste
    Joseph
    Lubin
    Paul
SINDOS, Marie Céleste   See DROUET
SIRONDELLE, Marie Anne   See François PORTE (POETE)
SKIPWITH, Fulwar   See Sébastien HIRIART
SMITH, Henriette Antoinette   See Jean B. MERCIER
SMITH, Marie Julie   See Bertrand LABARRIERE
SMITH, Richard   See Raphaël SMITH
    Robert
    William
SOLOMON, Aaron   See Maurice BARNET, Sr.
    Joseph
SOMEREAU, Monsieur   See Louis FERIET
SOUBERCAZE, Pierre   See Antoine SOUBERCAZE
SOUBLE, Victoire   See Bernard TREMOULET
SPERRIER, Charles   See E. SPERRIER
STABLE, F.   See Richard STABLE
STERLIN (STERLING), Louis   See Lotrege STERLIN
STERLING, Susana   See Pierre D. HENRY
STUART, Oliver   See S. STUART
SUIZA, Barthelemy   See Barthelemy SUISSE
SYLER, Edward   See Valentin SYLER
TANGUY, Widow   See Bernard DUCHAMP
TANNERET, Monsieur   See Jean GOURSON
TASSIER, Rose   See John A. MASCEY
TAUCHET, Jean   See Thomas FOUCHET
    E. TOUCHET
TAUNOU, Louis   See Nicholas VASSEL
TAUSIA, Joseph   See Joseph BOURNOS, Jr.
TERRIER, François   See Henry RAMEL

TESSIER, Antonio Nicolas	See Auguste TESSIER
TESSIER, Monsieur	See Jean B. DURU (DURIEUX)
TETE, Auguste	See Angel TOURLA
TETE, Marie Louise	See Auguste TETE
TEXIER DUPATY, Aveline	See P. FERRIER
THEARD, Charles	See René THEARD
Jean	
René	
THESIER, Monsieur	See Jean B. DURU
THIERY, Monsieur	See Jean DESVIGNES
THOLOZAN, Auguste	See J. S. THOLOZAN
Garrigue	
Martin	
Thomas	
THOMAS, Pérrine	See Jacques BRAVAXT
THOMAS, Philemon	See Bernard GENOIS, Sr.
THOMPSON, Nicholls	See Nathan THOMPSON
TIMBALIER, Marie A.	See Barthelemy GRIMA
TOAS, Jane	See James WIDNUY (WIDNEY)
TOLEDANO, Adolphe	See Christoval TOLEDANO
Antoine	
Arsène	
Sosthénes	
TOLEDANO, Anne	See Raphaël TOLEDANO
Fergus	
TOLEDANO, Manuel	See Eustache FREMONT
TOMACHICHI, Marie Lucie	See Jacques BRAVAXT
TONNELIER, Justine	See P. L. BERLUCHAUX
TONNELIER, Santiago	See Pierre HENO, Jr.
TOSSIE, Caroline	See Jean B. CRUZEL
TOUCHES, Thomas	See E. TOUCHET
TOURNE, Genevieve	See RIVIERE
TOWNSLEY, Thomas F.	See Germain MUSSON
TRAHAN, Marie	See Maurice BARNET, Sr.
TREME, Benoit	See TREME

TREME, Marie D.	See Antoine P. LANAUX, Sr.
TREMOULET, Antoine	See Bernard TREMOULET
Bernard (Jr.)	
Charles	
Cyprien	
TREMOULET, Bernard	See Philip ALVAREZ
	Jean B. TURPIN, Jr.
TREMOULET, Charles (Jr.)	See Charles TREMOULET
Louise Aimée	
TREMOULET, Henriette	See Jean B. TURPIN, Jr.
TREPAGNIER, F. B.	See F. TREPAGNIER
Fulgence	
François	
TRICOU, Eugénie Félicité	See Louis M. SAGORY
TRICOU, Joseph Adolphe	See Pierre J. TRICOU
Marie	
Pierre Joseph (Jr.)	
TRIME, Benoit	See Edouard TREME
Henry	
TRUDEAU, Genevieve	See Jules DREUX
TURCUIT (TERCUIT), Francis J.	See F. THERCOUT
TURPIN, Desirée	See Jacques TURPIN
TURPIN, Jean	See Bernard TREMOULET
TURPIN, Jean Baptiste (Sr.)	See Jean B. TURPIN, Jr.
VALENTINE (VALENTIN), François S.	See VALENTINE
Sallue	
Samuel	
Santiago	
VALET, Pierre	See Amand C. VALLE
VALLEE, P. R.	See Amand C. VALLE
Pierre	
VALLET, Emilie	See Andrew ARMSTRONG
VALMONT, Emile	See VILLEMONT

VALTON, Marie	See Henry MERCIER
VANEL (VANNEL), Emilie	See Joseph François VANEL
Théodore	
VARION (VARIAN), François	See Jean B. VERRON
VATEL (VATELLE), Margaret	See Nicolas Jean PIERRE
VAUGINE, Victoria	See Ignacio CHALMETTE
VEAU, Octavie	See Pierre VEAU
VEDIE, Elizabeth	See Eustache FREMONT
VERLOIN DeGRUY, Marie	See Pierre St. PE
VERON, Cecilia	See Jean B. VERRON
VERRASONE, Martha	See Pierre J. DULCOT
VERRETE, Catherine	See François DUCOIN
VIDAL, G.	See Rolland BOULLEMET
VIEL, Anne Marie	See Yves LEMONNIER
VIEL, Jeanne Clémence	See Pierre G. DeBUYS
VIENNE, Louis	See Philip VIENNE
VILLEMONT, A.	See VILLEMONT
Charles	
Emile	
Louis Célestin	
VINET, Céleste	See Michel MAGNOL
François	
VINICK, Madame	See Nicolas POLITY (POLITE)
VINOT, Louise	See Arnaud ROBERT
VION, Marie Thérèse	See Joseph C. St. ROMES
Michel	
VISINIER, Nicolas Victor	See Charles F. VISINIER
VITRAC, Charles	See Alphonse VITRAC
Hyppolite	
P.	
VITRAC, Hyppolite	See Victorin DUSSAC
VOISIN, Angeliae	See Jean B. VOISIN
Délphine	
Jeanne Célestine	
Pétronile	
Pierre	

VON KUEBECK	See Vincent NOLTE
WALE, Marie	See Patrick WALE
Patrick (Jr.)	
Patrick Alexander	
WARFIELD, C. A.	See Eliphalet WACHFIELD
WEDERSTRANDT, John	See Charles F. VISINIER
WEST, John K.	See François A. DUPLESSIS, Jr.
WHITE, Thornley Lee	See Lee WHITE
WIDNEY, Elizabeth	See James WIDNUY (WIDNEY)
WILKINSON, James	See Jean St. AVID
WILLIAMS, Justin	See William H. HAYS
WILLIAMSON, James	See J. WILLIAMSON
John	
Joseph	
WILLIE, John	See John WILLIGIE
WILPOLES, Widow	See Louis DUBIGNON
WILSON, Thomas	See Marius MICHEL
WILTZ, Marguerite	See Pierre A. ROUSSEAU
WINTER, Samuel	See René THEARD
YOUX, Dominique	See Henry St. GEME
ZERINGUE, Emilie	See Dionis MORTIMER
ZERINGUE, Eulalie	See Jean B. PLAUCHE

BIBLIOGRAPHY

I. MUSTERS AND PAYROLLS
- A. Casey, Powell A. *Louisiana in the War of 1812.* Baton Rouge, 1963.
- B. Casey, Powell A. Papers, Howard-Tilton Memorial Library, New Orleans, Louisiana.
  - a. Muster Roll: Captain Pierre Roche, Company of Carabiniers, 10 December 1814 to 28 February 1815.
  - b. Muster Roll: Captain Henry de St. Géme, Company of Dragoons, 16 December 1814 to 28 February 1815.
  - c. Payroll: Captain Jean Hudry, Company of Francs, 17 December 1814 to 20 March 1815.
  - d. Payroll: Captain Maunsel White, Company of Blues, 17 December 1814 to 28 February 1815.
  - e. Muster Roll: Captain Auguste Guibert, Company of Chasseurs, 10 December 1814 to 28 February 1815.
  - f. Payroll: Musicians, 10 December 1814 to 20 March 1815.
  - g. Payroll: Staff of the Battalion, 16 December 1814 to March 1815.
- C. Moreland, C. C. (Comp.). "Index to Compiled Service Records of Volunteer Soldiers Who Served During the War of 1812," *Louisiana Genealogical Register:*
  - a. VII (June, 1960), 29-30.
  - b. VII (December, 1960), 60-61.
  - c. VIII (June, 1961), 22-24.

- D. Pelletier, J. B. (Mrs.). "Copy of Muster Roll of the Battalion of Orleans Volunteers During the Invasion of Louisiana by the English Army in 1814-1815." Typescript copy made by the Louisiana Historical Society from a document loaned by Mrs. J. B. Pelletier, Louisiana Historical Center, Louisiana State Museum, New Orleans, Louisiana.
- E. Pierson, Marion John Bennett (comp.). *Louisiana Soldiers in the War of 1812.* Louisiana Genealogical and Historical Society, 1963.
- F. "Roster of the Orleans Battalion," in Genealogical Records, Louisiana Daughters of the American Revolution, 1931-1932. Copy in Louisiana Historical Center, Louisiana State Museum, New Orleans, Louisiana.
- G. "Muster Rolls and Communications Pertaining to the Battle of New Orleans." Typescript copy in Louisiana Historical Center, Louisiana State Museum, New Orleans, Louisiana.

II. CEMETERY FILES AND TOMBSTONE INSCRIPTIONS

- A. "St. Louis Cemetery Number I of New Orleans." Vertical Files of the tombstone inscriptions at the Louisiana Historical Center, Louisiana State Museum, New Orleans, Louisiana.
- B. "St. Louis Cemetery Number II of New Orleans." Vertical Files.
- C. "Girod Cemetery of New Orleans." Vertical Files.
- D. *Louisiana Tombstone Inscriptions.* 10 vols. Compiled and Published by the Louisiana Society-NSDAR, 1954-1957. VII.

III. DIRECTORIES AND CENSUSES

- A. *New Orleans in 1805: A Directory and a Census. Together with Resolutions Authorizing Same, Now Printed* for the First Time from the Original Manuscript. A Facsimile. New Orleans, The Pelican Gallery, Inc., 1936.

B. "New Orleans First Directory, 1807." Louisiana Historical Center, Louisiana State Museum, New Orleans, Louisiana. The Museum has a typescript copy compiled by Stanley C. Arthur.

C. Lafon, B. *Annuaire Louisianais Pour L' Année 1809.* New Orleans, 1808.

D. *Whitney's New-Orleans Directory and Louisiana & Mississippi Almanac for the year 1811.* New Orleans, 1810.

E. Paxton, John Adems. *Paxton's New-Orleans Directory, List of Names Containing the Heads of Families and Persons in Business, Alphabetically Arranged.* New Orleans, 1822.

F. Paxton, John Adems. *Supplement of the New Orleans Directory of the Last Year, 1824.* New Orleans, 1824.

G. *The New-Orleans Annual Advertiser, for 1832, Annexed to the City Directory.* New Orleans, Stephen E. Percy & Co., 1832.

H. Michel, Edward Augusta. *Michel's New Orleans Annual and Commercial Register Containing the Names, Professions and Residences of all the Heads of Families and Persons in Business of the City and Suburbs with other Useful Information and a List of Removals and Commercial Houses Lately Established for 1834.* New Orleans, Gaux, et Sollee, 1833.

I. Jackson, Ronald V., Gary Ronald Teeples, David Schaefermeyer (eds.). *Louisiana 1810 Census Index.* Utah, Accelerated Indexing Systems, Inc., 1976.

J. ———. *Louisiana 1820 Census Index.* Utah, Accelerated Indexing Systems, Inc., 1976.

K. ———. *Louisiana 1830 Census Index.* Utah, Accelerated Indexing Systems, Inc., 1976.

IV. MARRIAGES, CONFIRMATIONS, AND BAPTISMS

A. Hebert, Donald J. (Rev.). *Southwest Louisiana Records: Church and Civil Records of Settlers.* 8 vols. Eunice, Louisiana: 1974-197—.
   - a. I (1756-1810)
   - b. II (1811-1830)
   - c. III (1831-1840)
   - d. IV (1841-1847)
   - e. V (1848-1854)
   - f. VI (1855-1860)

B. *Libro primero de confirmaciones de esta parroquia de Sn Luis de la Nueva Orleans.* Genealogical Research Society of New Orleans. New Orleans, 1967.

C. Maduell, Charles R. (Jr.). *Marriage Contracts, Wills and Testaments of the Spanish Colonial Period in New Orleans, 1770-1804.* New Orleans, 1969.

D. ———. *Marriages and Family Relationships of New Orleans, 1830-1840.* New Orleans, 1969.

E. Orleans Parish Minute Book, June 18, 1814 to September 21, 1815. Including Record of Marriage Licenses Issued from April 30, 1807 to December 31, 1808. Archives of the Louisiana Division, New Orleans Public Library, New Orleans, Louisiana.

V. WILLS, SUCCESSIONS, AND INVENTORIES

A. Archives of the Louisiana Division, New Orleans Public Library, New Orleans, Louisiana.
   - a. Judicial Records: Court of Probate for the Parish of New Orleans, IX, September 10, 1811 to February 10, 1813.

    b. Judicial Records: Court of Probate for the Parish of Orleans, May 13, 1816 to September 5, 1818.
    c. Inventories: Court of Probate for the Parish of Orleans, October 15, 1816 to September 2, 1818.
    d. Oaths of Partie Parts: Probate Proceedings for Orleans Parish, December 27, 1834 to October 23, 1835.
    e. Minute Book: Court of Probate for the Parish of Orleans, 1841-1842.

B. Bertin, P. M. (Comp.). *General Index of All Successions, Opened in the Parish of Orleans, for the Year 1805, to the Year 1846.* New Orleans, 1849.

[The writer chose to utilize the compilations of the *General Index*, which appeared in the issues of the *New Orleans Genesis*, for it was better organized alphabetically rather than by the cumbersome chronological-alphabetical method used by P. M. Bertin.]

a.	I,	No. 2	(March, 1962), 141-150.
b.	I,	No. 3	(June, 1962), 237-252.
c.	I,	No. 4	(September, 1962), 365-370.
d.	II,	No. 5	(January, 1963), 57-66.
e.	II,	No. 6	(March, 1963), 111-120.
f.	II,	No. 7	(June, 1963), 233-244.
g.	II,	No. 8	(September, 1963), 346-355.
h.	III,	No. 11	(June, 1964), 253-262.
i.	III,	No. 12	(September, 1964), 360-371.
j.	IV,	No. 14	(March, 1965), 108-120.
k.	IV,	No. 16	(September, 1965), 346-352.
l.	V,	No. 17	(January, 1966), 89-92.
m.	V,	No. 18	(March, 1966), 138-147.
n.	VII,	No. 25	(January, 1968), 75-84.
o.	VII,	No. 26	(March, 1968), 183-192.
p.	VII,	No. 27	(June, 1968), 235-244.

q. VII, No. 28 (September, 1968), 341-350.
r. VIII. No. 29 (January, 1969), 32-42.
s. X, No. 37 (January, 1971), 9-20.
t. X, No. 38 (March, 1971), 116-127.

VI. GOVERNMENT PUBLICATIONS AND DOCUMENTS
NATIONAL:
A. *American State Papers, Documents, Legislative, and Executive of the Congress of the United States, in Relation to Public Lands:*
  a. II—*From the First Session of the First Congress to the First Session of the Twenty-Third Congress. March 4, 1789 to June 15, 1834.* Washington, 1834.
  b. III—*From First Session of the Fourteenth Congress to the First Session of the Eighteenth Congress. December 4, 1815 to May 27, 1824.* Washington, 1834.
  c. IV—*From the First Session of the First Congress to the First Session of the Twenty-third. March 4, 1789 to June 15, 1834.* Washington, Duff Green, 1834.
  d. V—*From the First Session of the Twentieth to the Second Session of the Twentieth, Inclusive: Commencing December 3, 1827, and Ending March 3, 1829.* Washington, Gales and Seaton, 1860.
  e. VI—*From the First Session of the Twenty-First to the First Session of the Twenty-Third Congress, Commencing December 1, 1828, and Ending April 11, 1834.* Washington, Gales and Seaton, 1860.
  f. VII—*From the First Session of the Twenty-Third to the Second Session of the Twenty-Third Congress, Commencing April 11, 1836, and Ending March 3, 1835.* Washington, Gales and Seaton, 1861.
  g. VIII—*From the First Session of the Twenty-Fourth to the Second Session of the Twenty-Fourth Con-*

gress, *Commencing December 8, 1835, and Ending February 28, 1837.* Washington, Gales and Seaton, 1861.

B. *Digested Summary and Alphabetical List of Private Claims Which Have Been Presented to the House of Representatives From the First to the Thirty-First Congress, Exhibiting the Action of Congress of Each Claim with Reference to the Journals, Reports, Bills, S. c. Elucidating its Progress.* 3 vols. Baltimore, Genealogical Publishing Co., Inc., 1970. II

C. Carter, Clarence Edwin (Comp. and Ed.). *The Territorial Papers of the United States:*
    a. IX—*The Territory of Orleans, 1803-1812.* Washington, 1940.
    b. XV—*The Territory of Louisiana-Missouri, 1815-1821.* Washington, 1951.

D. Jackson, Andrew Papers, 1767-1845. Microfilm copy in Louisiana State University, Baton Rouge, Louisiana. 78 reels. Film No. 2752.
    a. Reel No. 15 (December 24, 1814 to January 26, 1815)
    b. Reel No. 16 (January 27, 1815 to February 20, 1815)
    c. Reel No. 17 (February 21, 1815 to April 1, 1815)

E. McMullin, Philip W. *Grassroots of America: A Computerized Index to the American State Papers: Land Grants and Claims (1789-1837)* [?] *with Other Aids to Research.* Salt Lake City, 1972.

F. Rowland, Dunbar (ed). *Official Letter Books of W. C. C. Claiborne, 1801-1816.* 6 vols. Jackson: Mississippi, 1917.
    a. I (1801-1804)
    b. II (1804-1806)

    c. III (1804-1806)
    d. IV (1806-1809)
    e. V (1809-1811)
    f. VI (1811-1816)

STATE:
  G. Acts Passed by the Legislature of Louisiana:
    a. *Acts Passed at the Second Session of the Second Legislature of the State of Louisiana, 1816.* New Orleans, 1816.
    b. *Acts Passed at the Second Session of the Fourth Legislature, 1820.* New Orleans, 1820.
    c. *Acts Passed at the First Session of the Fifth Legislature, 1821.* New Orleans, 1821.
    d. *Acts Passed at the Second Session of the Fifth Legislature, 1822.* New Orleans, 1822.
    e. *Acts Passed at the First Session of the Sixth Legislature, 1823.* New Orleans, 1823.
    f. *Acts Passed at the First Session of the Seventh Legislature, 1824.* New Orleans, 1824-1825.
    g. *Acts Passed at the Second Session of the Seventh Legislature, 1825.* New Orleans, 1826.
    h. *Acts Passed at the First Session of the Eighth Legislature, 1827.* New Orleans, 1827.
    i. *Acts Passed at the First Session of the Eleventh Legislature, 1833.* New Orleans, 1833.
    j. *Acts Passed at the First Session of the Twelfth Legislature, 1833.* New Orleans, 1835.
    k. *Acts Passed at the Second Session of the Twelfth Legislature, 1836.* New Orleans, 1836.
    l. *Acts Passed at the Second Session of the Thirteenth Legislature, 1837.* New Orleans, 1838.
    m. *Acts Passed at the First Session of the Fourteenth Legislature, 1839.* New Orleans, 1839.

n. *Acts Passed at the Second Session of the Fourteenth Legislature, 1840.* New Orleans, 1840.
o. *Acts Passed at the First Session of the Sixteenth Legislature, 1843.* New Orleans, 1843.
p. *Acts Passed at the Second Session of the Sixteenth Legislature, 1844.* New Orleans, 1844.
q. *Acts Passed at the First Session of the Seventeenth Legislature, 1845.* New Orleans, 1845.
r. *Acts Passed at the First Session of the First Legislature, 1846.* New Orleans, 1846.
s. *Acts Passed at the Second Session of the First Legislature, 1847.* New Orleans, 1847.
t. *Acts Passed at the First Session of the Second Legislature, 1848.* New Orleans, 1847.
u. *Acts Passed at the First Session of the Third Legislature, 1850.* New Orleans, 1850.

LOCAL:
H. Orleans Parish Minute Book, June 18, 1814 to September 21, 1815. Archives of the Louisiana Division, New Orleans Public Library, New Orleans, Louisiana.
I. New Orleans City Court Records of Cases Tried Before the Court of Mayor Joseph Roffignac and the City Council, 1823-1827. Archives of the Louisiana Division, New Orleans Public Library, New Orleans, Louisiana.

VII. MILITARY PENSIONS AND APPOINTMENTS
A. Casey, Powell A. (Comp.). "Militia Appointments in the Orleans Territory Between April, 1805, and May, 1806," *Louisiana Genealogical Register,* XVIII (June, 1970), 170-175.
B. Clinton, Charles (Auditor). "Veterans of 1814 and 1815," *Louisiana Genealogical Register,* XIII, No. 4 (December, 1966), 61-62.

  C. Davis, Edwin A. Collection, c. 1870, Louisiana State University Department of Archives, Baton Rouge, Louisiana.
  D. Haase, W. E. (Mrs.). "Applicants for the State Pensions Granted to Louisiana Soldiers who Served in the War of 1812," *Louisiana Genealogical Register,* XV:
    a. No. 1 (March, 1968), 1-3.
    b. No. 2 (June, 1968), 14-16.
    c. No. 3 (September, 1968), 125-36.
    d. No. 4 (December, 1968), 147-48.

VIII. NEWSPAPERS:
  A. New Orleans *Bee,* 1825-1829.
  B. *Courrier de la Louisiane,* 1810-1818.
  C. *Louisiana Gazette and New Orleans Advertiser,* 1813.

IX. MISCELLANEOUS:
  A. Brown, Wilbur S. *The Amphibious Campaign for West Florida and Louisiana, 1814-1815.* Alabama, University of Alabama Press, 1969.
  B. Casey, Powell A. (Comp.). "Signers of Notice by members of the Louisiana Guards Company of the Louisiana Legion of the Louisiana Militia in New Orleans, Dated August 2, 1823," *Louisiana Genealogical Register,* XIX (March, 1972), 117.
  C. ———"Register of Civil Appointments, Territory of Orleans, December, 1804 to January, 1806," *Louisiana Genealogical Register,* XVIII, no. 2 (June, 1971), 175-176.
  D. Clark, John G. *New Orleans, 1718-1812: An Economic History.* Baton Rouge, Louisiana State University Press, 1970.
  E. Conrad, Glenn R. *St. Charles: Abstracts of Civil Records of St. Charles Parish, 1700-1803.* Lafayette, University of Southwestern Louisiana Press, 1974.

F. ———. *Saint-Jean des Allemands: Abstracts of the Civil Records of St. John the Baptist Parish, with Genealogy and Index, 1753-1803.* Lafayette, University of Southwestern Louisiana Press, 1972.

G. DeVerges, Marie Cruzat (Mrs. Edwin X.). *American Forces at Chalmette: Veterans and Descendants of the Battle of New Orleans, 1814-1815.* Published by the Battle of New Orleans 150th Anniversay Committee (Women's Committee), 1966.

H. Kmen, Henry A. *Music in New Orleans: The Formative Years, 1791-1841.* Baton Rouge, Louisiana State University Press, 1966.

I. Hatfield, Joseph T. *William Claiborne: Jeffersonian Centurion in the American Southwest.* Lafayette, University of Southwestern Louisiana History Series, 1976.

J. Holmes, Jack D. L. *Honor and Fidelity: The Lousiana Infantry Regiment and the Louisiana Militia Companies, 1776-1821.* Birmingham, Alabama, 1965.

K. King, Grace. *Creole Families of New Orleans.* New York, 1921.

L. Latour, A. Lacarrière. *Historical Memoirs of the War in West Florida and Louisiana on 1814-1815 with an Atlas.* Facsimile Reproduction of the 1816 Edition with Introduction by Jane Lucas DeGrummond. Gainesville, University of Florida Press, 1964.

M. LeBreton, Marietta Marie, "A History of the Territory of Orleans, 1803-1812." Unpublished Ph. D. dissertation, Louisiana State University, 1969.

N. Maduell, Charles R. (Jr.). *Federal Land Grants in the Territory of Orleans: The Delta Parishes. A Digest from the American State Papers, Public Lands, Volume II.* New Orleans, 1975.

O. Marchand, Sidney A. *Pioneer Settlers in the Second*

   Acadian Settlement: Ascension Parish, Louisiana 1772-1829. Donaldsonville: Louisiana, 1959.
P. Morazán, Ronald R. "Letters, Petitions, and Decrees of the Cabildo of New Orleans, 1800-1803: Edited and Translated." Unpublished Ph. D.dissertation,Louisiana State University, 1972:
  a. Volume I (1800)
  b. Volume II (1801-1803)
Q. Nolte, Vincent. *The Memoirs of Vincent Nolte Reminiscences in the Period of Anthony Adverse or Fifty Years in Both Hemispheres.* Translated from German. Originally published in 1854. New York, 1934.
R. Seebold, Herman de Bachelle. *Old Louisiana Plantation Homes and Family Trees.* 2 vols. New Orleans, 1941.
S. Warren, H. Gaylord. *The Sword was Their Passport.* Baton Rouge, Louisiana State University Press, 1943.